Transforming Gaming and Computer Simulation Technologies across Industries

Brock Dubbels
McMaster University, Canada

A volume in the Advances in Multimedia and
Interactive Technologies (AMIT) Book Series

www.igi-global.com

Published in the United States of America by
    IGI Global
    Information Science Reference (an imprint of IGI Global)
    701 E. Chocolate Avenue
    Hershey PA, USA 17033
    Tel: 717-533-8845
    Fax: 717-533-8661
    E-mail: cust@igi-global.com
    Web site: http://www.igi-global.com

Library of Congress Cataloging-in-Publication Data

Names: Dubbels, Brock Randall, editor.
Title: Transforming gaming and computer simulation technologies across
  industries / Brock Dubbels, editor.
Description: Hershey PA : Information Science Reference, [2017]
Identifiers: LCCN 2016045760| ISBN 9781522518174 (hardcover) | ISBN
  9781522518181 (ebook)
Subjects: LCSH: Management games. | Educational games. |
  Management--Simulation methods. | Organization--Simulation methods.
Classification: LCC HD30.26 .T73 2017 | DDC 658.001/51932--dc23 LC record available at https://lccn.loc.
gov/2016045760

This book is published in the IGI Global book series Advances in Multimedia and Interactive Technologies (AMIT) (ISSN: 2327-929X; eISSN: 2327-9303)

British Cataloguing in Publication Data
A Cataloguing in Publication record for this book is available from the British Library.

All work contributed to this book is new, previously-unpublished material. The views expressed in this book are those of the authors, but not necessarily of the publisher.

For electronic access to this publication, please contact: eresources@igi-global.com.

Advances in Multimedia and Interactive Technologies (AMIT) Book Series

Joel J.P.C. Rodrigues

National Institute of Telecommunications (Inatel), Brazil &
Instituto de Telecomunicações, University of Beira Interior,
Portugal

ISSN:2327-929X
EISSN:2327-9303

Mission

Traditional forms of media communications are continuously being challenged. The emergence of user-friendly web-based applications such as social media and Web 2.0 has expanded into everyday society, providing an interactive structure to media content such as images, audio, video, and text.

The **Advances in Multimedia and Interactive Technologies (AMIT) Book Series** investigates the relationship between multimedia technology and the usability of web applications. This series aims to highlight evolving research on interactive communication systems, tools, applications, and techniques to provide researchers, practitioners, and students of information technology, communication science, media studies, and many more with a comprehensive examination of these multimedia technology trends.

Coverage

- Multimedia Services
- Digital Communications
- Digital Games
- Web Technologies
- Audio Signals
- Mobile Learning
- Gaming Media
- Digital Watermarking
- Digital Images
- Multimedia Streaming

IGI Global is currently accepting manuscripts for publication within this series. To submit a proposal for a volume in this series, please contact our Acquisition Editors at Acquisitions@igi-global.com or visit: http://www.igi-global.com/publish/.

Titles in this Series

For a list of additional titles in this series, please visit: www.igi-global.com

Feature Detectors and Motion Detection in Video Processing
Nilanjan Dey (Techno India College of Technology, Kolkata, India) Amira Ashour (Tanta University, Egypt) and Prasenjit Kr. Patra (Bengal College of Engineering and Technology, India)
Information Science Reference • copyright 2017 • 328pp • H/C (ISBN: 9781522510253) • US $200.00 (our price)

Mobile Application Development, Usability, and Security
Sougata Mukherjea (IBM, India)
Information Science Reference • copyright 2017 • 320pp • H/C (ISBN: 9781522509455) • US $180.00 (our price)

Applied Video Processing in Surveillance and Monitoring Systems
Nilanjan Dey (Techno India College of Technology, Kolkata, India) Amira Ashour (Tanta University, Egypt) and Suvojit Acharjee (National Institute of Technology Agartala, India)
Information Science Reference • copyright 2017 • 321pp • H/C (ISBN: 9781522510222) • US $215.00 (our price)

Intelligent Analysis of Multimedia Information
Siddhartha Bhattacharyya (RCC Institute of Information Technology, India) Hrishikesh Bhaumik (RCC Institute of Information Technology, India) Sourav De (The University of Burdwan, India) and Goran Klepac (University College for Applied Computer Engineering Algebra, Croatia & Raiffeisenbank Austria, Croatia)
Information Science Reference • copyright 2017 • 520pp • H/C (ISBN: 9781522504986) • US $220.00 (our price)

Emerging Technologies and Applications for Cloud-Based Gaming
P. Venkata Krishna (VIT University, India)
Information Science Reference • copyright 2017 • 314pp • H/C (ISBN: 9781522505464) • US $195.00 (our price)

Digital Tools for Computer Music Production and Distribution
Dionysios Politis (Aristotle University of Thessaloniki, Greece) Miltiadis Tsalighopoulos (Aristotle University of Thessaloniki, Greece) and Ioannis Iglezakis (Aristotle University of Thessaloniki, Greece)
Information Science Reference • copyright 2016 • 291pp • H/C (ISBN: 9781522502647) • US $180.00 (our price)

Contemporary Research on Intertextuality in Video Games
Christophe Duret (Université de Sherbrooke, Canada) and Christian-Marie Pons (Université de Sherbrooke, Canada)
Information Science Reference • copyright 2016 • 363pp • H/C (ISBN: 9781522504771) • US $185.00 (our price)

Trends in Music Information Seeking, Behavior, and Retrieval for Creativity
Petros Kostagiolas (Ionian University, Greece) Konstantina Martzoukou (Robert Gordon University, UK) and Charilaos Lavranos (Ionian University, Greece)
Information Science Reference • copyright 2016 • 388pp • H/C (ISBN: 9781522502708) • US $195.00 (our price)

www.igi-global.com

701 E. Chocolate Ave., Hershey, PA 17033
Order online at www.igi-global.com or call 717-533-8845 x100
To place a standing order for titles released in this series, contact: cust@igi-global.com
Mon-Fri 8:00 am - 5:00 pm (est) or fax 24 hours a day 717-533-8661

As in everything I do,
this is dedicated to my wife Lisa,
and our children Liam and Rowan.

Table of Contents

Preface xv

Section 1
User Research

Chapter 1
Quantifying "Magic": Creating Good Player Experiences on Xbox Kinect 1
 Kristie J. Fisher, Google, USA
 Timothy Nichols, Microsoft, USA
 Katherine Isbister, University of California – Santa Cruz, USA
 Tom Fuller, Tableau Software, USA

Chapter 2
Gamification Transformed: Gamification Should Deliver the Best Parts of Game Experiences, Not
Just Experiences of Game Parts 17
 Brock Randall Dubbels, McMaster University, Canada

Chapter 3
The Relationship between Avatar-Based Customization, Player Identification, and Motivation 48
 Selen Turkay, Harvard University, USA
 Charles K. Kinzer, Teachers College, Columbia University, USA

Chapter 4
An Experiment on Anonymity and Multi-User Virtual Environments: Manipulating Identity to
Increase Learning 80
 Richard N. Landers, Old Dominion University, USA
 Rachel C. Callan, Old Dominion University, USA

Chapter 5
Digital Divide: Comparing the Impact of Digital and Non-Digital Platforms on Player Behaviors
and Game Impact 94
 Geoff Kaufman, Carnegie Mellon University, USA
 Mary Flanagan, Dartmouth College, USA

Section 2
Learning Applications

Chapter 6
Making Lifelike Medical Games in the Age of Virtual Reality: An Update on "Playing Games
with Biology" from 2013 103
Thomas B. Talbot, University of Southern California, USA

Chapter 7
Using Serious Gaming to Improve the Safety of Central Venous Catheter Placement: A Post-
Mortem Analysis 120
Daniel Katz, Icahn School of Medicine at Mount Sinai, USA
Andrew Goldberg, Icahn School of Medicine at Mount Sinai, USA
Prabal Khanal, 3D Systems Inc., USA
Kanav Kahol, Arizona State University, USA
Samuel DeMaria, Icahn School of Medicine at Mount Sinai, USA

Chapter 8
Making Learning Fun: An Investigation of Using a Ludic Simulation for Middle School Space
Science 130
Min Liu, The University of Texas at Austin, USA
Lucas Horton, The University of Texas at Austin, USA
Jina Kang, The University of Texas at Austin, USA
Royce M. Kimmons, Brigham Young University, USA
Jaejin Lee, The University of Seoul, South Korea

Section 3
Health Enhancement and Clinical Intervention

Chapter 9
Teaching Childbirth Support Techniques Using the Prepared Partner and Digital Birth: The
Design and Development of Games for Dads-To-Be 154
Alexandra Holloway, University of California – Santa Cruz, USA

Chapter 10
Beyond Gaming: The Utility of Video Games for Sports Performance 183
Roma P. Patel, UC Davis Eye Center, USA
Jerry Lin, USC, USA
S. Khizer R. Khaderi, University of Utah Moran Eye Center, USA

Chapter 11
Games and Other Training Interventions to Improve Cognition in Healthy Older Adults 192
Elizabeth M. Zelinski, University of Southern California, USA

Chapter 12
Computer-Presented and Physical Brain-Training Exercises for School Children: Improving
Executive Functions and Learning.. 206
    Bruce E. Wexler, Yale University, USA

Chapter 13
Promoting Physical Activity and Fitness with Exergames: Updated Systematic Review of
Systematic Reviews... 225
    Tuomas Kari, University of Jyvaskyla, Finland

Chapter 14
Is Artificial Intelligence (AI) Friend or Foe to Patients in Healthcare? On Virtues of Dynamic
Consent – How to Build a Business Case for Digital Health Applications 246
    Veronika Litinski, MaRS Discovery, Canada

Compilation of References 258

About the Contributors 290

Index.. 295

Detailed Table of Contents

Preface.. xv

Section 1
User Research

Chapter 1

Quantifying "Magic": Creating Good Player Experiences on Xbox Kinect.. 1
 Kristie J. Fisher, Google, USA
 Timothy Nichols, Microsoft, USA
 Katherine Isbister, University of California – Santa Cruz, USA
 Tom Fuller, Tableau Software, USA

In November 2010, Microsoft released the Kinect sensor as a new input device for the Xbox 360 gaming console, and more recently the "next generation" of Kinect was released in November 2013 as part of the Xbox One entertainment system. Kinect enables users to control and interact with on-screen elements by moving their bodies in space (e.g., move characters, select menu items, manipulate virtual objects) and via speech input. The team at Microsoft Studios User Research (SUR) has worked with game designers, programmers, and hardware developers on games and other applications that use Kinect. In this article the authors leverage data SUR has collected over the development cycles of many different games created for many different audiences to summarize the unique user experience challenges that the Kinect sensor brings to game development. The authors also propose principles for designing fun and accessible experiences for Kinect.

Chapter 2

Gamification Transformed: Gamification Should Deliver the Best Parts of Game Experiences, Not Just Experiences of Game Parts.. 17
 Brock Randall Dubbels, McMaster University, Canada

Gamification may provide new venues for offering customer experiences. The chapter compares three models of game play analyzed through user experience research. In section 1, the three models are presented: Grind Core, Freemium, and Immersion. These models are differentiated as value delivered, and user experience. Value and experience are defined across four categories: function, emotion, life change and social impact. In section 2, the role of emotion, value, and experience are described to inform how games can be transformative, providing the life change and social impact through the immersion experience model. This chapter is intended to help developers identify what kind of value experience they want to provide their customers, and provide a new view of gamification.

Chapter 3

The Relationship between Avatar-Based Customization, Player Identification, and Motivation 48

Selen Turkay, Harvard University, USA

Charles K. Kinzer, Teachers College, Columbia University, USA

Player identification is an outcome of gameplay experiences in virtual worlds and has been shown to affect enjoyment and reduce self-discrepancy. Avatar customization has potential to impact player identification by shaping the relationship between the player and the character. This mixed method study examines the effects of avatar-based customization on players' identification with their characters, and the effects of identification dimensions (i.e., perceived similarity, wishful identification, embodied presence) on their motivation in a massively multiplayer online game, Lord of the Rings Online (LotRO). Participants (N = 66) played LotRO either in customization or in no-customization group for ten hours in four sessions in a lab setting. Data were collected through interviews and surveys. Results showed both time and avatar customization positively impacted player identification with their characters. Player motivation was predicted in different sessions by different identification dimensions, which shows the dynamic and situational impact of identification on motivation.

Chapter 4

An Experiment on Anonymity and Multi-User Virtual Environments: Manipulating Identity to Increase Learning... 80

Richard N. Landers, Old Dominion University, USA

Rachel C. Callan, Old Dominion University, USA

Little prior research has empirically examined anonymity in learning. In this study, we manipulated learner identity by experimentally assigning learners to participate in online discussion either anonymously or using their actual name, crossed with learning medium (OpenSim/Second Life vs. real-time chat), with the goal of determining if anonymous discussion in multi-user virtual environments (MUVE) provides unique value to learning (a 2x2 between-subjects design). Results from a quantitative hierarchical multiple regression analysis revealed both main effects: participants who were anonymous scored lower (d = -0.46) and participants discussing in a MUVE scored lower (d = -0.47) on the learning measure without interactive effect, suggesting that anonymizing participants during content-related discussion may reduce learning under certain circumstances. We suggest instructors encourage learners to represent themselves authentically in any VEs to maximize learning and also discourage instructors from adopting MUVEs if their only reason to do so is to host synchronous discussion.

Chapter 5

Digital Divide: Comparing the Impact of Digital and Non-Digital Platforms on Player Behaviors and Game Impact 94

Geoff Kaufman, Carnegie Mellon University, USA

Mary Flanagan, Dartmouth College, USA

With a growing body of work demonstrating the power of games to transform players' attitudes, behaviors, and cognitions, it is crucial to understand the potentially divergent experiences and outcomes afforded by digital and non-digital platforms. In a recent study, we found that transferring a public health game from a non-digital to a digital format profoundly impacted players' behaviors and the game's impact. Specifically, players of the digital version of the game, despite it being a nearly identical translation, exhibited a more rapid play pace and discussed strategies and consequences less frequently and with less depth. As a result of this discrepancy, players of the non-digital version of the game exhibited significantly higher post-game systems thinking performance and more positive valuations of vaccination, whereas players of the digital game did not. We propose several explanations for this finding, including follow-up work demonstrating the impact of platform on basic cognitive processes, that elucidate critical distinctions between digital and non-digital experiences.

Section 2
Learning Applications

Chapter 6

Making Lifelike Medical Games in the Age of Virtual Reality: An Update on "Playing Games with Biology" from 2013 103
Thomas B. Talbot, University of Southern California, USA

Medical simulations differ from other training modalities in that life procession must be simulated as part of the experience. Biological fidelity is the degree to which character anatomical appearance and physiology behavior are represented within a game or simulation. Methods to achieve physiological fidelity include physiology engines, complex state machines, simple state machines and kinetic models. Games health scores that can be used in medical sims. Selection of technique depends upon the goals of the simulation, expected user inputs, development budget and level of fidelity required. Trends include greater availability of physiology engines rapid advances in virtual reality (VR). In VR, the expectation for a naturalistic interface is much greater, resulting in technical challenges regarding natural language and gesture-based interaction. Regardless of the technical approach, the user's perception of biological fidelity, responsiveness to user inputs and the ability to correct mistakes is often more important than the underlying biological fidelity of the model.

Chapter 7

Using Serious Gaming to Improve the Safety of Central Venous Catheter Placement: A Post-Mortem Analysis 120
Daniel Katz, Icahn School of Medicine at Mount Sinai, USA
Andrew Goldberg, Icahn School of Medicine at Mount Sinai, USA
Prabal Khanal, 3D Systems Inc., USA
Kanav Kahol, Arizona State University, USA
Samuel DeMaria, Icahn School of Medicine at Mount Sinai, USA

Serious gaming a tool that can be used to train new physicians in a manner that keeps patients out of harm's way. This is especially true when teaching procedures, which in the medical community if often done in a "see one, do one, teach one" manner. Additionally, many teachers focus on technical aspects of the procedure and may leave out or de-emphasize non-technical portions of the procedure such as hand washing and patient positioning. This chapter per the authors investigates the utility of serious gaming in teaching physicians technical procedures. The chapter begins with game development and will end with a discussion of the results of the prospective randomized study.

Chapter 8

Making Learning Fun: An Investigation of Using a Ludic Simulation for Middle School Space
Science 130

Min Liu, The University of Texas at Austin, USA
Lucas Horton, The University of Texas at Austin, USA
Jina Kang, The University of Texas at Austin, USA
Royce M. Kimmons, Brigham Young University, USA
Jaejin Lee, The University of Seoul, South Korea

We examine the use of a ludic simulation designed for middle school space science to support students'
learning and motivation. A total of 383 sixth graders and 447 seventh graders participated in this study.
The findings showed that sixth- and seventh-graders perceived the simulation as having substantial ludic
characteristics and educational value. The results indicated that having a playful experience is important
for this age group and that participating in a ludic simulation can help motivate students to learn school
subjects. Results also indicated that incorporating ludus into the learning experience can improve students'
attitudes toward the subject matter. Implications of policy, research, and practice with regard to using
ludic simulations to support classroom-based learning were discussed.

Section 3
Health Enhancement and Clinical Intervention

Chapter 9

Teaching Childbirth Support Techniques Using the Prepared Partner and Digital Birth: The
Design and Development of Games for Dads-To-Be.. 154

Alexandra Holloway, University of California – Santa Cruz, USA

In today's California, a mother's primary social support person in childbirth is her partner, guiding her
through a multidimensional experience, helping her make sense of unforgettable emotions and sensations.
Preparing the partner is an integral step to making sure that the mother is well-supported in her birth.
Because the mother's experience is influenced by the support she receives, and because birth partners
need more support than is recognized, we target birth partners with a learning intervention. We investigate
video games as a vehicle for knowledge transfer to the birth partner, both as currently available and as
a positive learning tool. To address the problem of limited access to childbirth preparation methods,
we investigated, designed, and evaluated two games: The Prepared Partner, an online Flash game, and
Digital Birth, an iPhone application. Both games allow the user to practice various supportive actions
in the realm of childbirth support for a mother in labor. We found that players of The Prepared Partner
met learning goals while enjoying the game.

Chapter 10

Beyond Gaming: The Utility of Video Games for Sports Performance 183

Roma P. Patel, UC Davis Eye Center, USA

Jerry Lin, USC, USA

S. Khizer R. Khaderi, University of Utah Moran Eye Center, USA

The interest around the utilization of video games as a component of rehabilitative therapy has dramatically increased over the past decade. Research efforts have confirmed the positive effects of repetitive gaming in improving visual outcomes; however, there is limited knowledge on the mechanism of action delivered by repetitive gaming. Utilizing knowledge of the visual system, including targeting specific cells in the retina with visual stimuli, the authors captured the training effects of gaming to augment pre-selected skills. Specifically, the authors embedded a homerun derby style baseball game with a contrast threshold test, to stimulate parvocellular retinal ganglion cells. Parvocellular cells are the first line of the ventral, or "what" pathway of visual processing. Repetitive stimulation of the parvocellular system shows promising preliminary results in improving batting performance.

Chapter 11

Games and Other Training Interventions to Improve Cognition in Healthy Older Adults 192

Elizabeth M. Zelinski, University of Southern California, USA

Many of the cognitive declines in healthy aging are moderated by experience, suggesting that interventions may be beneficial. Goals for aging outcomes include improving performance on untrained tasks, remediating observed cognitive declines, and ensuring preservation of functional ability. This selective review evaluates current progress towards these goals. Most research focuses on untrained tasks. Interventions associated with this outcome include games and exercises practicing specific cognitive skills, as well as aerobic exercise, and modestly benefit a relatively narrow range of cognitive tasks. Few studies have directly tested improvements in tasks on which individuals have been shown to experience longitudinal decline, so this goal has not been realized, though remediation can be examined rather easily. Little work has been done to develop psychometrically strong functional outcomes that could be used to test preservation of independence in everyday activities. Virtual reality approaches to functional assessment show promise for achieving the third goal.

Chapter 12

Computer-Presented and Physical Brain-Training Exercises for School Children: Improving

Executive Functions and Learning 206

Bruce E. Wexler, Yale University, USA

This chapter reviews the neuroscience foundation for understanding and harnessing neuroplastic processes that shape the structure and function of the human brain after birth, describes a newly developed, integrated series of computer presented and physical exercises to promote activity-related development of neurocognitive systems of attention and executive function in elementary school children, and reviews evidence of the efficacy of the program. The computer-presented brain exercises have new functionalities that more fully shape the training to each user's individual profile of cognitive strengths and weaknesses than was previously possible. The programs also provide assessments of each child's cognitive strengths and weaknesses based on built in formal tests of cognition and error analytic algorithms applied to 15-20,000 responses from each child while using the brain training program.

Chapter 13
Promoting Physical Activity and Fitness with Exergames: Updated Systematic Review of
Systematic Reviews 225
Tuomas Kari, University of Jyvaskyla, Finland

This updated systematic review of systematic reviews evaluates the effectiveness of exergaming on physical fitness and physical activity. A systematic literature search was conducted on 10 databases, first in 2014 and then repeated in 2016. In total, 1040 and 287 articles were identified. 68 and 31 articles were found potentially relevant and selected for closer screening. The quality of all relevant articles was evaluated using the AMSTAR tool. After the duplicates were removed and inclusion, exclusion, and quality criteria were implemented, six and three articles remained for review. The results indicate that exergaming is generally enjoyed and can evoke some benefits for physical fitness and physical activity, but the current evidence does not support the ability of exergaming to increase physical fitness or physical activity levels sufficiently for significant health benefits. This systematic review also revealed gaps in previous research. Additional high-quality research and systematic reviews concerning exergaming are needed.

Chapter 14
Is Artificial Intelligence (AI) Friend or Foe to Patients in Healthcare? On Virtues of Dynamic
Consent – How to Build a Business Case for Digital Health Applications 246
Veronika Litinski, MaRS Discovery, Canada

Failure to appropriately measure Value is one of the reasons for slow reform in health. Value brings together quality and cost, both defined around the patient. With technology we can measure value in the new ways: commercially developed algorithms are capable of mining large, connected data sets to present accurate information for patients and providers. But how do we align these new capabilities with clinical and operational realities, and further with individual privacy? The right amount of information, shared at the right time, can improve practitioners' ability to choose treatments, and patients' motivation to provide consent and follow the treatment. Dynamic Consent, where IT is used to determine just what patients are consenting to share, can address the inherent conflict between the demand from AI for access to data and patients' privacy principles. This chapter describes a pragmatic Commercial Development framework for building digital health tool. It overlays Value Model for healthcare IT investments with Patient Activation Measures and innovation management techniques.

Compilation of References 258

About the Contributors 290

Index 295

Preface

INTRODUCTION

Video games and digital experiences have come to have an important place in modern society. Game experiences have become ubiquitous. Games have been adapted for enhancing productivity tools, customer experiences, marketing, communication, teaching and learning, data collection, and even medical interventions. Games are still games, and thanks to computers and communications infrastructure, we can now experience a wide variety of gaming experiences with a great variety of content, purpose, and participation. Articles in these sections present insight and exploration, extending what we know about games, gamification, and simulations. This collection is drawn from articles selected as enhanced, top-articles published in a leading, peer-reviewed journal.

This preface begins with a brief background about the journal, and then provides an overview and summary of the 14 chapters in this book. The book is organized in three sections by theme: User Research, Learning Applications, and Health Enhancement. Each section is briefly defined, and each chapter is given an overview related to that section theme. This preface concludes with some recommendations and goals for future research, policy, and practice.

IJGCMS

The International Journal of Games and Computer-Mediated Simulations (IJGCMS) was launched in 2009 (http://www.igi-global.com/ijgcms). The journal is devoted to the theoretical and empirical understanding of electronic games and computer-mediated simulations. The journal is interdisciplinary in nature; it publishes research from fields and disciplines that share the goal of improving the foundational knowledge base of games and simulations. The journal publishes critical theoretical manuscripts, qualitative and quantitative research studies, meta-analyses, worked examples, industry post mortems on product research and implementation for development, and methodologically sound case studies.

The journal also includes book reviews to keep readers on the forefront of this continuously evolving field. Occasional special issues from the journal provide deeper investigation into areas of interest within either gaming or simulations.

The main goal of this peer-reviewed, international journal is to promote a deep conceptual and empirical understanding of the roles of electronic games and computer-mediated simulations across multiple disciplines. A second goal is to help build a significant bridge between research and practice on electronic gaming and simulations, supporting the work of researchers, practitioners, and policymakers.

In the following paragraphs, the editorial policy of IJGCMS, and five guiding principles are presented.

Principle 1: Quality and Rigor in Content and Review

The first important principle is. IJGCMS follows a double-blind review process to ensure anonymity and a fair review. The review process is intended to be critical, but helpful and instructive. We want the journal to provide high-value function, positive emotional experience, and potentially, transformation, and social impact.

Research articles that are published may contain either quantitative or qualitative data collection and analyses. However, articles using either method must present data to support and justify claims made within the article. Articles that simply summarize data without presenting it or the analytical techniques used, are not considered.

Theoretical manuscripts are also published. However, these theoretical reviews must create new knowledge by synthesizing and critiquing past research. Simple summaries of existing literature without thoughtful and considerate analyses are not considered.

Principle 2: Interdisciplinary Focus

IJGCMS seeks to publish about games and simulations within and across the numerous fields and disciplines that undertake research related to games and simulations. Psychology, Education, History, Journalism, Literature, Computer Science, Engineering, Fine Arts, and Medicine are just a few of the areas where one could find gaming and simulation research. Unfortunately, in academia, the notion of standing on the shoulders of giants has implied an historical perspective, but often only within the well-defined academic fiends. There are often well-defined boundaries, useful for maintaining traditions, and content-domain-specific concepts and methods. The journal seeks to celebrate history and progress. This is an important part of moving the field forward. But the journal is intended to cross traditional boundaries, and include parallel work in other fields to address and explore the complex natures of games and simulations.

IJGCMS publishes articles from any discipline as long as the content of the work is related to games and simulations. Including multiple fields helps researchers recognize their similarities as well as introducing them to colleagues from distinctly different backgrounds.

Principle 3: International Contributions

A third principal of this journal is its international focus. The journal editorial board seeks and recruits scholars to represent different international perspectives on the Editorial Board of IJGCMS. Having diverse, international perspectives provides two interesting opportunities. First, readers are able to see how researchers from various countries conduct and report scientific inquiry, and their interests on games and simulations. For example, what are the current inquiries and interests on games in various countries around the world?

Principle 4: Innovation

Gaming and simulation researchers often create new concepts, new methods, new implementation, and new technologies in their work. IJGCMS is a journal where authors who create new approaches can publish their findings. IJGCMS is also a resource for readers who want to keep up with the latest and most cutting edge technologies. Special, focused issues with guest editors promote new insights; connect readers with new ideas, new researchers, and new topics for in-depth analyses of conceptual or technological innovations. As part of the journal mission, proposals for special issues are welcomed at any time.

Principle 5: Implication for Practice and Theory

Research should inform theory and application. We seek the betterment of humanity. Our intent to provide some improvement in whatever means possible: entertainment, research methods, our interactions with contributors and readers; we seek to examine and share cultural issues ranging from gender bias and misogyny, cultural diversity, and representation (or the lack thereof) as race, age, and gender. Games and entertainment have much to teach us about our society, and provide a mirror report on our culture. How we play and what we seek for entertainment can be indicative of our cultural values.

Developing a strong research foundation for games and simulations is important, but only to the extent that the research provides a positive impact. We ask our reviewers directly:

- "What are the implications of this work on other research, policy, and practice?"

Recommended topics for the journal include (but are not limited to) the following:

- User research: Psychological aspects of gamers
- Cognitive, social, and emotional impact of games and simulations
- Critical reviews and meta-analyses of existing game and simulation literature
- Current and future trends, technologies, and strategies related to game, simulation development, and implementation
- Electronic games and simulations in government, business, and the workforce
- Electronic games and simulations in teaching and learning
- Frameworks to understand the societal and cultural impacts of games and simulations
- Impact of game and simulation development use on race and gender game and simulation design
- Innovative and current research methods and methodologies to study electronic games and simulations
- Teaching of games and simulations at multiple age and grade levels
- Medical usage of games for clinical assessment and intervention
- Postmortems on game development

Additionally, IJGMCS partners with academic and professional conferences. A tremendous amount of cutting-edge research in games and simulations is first presented at conferences. In an attempt to capture these findings, IJGCMS often partners with conferences and organizations to create special issues focused on the leading research from conferences including the Meaningful Play Conference, Serious Games Conference, Ludica Medica, and the American Education Research Association (AERA) Games Special Interest Group.

This book includes top articles from four regular issues, and four special issues. The special issue topics were:

- Gamification, Serious Games, and Ludic Simulations
- Teacher Education
- HFACS (Human Factors Analysis and Classification System)
- Ludica Medica, a special issue drawn from the Games for Health Conference subgroup called, which specialized on Health Care simulations.

The IJGCMS' editorial board consists of four separate groups (http://www.igi-global.com/ijgcms).

1. The international advisory board consists of a panel of leading experts from around the world. The advisory board provides insight and helpful recommendations to the editor; they are also available for suggestions and recommendations of future journal goals and special issues.
2. IJGCMS has a panel of associate editors. Each submission goes to one associate editor. Having a smaller number of associate editors has provided a way to maintain consistency in reviews.
3. Each submission receives three double blind, peer reviews. The associate editor and the editorial review board members are matched as closely as possible based on the topic of the submission and the expertise of the reviewer. However, the reviews are double blind. In other words, the authors do not know the identity of the reviewers assigned to their paper, nor do the reviewers know the author.
4. The fourth group is a panel of co-book review editors who help select books, solicit reviewers, and edit reviews. IJGCMS publishes a book review with almost every issue.

Journal special issues are also peer-reviewed. This can be done in a number of different ways. Often, for conference special issues, submissions are reviewed once at the submission stage, where they are accepted or rejected for presentation. Accepted papers are then offered the chance to submit for journal submission, where they are again reviewed either by the conference review panel or IJGCMS' own review board.

The four issues for 2012 and 2013 produced a total of 46 peer-reviewed papers. The editorial board selected fourteen articles as the top articles. Upon selection the authors were given the opportunity to update their paper with new data, new findings, or related articles since the original publication of their paper. The purpose and goal of this book is to highlight the work of those authors, presenting findings that will impact the field of gaming and simulations in multiple ways.

The book itself is divided into three themes sections:

- Section 1: User Research
- Section 2: Learning Applications
- Section 3: Health Enhancement

It should be noted that the purpose of this summary is to highlight the main ideas. It is not intended to take away from the rich insights or deep conversations included in each chapter. For instance, one of the goals of IJGCMS is to publish articles that directly impact policy, research, and practice. Each chapter in this book contains a rich description of the 'so what?' for those working in various fields. A thorough reading of each chapter will provide such detailed information.

SECTION 1: USER RESEARCH

User research focuses on understanding user behaviors, needs, and motivations through observation techniques, task analysis, and other feedback methodologies. In 2013 and 2014, there were five articles selected that develop around the theme of user research.

Chapter 1: Quantifying "Magic" – Learnings from User Research for Creating Good Player Experiences on Xbox Kinect

In our first chapter, Drs. Fisher, Nichols, Ibister, and Fuller offer insight into their work as part of the Microsoft Studios User Research (SUR) team, and their role in creating the first full-body gaming experiences for the Kinect system. They describe outcomes of internal research for the development of Kinect, describing the method and practice SUR has created for working with game designers, programmers, and hardware developers on games and other applications that use Kinect.

Chapter 2: Gamification Transformed – Gamification Should Deliver the Best Parts of Game Experiences, Not Just Experiences of Game Parts

In the second chapter the author presents a new perspective on gamification. The article proposes that gamification should deliver the best parts of game experiences, not just experiences of game parts. The chapter examines commonly held views that gamification is the use game elements used in a non-game context, often to amplify a user's engagement in an activity that may be tedious or repetitive. The problem with this definition is that it does not define which game elements that make for great experiences.

The author presents three game models predicated upon the experience of the user. Where Grind Core and Freemium games rely heavily on compulsion loops, the Immersion model is constructed around reward action contingencies. These three experiential models are compared to examine potential to deliver value across four categories: function, emotion, life changing, and social impact.

Chapter 3: The Effects of Avatar-Based Customization on Player Identification

In article three, Drs. Turkay and Kinzer explore the way that games allow players to perceive themselves in alternate ways in imagined worlds. This mixed method study aims to examining the effects of avatar-based customization on players' identification and empathy with their characters in a massively multiplayer online game, Lord of the Rings Online (LotRO). The authors use Self-Determination Theory to interpret results and found that avatar-based customization positively impacted players' identification with their avatars, and had significant influence on player behavior. Through avatars, games allow players to explore themselves in alternate ways in imagined worlds. They explain that player identification with an avatar –how the player is represented—as an important part of gameplay experience, and how it affects player enjoyment.

Chapter 4: An Experiment on Anonymity and Multi-User Virtual Environments – Manipulating Identity to Increase Learning

The fourth article in the section was an experimental study that compared the effect of having students hold a discussion though a multi-user virtual environment (MUVE; OpenSim) vs. a chat room and whether these discussions were anonymous or not. Their results and discussion provide valuable context for researchers and educators to use in considering when and how to use MUVEs and features of (e.g., anonymity). More generally, Landers and Callan's research emphasizes that MUVE environments require an abundance of context-sensitive and descriptive empirical research to help identify best use, and the boundaries of their use.

Chapter 5: Digital Divide – Comparing the Impact of Digital and Non-Digital Platforms on Player Behaviors and Game Impact

In Chapter 5, authors Kaufman and Flannagan examine whether transferring a board game from an analog to a digital format would impact players' perceptions of the game and still be as effective in changing player beliefs about the role of vaccines. Small changes in game presentation were accounted for, yet players reported that playing the same game, when the game board was presented on a digital tablet made the game more complex. Studies of how small changes can yield markedly different user experience are important for understanding development and design issues in the creation and implementation of games. The authors propose several explanations for this finding, including follow-up work demonstrating the impact of platform on basic cognitive processes, to help elucidate critical distinctions between digital and non-digital game play experience and impact.

SECTION 2: LEARNING APPLICATIONS

In Section 2, the theme of learning applications provides research on the use of games and simulations for training and learning in a variety of educational contexts, ranging from children in science and mathematics classrooms, to adults in medical school. These chapters look at the potential for using computer games and simulations to enhance learning through interactive content.

Chapter 6: Making Lifelike Medical Games in the Age of Virtual Reality – An Update on "Playing Games with Biology"

In Chapter 6, the author addresses this question "How much fidelity is really necessary in a medical simulation?" by presenting a rich review of best-case scenarios for efficacy of realism, immersion, and narrative. In medical education, high fidelity is important for training practitioners to care for people. This is because the learning that happens in games must result in better-prepared doctors, nurses, caregivers, and responders. In some situations, this training could make the difference in someone's life. This chapter provides insight on simulating biological processes for medical training and education.

Chapter 7: Using Serious Gaming to Improve the Safety of Central Venous Catheter Placement – A Post-Mortem Analysis

In Chapter 7, Katz, Goldberg, Khanal, Kahol, and DeMaria provide a post-mortem, describing the need, process, and development of a serious game for medical training. They describe the need for a realistic and highly interactive simulated environment; so medical students can learn not only psychomotor skills (e.g., lumbar puncture, endotracheal intubation), but also key management and non-technical steps, which make their tasks safer. Their game trains in the placement of central venous catheter (CVC). The chapter provides an examination of the challenges encountered while designing and executing their serious game as medical research. Evaluation of the CVC game showed the game to be an effective teaching tool, and the authors provide insight for similar projects in the future.

Chapter 8: Making Learning Fun – An Investigation of Using a Ludic Simulation for Middle School Space Science

Chapter 8 provides observations on the use of ludic simulations for middle school space science instruction. They present a brief overview of previous research on simulation and then explore some intricacies of students' ludic experiences within it. The purpose of the chapter is to better understand the value of ludic simulations in education. Play is an organizing principle in ludic simulation.

Unlike true simulations, which would replicate a system with absolute fidelity and realism, ludic simulations hold ludic (playful) activity to be as important as fidelity or realism. They offer observations of student experiences with ludic simulations for engagement and education rigor.

SECTION 3: HEALTH ENHANCEMENT AND CLINICAL INTERVENTION

Section 3 provides six chapters covering topics such as childbirth education, sports therapy for rehabilitation and enhancement of vision, and improving cognition for healthy aging for the elderly and for children. These chapters are followed by a meta-analysis on the effectiveness for using games to improve physical fitness, and a case study, which provides insights into building a business case for using games and artificial intelligence for medical services and data collection.

Chapter 9: Teaching Childbirth Support Techniques Using the Prepared Partner and Digital Birth – The Design and Development of Games for Dads-to-Be

Chapter 9 provides insight into user research methods that inform the development of a serious game to prepare first-time parents for childbirth. Ethnography was used in a mixed-methods approach, which included interview, observation, and survey techniques to document the practice of childbirth preparation. The data collected was used to construct software requirements to inform the game design. Prepared Partner was developed as an online Flash game, and Digital Birth, was developed as a free iPhone application. Both games are described as tools to help birth parents prepare for supportive actions and behavior in labor in birthing. Outcomes in the analysis indicated that the games were effective in helping players met learning goals for birth preparation, and players reported enjoyment in playing the games.

Chapter 10: Beyond Gaming – The Utility of Video Games for Sports Performance

In Chapter 10, the authors created a game to look at the potential to improve vision with a video game. They grounded their study in vision research, building their variables around the psychophysics of vision. Specifically, they target research that has shown that repetitive stimulation of the parvocellular system shows promising preliminary results in improving vision related to batting performance in baseball. To examine this, they embedded a homerun derby style baseball game with a contrast threshold test, to stimulate parvocellular retinal ganglion cells.

Chapter 11: Games and Other Training Interventions to Improve Cognition in Healthy Older Adults

In Chapter 11, the author presents a review offering insight into how games may be used to help older populations maintain independence and autonomy through improving cognition. Dr. Zelinsky makes the case that games and exercises can serve as interventions for healthy aging, and provides specific areas that need to be researched to fulfill that promise.

Chapter 12: Computer-Presented and Physical Brain-Training Exercises for School Children – Improving Executive Functions and Learning

In Chapter 12, Bruce Wexler of Yale University examines academic and cognitive outcomes in a study of C8 games, which were developed to examine the use of video games for improvements in attention, executive function, and their relationship to the academic performance of elementary school children. The article, "Integrated Brain and Body Exercises" presents the neuroscience foundation for understanding and enhancing performance, as well as study outcomes, which offer insight into cognitive training, diagnostic feedback, and the value of informing each child of their cognitive strengths and weaknesses. The training outcomes were then related to improved academic outcomes for elementary children in two schools

Chapter 13: Promoting Physical Activity and Fitness with Exergames – Updated Systematic Review of Systematic Reviews

In Chapter 13, a systematic review is provided to offer insights and precedent. With the increase in new media, there is also a significant decrease in the level of physical activity in people. The purpose of this chapter is to answer the following research questions: (1) What levels of exertion are typical for exergaming? (2) Can exergaming contribute to increasing physical activity? (3) Can exergaming be used to increase physical fitness? This study also identifies relevant gaps in previous research and gives recommendations for future studies.

Chapter 14: Is Artificial Intelligence (AI) Friend or Foe to Patients in Healthcare? On Virtues of Dynamic Consent – How to Build a Business Case for Digital Health Applications

In Chapter 14, the author presents a process for developing a business model. This is done with examples and best practice through a case study called the Home Assessment Tool (HAT). To understand, design, and implement, she describes a method called the Patient Journey Mapping. This technique is used for tracking and gaining insights into consumers' day-to-day experiences, i.e. the full complexity of their decisions regarding aging-related cognitive change.

CONCLUSION

The work that has been published on games and simulations in IJGCMS is continuing to advance research, policy, practice, and improve people's lives. In conclusion, one could ask, what can we learn about the current state of the field from these 14 publications? Listed below are some of the key findings from each of these studies:

1. User experience research is essential in game development. Developers need research data to understanding the user for the design, development, and implementation of software as games and simulations.
2. Digital games and simulations exist in many forms, but those that provide high-value experiences to the user are more likely to lead to optimal experience. These experiences are built upon delivering intuitive functionality, positive emotional tone, and personal transformation, resulting in trust and loyalty in customers, leading to social impact.
3. There is a difference between making a difficult game, and a challenging game. Challenging games have activities that can be overcome in the flow of game play, difficult activities must be over powered – to do this the player leaves the focus and flow of the game
4. Software, products, and services should look beyond enhancing tedious activities with parts of games, and consider how to deliver the best experiences that games offer.
5. Avatar creation and play creates self-exploration and provides the potential for life-changing experience.
6. Gamification and the use of MUVES require an abundance of context-sensitive and descriptive empirical research that identifies the boundaries of their use and replicates findings.
7. Small differences in game presentation can alter the beliefs and approach to a game experience. Platform and presentation provide a demonstrable difference in response in basic cognitive processes between digital and non-digital game play experience and impact.
8. Games can increase contact and accessibility for sharing important information, and learning about life transitions.
9. Games for medical education and training should be planned based upon how much fidelity is necessary.
10. Game and simulation designers can improve learning outcomes by considering the interaction and representation– not just the content. In well-designed games and gamification, the interaction is the content.

11. Consistency, feedback, and the appropriate use of representations through game interfaces can positively impact user learning and cognitive development.
12. Games and game-play can be used as hooks to help students then help students understand and explore real-world rites of passage.
13. Play is an important part of learning content in simulations and gaming. The ability to practice and explore can be signaled through design and provide a playful approach. Play can increase motivation in academic learning.
14. Simulations can be playful (ludic) and fun. Students who are unmotivated to participate and engage in learning often change their mind when presented with playful, game-like experiences.
15. Games have the potential to provide complex experiences to present a new frontier in cognitive aging and quality of life
16. Physical behavior aligned with digital game play can be motivating, and potentially lead to cognitive enhancement, improved academic learning, and improved well-being
17. New digital delivery systems can help improve physical health outcomes through data collection and artificial intelligence to inform the individual user for behavioral modification, as well as provide broader patters for institutional insights to provide broader health care initiatives.

Brock Dubbels
McMaster University, Canada

Section 1
User Research

Chapter 1
Quantifying "Magic":
Creating Good Player Experiences on Xbox Kinect

Kristie J. Fisher
Google, USA

Katherine Isbister
University of California – Santa Cruz, USA

Timothy Nichols
Microsoft, USA

Tom Fuller
Tableau Software, USA

ABSTRACT

In November 2010, Microsoft released the Kinect sensor as a new input device for the Xbox 360 gaming console, and more recently the "next generation" of Kinect was released in November 2013 as part of the Xbox One entertainment system. Kinect enables users to control and interact with on-screen elements by moving their bodies in space (e.g., move characters, select menu items, manipulate virtual objects) and via speech input. The team at Microsoft Studios User Research (SUR) has worked with game designers, programmers, and hardware developers on games and other applications that use Kinect. In this article the authors leverage data SUR has collected over the development cycles of many different games created for many different audiences to summarize the unique user experience challenges that the Kinect sensor brings to game development. The authors also propose principles for designing fun and accessible experiences for Kinect.

INTRODUCTION

Video games can provide players with a wide range of experiences, from the thrill of shooting enemies in a highly-realistic combat scenario to the challenge of solving complex spatial puzzles, to the simulation of racing a Formula 1 car, to the simple joy of beating a friend in virtual Scrabble™. A common goal for all video games, though, is to either allow players to experience things that they cannot do or that do not exist in real life, or to greatly enhance the fun, reward, or challenge of real life experiences by creating a "game-ified" version of them. The Kinect full-body motion gaming sensor for the Xbox 360[1] allowed for the creation of new types of games based on experiences that had been difficult to "game-ify" in

DOI: 10.4018/978-1-5225-1817-4.ch001

the absence of such full-body motion input technology, such as dance, fitness, and augmented reality. It also has the potential to make video games from more "traditional" genres (action, combat, racing, etc.) more immersive by allowing users to more "directly" interact with them.

The Vision of Kinect

Kinect was designed with a few specific goals in mind. First, Kinect was meant to expand the technical capabilities of motion gaming. While Kinect was being developed, an extremely popular motion gaming device was the Nintendo Wii[2]. The Wii requires the player to move a handheld controller through space in order to interact with its games. This constrains the user experience in some ways, because Wii games are programmed to attend only to the location of the controller relative to the sensor, meaning that the rest of the player's gestures are irrelevant. Typically the player uses the standard "Wii-mote" controller to interact with the system, but some games require a secondary controller accessory, which requires users to have a collection of input devices. Similarly, the Sony EyeToy, which was a motion input device for the Playstation 2 that pre-dated the Wii[3], allowed for some controller-free gesture input, but its functionality was extremely limited. There was therefore an opportunity to advance motion gaming to include inputs derived from full body tracking of multiple players in 3D space as well as speech inputs. In expanding the technical capabilities of motion gaming, the possibilities for player experience could also expand.

As one result of this increased technical capability, the creators of Kinect wanted using it to feel "magical." The design philosophy behind this was that when a game removes the intermediate input device between the user and the system – the game controller – then the players' ability to interact with games "directly" using their bodies would inherently be more immersive than traditional controller gaming experiences. Indeed, the idea that movement can enhance the engagement and emotion of players

Figure 1.

is supported by some researchers in the field of human-computer interaction (e.g., Bianchi-Berthouze, Kim, & Patel, 2007; Lindley, Le Couteur, & Berthouze, 2008).

Kinect also had the potential to broaden the Xbox 360 audience beyond the "traditional" console gamer audience, as the target audience for most games created at Microsoft Studios for the Xbox 360 is males between the ages of 18-40. That is, with Kinect there were new opportunities to create casual gaming experiences that could appeal to whole families and to individuals who were intimidated by popular video game genres, such as shooters, and/or by the steep learning curve of the Xbox 360 controller. One of the advertising slogans for Kinect is "All you need is you," and the official Xbox website explains, "You already know how to play" (http://www.xbox.com/en-US/kinect), which implies that no previous gaming experience is required in order for players to play and enjoy games made for the Kinect. More specifically, part of the creative vision for Kinect was that players could "intuitively" know what to do in order to play the games without being given any instructions.

The Role of User Research at Microsoft Studios

The user research group was one of the teams at Microsoft Studios tasked with helping to realize the design goals for Kinect. Microsoft Studios is responsible for creating games and other entertainment content for Microsoft's platforms, and Microsoft Studios User Research (SUR) has existed at Microsoft since 2000. The group was created during the development of the original Xbox console[4] with the task of determining whether the games being created for the Xbox would be fun for players. Its function is to work in close partnership with game designers from the earliest stages of the production cycle to ensure that players are having the experience that the game creators intend for them to have[5]. To do this, SUR operationally defines relevant aspects of user experience (for example, "fun," "mastery," "pace," "frustration,") and gathers behavioral, attitudinal, game telemetry, and other data from users via a variety of methods derived from academia and industry. SUR then collaborates with the game creators to iterate on the game experience in response to those data (see Pagulayan et al., 2007, for a more detailed summary of games user research work at Microsoft Studios).

SUR has been involved in the development of Kinect games from their early incubation through the present. In light of the new gesture- and speech-based interaction models, new types of game experiences, and new types of players that Kinect introduced to the Xbox system, SUR adapted its methodologies to provide the same type of data and insights to game development teams that it had for traditional controller games. In the remainder of this article, we first describe the learnings SUR has assimilated throughout the last 5 years regarding how the unique capabilities and limitations of Kinect affect player experience. We then describe best practices for designing games for Kinect that are most likely to create good experiences for users. Most of the findings discussed here are distilled from numerous usability studies of Kinect games conducted at Microsoft, and all games described here that were developed by Microsoft Studios have been released to the public. It is important to note, however, that specific data and detailed methodology from usability studies and other research on internal in-development titles or on competitor titles is considered Microsoft confidential. Therefore, in the remainder of the article we present our view on full-body motion gaming as industry experts, but we are able to describe only our high-level learnings from our studies.

KINECT'S UNIQUE USER EXPERIENCE CHALLENGES

Kinect presented players with entirely new interaction models, and while novelty alone can present a challenge to user experience, the inherent nature of the system presents additional challenges, especially in light of the design vision for Kinect.

Very Few Gestures Are "Intuitive," and Gestures Are Hard to Teach

One of the user experience goals for Kinect was that using it should feel "intuitive." Instructions and tutorials should be unnecessary, and players should simply know what to do as soon as they step up to use the system. In the fields of cognitive psychology and human computer interaction, the term "intuitive" typically implies that within a given system there are proper affordances to guide the user to the correct action and/or that the user has prior knowledge that he or she can apply to interact with the system (e.g., Norman, 2010, 2013). The work done by SUR during the development of many Kinect games revealed that, even with good affordances, it was generally difficult for users to correctly guess the exact gestures the system was expecting. For example, given an on-screen virtual ball and a target, it might be "intuitive" that the object of the game is to throw the ball at the target, but there are a variety of ways that one can "throw" a ball (overhand, underhand, "push", two handed, spinning around first to get momentum, etc.). If only one of those ways is "correct" according to the input the system is expecting, then the system will only work for the handful of users who happens to have the correct "intuition."

For example, several early Kinect games required users to initiate engagement with the game by "waving" at the Kinect sensor. The template wave gesture that the Kinect was programmed to detect was performed as follows: the user held his or her hand up parallel with the body (with the elbow bent and the open palm facing the television) and steadily moved the hand to the side, away from the body, and back, for a range about 90 degrees. However, users of all ages and levels of experience with video games and technology interpreted the instruction to wave at Kinect in a numerous, distinct ways (see Figure 2).

Figure 2.

This inability of players to have an "intuitive" experience with Kinect's gesture inputs is exacerbated by the inherent limitations of the Kinect system to distinguish player intentions from player inputs and by the inherent variability of individuals, as described in the section below. Because having an inherently "intuitive" system was practically impossible for most Kinect games, the focus of SUR and the game development teams when creating the first games for Kinect shifted to providing players with comprehensive gesture instruction and in-game feedback (see Figure 3 for an example).

Gesture instruction has its own challenges, however, because learning to perform a gesture precisely and accurately is very difficult for people generally (e.g., Allard & Starkes, 1991); athletes, dancers, and musicians dedicate lifetimes to mastering precise muscle movements. SUR found that creating good learning systems for Kinect not only involved having clear instructions for players, but also having relatively loose gesture input requirements to accommodate variability in how players executed the gestures that they learned. Hinrichs and Carpendale (2011) came to a similar conclusion in a field study of a "natural user interface" (NUI) system requiring gesture inputs, that is, that flexibility of the system to respond to multiple types of user input is important for creating an accessible and enjoyable user experience. We further discuss player instruction in the Creating Good Player Experiences with Kinect section. Clear feedback to players regarding gesture execution is also difficult to provide because in order to do so the game needs to make accurate assumptions around what the user's intentions are, which is difficult for Kinect, as discussed below. A best practice developed by SUR was that every input gesture a user executes should have some type of feedback associated with it; furthermore, all intended user behaviors should have visual and/or auditory feedback. Conducting extensive user testing on Kinect games can also reveal common types of "mistakes" people will make, which can help to improve instruction and feedback.

User Intent Is Ambiguous and User Input Is Variable

With a gamepad controller, the ways in which user input can be variable are constrained by the nature of the system, and the system can be easily programmed to recognize and respond to nearly all input variations. On the Xbox 360 controller there are 15 buttons and two analog joysticks, and user input is comprised of which buttons are pressed, the order in which they are pressed, and the duration with which they are pressed. With gesture inputs, however, there are infinite degrees of freedom in how a user might execute a given gesture, even when the user has a correct understanding of what gesture he or she

Figure 3.

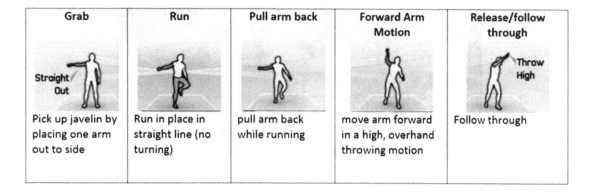

is meant to perform. Additional variations in the size, shape, and mobility of human players themselves further add to the variability of gesture inputs.

Moreover, with the console gamepad controller, player intent almost always matches player input. For example, if a player approaches an in-game enemy and hits the attack button, the game will register that the button was pressed and will respond according to the programmed game rules. It is safe for the game to "assume" that when a specific button press is registered, the user intended to execute the corresponding action (excepting cases in which the user does not know which actions are mapped to which buttons or accidentally presses the wrong button). If during game development it is observed that a player's attempt at executing an attack repeatedly fails, then the player inputs can be examined within the game context to determine why the failure occurred and what design solution, if any, is required to ameliorate it.

In the case of this attack example, perhaps the player did not execute the attack at the appropriate distance from the enemy, which may mean that player training was ineffective or that the game's logic should be revised to adjust the attack range to match player expectations. Alternatively, perhaps the attack is designed to require a level of precision in execution that the player must learn to master over time. In this case there would be no "issue" to fix as long as the player is aware of this mastery aspect of gameplay. When user intentions are known (the game detects the attack button input, so it "knows" the player wants to attack), then comparing design intent to player experience can be done simply and directly in most cases.

In a full-body gesture controlled game, however, the input registered by the game may not be an accurate representation of what actions the user is actually doing or intending to do. This is a broader problem with gesture-based NUIs in that what the machine can "sense" usually does not encompass everything the user can do, and what the user is doing at a given moment may not be the input that the machine desires (Benford et al., 2005). For example, when a user is intending to swipe his or her hand from the right to the left side of the screen, the mere act of raising the hand and positioning the arm to perform the swipe may be interpreted by Kinect as an input gesture. In many cases, this might trigger an unintended action from the system (see Figure 4).

Figure 4.

When the system responds to the user in unexpected ways, due to an incorrect interpretation of intent, players can develop a flawed mental model of how to interact with a game. For example, in the game Kinect RUSH: A Disney Pixar Adventure (2012), players control the movements of an avatar in 3D space. One of the most frequently used avatar actions was the "run" action. For the run input gesture, the speed of the avatar was controlled by the player swinging his or her arms in a run motion. In one area of the game, players were meant to perform a "swim," gesture, which resembled a breast stroke. While the game was still in development, it was observed during testing that some players (who were young children, the target audience) would forget the correct gesture in these swim areas and would default to using the gesture they were most familiar with, run (see Figure 5). Because the run gesture and the swim gesture both involve forward arm movement, the system occasionally responded to it, but not reliably, and not in proportion to the increased intensity of players' run gesture input, which led to a kind of "start-stop" partial progression of the on-screen avatar. In this way, players could become frustrated or could feel like they did not have control over their avatar. However, because the system was responding *at all*, the users didn't realize that they were performing the incorrect gesture.

The user experience issues caused by the variability in player inputs and the inherent limitations of the Kinect system in interpreting player intent can be mitigated somewhat by good instruction and feedback. However, these limitations should also be considered in the initial phases of conceptualizing and designing games, as discussed in the Creating Good Experiences with Kinect section of this article.

Kinect Must Manage Players in 3D Space

Players interact with Kinect by moving their bodies through space and/or by speaking to it, and multiple players can interact with Kinect at once. Because of this, a Kinect game has the added challenge of player management—knowing which player is which and where players are in the room and relative to one another—which controller games do not. Because Kinect was meant to appeal to families and casual gamers, being able to play with friends or family members as a group was an important capability. However, all of the issues described above with player instruction, in-game feedback, player intent, and

Figure 5.

gesture variability, are compounded when multiple users are interacting with the system. The Kinect first needs to communicate to players how to initiate interaction with it (e.g., "Player 1 – Raise hand to start!"), then it needs to determine which players are attempting to engage, and lastly it needs to ignore inputs form other individuals who may be in the room but not actively playing the game.

Once a game has begun, Kinect needs to keep track of player identity and location and to differentiate gesture inputs from each active player, which can be a technical challenge if players' limbs or bodies overlap as they move about to interact with the game. Kinect must also keep players within the boundaries of the "playspace" (the area in which Kinect can detect players), and it must alert players when they have moved outside of the ideal boundaries (see Figures 6 and 7). All of these player management features can impact player experience and have design implications. Furthermore, in any kind of social situation, players' attention is likely to be divided between the game and the other individuals in the room, which creates additional constraints for providing effective instruction and feedback.

Figure 6.

Figure 7.

CREATING GOOD PLAYER EXPERIENCES WITH KINECT

The new types of game experiences enabled by Kinect are accompanied by new user experience challenges. Creating good player experiences in Kinect games requires designing games that leverage the unique capabilities of Kinect while circumventing its limitations and avoiding some of the potential issues described above. The following best practices are specific to Kinect, but are aligned with more generalized motion game design principles recently suggested by Mueller and Isbister (in press).

In Kinect Games, the Gestures Should Be Fun in and of Themselves

Given that Kinect differentiates itself from its competitors with its 3D camera and its ability to use full-body gestures as inputs without the aid of a secondary device, players' gestures should be at the center of any good Kinect experience.

- *The gesture controls themselves should be enjoyable to execute.* In Kinect Sports Season 2 (2011), players in SUR studies reported that it was fun to make throw gestures when playing football, because it allowed them to feel like they were really playing the game in a way that went above and beyond the feeling of throwing a football in a controller game.
- *Gesture controls should correspond to the experience of the game.* For example, performing squats as an input gesture is appropriate for a fitness game, but probably not for a shooter game.
- *Gesture controls should not cause discomfort or inappropriate fatigue during the duration of expected play sessions.* The goal of some full-body motion games may be for players to be active or to exercise, and in this case feeling fatigued or having sore muscles after playing would be appropriate, but this should not be the case for games in which physical exertion is not a design goal. For example, in Child of Eden (2011) players stand in front of Kinect and move one or both of their arms around a screen to control the reticles of weapons used to destroy enemies. Maintaining this kind of standing position for a 30 minute gaming session can cause fatigue and back ache.
- *"Enhance" the players' experience of executing a gesture, rather than to simply providing an on-screen representation of that movement.* In Dance Central (2010), a "model dancer" avatar (rather than a representation of the player) is at the forefront of the screen so that players can feel that they are embodying a stylish dancer who is executing the moves perfectly, whether or not that is actually the case. In Kinect Disneyland Adventures (2011) there is a park "attraction" in which players control a character flying through the sky. The feeling of controlling a character who is flying is enhanced by using gesture inputs because of the unique "first person" perspective achieved when the player's body movements control the game camera. In Puss in Boots (2011) players have partial control over an on-screen character, and when they perform sword fighting moves the on-screen character does not match player movements exactly, but rather performs exciting animations in response to players' inputs, which enhances the feeling of combat.
- *Give players the opportunity to express themselves through movement when possible.* In Kinect Sports Season 2 (2011) the movements of the on-screen character closely match the movements that a player performs, so if after winning a player jumps up and down to celebrate, the on-screen character will do the same. Similarly, Dance Central 3 (2012) has modes that allow players to earn points through "free style" dancing.

If a Game Might Be Easier or More Fun for Players to Control with a Gamepad Controller, then It Is Probably Not Appropriate for Kinect

In short, a game should have appropriate precision and timing requirements based on Kinect and player limitations. If players are asked to perform complex sequences of gestures with the same precision and timing with which they are asked to perform complex sequences of button presses on a gamepad, then they are highly likely to fail and become frustrated.

- *What Kinect defines as a "successful" input should incorporate both player variability and the game context in which it must be performed.* For example, if a gesture must be performed quickly while under pressure, then the required gesture input should be more loosely defined in the system. Kinect Star Wars (2011) requires players to perform sequences of complex gestures in rapid succession during combat, which strains the capabilities of players and the Kinect; as a result, in SUR studies many players reported that controls could feel unresponsive. In contrast, the game Puss in Boots (2011) essentially equates *amount* of gesture activity (speed and frequency) with amount of damage that the player does to the enemies during combat, and it accepts as input nearly any type of arm "swipe" gesture in any direction, facilitating player success.
- *Input gestures should be as distinct from one another as possible with respect to the system's capabilities, and "big," simple gestures should be favored over subtle, complex ones.* While still in development, Fable the Journey (2012) experimented with various types of gestures for players to use to cast spells. SUR observed that complex, multi-step gestures were often mis-interpreted by the Kinect sensor. The Kinect especially confused the inputs from gestures that required the player to bring his or her hands together in front of the chest, because Kinect detection of overlapping limbs was relatively less robust. These complex gestures were eventually abandoned for very simple spell casting gestures.
- *Avoid "Kinect-ifying" an existing gamepad controller experience.* Many "traditional" console games are not designed in a way that affords "translating" button presses into gesture inputs. In Kinect Disneyland Adventures (2011), character navigation was difficult for many players in SUR studies. Moving a character through 3D space with precision (which requires 360 degree turning, quick direction changes, avoiding obstacles, etc.) is something that is easily accomplished with gamepad button or joystick inputs. With gesture inputs, in contrast, it is impossible to create a one-to-one mapping of movement, as it is with a joystick, because players must face the screen and must stay within the Kinect playspace in order to play the game (in this game, players bend the arm at the elbow and use the hand to direct the movement of the character). These limitations make it very challenging to create good 3D character navigation experiences for Kinect.
- *If the game experience requires lots of graphical user interface menu navigation, leverage speech inputs as much as possible.* This applies to both Kinect games and controller games "augmented" with Kinect inputs. For example, in The Elder Scrolls V: Skyrim (2011), a detractor of fun reported by players in post-release competitor studies conducted by SUR was that the Inventory and Favorites menus were difficult to learn how to use and that navigation through the menus could be slow and tedious. This could cause problems for players attempting to use the menus quickly to execute important in-game actions. The use of Kinect speech commands allows players to bypass the use of these menus.

Ensure Appropriate Player Instruction

As discussed in earlier sections, effective player instruction around gesture inputs is essential for a good Kinect user experience.

- *The gesture instruction should be primarily visual in nature.* As discussed above, learning a gesture is inherently difficult, and the best way to teach is to show.
- *Highlight the parts of the body that are most important for executing a gesture.* When presented with a visual demonstration of a gesture, players may not spontaneously attend to the part of the gesture that is most relevant to the input the system is expecting, so gesture instructions should emphasize the parts of the body that are most important (see again Figure 3).
- *Text or audio cues should describe important aspects of the gesture that are difficult to illustrate or emphasize visually.* For example, in Kinect Sports (2010), players are told via voice over instructions that lifting their knees high while running in place will increase their character's speed.
- *User testing can help to determine the range of gesture inputs that the system should accept, given player variability, and can help guide the creation of effective player instruction tools.* Because children have no "real world" experience driving cars, when attempting to use a "steering wheel" gesture during the development of Kinect RUSH: A Disney Pixar Adventure (2012) and Kinect Joyride (2010), children were often observed during SUR tests to make very large gestures with their arms and to cross their hands when trying to turn. User testing helped to determine an appropriate sensitivity for steering and informed the look of the animated gesture instruction figures.
- *Provide players with an opportunity to practice gestures and receive feedback without risking failure.* A universal best practice for all types of video games is providing a place for players to learn and practice game controls without the risk that their actions will result in failure. For example, in the original Halo: Combat Evolved (2001), players are given the opportunity to practice moving their character and controlling the camera before ever encountering an enemy or acquiring a weapon. Given the difficulty of learning to perform gestures, this principle is even more salient for Kinect games.
- *When possible, provide feedback not just on whether or not the player is doing a gesture correctly, but also on how the player needs to adjust his or her motions.* Because mastering kinesthetic awareness and executing gestures with precision is so inherently difficult (e.g., Allard & Starkes, 1991), it is not helpful for the game to simply tell the player that their input is incorrect. Rather, it needs to tell the player what to do to correct his or her action (see again Figure 6, which shows how Kinect Adventures, 2010, instructs players on how to move back into the playspace).
- *Do not require users to memorize too many gestures, and provide frequent cues to players to remind them of required gesture inputs.* Human working memory is limited (e.g., Baddeley, 1992), so games should provide users with frequent cues reminding them of the appropriate gesture to perform (especially during a user's initial experience with the game) so that the user does not become "stuck." For example, in the Kinect Sports (2010) hurdles event, the player must only perform two gestures, running and jumping, and there is a multi-faceted jumping cue so that players can prepare to jump and execute the jump with correct timing.

Kinect Should Leverage a User's Social Context when Possible

Kinect games can be a better group experience compared to controller games because individual controllers are not required to accommodate each player, and because the lines between "players" and "observers" are often blurred. That is, Kinect can accommodate a "jump in, jump out" player-switching model and can detect speech inputs from any nearby individuals.

Therefore, whenever possible, games should find ways to include others in the room in the fun, even if indirectly (a design best practice that is also supported by Reeves, Benford, O'Malley, & Fraser, 2005). Games should also strive to make the experience of watching others play enjoyable (see Figure 8 for an example). Kinect's ability to entertain a large group by providing a fun observer experience, by "knowing" about other players in the room, and by allowing others to participate in the experience in some way is something that can contribute to the feeling of "magic" that is part of Kinect's design vision.

Kinect "Augmentation" Should Not Be Disruptive

Some Xbox 360 controller games (e.g., Elder Scrolls V: Skyrim, 2011; Mass Effect 3, 2012; Halo: Combat Evolved Anniversary Edition, 2011) have used Kinect's speech input capabilities to augment the game experience, for example by allowing players the option of using speech commands for menu navigation or as shortcuts to performing some in-game actions. Though speech inputs are inherently simpler and faster for players to execute than gesture inputs, for each game there exists a unique syntax for how speech commands need to be executed in order for the system to recognize them; this creates the same need for player instruction and feedback as with gesture inputs. The Xbox 360 dashboard provides a good example for how to cue users to the existence and proper use of speech commands (see Figure 9). More recently, Dead Rising 3 (2013) for the Xbox One[6] allows players to direct non-player characters by pointing at the screen, in addition to using speech commands. Zoo Tycoon (2013) allows players the option to use Kinect to interact "directly" with the animals in their virtual zoo.

Figure 8.

All of these types of Kinect-augmented experiences have the potential to enhance players' gameplay by allowing them to accomplish some tasks more efficiently and/or by allowing them to interact with the game in ways that are more realistic or engaging (for example, actually speaking to a character rather than pressing a button to "have a conversation"). However, it is important that a given Kinect augmentation does not require the player to shift his or her attentional focus from the primary game experience and does not put the player at risk of failure if the player is required to put down the controller in order to interact with Kinect. The best Kinect augmentations for games explicitly inform players of their existence, have a system for teaching players how to use them, and provide players with affordances and feedback that they are able to attend to given their current gameplay context. Lastly, Kinect features should be optional to accommodate players who cannot or do not want to use them.

CONCLUSION

Kinect is a unique technology with both amazing capabilities and inherent limitations. These capabilities and limitations, and how they intersect with human cognitive abilities when it comes to learning and executing gestures, need to be considered carefully when creating games. Even as the technical power of Kinect increases in the "new generation" of gaming consoles, such as the Xbox One and beyond, there are some user experience challenges that will remain despite any new technical achievements.

Specifically, players will always need clear affordances, effective instructions, and timely, informative feedback in order to properly execute gesture and speech inputs. Furthermore, gesture and speech controls that are too complex to teach players or that are too similar to one another given innate human variability and system limitations will always cause problems for the player and the system.

Figure 9.

ACKNOWLEDGMENT

The authors would like to acknowledge all of the members of the Microsoft Studios User Research team, whose work contributed to the learnings described in this article. We would also like to acknowledge Microsoft Studios design director Clayton Kauzlaric for his insights and feedback.

REFERENCES

Allard, F., & Starkes, J. L. (1991). Motor-skill experts in sports, dance, and other domains. In *Toward a general theory of expertise: Prospects and limits*, (pp. 126-152). Academic Press.

Baddeley, A. (1992). Working memory. *Science, 255*(5044), 556–559. doi:10.1126/science.1736359 PMID:1736359

Benford, S., Schnadelbach, H., Koleva, B., Anastasi, R., Greenhalgh, C., Rodden, T., … Steed, A. (2005). Expected, sensed, and desired: A framework for designing sensing-based interaction. *ACM Transactions on Computer-Human Interaction, 12*(1), 3-30. doi: 1073-0616/05/0300-003

Bianchi-Berthouze, N., Kim, W. W., & Patel, D. (2007). Does body movement engage you more in digital game play? and why? In *Proceedings of the 2nd international conference on Affective Computing and Intelligent Interaction, ACII '07*. Berlin: Springer-Verlag. doi:10.1007/978-3-540-74889-2_10

Child of Eden [Computer software]. Montreuil-sous-Bios, France: Ubisoft.

Dance Central [Computer software]. Redmond, WA: Microsoft.

Dance Central 2 [Computer software]. Redmond, WA: Microsoft.

Dance Central 3 [Computer software]. Redmond, WA: Microsoft.

Dead Rising 3 [Computer software]. Redmond, WA: Microsoft.

Elder Scrolls, V. *Skyrim* [Computer software]. Rockville, MD: Bethesda Softworks.

Fable the Journey [Computer software]. Redmond, WA: Microsoft.

Halo: Combat Evolved [Computer software]. Redmond, WA: Microsoft.

Halo: Combat Evolved Anniversary Edition [Computer software]. Redmond, WA: Microsoft.

Hindrichs, U., & Carpendale, S. (2011). Gestures in the Wild: Studying Multi-Touch Gesture Sequences on Interactive Tabletop Exhibits. In *Proceedings of the SIGCHI Conference on Human Factors in Computing Systems, CHI '11*, (pp. 3023-3032). New York: ACM.

Kim, T. (2008, November 6). In-Depth: Eye To Eye – The History of EyeToy. *Gamasutra*. Retrieved from http://www.gamasutra.com/php-bin/news_index.php?story=20975

Kinect Adventures [Computer software]. Redmond, WA: Microsoft.

Kinect Disneyland Adventures [Computer software]. Redmond, WA: Microsoft.

Kinect Joyride [Computer software]. Redmond, WA: Microsoft.

Kinect Party [Computer software]. Redmond, WA: Microsoft.

Kinect Rush: , *A Disney Pixar Adventure* [Computer software]. Redmond, WA: Microsoft.

Kinect Sports [Computer software]. Redmond, WA: Microsoft.

Kinect Sports Season 2 [Computer software]. Redmond, WA: Microsoft.

Lindley, S. E., Le Couteur, J., & Berthouze, N. L. (2008). Stirring up experience through movement in game play: effects on engagement and social behaviour. In *Proceedings of the SIGCHI Conference on Human Factors in Computing Systems, CHI '08*, (pp. 511–514). New York: ACM. doi:10.1145/1357054.1357136

Mass Effect 3 [Computer software]. Redwood City, CA: Electronic Arts.

Mueller, F., & Isbister, K. (in press). Movement Based Game Guidelines. In *Proceedings of the SIGCHI Conference on Human Factors in Computing Systems, CHI '14*. New York: ACM.

Nintendo. (2009). *Nintendo Annual Report 2009*. Retrieved from http://www.nintendo.co.jp/ir/pdf/2009/annual0903e.pdf

Norman, D. (2010). Natural User Interfaces are Not Natural. *Interaction*, *17*(3), 6–10. doi:10.1145/1744161.1744163

Norman, D. (2013). *The Design of Everyday things, Revised and Expanded Edition*. New York: Basic Books.

Pagulayan, R., Keeker, K., Fuller, T., Wixon, D., & Romero, R. (2007). User-centered Design in Games. In A. Sears & J. Jacko (Eds.), *The Human-Computer Interaction Handbook: Fundamentals, Evolving Technologies, and Emerging Applications* (pp. 742–758). Hillsdale, NJ: Earlbaum. doi:10.1201/9781410615862. ch37

Puss in Boots [Computer software]. Agoura Hills, CA: THQ.

Reeves, S., Benford, S., & O'Malley, C. (2005). Designing the Spectator Experience. In *Proceedings of CHI 2005*.

Zoo Tycoon [Computer software]. Redmond, WA: Microsoft.

ENDNOTES

[1]   The Xbox 360 gaming console was released in November, 2005. The Kinect sensor was released in November, 2010.

[2]   According to the earnings report released by Nintendo in 2009, by the end of the 2009 fiscal year the Nintendo Wii had sold 50.39 million units since its release in November 2006 (Nintendo, 2009).

[3]   The Sony EyeToy was released in 2003, and as of 2008 it had sold 10.5 million units (Kim, 2008).

[4]   The first Xbox console was released in North America on November 15, 2001.

[5]   More information about Studios User Research can be found at their website, www.studiosuserreearch.com

[6]   The Xbox One was released in North America on November 22, 2013.

Chapter 2
Gamification Transformed:
Gamification Should Deliver the Best Parts of Game Experiences, Not Just Experiences of Game Parts

Brock Randall Dubbels
McMaster University, Canada

ABSTRACT

Gamification may provide new venues for offering customer experiences. The chapter compares three models of game play analyzed through user experience research. In section 1, the three models are presented: Grind Core, Freemium, and Immersion. These models are differentiated as value delivered, and user experience. Value and experience are defined across four categories: function, emotion, life change and social impact. In section 2, the role of emotion, value, and experience are described to inform how games can be transformative, providing the life change and social impact through the immersion experience model. This chapter is intended to help developers identify what kind of value experience they want to provide their customers, and provide a new view of gamification.

GAMIFICATION: TWO VIEWS

Games can offer user experiences that build customer loyalty through providing value to the user. However, there is some confusion about how to translate great game experiences into gamification. Traditionally, there have been two views of gamification that are similar (Figure 1).

These two views are problematic. Neither of these views describes which game elements deliver great user experience, how to provide value to the user, or how to deliver these experiences. For example:

- Using game elements in non-game contexts can lead to a confusing user experience. Which elements of games are useful? Digital experiences require an investment of time and resource, and adding game elements to an experience may result in a lack of coherence. What if those game elements don't deliver a game-like experience? This definition could result in providing chocolate-

DOI: 10.4018/978-1-5225-1817-4.ch002

Figure 1. Two views of gamification

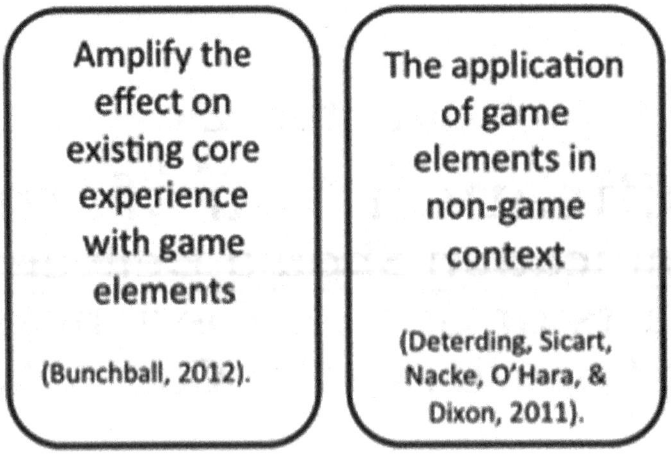

Amplify the effect on existing core experience with game elements

(Bunchball, 2012).

The application of game elements in non-game context

(Deterding, Sicart, Nacke, O'Hara, & Dixon, 2011).

covered broccoli as gamification. Will chocolate make the broccoli better? If there is no game experience, then is it gamification?

• Amplification often depends upon behavioural modification techniques to increase engagement. In high-value interactions with customers, employees, patients, and partners this approach can backfire. User research data has shown that behavioural techniques may lead to short-term engagement, but create long-term resentment and feelings of manipulation.

Gamification: A New Perspective

Today the concept of selling experiences has spread beyond theaters and theme parks (Pine & Gilmore, 1998). Customer experience is an interaction that begins with a customer's first attraction, and evolves into awareness, cultivation, purchase, and advocacy. Customer experience implies a holistic perspective, with customer involvement at different levels - such as rational, emotional, sensorial, physical, and spiritual. Customers are able to recall interactive experiences much more effectively and accurately than passive activities. However, this can also have a negative effect on the customer's experience. Just as interactive, hands-on experiences can greatly develop value creation; it can also greatly facilitate value destruction (Tynan, McKechnie, & Hartley, 2014). This is related to a customer's satisfaction of their experience. By understanding what causes satisfaction or dissatisfaction of a customer's experience, one can adapt and provide optimal experiences to customers(Ren, Qiu, Wang, & Lin, 2016). Digital games offer similar interactive high value experiences to customers, and can extend reach and influence by providing users with meaningful experiences. To provide a meaningful experience, which may provide a sensational, emotional, and even spiritual experience, research on the user experience can provide insight and evidence into how the user experiences all dimensions of an experience.

Traditionally, customer value has been examined from the perspective of business requirements and performance. Many companies now understand that they are providing services to increase the perceived and experienced value of their product. A customer-based approach that considers value within the broader context of a customer's life world (Tynan et al., 2014). Companies that invest in providing excellent customer service are consistently invested in ways to grow and improve how they can add value through providing experience. When companies use cunning and manipulation to stimulate a purchase, the result may lead to customer regret, and a decision to take their business elsewhere (Meyer & Schwager, 2007). Successful companies seek to provide experiences to increase loyalty and enhance enjoyment. The same is true for user experience research in video games.

However, it is common to see incoherence between the design and the goals of an intended game experience (Mitgutsch & Alvarado, 2012). This is because game play encourages the user to interact with the things they might read about in books, or watch on a screen. In games, interactions act as content – the story is told through experience. For the purposes of this chapter, three experiential models of gameplay are presented and compared for functionality, emotional value, and experience. The intent of this comparison is to identify what truly makes game experiences worthy of story, memory, and sharing that experience with others. Games have the potential to provide experiences to users that will build loyalty. To do this, the experience must provide value to the user. For many companies, the goal is to provide a transcendent customer experience, which is transformative, and even spiritual. This experience can generate lasting shifts in attitudes and beliefs, including subjective transformation and flow experience (Schouten, McAlexander, & Koenig, 2007).

THE CREATION OF VALUE IN EXPERIENCE

According to Almquist, Senior, and Bloch (2016), user experiences that deliver high value in four categories specific to their product (Figure 2) will have revenue growth four times greater than that of companies with only one high score (Almquist, Senior, & Bloch, 2016). A successful brand shapes customers' experiences by embedding the fundamental value proposition in every feature (Meyer & Schwager, 2007b).

Value is additive. Companies that provide value in function and emotion are much more likely to provide experiences that are life changing or provide social impact. Many games provide value across these categories, while other provide high-level, even transformative user experiences. Any attempt at gamification should offer the best what games have to offer:

- High-value function,
- Positive emotional experience,
- Potentially transformation, and
- Social impact.

THREE EXPERIENTIAL GAME MODELS

In this section, three game experience models are presented:

- Grind Core,
- Freemium, and
- Immersion.

Figure 2. The Elements of Value
From Almquist, Senior, & Bloch.

These models are presented in the context of a hypothetical game presented in section four. Two of the three models are predicated upon a token economy, where the player can collect, purchase, and trade seeds in place of money.

All three of these experiential models use an engagement loop. An engagement loop refers to reinforcement as feedback loops that keep the player engaged in the game. What matters is how the engagement loop is used.

In general, the engagement loop provides motivation through a call to action. An engagement loop can be expressed in two ways: a compulsion loop (used in Grind Core and Freemium), and Reward Action Contingency (used in the immersion model). The call to action provides details how to participate, and indicates the reward:

- **A Compulsion Loop:** Refers to the game challenge compelling the user into predictable, tedious, and repetitive tasks, undertaken in order to obtain items. The user participates in non-desirable activities to obtain a desirable object. The value of a compulsion loop is that it distracts the player from undesirable activities. The problem with a compulsion loop is that it directs the focus of the user towards the desirable object, a form of extrinsic motivation. This emphasis on extrinsic motivation means that after the desirable object is obtained, the reward is delivered, and if is not absolutely awesome, the user will experience remorse and resentment (Meyer & Schwager, 2007).

Figure 3. Three game experience models

Grind Core Represented by a *hamster wheel.*	Freemium Represented by a *hamster ball.*	Immersion Represented by a *hamster.*
The game play is difficult and requires the user to go on sidequests to collect powerful skills, objects, and companions to overpower the difficult game play. Sidequests often involve tedious repetitive activities similar to running on a hamster wheel, but also act to increase content. The focus of the main quest is often lost in pursuit of objects, items, and companions.	The game play is difficult, and grinding may be tedious and repetitive. The user can make in-game purchases instead of grinding for objects, skills, and extra turns to overpower the challenges. For example, the purchase of the hamster ball makes a hamster invulnerable and allows the player to overpower the challenges of the main quest.	The game play is challenging, but not difficult. The user is given some guidance to develop the skills and knowledge to overcome each obstacle, with the intent of immersing the player in the flow of game play. The user participates in the main quest, and is encouraged to overcome the challenges of the main quest through trial and error.

Figure 4. Engagement loop

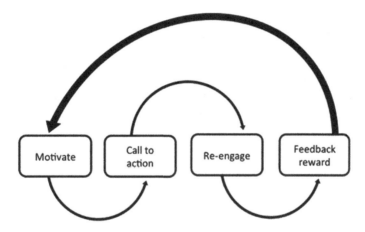

In a video game, this focus and reward system takes the player out of the flow of game play, and replaces the main quest with goals to obtain items. This can reduce the perceived value experience that is delivered.

The compulsion loop also serves as a replacement to game content. The compulsion loop acts as a treadmill, as an habitual, designed chain of activities that will be repeated to gain a neurochemical reward: a feeling of pleasure and/or a relief from pain (Kim, 2014). The compulsion loop has its origins in behavioural modification, and has been called a Skinner Box. As the reward becomes more desirable, the motivation becomes stronger. The user participates in clicking and other repetitious behaviour to gather tokens. Those tokens are then used to obtain powerful objects. This technique is a form of behavioural modification, and has been purposefully integrated into games (Hopson, 2001) to provide content, increase playing time, and habituate the user. The compulsion loop is one of the core features of the Grind Core experience model.

- **Reward Action Contingency:** Where grinding is a vicious cycle, the RAC is a virtuous cycle. The RAC provides reinforcement and reward in service to the game. The RAC provides clear signals of progress to increase the player's sense of empowerment, knowledge, control and potential, and can serve as a conceptual model (Green, Benson, Kersten, & Schrater, 2010). RACs aid the user in overcoming game challenges, rather than redirecting the user to engage in predictable, tedious, and repetitious activities motivated by objects. In contrast to compulsion loops, RACs provide insight through the experience of a canonical example.

A canonical example provides a general experience representative of future activities (Acunas & Schrater, 2010). By engaging with a canonical example, the user gets a sense of future cause and effect relationships, and may form a belief system about similar tasks encountered in future play (Andersen, Zeng, Christensen, & Tran, 2009; Andrade, Ramalho, Santana, & Corruble, 2005; Merrick & Maher, 2007). Although a canonical example is similar to repetition, there is a difference. The RAC must evolve and change so that it is not predictable. The experience of a RAC offers a generalizable model, which results in the creation of a cognitive theory of action (Dubbels, 2010). A cognitive theory of action is simply the user creating an explanation of cause and effect.

EXAMPLE OF THREE GAME MODELS

In the following hypothetical game, the user must return a magic sunflower seed to save their world. The user must travel the golden Road, which is fraught with challenge and danger, and plant the seed in the Sacred Garden. This hypothetical game provides three experience models to play the game: Grind core, Freemium, and Immersion.

Figure 5. The quest of the magic sunflower
Source: Will Cross-Bermingham, 2016.

Experiential Model: Grind Core

Some people like the grind, others do not. This model is common in open world game play, where the player has the option to go where they want, and do what they want. The success of this design is undeniable. Many of the top games are open worlds, where the player can step away from the main quest, and pursue activities that provide opportunities to collect objects, build skills, and recruit companions. However, many open world games depend upon behavioral game mechanics such as explore and gather, craft and sell, build and hoard, combat, and much walking around in the world. These activities provide a lot of content for the user, but may distract from the main quest.

Developers of Grind Core games make the main quest intentionally difficult, and this may require the user to participate in activities not in service to the story. These activities provide rewards, but require participation in predictable, tedious, and repetitive activities. One reviewer described this type of game play as a "junk-hording-crafting grind-loop fetish" (What, 2015). By design, the player is forced into side quests and related stories.

Game Play Content as Junk-Hording-Crafting Grind-Loop Fetish

The user has arrived at Area 2, and must scale the great stones to speak with the spirit guide. Unable to scale the stones, the user runs around looking for ideas (clicking things), and he meets a traveler. The traveler describes a merchant wagon with many amazing objects in Area 3.

Upon finding the merchant, the user discovers the merchant has flying boots, but the user does not have enough seeds to buy the flying boots. The merchant gives the user a bucket, and tells them to go to Area 4 and to gather 40 sparkle stones to trade for the flying boots. When the bucket is full of sparkle stones, he can return and trade for the boots. This is known as a side quest. The user must range far and wide looking for sparkle stones to trade for the boots of flying.

This is a simple quest, but time consuming and tedious. It is also repetitive, as the player must search and click to fill the bucket. The user finds no sparkle stones, but discovers a powerful magician camped outside a cave in Area 4. The magician tells the user that sparkle stones are actually found in Area 5, but it is very dangerous. The magician is very busy, but offers to instruct the user in magic to survive Area 5. For this, the user must bring back food and collect ingredients for the magician. The ingredients are found in Area 6 and Area 7.

Figure 6. Grinding and distraction

Sound confusing?

Now the user is on two side quests:

1. A side quest for the magic teacher,
2. A side quest for the merchant.

This kind of activity is how grinding takes the place of actual content. Sure, the user has many more experiences in the game world, but the activities are all predicated upon a token economy (for definition and history, read Appendix B). The user collects something in the game to trade or create something else. In this case, the tokens are sparkle stones for the merchant, and food and supplies for the magician. In this model of game play experience, the user is given an item to collect, and the item can be used in trade to obtain items to overpower the challenge. To obtain items, the user participates in repetitive, predictable, and tedious activities to earn tokens that can be used to obtain powerful skills and objects.

As the user begins to shift their focus to the acquisition of powerful objects from the merchant, and magic ability from the magician, the user my switch their focus to side quests, and provide a very different user experience. The game is no longer about the story, and overcoming the challenges; instead, the user becomes focused on the desirable items in the token economy, and using them to overpower the challenges.

Grinding focuses the user on earning objects. This approach actually saves developers time and effort, as they are no longer required to create game content in service to the story. They simply make the game challenges too difficult to overcome, and send the user on side quests to earn objects so that they can overpower the challenges. There is an important distinction to be made between overpowering a challenge, and overcoming a challenge.

Figure 7. Map of quests

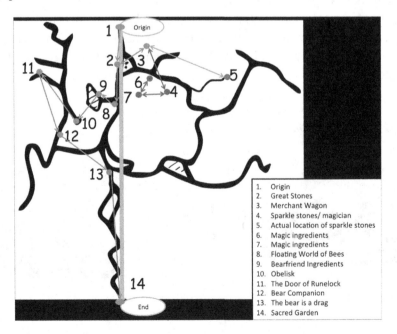

1. Origin
2. Great Stones
3. Merchant Wagon
4. Sparkle stones/ magician
5. Actual location of sparkle stones
6. Magic ingredients
7. Magic ingredients
8. Floating World of Bees
9. Bearfriend Ingredients
10. Obelisk
11. The Door of Runelock
12. Bear Companion
13. The bear is a drag
14. Sacred Garden

Figure 8.

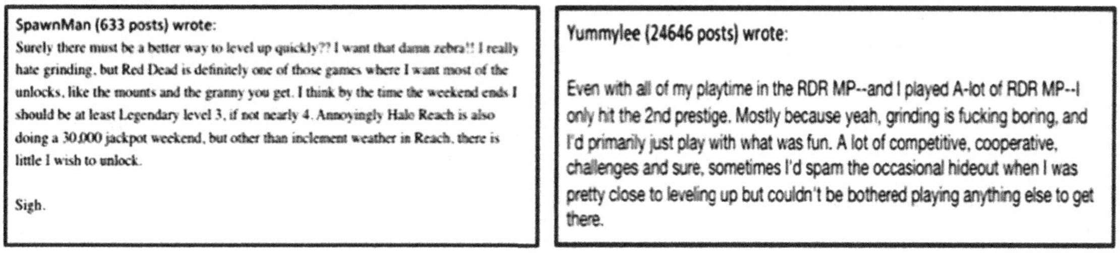

> **SpawnMan (633 posts) wrote:**
> Surely there must be a better way to level up quickly?? I want that damn zebra!! I really hate grinding, but Red Dead is definitely one of those games where I want most of the unlocks, like the mounts and the granny you get. I think by the time the weekend ends I should be at least Legendary level 3, if not nearly 4. Annoyingly Halo Reach is also doing a 30,000 jackpot weekend, but other than inclement weather in Reach, there is little I wish to unlock.
>
> Sigh.

> **Yummylee (24646 posts) wrote:**
>
> Even with all of my playtime in the RDR MP--and I played A-lot of RDR MP--I only hit the 2nd prestige. Mostly because yeah, grinding is fucking boring, and I'd primarily just play with what was fun. A lot of competitive, cooperative, challenges and sure, sometimes I'd spam the occasional hideout when I was pretty close to leveling up but couldn't be bothered playing anything else to get there.

Figure 9.

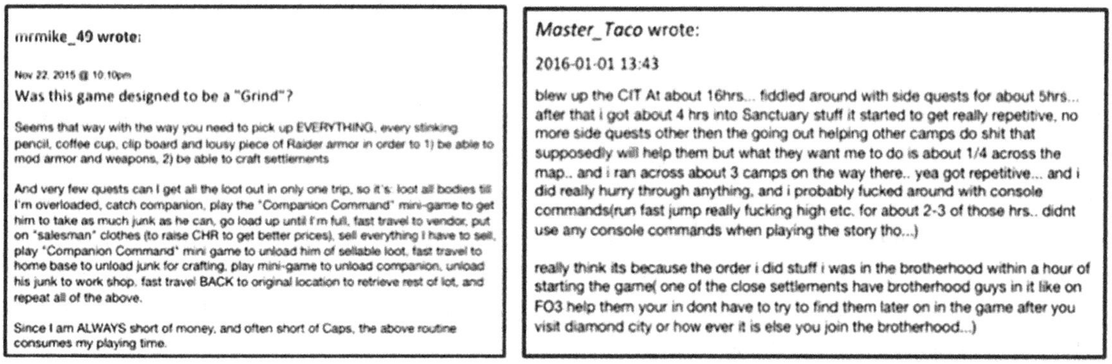

> **mrmike_49 wrote:**
>
> Nov 22, 2015 @ 10:10pm
> Was this game designed to be a "Grind"?
>
> Seems that way with the way you need to pick up EVERYTHING, every stinking pencil, coffee cup, clip board and lousy piece of Raider armor in order to 1) be able to mod armor and weapons, 2) be able to craft settlements
>
> And very few quests can I get all the loot out in only one trip, so it's: loot all bodies till I'm overloaded, catch companion, play the "Companion Command" mini-game to get him to take as much junk as he can, go load up until I'm full, fast travel to vendor, put on "salesman" clothes (to raise CHR to get better prices), sell everything I have to sell, play "Companion Command" mini game to unload him of sellable loot, fast travel to home base to unload junk for crafting, play mini-game to unload companion, unload his junk to work shop, fast travel BACK to original location to retrieve rest of lot, and repeat all of the above.
>
> Since I am ALWAYS short of money, and often short of Caps, the above routine consumes my playing time.

> **Master_Taco wrote:**
>
> 2016-01-01 13:43
>
> blew up the CIT At about 16hrs... fiddled around with side quests for about 5hrs... after that i got about 4 hrs into Sanctuary stuff it started to get really repetitive, no more side quests other then the going out helping other camps do shit that supposedly will help them but what they want me to do is about 1/4 across the map.. and i ran across about 3 camps on the way there.. yea got repetitive... and i did really hurry through anything, and i probably fucked around with console commands(run fast jump really fucking high etc. for about 2-3 of those hrs.. didnt use any console commands when playing the story tho...)
>
> really think its because the order i did stuff i was in the brotherhood within a hour of starting the game(one of the close settlements have brotherhood guys in it like on FO3 help them your in dont have to try to find them later on in the game after you visit diamond city or how ever it is else you join the brotherhood...)

- **Overpower:** To have more strength of force, or effect.
- **Overcome:** Suggests getting the better of adversity with difficulty or after hard struggle.

Games that depend upon overpowering challenges are called Grind Core. Grind Core is named this because the core of the game play is grinding: the user is engaged in tedious, predictable, repetitive activities motivated by desirable objects to overpower in-game challenges. The developer does not need to make clever challenges; the developer just gives the user a bucket to fill with tokens, and the user can trade these tokens for powerful objects. Grind Core experience models work. They save developers time from developing content, and use motivational hooks from behaviour modification to engage the user through compulsion loops (Hopson, 2001).

Grinding and Game Abandonment

According to Snow (2011), only 10% of players finished the final mission of Red Dead Redemption, the 2010 game of the year. Red Dead Redemption took over 800 people and nearly six years to complete, with a total cost estimated at approximately $80-$100 million, making it one of the most expensive games ever developed ("*Red Dead Redemption*," 2013). Although the game was celebrated by many reviewers, and sold well, it is also known for tedious grinding. One need only search for user comments with the name of a celebrated title to learn about the player experience. A simple search on a game title and grinding will provide ample evidence about how users really feel about Grind Core. The following player quotes comes from the review site Giant Bomb (2011).

According to Yummy Lee and SpawnMan, the Red Dead Redemption game relied upon grinding for much of its content. They are not the only people in the world that felt this way. Complaints about grinding are actually pretty common. Fallout 4 is another example of a very popular game that utilizes a lot of grinding.

People are drawn to these games because of the fantastic open worlds that they can explore. Although the story, the world, and the in-game items are fantastic, the game often forces the user to seek side quests to gain objects and skills from the token economy to succeed in overpowering the story challenges. Developers reinforce grinding by creating very difficult story challenges so that the players must grind on side quests. Although compulsion loops do provide activities and experience in the world, compulsion loops rarely serve to advance the experience of the story. Instead, they create more time on tasks unrelated to the main quest.

Some People Like Grind Core

Many players do love the grind. For some, the grind *is* the story. However, the certainty and repetition of grinding makes the gameplay experience predictable and tedious. If the game is simply repetition and maintenance, the user may cut their losses and abandon the game. The rate of game abandonment of acclaimed video games is high (see Appendix A).

However, behaviorist techniques are efficient. By making the main quest difficult, the user must seek out simple grinding activities to collect skill enhancement, such as super weapons, vehicles, magic powers, and powerful companions to over power main quest challenges. This is a very effective strategy, because after the user has made an investment of time and effort grinding, they will become less likely to quit. In behavioural economics, this is called loss aversion. The big idea is that "losses loom larger than gains" (Kahneman & Tversky, 1979). Quitting the game is a loss of invested time, effort, and energy. However, when loss aversion is the motivator, the user rarely perceives the game as a positive emotional experience.

When games utilize compulsion loops, users do report feeling powerful with new skills and objects, but they also report negative emotional experience (Ryan, Rigby, & Przybylski, 2006). These negative emotional experiences result from tedious repetitive side quests. Game developers understand the power of compulsion loops (for more detail on structure, see Appendix B), and their origin in behaviour modification (Hopson, 2001). The problem is that the user may experience a limited number of the possible emotional values identified in Figure 1, and when they do, the valence of those emotions is negative (for more on valence and emotion, see section 6, this chapter).

Experiential Model: Freemium

A hamster ball represents this experiential model. A hamster ball is a hollow plastic ball, which allows the user to freely roll around in the game world to explore and exercise, while preventing injury, and allowing the user to roll over any adversaries. In the hypothetical game, the hamster ball makes the user invincible for an easy in-game purchase of 399 seeds. What do 399 seeds cost? That depends upon the user agreement. What user agreement? The one that was clicked when the user installed the game. By agreeing, the game is connected to a credit card in iTunes, Google Play, Steam, Xbox Live, etc. Then the user can make in-game purchases in the flow of the game play with seeds, rather than seeing the actual dollar amount (this is another form of token economy). With a token economy, things lose their determining force, and the consequences are obscured with tokens, rather than actual cost. This form of cunning is very effective. The user may not understand the cost of a seed until after the purchase, and thus, experience remorse and resentment after the purchase.

Pay to Stay in the Flow of Game Play

The lesson from the Freemium experience model is that people will pay to avoid grinding, and to stay in the flow of the game. Freemium experiential models have evolved a "buy-instantly" button with little disruption. When the user's health is low, or faces a challenge, such as getting to the top of the Great Stones, the user's spirit guide may appear to suggest making a seed offering.

In this hypothetical game, seeds are tokens that can be earned through grinding, or purchased with a linked credit card. When the spirit guide appears, the user can choose one of the options by pressing a button. It is super-easy. The user can choose *Beanstalk* to be easily lifted up, or *Seedfriend* will give him a super energy boost to climb. In-game purchases are easy. Now the user does not need to run around looking for sparkle stones. No tedious, predictable, repetitive searching and clicking.

So, how easy is it to make an in-game purchase? It depends upon the game. But there are many examples of parental tales of horror categorized in search engines as "you spent what on my credit card!"

Just imagine a five-year old. The child wants to play a game. They go to their parents and point out that it is free, and the parent agrees. To download the game, the parent enters their iTunes / Google Play / Xbox Live password, and the child can begin playing their Freemium game.

But here's where it goes bad. Within five minutes the child has spent a significant amount of money on in-game purchases, such as magical seeds, rainbow unicorns, and stealth weapon packs. The following are a small sampling of the many real stories that show just how easy it is:

Why does this happen? Game makers understand that users don't want to think about the purchase, they want to stay in the flow of the game. They would prefer not to spend time grinding when given the option to spend money instead. The game is still predicated upon grinding, but the user can pay for the powerful object rather than grind.

The Freemium experiential model is evidence of the importance of keeping the user in the flow of game play. However, Freemium still redirects the user to make a purchase. The user makes the purchase

Figure 10. Buy instantly from your spirit guide

Figure 11. Examples of children spending thousands on in-game purchases

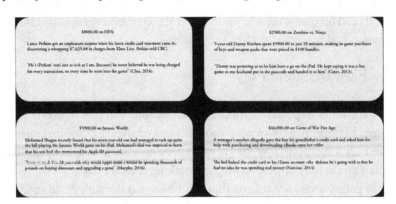

to overpower a game challenge, rather than staying in the flow of the game to overcome it. However, if the developer has made the challenge intentionally difficult, the user may be forced into a choice to spend or grind.

There is great benefit to the Freemium model. Game companies are making billions in microtransactions. In-game purchases were the biggest driver of revenue growth for video games, increasing 21 percent in 2015 to reach USD $44.6 billion ("In-Game Purchases and Construction Toys Drive Global Growth for Toys and Games in 2015 | Business Wire," 2016). This trend has led to concern about the messaging around in-app purchases in similar free-to-play games, which has led the European Commission to strongly recommend that apps built on the business model no longer call themselves 'free' ("European Commission - In-app purchases: Joint action by the European Commission and Member States is leading to better protection for consumers in online games," 2014), and game companies have begun to take more responsibility for in-game purchases. They realize the short-term profit might lead to long-term customer distrust and resentment. The emotional values offered for the Freemium experience model may not increase trust or future loyalty. It may result in a remorseful and even vindictive customer.

Experiential Model: Immersion

This experiential model emphasizes keeping the user in the flow of game play. In an immersion model, all activity is in service to the goals of the game. Many professional game user researchers are employed to conduct play testing to make sure that the user enjoys the game play experience. Fisher, Nichols, Isbister, & Fuller (2014), share that the creators of the Kinect wanted to remove distractions from their games and to make the games feel "magical". To do this, the goal was to increase the players' feelings of immersion by improving the feeling of being in the flow of the game.

The Immersion experiential model still uses engagement loops, but they are implemented as Reward Action Contingencies (RAC). The main difference between a RAC and a compulsion loop is that the RAC can be overcome, where the compulsion loop must be overpowered. This is the difference between challenging and difficult:

- **Difficult:** The activity is hard. The user may not be able to advance.
  - Difficulty is often intentional.
    - To direct the user to grinding or an in-game purchase.

- ◦ Difficulty is inadvertent.
  - ▪ The game is too hard, or doesn't make sense
- **Challenge:** The activity is hard, but can be overcome with correct strategy.
  - ◦ The designer scaffolds the user through reward action contingency (RACs) to acquire and implement a strategy.

Reward Action Contingency (RACS)

The Reward Action Contingency is a type of engagement loop. Where grinding is the vicious cycle, the RAC is a virtuous cycle. The difference is that RACs are designed to provide clear signals in the engagement loop that increase the user's ability to overcome the challenge through strategy, and increase the user's sense of empowerment, knowledge, control and potential (Green, Benson, Kersten, & Schrater, 2010). These elements are very similar to grinding, and provide the same motivational hooks. However, a RAC should be in service to the story, help the user understand the strategy to overcome the in-game challenge, and avoid predictability, tedium, and repetition.

What a RAC does is to provide insight for overcoming game challenges through the experience of a canonical example. A canonical example provides a general experience representative of future activities (Acunas & Schrater, 2010). By engaging with a canonical example, the user gets a sense of future cause and effect relationships, and may form a belief system about similar tasks encountered in future play.

RAC Example

For example, the user learns from his spiritual guide that he must seek out the Floating World, and speak to the Queen of Bees. The user must first find the Obelisk in Area 8, leave Polygon, and visit the Floating World in Area 9. The user undergoes the challenges of finding the Obelisk in Area 8 (Figure 12), transitions to the floating world in Area 9, and learns from the Queen that he will need a powerful companion. For this, the user must become a *Bearfriend*.

Figure 12. The Obelisk and the floating world of Bees

The bees tell the user that to become a Bearfriend, the user must:

1. Claim the Rune Scroll --which offers translation and meaning of runes -- from the ancient hive.
2. Collect blueflower berries found by the Salmonsage River (area 10).
    a. When this is achieved, the queen will give an incantation to the user, which the user must translate with the Rune Scroll.
3. Return to the Obelisk to mix the ingredients.
    a. To mix, the user must recite the incantation in the right order and rhythm by pushing the runes on the Obelisk.
4. Bearfriend potion completed.

Does this sound questy? Yes, very questy.

Does it look like Grind Core? Perhaps it is a bit grindy, but the user is still focused on the main quest, and this challenge can be overcome in service to the story. In this scenario, the user is not filling a bucket with sparkle stones for the merchant, or gathering food and materials for the magician. The focus is on moving forward and overcoming a challenge. This contrasts Grind Core and Freemium, where the focus is on powerful objects to overpower the challenge. Also, the game challenge does not need to be tedious, repetitive, or predictable. A Reward Action Contingency (RAC) is different, as it is not predictable, and is designed to help the user over come the challenge through in-game learning, and keeps the user in the flow of game play, and in service to the main quest.

RACs Are Unpredictable

Although a canonical example is similar to repetition, there is a difference. The RAC must evolve and change so that it is not predictable. The experience of a RAC offers a generalizable model, which results in the creation of a cognitive theory of action (Dubbels, 2010). Recall the activity where the user must collect objects to make the Bearfriend potion? That activity provides a basis for future quests in service to the main quest as a canonical example. Now that the user has made the Bearfriend potion at the Obelisk, they must find the Door of Runelock to return to Polygon.

The Door of Runelock works as a RAC, and the Obelisk served as the canonical example; the Door of Runelock is a variation of the Obelisk, but the Door is a little more challenging. The user recalls that the Rune Scroll provides a translation, and that the runes have to be chanted in the correct sequence and rhythm to say something, like "open the door please."

The user tries clicking a rune. It lights up. The user refers to the Rune Scroll, and sees that they must click a sequence of runes on the door. The user clicks the runes for "open the door please". The door gives feedback that the runes were not clicked in the correct order. The user clicks "please open the door", and the door opens.

This is an example of a RAC. It is similar to previous challenges, but not predictable or repetitive. It requires that the user utilize prior knowledge in a new way. The RAC can scaffold the user and provide learning in the flow of the game. RACs are not predictable, and can provide some surprise.

Figure 13. The Runelock Door

RACS Provide Surprise

Imagine the user has opened the door, but a bear is blocking the passageway. The user remembers what the spirit guide told him about a powerful companion. The user can choose to try out the Bearfriend potion and wake the bear up, or the user can try to sneak around him. The user drinks the potion and wakes the bear.

The bear thanks the user for waking him. He has overslept. Like the user, he must go to the east, offers to escort the user on their mission as long as the user helps him find honey and berries. Good job Bearfriend. Good thing that potion worked!

The user feels rewarded. The simple actions reinforced by the RAC (from the Bees, Figure 8) have led to the fulfillment of the side quest Bearfriend. A RAC is different from a compulsion loop, as it works to provide intermediate goals in service to the larger goal – taking the seed to the garden. The user now has a powerful companion to share and overcome the challenges of the Golden Road. The RAC should provide a cognitive theory of action. In this case, the user has seen that the recommended

Figure 14. The bear companion

course of action is a good course of action, and will lead them to their greater goal. However, a RAC is not predictable. Even though the intermediate goal Bearfriend was accomplished, the terms of the reward should be unpredictable. Juxtaposition and compromise can provide a range of experience, where the perfect solution is never available.

Juxtaposition: An Unpredictable Reward Action Contingency

An example of an unpredictable RAC is juxtaposition. For example, the user is beginning to realize that the bear is very helpful in keeping away adversaries, but the bear also requires a lot of food. At least half of the game seems to be foraging for the bear (grinding). The short-term gain of the bear actually provides long-term loss! The player has a moment of realization, and begins to see things from a new perspective. In this case, the reward becomes a punishment, and the player must weigh the pros and cons of the bear. At this point, the user has almost reached their destination: the Sacred Garden.

Immersion, RACs, and the Sacred Garden for Game Design

At this point, the user has traveled the most of the main quest, and has the experience of losing focus on some side quests (Grind Core and Freemium, points 4-7), and then returning to the Golden Road.

RACs (Reward Action Contingency): A Final Look

As an example, perhaps the user needs to cross a brook. As he gathers up his courage to swim across, he notices turbulence, a fin, and then a close encounter with a large and hungry pike. Pike are willing carnivores, and eat small creatures like hamsters whenever they can. The user becomes unnerved.

Figure 15. The Golden Road

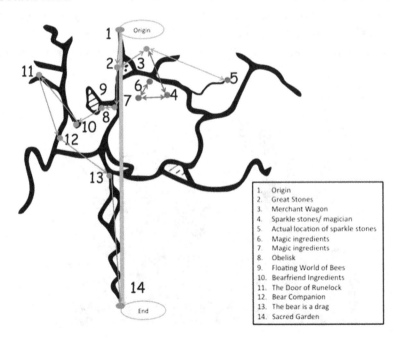

1.	Origin
2.	Great Stones
3.	Merchant Wagon
4.	Sparkle stones/ magician
5.	Actual location of sparkle stones
6.	Magic ingredients
7.	Magic ingredients
8.	Obelisk
9.	Floating World of Bees
10.	Bearfriend Ingredients
11.	The Door of Runelock
12.	Bear Companion
13.	The bear is a drag
14.	Sacred Garden

In this challenge, perhaps the game designer seeks to draw from one of the challenges in the novel Watership Down (Adams, 2009), and use a story within the game to provide a RAC. In the novel, the rabbits of Watership Down were very enterprising, and drew courage from the lore of a mythical rabbit named El-ahrairah. Perhaps the spirit guide comes to the user with a message (Figure 17).

The goal is to further the narrative with this story from the guide. Through the story, the player is scaffolded into building a canonical model that provides a general analogy to help the user. Rather than making the player grind or pay for the power of flight, the game might highlight a hint.

Figure 16. Learning from lore as RACs

Child, open your mind.
Hear me tell the tale of the trickster El-ahrairah.
See how he tricked the hungry pike and crossed the brook

Figure 17. The Sacred Garden

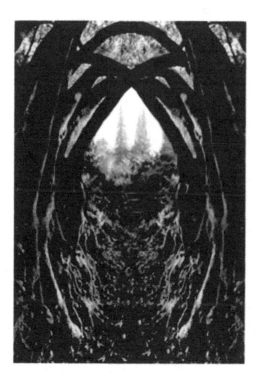

One example of such a story-within-a-story comes from the novel Watership Down. In the novel, the rabbits have a mythical hero that provides the foundation of their culture as rabbits. El-ahrairah is a clever trickster, which must outwit his adversaries rather than overpower them. The stories serve as teaching tales and help the rabbits overcome challenges in the story experience:

Once, so they say, he had to get home by swimming across a river in which there was a large and hungry pike. El-ahrairah combed himself until he had enough fur to cover a clay rabbit, which he pushed into the water. The pike rushed at it, bit it and left it in disgust. After a little, it drifted to the bank and El-ahrairah dragged it out and waited a while before pushing it in again. After an hour of this, the pike left it alone, and when it had done so for the fifth time, El-ahrairah swam across himself and went home. Some rabbits say he controls the weather, because the wind, the damp and the dew are friends and instruments to rabbits against their enemies. (Adams, 2009, p. 14)

As a RAC, the user can follow this example, and the developer can also design multiple paths to solve the problem. So in addition to the mud bunny, the designer can highlight objects that are clickable, and encourage the user to play around by clicking on things.

For example, perhaps there is a flat piece of wood that might turn up with a little searching around. With a combination of clicking and moving, the wood is in the water, and the user is floating across. But perhaps the user needs an oar? There are many ways to engage the user and create meaningful experiences in service to the main quest.

The idea is to lead the user to take action through a Reward Action Contingency (RAC). This might involve lots of clicking, but through trial and error they may discover a tactic or strategy that works – such as floating across on a board, or making a clay replica covered in fur. The user will remember this story, and find the workload is reduced, and have the sensation of ease and play, leading to positive emotional tone, and a greater likelihood of staying in the flow of the game. Stories come with a grammar that many people inherently identify. We look for elements such as "once upon a time", and "happily ever after"; and in between we ask with anticipation, "and what happened next?" Memory is story shaped, so stories are easier to remember.

Memory Is Story-Shaped

The presentation of new information should be done in the form simple story, and action should be experienced in small chunks. Stories are made of predictable structural sequences, and a user might expect a predictable action based upon their prior knowledge of stories, but stories have the ability to surprise. The RAC taps into this prior knowledge and may use juxtaposition to subvert the user's expectations. For example, the intermediate goals of Bearfriend worked counter to the long-term goal of planting the seed. The bear created a lot of work for little return on value. The user expectation was that the wise Queen Bee told the user the intermediate goal; but perhaps the goal was not to keep the bear as a companion, but to show the player that they might be better off trusting themselves to solve the challenges on the Golden Road.

When a RAC uses story, and invokes the use of trial and error and play, the user is more likely to predict and act upon their expectations, and infer what comes next in the sequence. The user gathers limited action and experience, generates tactics, and those tactics may evolve into strategies—this builds player confidence, skills, knowledge, and generates positive emotional tone (Dubbels, 2008). The use of a RAC can help to create intermediate goals that highlight process, provide possible solutions to challenges, and even provide an easier chunk of information to store in memory. They may also serve to surprise and delight.

The Sacred Garden and Planting the Seed

By now the user has reached Area 14 on the map, and stands at the entrance to the Scared Garden; upon entry, the seed can be planted. This hypothetical game is intended to show the difference across the three experiential models through examples. Although the Grind Core and Freemium model are both very successful models for game play, they may not provide the emotional experiences that provide value leading to loyalty, and the potential for life change and social impact. The Immersion model is the gold standard, and may provide the best long-term return on investment. The Immersion model is more difficult to create, but it has the potential to deliver the positive emotional experiences that add value to the user experience, and their feelings about that particular brand. This is a powerful way to provide value through experience.

Summary: Immersion Model for Experience and Value

The Immersion experience model depends upon an engagement loop called a reward action contingency (RAC). A RAC may involve some tedious activities, but they are not repetitive, they are not predictable, and they do not change the user's focus from the main quest. When a user loses goal coherence, the game can become tedious, repetitive, predictable, and more like work than play. Even though loss aversion is a powerful motivator, Grind Core and Freemium can quickly lead to frustration and user abandonment.

The Immersion experience model delivers more value, can surprise and delight, and can potentially lead the user to new perspectives and insights beyond Function and Emotion. The Immersion model can potentially provide experiences that lead to transformation through the values listed at the top tier of the value pyramid (Figure 1). Games can help people look at things differently through experience; and a user is more like to have a transformative experience in an Immersive experiential model utilizing RACs. The key to creating an effective RAC, and the creation of an Immersive experiential model is successful delivery of values of Function (Figure 1), and setting the emotional tone.

EMOTIONAL TONE, AROUSAL, AND VALENCE

The James-Lange theory of emotions posits that emotional experiences start as physiological change (arousal) experienced via the body's nervous system to make decisions (valence) about their feelings (Cannon, 1987). Emotional experience begins with arousal, which is a stress response from the bodies hormonal system.

There are two types of stress, and these are measured in valence for categorization as emotional experience (Figure 18).

- **Distress (White):** Negative arousal, negative emotional tone,
- **Eustress (Blue):** Positive arousal, positive emotional tone.

Figure 18. Spectrum of arousal and emotional response

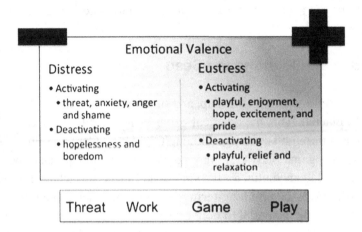

Distress: Negative Arousal as Emotion

Negative activating experiences can lead to distress, and lead to maladaptive social interaction such as aggression, passivity, and even withdrawal. When distress is triggered, the body responds with fear, anxiety, and shame; when eustress is triggered, the positive activating experiences lead to enjoyment, excitement, hope and pride.

Emotions are also triggered when signals from the environment activate prior experience as memories. If the memory is a story of shame or anger, it may signal a fight-or-flight response. The outcome of this may result in a deactivating response that is called learned helplessness – giving up (Overmier, 2002).

Eustress: Positive Emotional Arousal

When people are experiencing positive emotions or states as eustress, they feel like time is passing faster as compared to when they experience negative feelings (Sackett, Meyvis, Nelson, Converse, & Sackett, 2010). Along with filtering information, emotions can influence the recall of information (Schwarz, 1998) and the ability to learn new information (Winkielman, Schwarz, Fazendeiro, Reber, 2003). Additionally, if learning new information is experienced as easy, processing is experienced as pleasant (Winkielman & Cacioppo, 2001) and the result of this being greater likelihood to recall that information and to process related information (Winkielman et al., 2003). The use of the Immersion Experience Model uses RACs (Reward Action Contingency) to create the positive emotional experience that create the feeling of play, and increase the likelihood of Flow (Skinner and Belmont 1993).

Pleasant activating experiences as eustress do not have deleterious physiological effects. Eustress can increase physiological parameters of arousal as heart rate, or it can provide deactivation through relaxation. Positive emotions influence learning by affecting attention, motivation, use of learning strategies and self-regulation of learning. When people are experiencing positive emotions or states like Flow and fun, they feel like time is passing faster as compared to when they experience negative feelings.

Play, Positive Emotional Tone, and Flow

The experience of Flow is a transformative cognitive restructuring. In this sense, Flow is said to provide the "ultimate eustress experience", it is a state of being fully present and focused on a challenge, supported with positive arousal expressed as exhilaration (Hargrove, Nelson, & Cooper, 2013, p. 67). Flow is much like how children experience imaginative play, and much more likely to happen during play. In play, the individual may experience ambiguity, and through this, creates the goal structure and imbues it with intrinsic meaning and motivation. This ambiguity in play allows the user to create coherence in goals and process, a positive emotional tone, making an immersive game play, where a Flow experience becomes more likely (Figure 19).

Figure 19 depicts the spectrum between Play and Threat based upon signaling and motivation.

- **Threat:** When signaling is directive-- as in a command or a threat-- there is greater coherence, and the activity becomes serious and perhaps threatening. When motivation is extrinsic as a threat of direct or implied consequence, the activity increases in coherence as a threat.
- **Play:** When the signal is subjective, and there is greater ambiguity, signaling am invitation, request or a conditional statement, the activity is more likely to result in play. When motivation is intrinsic, where the user creates their goals, and the motivation is internal, the activity is more self-directed as play.

Flow is more likely to occur when one is in a playful mindset (Csikszentmihalyi, 2014). But one cannot be forced to play. Play is a mindset. It is a mental state of exploration and openness to experience. In Flow, the user directs the activity and creates their goals. The playful approach to experience is internally motivated, based upon subjective signals from the context of the activity. The user attempts to explore, discover, and connect through trial and error. It is through this playful ambiguous process

Figure 19. The role of ambiguity and play

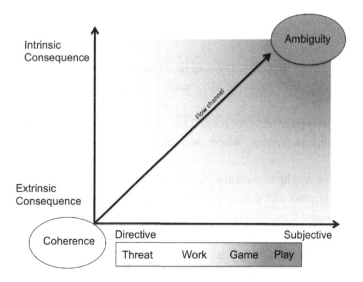

that the user creates coherence. The more ambiguous the goals and directions, the more likely the user will create them through trial and error, feedback, and the creation of intermediate goals that provide information about progress towards the larger goal.

Threat and Emotional Tone

The opposite is true of threat. Threat is signaled through directive signaling. Directive signaling indicates consequence for failing to comply, and is common in games predicated upon grinding. The user is being directed through behavioural means, and this does not allow for user agency through play, but motivates the user through offering desirable rewards. Most grinding content does not evolve to serve to advance a narrative, and seldom surprises the user. Grinding gameplay is often predictable, repetitive, and tedious behavior.

Rather than experience the joy of overcoming a challenge, users in grinding games overpower it. Users commit to tedious repetitive activities to earn desirable game items to overpower game challenges. User research on this experiential model of games indicates that players feel powerful, but report negative emotional arousal (Ryan, Rigby, & Przybylski, 2006).

These experiences work together collectively up the value pyramid (figure 1). Functional value will increase the likelihood that the user will experience emotional value. When functional and emotional value are both provided to the user, there is greater likelihood that the user will experience something of life-changing value, and perhaps even social impact as self-actualization. Again, value is additive. The foundations of the experience must be provided as functional and emotional value to experience immersion and Flow experience.

IMMERSION AND FLOW EXPERIENCE

One of the core goals of the immersion model is to keep the player engaged in the flow of game play. Csikszentmihalyi (1975; 1990) describes as Flow as an intrinsically enjoyable, self-rewarding experience. A review by Dormashev (in Osin, Malyutina, & Kosheleva, 2016) summarized the features of Flow, presented below:

1. **Clear Goals:** Clear, step-by-step awareness of the most immediate goals of actions being performed.
2. **Immediate Feedback:** Awareness of the results of actions undertaken is instantaneous, not postponed.
3. Perceived balance between actual challenges and available skills necessary to meet them.
4. Merging of action and awareness, where actions are consciously represented in an immediate manner.
5. Concentration on the task at hand with effortless concentration of attention on the actions performed.
6. A sense of potential control and confidence of success of current and future actions.
7. Loss of self-consciousness, or self-forgetfulness.
8. Altered sense of time, a feeling that time passes at a different pace than usual.
9. Acute and continuous enjoyment related to the process of activity that makes the experience autotelic.

The organizing principal of Flow is the feeling of focus. Focus is a narrowing of attention and an increase in arousal, which decreases the range of cues that an organism can take in and perceive from the stimulus and its environment (Easterbrook, 1959). This focus narrows our memory and attention processes, and shuts out thoughts and feelings that are not related to the experience of the activity (Elliot & Covington, 2001; Elliot, Gable, & Mapes, 2006; Gable & Poole, 2012). It is through this focus that feelings and emotion exert pressure on behavior and influences learning and perception (Greene, 2014). Focus does increase due to both positive and negative emotional arousal, but Flow is more likely to occur when experiencing positive emotional tone.

Skinner and Belmont (1993, p. 572), observed that engaged users show sustained behavioral involvement in activities when accompanied by a positive emotional tone. In this affective mode, the users engage in tasks at the border of their competencies, and are more likely to initiate action when given the opportunity, and exert intense effort and concentration. Flow experience is reported as happening in both positive and negative emotional tone. However, Flow is more likely when the user experiences positive emotional tone (Csikszentmihalyi, 2014). In order to facilitate emotional tone in an experience, developers should observe the interaction between user and their experience. User experience research is an important part of creating coherence between the game and the user to create an immersive Flow experience.

LEARNING AND DEVELOPMENT THROUGH USER EXPERIENCE RESEARCH

User experience researchers learn by observing users play games, and contribute to development as an iterative process. The game user researcher (GUR) gathers large amounts of behavioral data to share with designers, who can quickly interpret the data, implement analysis into design, and observe the effects of those changes for shaping the emotional experience of the user. The GUR studies users to provide a comparison analysis (Wixon & Pagulayan 2008, p. 3). This has resulted in greater emphasis on producing the Immersion Experience Model, which is intended to keep the user immersed in the flow of the game.

Here's the problem," Pagulayan mutters, motioning to a computer monitor that shows us the game from the player's perspective. He points to a bunch of grenades lying on the ground. She ought to be picking those up and using them, he says, but the grenades aren't visible enough. "There's a million of them, but she just missed them . . . Pagulayan makes a note of the problem. It is his job to find flaws in Halo 3 that its creators, who know what players should do, might not be able to see. He assesses whether the aliens have gotten too lethal, whether the revamped Needler guns are powerful enough, and — most important if and when players are getting bored or (as is more often the case) frustrated. Clicking away on his keyboard, Pagulayan brings up video of one of the first fights in the game, in which a Brute wields a ferocious gun. Neophyte players are getting massacred. "That enemy can kill the player in three shots," he says. "Imagine your mother playing, where she's barely learning how to move around in the game — bam, bam, bam — dead. That's not going to be a fun experience. (Thomson, 2007, p.3)

What Pagulayan is explaining is the importance of leading the player toward success, making the right tools available (and visible) at the right time to keep the user in the flow of game play. If one wants the user to have a good experience, the designer must identify the core experience being offered and lead them through it until the user can take the reins. The goal is to keep the player immersed in the flow of game play, and not to distract them with Grind Core and Freemium. An important distinction in these models:

- Grind Core and Freemium depend upon the user overpowering the challenges. This means to have more strength of force.
  - Design features (see Appendix b): Use of compulsion loops and token economy.
- Immersion depends upon in-game learning so the user can overcome the challenges by getting the better from being challenged and responding to adversity with new strategies.
  - Design feature: Use of RAC.

The goal for Pagulayan's team is to provide as much value as possible and immerse the user in positive experience, and avoid the grind. The method used is called Rapid Iterative Testing Evaluation (RITE). The team designs a prototype, conducts user testing research, applies the user data to make a design adjustment, tests the adjusted design, uses the research data to make a design adjustment (Medlock, Wixon, McGee, & Welsh, 2005; Medlock, Wixon, Terrano, Romero, & Fulton, 2002). What is important in the user experience testing process is to make sure the game challenges make sense. Do they serve in the interest of furthering the story, or do they distract? Will the game challenges work in service to the goals of the game? If the core experience is not well defined, the user may become distracted, frustrated, and never become immersed in play or Flow.

The workload in your game must be dedicated to the core experience you want to offer, not in figuring out menus for example, or icons. That's why defining your core pillars and sticking to this vision is crucial to offer a great User Experience (UX). There are always tradeoffs to make, and perfection is hardly reachable. UX is about making sure the tradeoffs make sense for the experience you intend. That doesn't mean your game must not be difficult or not have any challenges, quite the contrary: but the challenges must be about the core experience and nothing else. Think of it as playing golf with green ball. Might be spicing it up for some hardcore golfers maybe? But the golf experience is not about making it challenging to find the ball. (Hodent, 2015)

The developer must understand the difference between making things difficult as compared to making them challenging. Making the balls green really adds nothing to golf, except for increasing the difficulty of finding them. The idea is to use RACs to engage the user, not to use compulsion loops to force the user to find green golf balls in tall grass.

RESEARCH HELPS US SHAPE EXPERIENCE AND STORY FOR THE USER

Research can improve game play experience. By observing and collecting user data, the developer can adjust to user needs and modify the game design to increase positive feelings, invoke a playful mindset, and increase the likelihood of Flow. Data-informed design works to increase coherence for the intended game play experience by scaffolding the player through difficult challenges, and reducing activities that distract the player from the story, and reduce player immersion.

If the experience is complex, the user researcher can present the data to the development team, and perhaps make suggestions on how to off-load the work-load challenge onto the game (Dubbels, 2013). This can increase coherence, and provide a simple, challenging, and immersive experience to the user.

KEEP IT SIMPLE, INCREASE VALUE, INCREASE GOAL COHERENCE

Games can be made simple, challenging, and immersive. A challenging game can be simplified through off-loading complexity onto the game until the user becomes capable of taking on full control of their avatar. This is a form of game tuning, which adjusts the level challenge to meet the needs of the player, and become incrementally more complex as the user becomes more adept. Incremental learning allows for the player to learn without being overwhelmed. This is achieved through having a coherent core experience, understanding the user. This approach allows for positive emotional tone, and a greater probability of immersion and Flow experience.

CONCLUSION

This chapter presented three views of gamification as user experience models: Grind Core, Freemium, and Immersion. These models were presented to provide insight into what makes games valuable digital experiences. The Immersion user experience model was meant to provide the gold standard in game design, and provided examples of what should inform any attempt at gamification. In order to provide an immersive game experience, the game should provide value in function, emotion, and potentially, transformation as life change, and social impact. These categories are not mandatory, but provide a framework for optimal user experience in games and gamification.

Where Grind Core and Freemium experience models rely upon compulsion loops, the Immersion model utilizes Reward Action Contingencies. While the compulsion loop will provide short-term gain, it may result in long-term remorse and resentment. The use of loss aversion and behaviour modification techniques are effective and powerful, but not if the intent is to improve return on investment, loyalty, and increase customer satisfaction.

Users will recognize the use of compulsion loops as way to manipulate them through behaviour modification. The better approach is to provide value through the user experience, with the ultimate goal of making a social impact (see figure 1). This can occur through understanding how the user co-creates the experience. Gamification should deliver a sense of magic to the user. It should be capable of surprise and delight, and immerse the user in a Flow experience. Gamification should offer users the best of games, not parts of games to amplify tedious repetitive activities as chocolate-covered broccoli. Gamification should add emotional value, with the potential for transformation, for both life change, and social impact.

REFERENCES

Abernathy, T., & Rouse, R. (2014). *Death to the Three Act Structure! Toward a Unique Structure for Game Narratives*. Retrieved July 5, 2016, from http://www.gdcvault.com/play/1020050/Death-to-the-Three-Act

Adams, R. (2009). *Watership down: A novel.* Simon and Schuster. Retrieved from https://books.google. com/books?hl=en&lr=&id=ittzoegmRpAC&oi=fnd&pg=PA3&dq=watership+down&ots=RmUTuR NLZj&sig=LOGjx4-9kPRPKfDElmk-56ZNbeg

Business Wire. (2016, June 21). *In-Game Purchases and Construction Toys Drive Global Growth for Toys and Games in 2015.* Retrieved August 15, 2016, from http://www.businesswire.com/news/ home/20160621005113/en/In-Game-Purchases-Construction-Toys-Drive-Global-Growth

Cannon, W. B. (1987). The James-Lange theory of emotions: A critical examination and an alternative theory. *The American Journal of Psychology, 100*(3/4), 567–586. doi:10.2307/1422695 PMID:3322057

Csikszentmihalyi, M. (2014). Play and Intrinsic Rewards. In Flow and the Foundations of Positive Psychology (pp. 135–153). Springer. Retrieved from http://link.springer.com/chapter/10.1007/978-94-017-9088-8_10

Deci, E. L. (1971). Effects of externally mediated rewards on intrinsic motivation. *Journal of Personality and Social Psychology, 18*(1), 105–115. doi:10.1037/h0030644

Dubbels, B. (2008). Video games, reading, and transmedial comprehension. In Handbook of research on effective electronic gaming in Education (pp. 251–276). Academic Press.

Dubbels, B. (2013). Gamification, Serious Games, Ludic Simulation, and other Contentious Categories. *International Journal of Gaming and Computer-Mediated Simulations, 5*(2), 1–19. doi:10.4018/ jgcms.2013040101

European Commission. (2014, July). *In-app purchases: Joint action by the European Commission and Member States is leading to better protection for consumers in online games.* Retrieved August 15, 2016, from http://europa.eu/rapid/press-release_IP-14-847_en.htm

Giant Bomb. (2011, July). *So much grind... - Red Dead Redemption - Giant Bomb.* Retrieved August 11, 2016, from http://www.giantbomb.com/red-dead-redemption/3030-25249/forums/so-much-grind-505106/

Hargrove, M. B., Nelson, D. L., & Cooper, C. L. (2013). Generating eustress by challenging employees. *Organizational Dynamics, 42*(1), 61–69. doi:10.1016/j.orgdyn.2012.12.008

Hodent, C. (2015, March 31). *Gamer's Brain: Neuroscience, UX & Design.* Retrieved from http://celiahodent.com/the-gamers-brain/

Hopson, J. (2001, April). *Behavioral Game Design* [Gamasutra]. Retrieved from http://www.gamasutra. com/view/feature/131494/behavioral_game_design.php

Kazdin, A. E., & Bootzin, R. R. (1972). The token economy: An evaluative review. *Journal of Applied Behavior Analysis, 5*(3), 343–372. doi:10.1901/jaba.1972.5-343 PMID:16795358

Kim, J. (2014, March). *The Compulsion Loop Explained* [Gamasutra]. Retrieved from http://www. gamasutra.com/blogs/JosephKim/20140323/213728/The_Compulsion_Loop_Explained.php

Kumar, J., & Herger, M. (2016). *Gamification at Work: Designing Engaging Business Software.* Interaction Design Foundation. Retrieved from https://www.interaction-design.org/literature/book/gamification-at-work-designing-engaging-business-software

Lepper, M. R., & Greene, D. (1975). Turning play into work: Effects of adult surveillance and extrinsic rewards on childrens intrinsic motivation. *Journal of Personality and Social Psychology, 31*(3), 479–486. doi:10.1037/h0076484

Medlock, M. C., Wixon, D., McGee, M., & Welsh, D. (2005). The rapid iterative test and evaluation method: Better products in less time. In *Costjustifying Usability: An Update for the Internet Age*, (pp. 489–517). Academic Press.

Medlock, M. C., Wixon, D., Terrano, M., Romero, R., & Fulton, B. (2002). *Using the RITE method to improve products: A definition and a case study.* Usability Professionals Association. Retrieved from http://www.computingscience.nl/docs/vakken/musy/RITE.pdf

Meyer, C., & Schwager, A. (2007a). Customer Experience. *Harvard Business Review*, 1–11. PMID:17345685

Meyer, C., & Schwager, A. (2007b). Understanding customer experience. *Harvard Business Review, 85*(2), 116. PMID:17345685

Mitgutsch, K., & Alvarado, N. (2012). Purposeful by design?: a serious game design assessment framework. In *Proceedings of the International Conference on the Foundations of Digital Games* (pp. 121–128). ACM. doi:10.1145/2282338.2282364

Osin, E., Malyutina, A., & Kosheleva, N. V. (2015). Self-Transcendence Facilitates Meaning-Making and Flow Experience: Evidence from a Pilot Experimental Study (SSRN Scholarly Paper No. ID 2576658). Rochester, NY: Social Science Research Network. Retrieved from http://papers.ssrn.com/abstract=2576658

Osin, E. N., Malyutina, A. A., & Kosheleva, N. V. (2016). self-transcendence facilitates meaning-making and flow: Evidence from a pilot experimental study. *International Journal of Psychology, 5.* Retrieved from http://psychologyinrussia.com/volumes/pdf/2016_2/psychology_2016_2_7.pdf

Overmier, J. B. (2002). On learned helplessness. *Integrative Physiological and Behavioral Science, 37*(1), 4–8. doi:10.1007/BF02688801 PMID:12069364

Pine, B. J., & Gilmore, J. H. (1998). Welcome to the experience economy. *Harvard Business Review, 76*, 97–105. PMID:10181589

Ren, L., Qiu, H., Wang, P., & Lin, P. M. C. (2016). Exploring customer experience with budget hotels: Dimensionality and satisfaction. *International Journal of Hospitality Management, 52*, 13–23. doi:10.1016/j.ijhm.2015.09.009

Ryan, R. M., Rigby, C. S., & Przybylski, A. (2006). The motivational pull of video games: A self-determination theory approach. *Motivation and Emotion, 30*(4), 344–360. doi:10.1007/s11031-006-9051-8

Sackett, A. M., Meyvis, T., Nelson, L. D., Converse, B. A., & Sackett, A. L. (2010). Youre having fun when time flies the hedonic consequences of subjective time progression. *Psychological Science, 21*(1), 111–117. doi:10.1177/0956797609354832 PMID:20424031

Schouten, J. W., McAlexander, J. H., & Koenig, H. F. (2007). Transcendent customer experience and brand community. *Journal of the Academy of Marketing Science, 35*(3), 357–368. doi:10.1007/s11747-007-0034-4

Skinner, E. A., & Belmont, M. J. (1993). Motivation in the classroom: Reciprocal effects of teacher behavior and student engagement across the school year. *Journal of Educational Psychology, 85*(4), 571–581. doi:10.1037/0022-0663.85.4.571

Thomson, C. (2007, August 21). *Halo 3: How Microsoft Labs Invented a New Science of Play.* Retrieved July 7, 2016, from http://archive.wired.com/gaming/virtualworlds/magazine/15-09/ff_halo?currentPage=all

Tynan, C., McKechnie, S., & Hartley, S. (2014). Interpreting value in the customer service experience using customer-dominant logic. *Journal of Marketing Management, 30*(9–10), 1058–1081. doi:10.1080/0267257X.2014.934269

Vygotskiĭ, L. S. (1978). *Mind in society: The development of higher psychological processes.* Harvard Univ Pr. Retrieved from http://books.google.com/books?hl=en&lr=&id=RxjjUefze_oC&oi=fnd&pg=PA1&dq=mind+in+sociaety&ots=ogzWQZu1dv&sig=Gc_Qkp0dB85be_VBFRaTmuQnsgU

What, R. (2015, November 10). *The boring apocalyptic grind of Fallout 4 reviews.* Retrieved from https://robertwhat.com/2015/11/10/the-boring-apocalyptic-grind-of-fallout-4-reviews/

Wixon, D., & Pagulayan, R. (2008). Halo 3: The theory and practice of a research-design partnership. *Interactions, 15*(1), 52–55.

APPENDIX A: GAME ABANDONMENT

Game engagement and rate completion are important. Many game companies are taking a serious look at why players abandon their games through game user research. Abernathy & Rouse (2014), presented game completion rates at their Game Developer's Conference talk (Table 1).

Although Table 1 shows a definite reduction in game abandonment, the rate of abandonment is still surprising. We often think of games as addictive and that people cannot help but play. But it seems that we might be overly optimistic about the power of games to engage, as compared to the power of well-designed games that do actually engage.

Table 1. Rate of completion of games on steam

Game	Completion
The Walking Dead: Season 1, Episode 1	66%
Mass Effect 2	56%
Bioshock Infinite	53%
Batman: Arkham City	47%
Portal	47%
Mass Effect 3	42%
The Walking Dead: Season 1, Episode 5	39%
The Elder Scrolls V: Skyrim	32%
Borderlands 2	30%

Abernathy & Rouse (2014) .

APPENDIX B: COMMON GAME ELEMENTS OF GAMIFICATION

Token economy and/or leaderboard predate the gamification movement. In fact, the first documented use of these systems occurred in psychiatric hospitals in the 1960's (Kazdin & Bootzin, 1972). Prior to this, token economies had been used in in schools and prisons for behavior modification. In a token economy, an individual is rewarded with a token when they exhibit the target behavior. The tokens can then be exchanged for privilege, objects, and other reinforcers.

According to Kumar and Herger (2016) a token economy can offer tokens that reward:

- Self-esteem, leadership, conquest, mastery, access, praise.
- Fun, discovery, excitement, awe, delight, fantasy, surprise.
- Social capital, likes, friends, contribute, charity, groups, status.
- Things, points, cash, resources, rewards, prices.

There is a problem with this technique. When the reward system stops, the behaviour stops. Historically, token economies are very successful in closed institutional contexts such as mental hospitals, schools, and animal management. However, when an individual leaves the closed loop of the token economy, the user reverts back to their original behaviors (Csikszentmihalyi, 2014; Deci, 1971; Lepper

& Greene, 1975). This is also true of gamification. In gamification if an individual is rewarded for a specific behaviour, they will demonstrate it until the rewards stop. Once the rewards stop, the targeted behaviour stops.

Points are used to indicate progress in token economies. They are a unit of measurement used to track player behaviour in relation to the targeted behaviour. Tokens are often used to purchase desirable items and privilege. It is the purchase of desirable objects and privilege that motivate behaviour.

Badges are a form of virtual achievement by the player. There are a number of reasons that badges or other achievement systems might work. Badges, like leaderboards, provide feedback about performance. But badges for the sake of badges depend upon the status they represent in the larger community.

Leaderboards display and compare points and badges to increase motivation through social comparison. Leaderboards bring in the social aspect of points and badges, by displaying the players on a list, typically ranked in descending order with the greatest number of points at the top. The possible disadvantage of a leaderboard is that it could be demotivating to a new player. For example, if player A has 10,000 points, and is on top of the leaderboard, and a new player B has 10 points and is at the bottom, it is likely that player B may become demotivated and give up playing the game. She, or he, may believe that he/she is never going to compete with player A, and therefore why should he/she even try? Leaderboards can be problematic for creating motivation and loyalty.

Constraints can be presented in the form or rules, tools, roles, and choice (Dubbels, 2008). If you look at a game, it is generally composed of a number of constraints that are structured to create interaction and experience. Because there are only so many choices that one can make, even in open-world game experiences, there will always be limitations and constraint on behavior, and especially on how behaviour is rewarded (token economy). In true play, "things lose their determining force" and the child may understand the constraints of a condition but gain the ability to act independently of what they see—creating new choices (Vygotskiĭ, 1978). In games, all actions are constrained by the programming, and actual play is rare.

Constraints also refer to limitations such as deadlines, which motivate people to action. According to Kumar & Herger (2016), the use of time constraints and implications of scarcity increase engagement with targeted behaviour. They report that when a website limits simple tasks with time constraint, that customers are more likely to bid on items. However, using this technique to manipulate the user could cause user resentment.

Narrative can provide an imaginative reframing of an activity. The use of narrative and subjective language promotes the imaginative powers of pretense and actual play. One such example of this is in software is Zombies, Run! The user plugs in headphones to a portable device, and a fantasy narrative ensues. The narrative allows joggers to pretend that they are running in missions in a zombie adventure story. According to the description at GooglePlay,

Every run becomes a mission where you're the hero, our immersive audio drama putting you at the center of your very own zombie adventure story.

The use of narrative as pretense is an important part of learning and expression. In children's play, a stick can become an imagined object, such as a horse or a flying machine.

Engagement Loop refers to a combination of the previously described behavioural game mechanics combined with reinforcement as feedback loops that keep the player engaged in the game. There are two types of engagement loops:

- Compulsion loop,
- Reward Action Contingency (RAC).

Chapter 3

The Relationship between Avatar–Based Customization, Player Identification, and Motivation

Selen Turkay
Harvard University, USA

Charles K. Kinzer
Teachers College, Columbia University, USA

ABSTRACT

Player identification is an outcome of gameplay experiences in virtual worlds and has been shown to affect enjoyment and reduce self-discrepancy. Avatar customization has potential to impact player identification by shaping the relationship between the player and the character. This mixed method study examines the effects of avatar-based customization on players' identification with their characters, and the effects of identification dimensions (i.e., perceived similarity, wishful identification, embodied presence) on their motivation in a massively multiplayer online game, Lord of the Rings Online (LotRO). Participants (N = 66) played LotRO either in customization or in no-customization group for ten hours in four sessions in a lab setting. Data were collected through interviews and surveys. Results showed both time and avatar customization positively impacted player identification with their characters. Player motivation was predicted in different sessions by different identification dimensions, which shows the dynamic and situational impact of identification on motivation.

DOI: 10.4018/978-1-5225-1817-4.ch003

INTRODUCTION

Media researchers have been writing about the ramifications of assuming technologically mediated identities since the inception of online virtual worlds (see Turkle, 1994; 1995). These virtual environments can provide anonymity and the freedom from the conventions of our everyday identities in areas such as gender, age or social status. They also offer opportunities to users to take on various personas, create or adopt new identities without fear of disapproval by members in their real-life social circle (Turkle, 1995).

There are different types of virtual worlds (i.e., social, gaming, educational) with various affordances. Massively multiplayer online games (MMOs) have emerged to be one of the most popular gaming virtual worlds over the last decade, and have been studied from various perspectives (e.g., player demographics, addiction, socialization, player motivations). This popularity is partly because MMOs' affordances to allow players to temporarily become a game character and adopt the salient characteristics of that character (Looy, Courtois & de Vocht, 2010). As detailed in the following section, player identification with the avatar/character is central to how players experience the game (e.g., engagement and enjoyment; Klimmit, Hefner &Vorderer, 2009) and why they may continue to play the game (i.e., motivation). Determining aspects of games that influence and can improve players' identification with their characters would be of interest to game designers as well as educators who select games for their students.

Avatar customization is an understudied factor when it comes to identification. Yet, it allows making each character different in MMOs by providing various combinations of attributes, adornments/physical properties, skills, and traits (Dickey, 2007). Customization experiences may help players to get into the mindset of the character, immerse themselves in the game context, resulting in increased likelihood of affecting players' real self-identities. This paper examines players' identification with their characters over several gameplay sessions, varying the participants' ability to customize their characters, and poses the following main research question and two exploratory research questions:

RQ₁: Is there a relationship between engagement with initial avatar customization and players' identification with their avatars?
RQ₂: Does players' identification with their characters change over time?
RQ₃: How does identification and customization predict players' motivation to play over time?

The background section below clarifies the theories and present previous studies that guided the formation of the research questions. Following the background, the methods section introduces the participants and describes the study. Before proceeding, however, it is worth clarifying the difference between avatar and character. Avatar is defined as the embodiment of the user in virtual environments (e.g., Ducheneaut, Wen, Yee, & Wadley, 2009). Characters in games are fictional identities within the narrative setting of the game. In this paper, "avatar" and "character" are used interchangeably because the research design does not differentiate avatar customization from character customization.

BACKGROUND

In technologically mediated virtual environments, players establish digital identities using a combination of modalities including text, audio and visuals. These online identities in videogames and virtual worlds are important for self-exploration as well as to communicate with others and with the virtual environment (Turkle, 1995; Thomas 2007). Avatars are the most commonly used expression of identity in virtual worlds (Hamilton, 2009). Visual characteristics of an avatar, name, as well as abilities of player characters, provide users with an expression of identity and an opportunity for extended identity formation (Turkle, 1995).

Self-representation is intentional within the given choice structure of a virtual world. For example, initial character creation choices may indicate how the player expects the avatar to function as a channel for her identity. Considering part of identity formation is thinking about what type person we want to be (Arnett, 2010, p.340), virtual worlds can function as "identity construction environments" (Bers, 2001, p. 365). In these environments, users can explore and experiment with the dynamic nature of identity by interacting with and through their avatars (Kafai, Fields, & Cook, 2010). Similarly, Turkle (1995) describes the creation of an identity in virtual environments (MUDs) as fluid and multiple. She states that in virtual worlds, "people are able to build a self by cycling through many selves" (Turkle, 1995, p.178). Players manage their identities through playing different characters in MMOs (Taylor, 1999). In other words, people cycle through their possible selves, defined as "the cognitive manifestation of enduring goals, aspirations, motives, fears, and threats" (Markus & Nurius, 1986, p. 954). Such identification facilitates identity development, especially during adolescence (Erickson, 1968). In a similar vein, McDonald and Kim (2001) report that young videogame players perceive no distance at all relative to their game protagonists, and "identify quite closely" with them (p. 254).

Looy, Courtois and de Vocht (2010) call for more attention to the concept of identification in game studies. Playing computer games is enjoyable, partly because players can enter imagined worlds beyond their real-life experiences and perceive themselves in alternate ways. Consequently, studying players' identification with their avatars in a virtual environment can be crucial for understanding their gameplay experiences and motivation to play. Cohen (2001) defines identification with media characters as "an imaginative experience in which a person surrenders consciousness of his or her own identity and experiences the world through someone else's point of view (p. 248)." Adapting this definition to video games, some researchers state that identification allows for experimentation with one's identity by temporarily adopting aspects of the target videogame character's identity (e.g., a famous hero, a historical figure, a sportsman) (Klimmt, Heefter, &Vorderer, 2009; Looy et al., 2010). Identification, therefore, is conceptualized as a temporary shift in players' self-perception (Klimmt, Hefner, Vorderer, Roth, & Blake, 2010). However, player identification with characters is complicated because of the multiplicity of roles (e.g., subject, audience, director, user etc.) that a player takes during gameplay (Flannagan, 1999) and the game state (e.g., fighting, socializing; Giddings, 2007). For example, when someone plays a videogame with an avatar, she is both the avatar/player-character and the player at the same time. When players exert agency over their avatars to interact with objects, events and other players, this is mediated both by the player characters' abilities and players' abilities, and those have consequences to the avatar within the designer created game world (Murphy, 2004). In MMOs, players do not observe autonomous social entities performing on screen, instead they make characters perform through character-generated actions, also called emotes. An avatar's representation of the player's motions and intentions has a great impact on identification (Hamilton, 2009) and a perceptual integration with the avatar, namely the player's awareness of her presence both in her body and in the screen (Dove, 2002).

In addition to avatars' abilities to represent players' intentions, previous studies determined various player behaviors, features of avatars, and characteristics of virtual worlds, that facilitate identification. Among these features are fondness for a character (Cohen, 1999), attractiveness of avatars (Kim, Lee, & Kang, 2012), the capabilities of the character (Newman, 2002), sense-of-presence and transportability in narrative games (Christy & Fox, 2016), point-of-view (Lim & Reeves, 2009), openness to experience personality trait (Worth, 2015; Soutter and Hitchens, 2016), and physical resemblance of avatars to their users in body shape, race, age, and facial features (Maccoby & Wilson, 1957; Williams, 2011). Players' perceived similarity to their characters (or similarity identification) has been called the mirror hypothesis (Chandler & Griffith, 2004). The mirror hypothesis refers to the theory that viewers tend to relate favorably to on-screen characters who are either like themselves (the mirror), or ones who represent someone the viewer would like to be (the magic mirror). The magic mirror relates to another type of identification: wishful identification. In wishful identification, the observer desires to emulate the character, either in general terms as a role model for future action or identity development, or in specific terms which extend responses beyond the viewing situation or by imitating a particular behavior (Hoffner & Buchanan, 2005; Hoffner & Cantor, 1991; Von Feilitzen & Linné, 1975). Wishful identification provides a glimpse of "what if," and these glimpses are powerful predictors of future behavior (Cohen, 2001).

In addition to its role in identity development, researchers have discovered various psychological and behavioral effects of player identification. Studies have found that identification with player characters reduces self-discrepancy (e.g., Bessiere, Seay, & Kiesler, 2007; Lim & Reeves, 2009), and impacts players' self-efficacy and trust within their virtual communities (Kim, Lee, & Kang, 2012). In an online survey study, Ducheneaut, Wen, Yee and Wadley (2009) found that visitors of online virtual worlds who perceive a smaller psychological difference between their avatar and themselves are generally more satisfied with their avatars and spend more time online. In another survey study, Watts (2016) found a significant relationship between avatar self-identification in *WoW* and self-esteem in real world. The author proposes that the more deeply these online gamers identify with their avatars, the more their virtual communities are able to nurture players' emotional growth that extends into their everyday lives.

Studies also found a relationship between identification with an avatar and avatar-consistent behavior in the real world (Yoon & Vargas, 2014). For instance, Van Looy et al. (2012) found that participants who showed stronger identification with their character in an online health promotion game, more often reported that they started exercising or dieting because of their online experiences. Identification also positively affects players' intention and willingness to purchase game items to increase their competitiveness and improve avatars' appearance (Park & Lee, 2011; Zhong & Yao, 2012). Through such mechanisms, increased identification may enhance player engagement, enjoyment, and motivation. For instance, Klimmt et al. (2010) conducted two experimental studies with male players and showed that enacting a character or role in a military themed first-person shooter game affected players' identity state and increase their game enjoyment. Identification is not only important for male players in MMOs or in fighting games, but is also important for female players. Reijmersdal, Jansz, Peters, and Noort's (2013) survey study with female players of a pink game, *goSupermodel* (WatAgame ApS., 2013), showed that girls who spent more time playing the game reported more identification. Their survey results also indicated a positive relationship between identification with game characters and female players gaming motivation.

While player motivation is desired for both commercial games and games for change, studies found conflicting results related to the relationship between customization and identification with game characters and how they may relate to gameplay experiences that impacts players' gaming related motivation. In a single setting short term online study with Amazon Mechanical Turk participants, Birk, Atkins, Bowey and Mandryk (2016) found that all three dimensions of character identification (i.e., perceived similarity, embodied presence, wishful identification) predicted players sense of autonomy, immersion, enjoyment, positive affect, effort, persistence (as measured by gameplay time which is terminated in the 20-minute mark). Participants played a running game for 4 minutes at minimum and 24 minutes at maximum. Participants filled out the identification survey after either creating and customizing their avatar or watching their avatar being created. Participants who customized their avatars identified more closely with their avatars. Whereas Soutter and Hitchens (2016)' survey study found that customization did not relate to identification but flow was significantly positively related to identification. Zhao, Wang and Zhu (2010) suggested that the degree of character identification would be likely influence players' motivation and commitment to playing online games.

In this study, we are interested in exploring how customization and dimensions of identification predict player motivation. Motivation toward playing a game is indicated by a player's persistence and willingness to come back and put their time and energy into playing that game. Thus, we operationalize motivation as the desire of a player to come back and play a game repeatedly. In this sense, player motivation is related to loyalty, which can be viewed as a gamer's tendency to play a game repeatedly (Choi & Kim, 2004; Teng, 2010).

The degree of control players has over their avatars (e.g., character's movement, choice of avatar appearance) may affect their level of identification with their avatars. Direct control over their character can imbue players with a sense of agency and may also increase their positive affect in the game (Hefner, Klimmt & Vorderer, 2007) and motivation to play the game (Turkay & Adinolf, 2015). For instance, Schmierbach, Limperos, & Woolley (2012) showed that when participants customized their racecars in a racing game their enjoyment increased. Although players did not customize their avatars in this study, they played the game by controlling their racecar. Therefore, we may expect that customization of racecars in a race game and customization of avatars in a role playing game may have similar psychological impact on player experiences. In a similar vein, Ganesh et al.'s (2011) neuroimaging study revealed that avatar related self-identification is related to the experience of agency and control over the observed body. These results imply a relationship between control over the avatar and self-identification.

Despite the results and implications of the studies noted above, Shaw (2011) points to a lack of empirical research on the extent to which control over the avatar strengthens the relationship between the avatar and the player, especially in longer experimental studies. The majority of the literature written on such a relationship has been performed through either a theoretical approach (e.g., Murphy, 2004; Hamilton, 2009) or surveys/interviews that specifically address only the questions around identification (e.g., Shaw, 2011; Looy, Courtois & de Vocht, 2010; Reijmersdal et al., 2013). This study aims to contribute to the literature by examining the effect of player control, specifically avatar-based customization, on players' identification with their avatars and how different dimensions of identification may predict player motivation.

Avatar-Based Customization

Many virtual worlds offer users ways to customize their experiences, either through built-in options or the ability to create or obtain add-on software modules as seen in games such as *World of Warcraft (WoW)* (Blizzard, 2004) and *Star Wars: The Old Republic (SWTOR)* (Bioware, 2011). Avatar customization is a main form of customization in many MMOs and social virtual worlds. Several studies have found that avatar customization and playing with a customized avatar impact gaming experiences (e.g., Trepte & Reinecke, 2010; Turkay & Adinolf, 2010; Turkay, 2012), motivation to continue playing a game (Turkay & Adinolf, 2015), learning in games (Okita, Turkay, Kim, Murai, 2013), subsequent helping behaviors after gameplay (e.g. Dolgov, Graves, Nearents, Schwark, & Brooks Volkman, 2014), exercising behaviors after customizing their avatars (Waddell, Sundar, & Auriemma, 2015), and increase players' emotional attachment to their characters (Waggoner, 2009; Shaw, 2011; Turkay & Kinzer, 2014). A subset of these studies made connections between avatar customization and players' identification with their characters.

For instance, studies of aggression in videogames (Fischer, Kastenmuller, & Greitemeyer, 2010; Holligdale & Greitemeyer, 2013) found evidence that avatar customization may amplify the psychological effects of video games through increased identification with one's character. In their study with 30 children who played one of three advergames with differing levels of avatar customization, Bailey, Wise and Bolls (2009) found that customization of game avatars can affect both subjective feelings of presence and psycho-physiological indicators of emotion during game-play, which may make players' experiences more enjoyable. Bailey et al.'s (2009) study was one of the first to examine avatar customization with physiological measures. However, the games they used were not multiplayer, and the participants played the games for a very short time, making generalization difficult. There is also evidence that identification facilitates customization behavior. A survey study found that *WoW* players who strongly identify with their characters more often like to role-play, create background stories about their avatars, and have a stronger interest in customizing the appearance of their character (Looy et al., 2010).

There are different types of customization. Turkay and Adinolf (2010, p. 1841) suggested that customization is grouped into three broad categories in MMOs:

Type I: Customization that affects game mechanics and dynamics directly and therefore has a direct effect on individual player gameplay. Customizing talent trees in *WoW* is an example of this type of customization.

Type II: Customization that does not affect game mechanics and dynamics. Avatar appearance customization is an example of this type of customization. Although it does not directly affect gameplay, it may affect a player's enjoyment of the game.

Type III: Customization that does not affect game mechanics and dynamics directly but may affect player performance, such as interface customization, may have an effect on players' gameplay experience.

Players use different strategies to create and customize avatars depending on their goals, game developers' goals and affordances of virtual worlds. For example, players may customize their avatars' appearance (cosmetic customization) to reflect their aesthetic views or dress-up (Fron, Fullerton, Ford Morie, & Pearce, 2007; Kafai et al., 2010). Players may also customize their characters with a functional goal in mind. In Kafai et al.'s (2010) study, one type of functional customization for Whyville (1999) users was to disguise within the community (e.g. Gender swapping to hide one's actual gender). Van Looy (2015) talks about two different types of avatar creation: identity driven and instrumental. Identity driven avatar creation is related to emotions and avatar functionality as an extension of the player in the game world. Instrumental avatar creation is related to in-game performance, driven by conscious decisions. In MMOs, players who want to create an instrumental avatar may choose a certain character class to fit a desired role within the game such as being able to heal other players.

It is likely that functional and cosmetic customization may result in differing levels of identification with characters. For instance, when players customize their character appearance similar to their real life physical appearance, their perceived similarity with their characters may increase, whereas if they customize their characters to be strong and invincible their wishful identification may increase more than other identification aspects. However, in this study, cosmetic and functional customization (via choosing rewards, and character race) were not manipulated separately. Instead, players either customized both avatar appearance and avatar abilities or did not customize at all. Therefore, the rest of this paper refers to the combination of cosmetic and functional avatar customization as avatar-based customization, and explores the impact of avatar-based customization on players' identification with their characters.

Duration of the Study

Most empirical studies of games research (e.g., Schneider, Lang, Shin, & Bradley, 2004; Hitchens, Drachen, & Richards, 2012; Birk et al., 2016) rely on a relatively short play time (between 8 minutes and 45 minutes) to draw conclusion regarding players' identification with their characters and motivation. However, MMOs are long-term games, and gameplay experiences may change over time as players gain expertise, form relationships within the game community, and develop their goals (Schultheiss, 2007). Thus, a reliable study of player experiences in these games requires play over a significant period of time, and certainly for more than one experimental session. In a similar vein, Klimmt et al. (2010) suggested that game-character identification may emerge from significant playing time and Reijmersdal, Jansz, Peters, and Noort (2013) stated that this possibility should be further investigated. Based on data about players' gameplay time, the average time of play per character in one week is 10.2 hours (Ducheneaut, Yee, Nickell, & Moore, 2006), and a regular player plays about 100-150 minutes per game session (Mahmassani, Chen, Huang, Williams & Contractor, 2010). With this in mind, this study's procedure involved about 10 hours of gameplay for each subject, divided into four sessions of 2 to 2.5 hours per session over two weeks.

METHOD

Participants and Design

Volunteers were invited to participate in this study, which took place at a medium-sized university, using fliers that outlined the study and promised 50 US dollars to people who would be selected. Respondents were screened to ensure their availability for the duration of the study, and also to ensure they were not expert game players. Expertise was measured in prescreening with multiple-choice questions about gaming habits, number of MMOs they played, and how long they played those MMOs. Seventy-five people were selected after screening. After the study began, one participant experienced motion sickness, and eight had scheduling conflicts. Thus, sixty-six participants (32 males, 34 female) completed the study.

Based on the screening questionnaire, the majority of the participants were not expert MMO game players. None of the participants were current MMO players, none said they had played an MMO in the last year, and only three had played an MMO for more than a month. Participants' familiarity with Lord of the Rings was also measured by asking about their experience in, watching related movies, playing card, board and video games, and reading Tolkien's books. None of the players had played Lord of the Rings Online (*LotRO*) (Warner Bros., 2013). The participants' average age was 25.63, which is very close to the average age of MMO players (M = 26.6) as reported in a previous, large scale study (Yee, 2006).

The study employed a between-subjects design with 33 participants in the customization group (CG; 17 females, 16 males) and 33 participants in the no customization group (NCG; 17 females, 16 males). Participants were assigned to one of the two groups by gender. In the CG, participants were given various choices in the game, such as the opportunity to choose their game character's specialties, skills, gender,

Figure 1. LotRO characters: a CG character (left), a NCG character (right)

and appearance, as well as in-game rewards after they completed quests. In the NCG, the participants were assigned to well-constructed pre-designed avatars with efficient character skills and quest rewards were chosen for them that would maximize their character abilities. In the NCG, avatar gender and participant gender were matched (see Figure 1 for female avatar examples.)

A preliminary analysis showed no significant differences between groups in their age ($t = 0.72$, $p = .477$), Lord of the Rings familiarity ($t = 0.94$, $p = .348$) or MMO experiences ($t = 1.32$, $p = .195$).

Materials and Apparatus

Stimulus

Lord of the Rings Online (*LotRO*) was used for the study. *LotRO* is a fantasy type MMO based on the books by J.R.R. Tolkien. In searching for an appropriate stimulus, three factors were taken into consideration:

1. Availability of avatar-based customization (Turkay & Adinolf, 2010). For example, being able to customize the character appearance and character skills;
2. Usability and playability; and
3. The technical requirements of the game.

Three different game accounts were generated for the study. At the time of data collection, *LotRO* was housed on 19 different servers; each server appeared as different instances of the same world. Players can play in one of these *LotRO* worlds, and some servers are more populated than others. Each account allows five characters per server. Using multiple accounts made it possible for participants to play in populated servers. This maximized the possibility of social interaction within the game. Participants used gaming-optimized PCs for the study, and wore a headset while playing.

Identification and empathy were assessed with a 21-item 5-point Likert-type scale, developed and tested by Looy et al., 2010. Based on previous literature, three main dimensions were identified: Wishful Identification (6 items), e.g., If I could become like my character, I would; Perceived Similarity (6 items), e.g. My character is like me in many ways; Embodied Presence (5 items), e.g., I feel like I am inside my character when playing. Similar to Looy et al., (2010) study, this study also examined players' empathy towards their characters with 4 items, e.g., I am upset when my character dies. Cronbach's α for the three dimensions of the identification scale per session were measured in the current study and found to be satisfactory (ranging from 0.842 to 0.954).

Engagement with avatar customization was assessed with a 5-point Likert scale survey, which was developed and tested by O'Brian & Toms (2010). Cronbach's α for the adapted scale was 0.813. In addition, participants rated the importance of different avatar customization parts (e.g., hair style, weight, height) by using a 5-point Likert scale. As explained above, this study did not manipulate different types of customization. In order to investigate how the outcomes of two main avatar-based customization (appearance and skills) may correlate with different dimensions of the identification scale, participants were asked to rate two 5-point Likert scale items (i.e., "How my character looks is important", "what my character can do is important") after the first and the last play sessions.

Game motivation as operationalized in this paper was assessed with a single 7-point Likert scale item, "I would be willing to play this game again", taken from the *Intrinsic Motivation Inventory* (*IMI*; Ryan, Mims, & Koestner, 1983).

While survey questions asked about identification, motivation, and engagement directly, semi-structured interviews were conducted to allow participants to "tell" their gameplay experience without prompting them on the topic of identification. These interviews were conducted after the first and the last session with all participants. A subset of participants was interviewed after the second (n = 27) and third (n = 18) sessions as well. This resulted in a total of 12 people who were interviewed after every session. General, open-ended questions were asked (e.g., Tell me about your experience this session.) to determine the extent of player identification with their characters.

Setting

The study took place in a research lab. The gaming computer in the research lab used during this study was separated from the main area with screens and resided in its own cubicle to avoid distraction. The researcher had a table in an adjoining cubicle, where a second monitor, keyboard and mouse were placed. These were connected to and mirrored the participant's computer, allowing the researcher to directly observe gameplay, and manipulate the NCG's choices. Participants had no direct line of sight to the researcher during the session. The setting remained the same throughout the study.

Procedure

As noted earlier, potential participants were provided with an online survey after they showed interest in the study. This survey collected demographic data (e.g., gender, age, occupation) and gaming experiences. Participants who were invited to participate in the study were provided with an informed consent document upon first entering the laboratory for the experiment.

After each participant read and signed the informed consent document, they were placed in front of the gaming computer, and were briefed on the study's procedure. They were told that they were going to finish the game tutorial in the first gameplay session, lasting about 1.5 to 2 hours. Then, the CG participants created their *LotRO* game characters. There was no time limit for character creation. Upon completing the character creation process, CG participants filled out a survey to measure their engagement with character customization. Using a 5-point Likert scale survey, participants also rated the importance and the degree of similarity of the customized avatar to themselves in 12 different elements of avatar customization (e.g., height, weight, hair color). The study procedure was the same for the NCG, except that they did not create their avatars and did not answer subsequent avatar customization related questions. NCG participant were assigned to well formed, but pre-generated characters.

Throughout the study, participants in the CG were allowed to make choices to customize their character skills and equipment, and they saw how their choices reflected on their character after equipping of new gear. The researcher made choices for the NCG on avatar-based functional customizations through mirrored controls, as described above. NCG participants would also not be able to see the changes reflected on their avatars when they equipped new gear. This was accomplished by a function called "Cosmetic Outfit" in *LotRO*.

Data Analysis

Independent samples *t*-tests were conducted to test differences between CG and NCG per session. RM-MANOVAs were used to measure the possible change in players' identification with, and their empathy toward, their characters over four sessions. Pearson correlations were conducted to test the direction and strength of a relationship between engagement with initial avatar customization and CG players' identification with their characters after each session.

Semi-structured interviews were analyzed thematically. Also, a second set of analysis was conducted based on the participants' use of first or third person pronouns in discussing the player characters in the games they played. This method was used previously in Hitchens et al. (2012)'s study of identification with characters. They asked participants to discuss various events and actions in the games they played and analyzed the interview transcript based on their pronoun use. For more explanation about the analysis see Hitchens et al. (2012).

RESULTS

Avatar Customization/Character Creation (Only CG)

The average time spent on character creation was 12:23.018 (twelve minutes 23 seconds and 18 milliseconds). On average, participants spent 06:43.574 on race and class selection and 05:39.442 on avatar appearance and name selection.

In general, participants had a positive attitude toward customizing their avatars, and reported a moderate level of engagement with customization process ($M = 3.81$, $SD = 0.62$), and felt in control of their customization experience ($M = 4.00$, $SD = 1.03$). For example, one of the players [P35] talked about her engagement with avatar customization as, "I had no expectation and interest at the beginning of the task. However, I saw getting drawn into...started to care a lot."

Importance and Identification

The most important avatar customization aspect for participants was hairstyle ($M = 4.39$, $SD = 1.03$) followed by hair color ($M = 3.85$, $SD = 1.15$) and eye color ($M = 3.70$, $SD = 1.47$). When all the participants' results were examined, avatars' height ($M = 2.60$, $SD = 1.55$) was rated as the least important avatar customization element. On average, participants highly cared about how their character looked (M

= 4.15, *SD* = 1.23). In fact, there was a statistically significant positive correlation between importance score and engagement with avatar customization ($r = 0.491$, $p = .002$).

Significant correlations were found between the importance score and Wishful Identification after each of the four sessions, between importance and Perceived Similarity after all but the first session, between importance and Embodied Presence after the last two sessions (see Table 1 for Pearson correlation coefficients).

In order to examine the possible impact of different types of customization on identification, another set of correlations was conducted between the three dimensions of identification and on items "How my character looks is important" (outcome of cosmetic customization) and "What my character can do is important" (outcome of functional customization). Results indicate that character appearance is more strongly related to identification than character abilities (see Table 2.)

Engagement with Avatar Customization and Identification

Results show that there is no statistically significant correlation between engagement with avatar customization and subscales of identification after the first session. However, engagement was significantly correlated with all of the subscales of identification after the fourth session (see Table 3).

Table 1. Pearson correlations between importance of avatar customization and identification dimensions

	Session 1	Session 2	Session 3	Session 4
Perceived Similarity	0.270	0.391*	0.452**	0.645***
Embodied Presence	0.128	0.158	0.426*	0.463**
Wishful Identification	0.484**	0.454**	0.441*	0.591***

*p < .05; **p < .01; ***p < .001.

Table 2. Pearson correlations between outcomes of two main avatar-based customization (cosmetic and functional) and subscales of identification

	e		Session 4	
	Cosmetic	Functional	Cosmetic	Functional
Perceived Similarity	0.359*	0.289	0.663*	-0.007
Embodied Presence	0.311	0.262	0.358*	0.105
Wishful Identification	0.448**	0.241	0.569**	0.078

*p < .05; **p < .01; ***p < .001.

Table 3. Pearson correlations between engagement with avatar customization and subscales of identification

	Session 1	Session 2	Session 3	Session 4
Perceived Similarity	0.007	0.258	0.350*	0.509**
Embodied Presence	-0.085	0.145	0.425*	0.536**
Wishful Identification	0.267	0.487**	0.480**	0.513**
Empathy	-0.009	0.112	0.330	0.417*

*p < .05; **p < .01; ***p < .001.

These results imply a possible impact of time on player identification with their characters, which is examined below.

Effect of Customization on Identification

Independent samples *t*-tests revealed statistically significant differences between CG and NCG (see Table 4) for all three dimensions of the identification scale. After each session, participants statistically significantly differed in Perceived Similarity and Wishful Identification, in favor of CG. CG reported a significantly higher sense of Embodied Presence than NCG after the second, third and the fourth gameplay sessions.

Assuming the normality of the data, RM-MANOVA was conducted to test for a possible difference between the CG participants and NCG participants in the amount of change in their ratings on the three dimensions of the Identification scale. Table 5 summarizes the results of the multivariate tests.

Since the *Box's M* value of 176.23 is associated with a $p < .001$, *Pillai's Trace* was used for the multivariate tests. Statistically significant multivariate effects were found for the main effects of Group, *Pillai's Trace* $= .20$, $F(3, 61) = 4.96$, $p = .004$, $\eta^2_{partial} = .20$ and for Sessions, *Pillai's Trace* $= .26$, *F*

Table 4. Statistics for identification subsections for each session

	Levene's		Independent Samples t-Test			CG		NCG	
	F	*p*	*t*	*p*	η^2	*M*	*SD*	*M*	*SD*
Perceived Similarity 1	3.52	.065	-3.20	.002	.14	2.56	1.08	1.81	0.83
Perceived Similarity 2	1.46	.231	-3.54	.001	.17	2.53	0.98	1.76	0.77
Perceived Similarity 3	3.68	.060	-3.39	.001	.15	2.65	0.98	1.92	0.76
Perceived Similarity 4	10.39	.002	-4.07	.000	.21	2.79	1.09	1.85	0.75
Wishful Identification 1	2.57	.114	-2.15	.035	.07	2.34	0.93	1.89	0.79
Wishful Identification 2	1.92	.170	-3.23	.002	.14	2.37	0.91	1.71	0.73
Wishful Identification 3	2.65	.109	-3.03	.004	.13	2.52	0.98	1.85	0.81
Wishful Identification 4	2.76	.101	-3.21	.002	.14	2.61	1.14	1.80	0.90
Embodied Presence 1	0.02	.892	-1.94	.056	.06	2.51	1.06	2.02	0.98
Embodied Presence 2	0.19	.663	-2.05	.044	.06	2.53	1.02	2.04	0.92
Embodied Presence 3	3.01	.088	-2.60	.011	.10	2.84	1.07	2.21	0.89
Embodied Presence 4	0.19	.661	-4.07	.000	.16	3.08	1.11	2.19	1.00

Table 5. Multivariate tests

Effect		*Pillai's Trace*	*F*	*df*	*Error df*	*p*	*Partial* η^2
Between	Intercept	.895	173.73	3	61	.000	.90
Subject	Group	.196	4.96	3	61	.004	.20
Within	Sessions	.258	2.13	9	55	.042	.26
Subject	Sessions x Group	.123	.86	9	55	.569	.12

$(9, 55) = 2.13, p = .042, \eta^2_{partial} = .26$, but not for the interaction between Group and Sessions, *Pillai's Trace* $= .123, F(9, 55) = 0.86, p = .569$. The examination of the means shows why the interactions may not be significant; the groups differed significantly on dependent variables at the end of the first session.

Tests of the Between-Subjects effects table indicate that there is a significant main effect of Group on Perceived Similarity, Wishful Identification, and Embodied Presence (see Table 6). Tests of Within-Subjects Contrasts showed a statistically significant linear relationship between sessions and Embodied Presence, $F(1, 63) = 10.81, p < .002, \eta^2_{partial} = .15$.

In order to estimate mean differences between sessions for each dependent variable, repeated tests were conducted. Results show that there is a statistically significant difference between Sessions 2 and 3 for all of the dependent variables (see Table 7, Table 8, and Table 9). An examination of Figure 2, Figure 3 and Figure 4 also helps us to understand the change between sessions.

In summary, quantitative analyses showed that both avatar-based customization and time impacted participants' identification with and empathy towards their characters. For CG participants, importance of avatar customization was significantly correlated with identification with their characters. Most notably, there was a significant linear relationship between participants' experienced Embodied Presence (how much players felt like they were the characters embodied in the game) and sessions. There was

Table 6. Tests of between subjects effects of group on identification

Source	Measure	SS	df	MS	F	p	Partial η^2
Group	Perceived Similarity	10.55	1	10.55	15.11	.000	.19
	Wishful Identification	6.73	1	6.73	9.59	.003	.13
	Embodied Presence	6.40	1	6.40	8.13	.006	.11
Error	Perceived Similarity	43.96	63	0.70			
	Wishful Identification	44.23	63	0.70			
	Embodied Presence	49.62	63	0.79			

Table 7. Test of within-subjects contrasts for perceived similarity

	SS	F	p	Partial η^2
Session 1 vs. Session 2	0.10	0.28	.596	.00
Session 2 vs. Session 3	1.19	5.84	.019	.09
Session 3 vs. Session 4	0.17	0.50	.482	.01

Table 8. Test of within-subjects contrasts for wishful identification

	SS	F	p	Partial η^2
Session 1 vs. Session 2	0.37	1.12	.294	.02
Session 2 vs. Session 3	1.23	5.79	.019	.08
Session 3 vs. Session 4	0.05	0.22	.644	.00

Table 9. Test of within-subjects contrasts for embodied presence

	SS	F	βp	Partial η^2
Session 1 vs. Session 2	0.02	0.04	.847	.00
Session 2 vs. Session 3	3.49	8.44	.005	.12
Session 3 vs. Session 4	1.12	2.81	.099	.04

Figure 2. Estimated marginal means of Perceived Similarity over four sessions

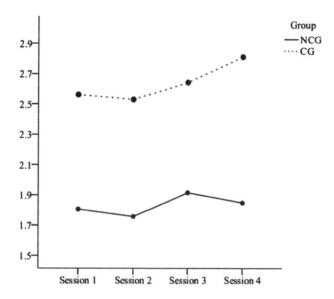

Figure 3. Estimated marginal means of wishful identification over four sessions

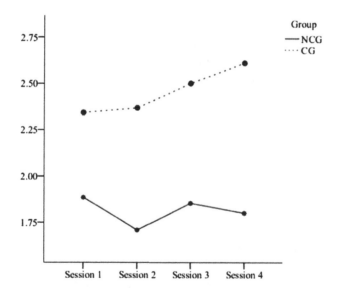

no interaction between groups and time meaning that, though CG started ahead, the change over time was similar for both groups in their identification with their characters. CG participants' engagement with character creation in the first session had a stronger relationship with their identification with their characters as the sessions proceeded.

The quantitative results indicate that since the rate of increase is about the same for both groups, there must be other factors, independent of the treatment, that impact identification.

Figure 4. Estimated marginal means of embodied presence over four sessions

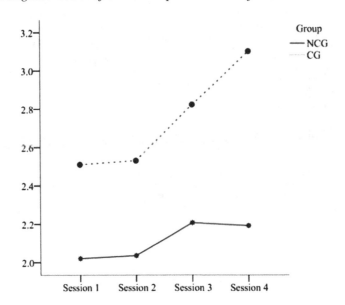

Predictors of Motivation

The third research question we ask is to what extent we can predict whether a player would be willing to re-play based on their character identification. For each session, a two stage hierarchical multiple regression was conducted with Motivation as the dependent variable. Customization (a dummy variable; coded as 0=no customization; 1=customization) was entered at the stage one of the regression to control for the experimental groups. Identification dimensions, Perceived Similarity, Embodied Cognition and Wishful Identification were entered at stage two. All correlations between the multiple regression variables were reported in Tables 10-11-12-13. Correlations between the predictor variables and the depended variable were weak to moderately strong.

For session 1, the first model was statistically significant, $F(1, 63)=10.25$, $p=.002$ and explained 14% of the variance in participants' motivation (see Table 14). After entering other predictors at Step 2, the total variance explained by the model as a while was 29%, $F(4, 60)=5.98$, $p<.001$. Introduction of the additional variables explained additional 15% variance in player motivation, after controlling for the experimental condition. In the final model, three predictor variables were marginally significant: customization, $\beta=.28$, $p=.021$, Embodied Presence, $\beta=.33$ $p=.065$ and Wishful Identification, $\beta=-.31$, $p=.085$.

For session 2, the first model was statistically significant, $F(1, 64)=8.59$, $p=.005$ and explained 12% of the variance in participants' motivation (see Table 15). After entering other predictors at Step 2, the total variance explained by the model as a while was 29%, $F(4, 60)=6.07$, $p<.0001$. Introduction of the additional variables explained additional 17% variance in player motivation, after controlling for the experimental condition. In the final model, two predictor variables were marginally significant: customization, $\beta=.21$, $p=.095$, Perceived Similarity, $\beta=.68$ $p=.003$ and Wishful Identification, $\beta=-.43$, $p=.029$.

For session 3, the first model was statistically significant, $F(1, 64)=13.03$, $p=.001$ and explained 17% of the variance in participants' motivation (see Table 16). After entering other predictors at Step 2, the total variance explained by the model as a while was 29%, $F(4, 61)=6.15$, $p<.001$. Introduction of the additional variables explained only additional 12% variance in player motivation, after controlling for the experimental condition. In the final model, only statistically significant predictor variable was customization, $\beta=.30$, $p=.015$.

For session 4, the first model was statistically significant, $F(1, 64)=23.48$, $p<.001$ and explained 27% of the variance in participants' motivation (see Table 17). After entering other predictors at Step 2, the total variance explained by the model as a while was 44%, $F(4, 61)=11.95$, $p<.001$. Introduction of the additional variables explained additional 17% variance in player motivation, after controlling for the experimental condition. In the final model, there were three statistically and marginally significant predictor variables: Customization, $\beta=.32$, $p=.005$, Perceived Similarity, $\beta=.41$, $p=.068$, and Embodied Presence, $\beta=.33$, $p=.043$.

Qualitative Findings

Both groups talked about their characters in the interviews when they were asked to recount their experiences. A comparison over time showed that almost twice as many participants mentioned their characters during the last interview ($n = 39$) than during the first interview ($n = 20$). Over four interviews, 90% of the CG mentioned their characters, compared to 50% of NCG players. CG Participants used the pronoun "I" (or "my character") more than NCG did while discussing their feelings about or events related to their game characters (72% vs. 35% of the time) (e.g. "I fought with a group of monsters"). NCG mostly used "s/he" or "the character" to refer to their avatars. However, both CG and NCG alternated between referring to their character in the first and third person while telling their experiences. This shift may indicate an ongoing process of forming a relationship with their characters, and shows identification can be situation dependent.

Compared to NCG, CG's conversation included more instances of similarity with their characters. For example, during the first interview, [P24] said "… If it [her character] looks like me I would be more interested in it. It is funny if the character has a similar look to me." Similarly, another participant, [P28], talked about her avatar as a perfect looking version of her "I wanted my avatar to look like an Elvin version of me, so similar to me but more perfect looking. I think my avatar looks the way I wanted it to." Perceived similarity was not only about appearance, but also about characters' behavioral characteristics. For example, [P08] said, "I think she is kind of like me… sometimes I get lost and I go off the wrong direction… sometimes ... [play] too bold." Another participant, [P59], was accepting all the quests in the game and when asked why she did that, she replied "… My character is kind of like me. She cannot say no." This association was facilitated by character creation in the first session and built up through customization and exploration over time. The majority of responses about perceived similarity came from their interviews in the last two sessions. For example, [P7] reflected on her character in the last interview as "I chose this character… So whether he's the kind of people I admire or the kind of people I think I am, there is some similar things that I have or I want to have…connected with me." This quote also exemplifies her choice of the character being a boundary between her ideal (other) and real self.

Wishful identification is about players' desire to be like their *LotRO* characters and was exemplified by several participants. The most common quotes in this category from CG participants were about how they wanted to be represented by aesthetically pleasing avatars. Some were more interested in their characters' skills or functionality. For example, [P53]'s quote shows how he chose his character based on what he wanted to do in the game:

...I chose my guy because I wanted to be right there in the middle of the fight... I didn't want to be the person in the back healing people or doing long-distance shots I think that had positive effect... I can sustain a lot more damage. I enjoyed that part I felt like I was my character...Being able to just give in and swing the axe... so that was rewarding... (P53, Interview 4, CG, M)

Although not as common as in CG, some NCG players bonded with their avatars. For example, [P18] felt quite immersed in the game, creating a strong connection with her alter ego, Aydal, over each session. In the last session, the game became more challenging and her character got killed. This experience made a big impact on her; she became very anxious and her hands shook. This connection to her avatar seemed to be extreme. Below [P18] explains how her character's increased competence might have contributed to such connection:

Hmmm... I don't know I feel like it is the small stuff... like when you trying to... you are growing in the beginning levels and when you get better when you reach another level you can do more things and you start to feel more than what you are and be happy for yourself... that kind of stuff contribute to how I built the connection... it is all the small stuff made me like the character more... (P18, Interview 4, NCG, F)

Achievements and experiences in the game help players "feel good" or "be proud" of themselves. For example, [P40] talked about how she liked non-player characters' compliments on her achievements "... I like that when they complemented my character... but I'm pretty sure it is standardized... it's like oh you did well very good fighter." Sense of competence and feeling of achievement are likely to contribute players' identification with their characters.

Character identification was likely to influence participants' identification and familiarity with the game which resulted in increased motivation to play the game. A CG player expressed her feeling of increased familiarity toward the game during the final interview.

[Laughter]... this game [LotRO] became a familiar thing for me now, not a house, not a home but something that is close to me. I was feeling happy when I was thinking about coming here. I was thinking that 'I will play and I will do something'. (P22, Interview 4, CG, F)

Social context was also an important factor for players' identification with their characters. Examples of two different perspectives are from [P59] and [P70]. In the third session, [P59] formed a fellowship (a group) with other players, which is a common practice in MMOs. She stated that "... I actually think that I am the character. But, before, I was not so connected with my character. Yeah, doing the quest together [with other players] I was very self-conscious..." Quite different from this experience was [P70]'s stance when she was asked and declined to join a fellowship consisting of higher level of players. She said "...if they think that my character is a novice then I'm also a novice player. I don't want to be seen that way by others. I don't want to reveal my identity [that I am a novice player]. I just pretend that I'm such a good player who is really skillful so they all want to be friends with me..." This shows that players' identification with character is strong to the point that she perceives how others may think about her character is equal to what they will think about her.

Participants talked about both functional and cosmetic character customization. Character creation and avatar customization at the beginning of the first session was mentioned mostly as cosmetic customization. Some participants talked about both. Customization was also continuous throughout the game. Here is a representative quote from [P64], "It was fun to create my own character to put multiple characteristics on it and it was also fun, as the game goes along, to keep customizing it by adding more weapons and all like changing colors and all."

Participants in NCG reported less attachment toward their characters. For example, [P3] talked about how she got used to her character dying in a battle "The character died once today… I think I'm getting used to watching my character dying, because I know she's going to come back." Similarly, [P9] talked about how, as time passed, she cared less about the character but more about the story that the character was embedded in. A similar comment came from [P23] emphasizing his apathy:

It [survey] was asking whether I would feel sorry when the character dies. No. I know that it's a game character…It is enjoyable to play that character as it is but there is no relationship between me and the character. I could not find anything in him to identify with myself. (P23, Interview 4, NCG, M)

When it comes to embodied presence, participants talked about a few different experiences that made them feel like their character was an extension of themselves. One of these experiences related to the game's first person view. *LotRO* provides players with two different view options: first person view and third person view. Third person view allows players see the back of their avatar on the screen and have the avatar present on the screen at all times. The first person view allows players to see the game world from their avatar's eyes without seeing the avatar on the screen. Participants who tried first person view when playing reported an elevated feeling of embodied presence. The game's 3D graphics and detailed real world modeling, incorporating animations and environmental details, facilitated such feelings as well. For example, [P70] talks about her enjoyment related to detailed graphics and how this impacted her feeling of embodiment.

I like the realistic characters and it is very detailed. I did not even imagine that I could laugh in the game. The gestures are so specific and detailed … makes me feel I get immersed in the character. (P70, Interview 4, CG, F)

In summary, a majority of the participants formed some form of a relationship with their characters, though this occurred more in the CG than NCG. It is implied in many cases that players would play the game to further this relationship. For some participants, the characters were a representation of themselves; for others, the characters were nothing but mere toys or vehicles. In all cases, this relation and identification with characters was dynamic and changed over time. Sometimes, players' sense of wishful identification with the character got quite strong, like in the case of [P18]. In addition to character creation and avatar customization, socialization, sense of accomplishment and the realistic game world increased participants' identification with their characters. Perceived similarity was attributed to both physical appearances of the characters and characters' personality assigned by thee player. Embodied presence was facilitated by the game design and graphics as well as the game's narrative.

DISCUSSION

Results showed that CG players identified with their characters significantly more than NCG did. The psychological aspect of making choices might explain this result: because players chose their avatars' aspects they felt more associated with the character by "taking ownership" of it. Another explanation might be related to the distance between real self and ideal self. Customization might have allowed players to create characters closer to their ideal self, which might have increased their identification with their characters. Within the CG, players spent considerable time customizing their character in the first session and their reported engagement was strongly related to their identification in the last session. This result implies that as players spent more time in the game with their customized avatars, their identification increases.

Correlational analysis between identification and two main outcomes of avatar-based customization (i.e., cosmetic and functional) indicates that cosmetic avatar customization was more strongly related to identification than functional customization for the players in this study. Considering players' low expertise with MMOs, this result is expected. It may take more time for players to understand the goals of the character as result of their choices and identify with them, than to identify with the characters through aesthetic manipulations.

Although NCG players, who were given a character, did not identify with those characters as much as CG players did, some of the NCG players showed identification with the characters they were given. According to previous studies, a match in gender and ethnicity influences identification (e.g., Lim, 2006). This may help us understand NCG players' identification with their characters. As mentioned previously, NCG players were assigned human avatars whose gender, hair color, skin color, and eye color matched with the players'. However, the impact of character creation/avatar customization was significantly more than mere gender match and appearance resemblance.

CG players felt their characters were more similar to themselves and wished to be like their characters more than their counterparts did. Players' Perceived Similarity (gauging how much players perceived themselves and their characters as having common characteristics, (e.g. physical appearance, social status), and Wishful Identification with their avatars as Within Subject variables did not significantly change over time. However, treatment had a moderate to large main effect on the differences in these variables.

Qualitative findings showed that many of the CG players chose their characters so that they possessed some aspect of themselves, such as a skill (e.g., playing an instrument) or physical characteristic (e.g., hair, eyes, built). Such matching along with the psychological aspect of the act of choosing might have increased CG players' identification with their characters by creating a channel to relate with their characters. Trepte and Reinecke's (2010) study supports this finding of the strong relationship between player-avatar similarity and identification. Character creation allowed players to create their own goals for the game. In turn, they started the game with a goal to accomplish for their characters. This initial goal setting might have motivated players as they engaged in goal related tasks (Latham & Locke, 1979).

Throughout the study, CG reported significantly higher Embodied Presence than NCG did. Players' Embodied Presence changed significantly over time. Treatment and sessions did not interact. This means that CG still felt more "present" in the game than NCG, but the rate of change in Embodied Presence was about the same for both groups. The significant change in Embodied Presence of CG players might be a result of increased player agency and social interaction through avatars (Taylor, 2002) as they progressed in the game. As players built a closer relationship with their avatars through continuous customization, their sense of being embodied by the avatars might have increased. Another reason for the increase might be that as players got more familiar with the game and with their characters, it became easier to immerse themselves in the game through their characters, and feel increased presence.

Players' identification with their characters increased over the four sessions as they built a profile for their avatars. This was evidenced both by qualitative and quantitative results. Although the rate of change was not significantly different for CG and NCG, customization corresponded to the initial variance among the players' identification and empathy. These differences between CG and NCG were maintained over four sessions.

Player motivation or retention depends on their emotional connection with the game and how meaningful that connection is to the players. For CG players, having opportunities to acquire unique, visually appealing items to customize their experiences might have facilitated this emotional connection (Koehne, Bietz, & Redmiles, 2013). The fact that NCG players could not see their choices being reflected on their characters might have inhibited the construction of a relationship between the player and the character. For NCG, increased responsibility (e.g., goals given to them) through the game narrative (Schneider et al., 2004) and interaction with their avatars might have resulted in increased identification with their characters.

Klimmit et al. (2009) propose that identification is never an absolute process in which the players' entire identity is replaced by the identity of the character, but rather a partial alteration in self-perception. This partial alteration may allow players to both experience empathy towards their characters (the character as the other) and experience a merge with their character (the character as the self). In a way, there is an emotional task switching during the gameplay.

One of the primary effects of identification is empathy towards the subject of identification (Nathanson, 2003; Looy et al., 2010). Perhaps, players feel empathy towards their characters after their identification process, or after the gameplay is over. This study asked participants to report their identification after their gameplay was over. When players are not actively involved in the game by controlling their characters, these characters may become "the other" for them. The current study was not designed to capture the possible shift in players' identifications and agency within a same session (see Giddings, 2007). Future studies should investigate ways to capture objective and subjective data during gameplay as well as via surveys after the gameplay is completed. For instance, Taylor, Kampe and Bell (2015) used a microethnographic method and showed participants video recordings of their gameplay sessions and invite them to comment on influential points in the game for close reading of their lived experiences.

Self Determination Theory (SDT, Deci & Ryan, 1985) posits that autonomy, competence and relatedness are necessary for people's well-being, and was used previously to explain motivational aspects of MMOs (Przybylski, Rigby & Ryan, 2010). As a meta-motivation theory, SDT can also be used as a lens to understand findings of the current study. Autonomy satisfaction, mostly utilized as the feeling of having control over an activity, is crucial in encouraging people to come back to do the same activity. The choice-making involved in customization may give people a sense of autonomy. In support of such an implication, Teng (2010) showed that customization increases gamer loyalty.

Third research question asked how different dimensions of identification predicts players' motivation. Motivation was operationalized by players' willingness to repeatedly come back to the gameplay. Birk et al. (2016) had found that all three dimensions of identification significantly positively predicted player motivation (time played). We found different results in the current study. Hierarchical linear regressions showed that the amount that the different dimensions of identification predicted motivation changed over sessions and customization was a significant predictor for players' motivation and can explain 12 to 17% of the variance in participant's willingness to play the game over the course of four sessions.

Perceived Similarity was a significant predictor of motivation after second and fourth sessions. Embodied Presence was only marginally significant predictor in the first session, not significant for the second and third sessions, and became significant in the fourth session. Perhaps the novice players realized that embodied presence is an enjoyable experience over time and they wanted to immerse themselves into the game through their characters. Wishful Identification was a significant negative predictor of motivation after second session and marginally significant predictor after the first session. If participants' wishful identification score was higher their motivation was lower. This results are aligned with the approach that characterize the player-avatar relationship as fluid rather than as a fixed state (Giddings and Kennedy, 2008; Taylor et al., 2015). In a similar, we found participants' shifting use of pronouns of "I" and "my character" when referring to participants' in-game character. This indicates of players' sense of agency and affiliation (see Giddings, 2007). Except the second gameplay session, customization remained a statistically significant predictor of motivation after we controlled for variables related to identification. This result implies that novice players will be willing to replay a videogame if they are exposed to customization opportunities.

In MMOs, players are introduced to more choices in the form of customization as they level up and gain expertise, but the most concentrated and impactful choice-making happens during character creation. In line with this, results showed that participants spent considerable amount of time making decisions about their avatar appearance and character skills. The positive relationship between CG participants' engagement with character creation in the first session, and their increased identification with their characters as the sessions proceeded, implies the character creation process has long-term effects on players' experience, such as identification. It is safe to put forward that CG participants' higher identification with their characters, compared to NCG participants, is due to the sense of agency and autonomy they felt as result of making various choices while customizing their characters in the first session. The improved sense of agency facilitated identification.

The across the board increase in players' identification with their characters over time may be due to an increased sense of competence as they accomplish goals in the game. For example, [P18], who was proud of her character's accomplishments, identified with her character closely—this temporarily reduced her self-discrepancy (Higgins, 1987) and getting defeated shook her relationship with her character. Previous work with young adults found that strong characters were attractive, implying the importance of feeling successful, for wishful identification (Janz, 2005). Players' need for relatedness might have encouraged them to create similar characters to themselves, thus fostering players' perceived similarity. Another form of relatedness is relating to other player characters in the game. Playing with others and having common missions might have fostered players embodied presence, thus increasing overall identification with their characters.

Results also showed significant differences between Sessions 2 and 3 for the dimensions of identification, whereas there was no difference between first two sessions and the last two sessions. The reason for this might be that during the first two sessions participants were still learning the game and the controls. Hamilton (2009) suggests that through the interaction with and via the avatar (through embodied interaction), players become coupled to the avatar. In such coupling, mastering the game controls is crucial, and it was after the second session that players got comfortable with game controls. In their SDT-based motivational model of video games, Przybylski, Rigby and Ryan (2010) emphasized the importance of mastery of game controls for player engagement and motivation. The findings of this study support this assertion. Mastery of controls might be the gateway to player's identification with their characters.

IMPLICATIONS FOR EDUCATIONAL GAMES

While not tested in an educational game, the results of this study imply that allowing learners to customize their avatars in educational virtual environments may have beneficial effects in the areas of motivation and other areas that correlate with learning.

This study shows that avatar-based customization may increase students' motivation. In educational settings, viewing identity as dynamic rather than static facilitates students' growth mindset (Kolb & Kolb, 2009). Virtual worlds give users imagined worlds and tools to test various identities through active processes of design. An avatar is the main tool users have for identity exploration. Strengthening the relationship between the player and the avatar can facilitate identification through which students can form their identities (Weinreich & Saunderson 2003). This study showed that avatar-based customization facilitates players' identification with their characters by increasing their sense of autonomy and agency. Such processes can build students' self-efficacy, resulting in higher achievement motivation (Ames, 1992). Considering that focused decision making during character creation in the beginning resulted in CG players' higher identification with their characters, educational game designers should consider giving players periodic chances to re-customize their characters' appearance and skills in addition to main avatar customization at the beginning of game-play. This may allow students to re-consider their characters' goals, as well as increase their sense of agency.

Second, avatar-based customization may catalyze students' learning. Mantovani and Castelnuovo (2003) state that identification might be an important factor in learning in virtual environments, increasing emotional impact and relevance, and Ganesh et al. (2011) showed that players remember avatar-related events more than non-avatar related events. The results of the current study suggest that when players customize their characters they will identify with their characters further and focus more on events related to their characters. When they don't customize, they focus on the game's narrative. We suggest that when teachers make decisions among different types of educational games to use in their classrooms, they should take into account both content and customization. If students learn best from the narrative, perhaps a game with less or no customization will help. If students learn best from the game system, or social interaction, customization may lend a helping hand. For instance, students may customize the appearance of their historical protagonist in a history themed video game. This should help them to recall more of the actions and the speeches of the historical character in the videogame via the mechanism of player identification (Cohen, 2001).

Analysis of pronoun use ("I" v.s. "she/he" or "my character") showed that CG participants used "I" more often to refer their characters when they were telling their game experiences. This perspective taking should increase students' recall. For instance, in a study of first person vs. third person perspective taking, Lozano, Hard, and Tversky (2007), showed participants a video clip of a person assembling a piece of furniture and told them to verbally describe the process in either the first-person perspective or third-person perspective. Later, participants who described the process in the first-person perspective made significantly fewer errors. We may expect similar effects in video games where students take characters' perspective rather than see their character as a separate entity.

Last, avatar-based customization may increase behavioral outcomes of serious games. For instance, if we aim to encourage students to exercise more or eat healthy through interactions within a game or virtual world, we should allow them to choose and customize their characters. Fox and Bailenson (2009) found that participants exercised more when they used a virtual representation of self rather than a virtual representation of other. We may expect that increased identification via customization would reinforce the effect of avatars on driving behavioral outcomes via gameplay. However, future research should investigate more clearly the impact of avatar-based customization on student learning, motivation and behavior, and examine whether customization increases player identification in various types of games (e.g., non-role playing games, games without narrative, educational games vs. commercial games).

LIMITATIONS

This study has multiple limitations. Its results may not be fully applicable to other types of virtual environments due to their structural differences, for example in their narrative and avatar customization processes. While MMOs are narrative driven gaming worlds, social virtual worlds such as Second Life usually do not have a built-in narrative. Narrative is known to impact player identification (Schneider, Lang, Shin, & Bradley, 2004), and future research should address the possible mediating role of narrative on the impact of customization on players' identification with avatars. They should ascertain under which conditions users identify more with their avatars in social virtual worlds. In a similar vein, implications for educational virtual environments should be viewed cautiously because *LotRO* is not an educational MMO and, while we believe educational-game implications can be (cautiously) made, this study did not test for learning.

Not all virtual worlds provide their users with similar types of customization options; some provide detailed customization (e.g., *City of Heroes*) others don't. Studies have shown that customization tools available to users when designing avatars (Turkay, 2012) and the type of virtual environment may affect players' online identity in absolute means (Koehne et al., 2013). For example, in Vasalou and Joinson (2009)'s study, participants were asked to create 2D avatars to represent themselves in an online forum (Yahoo! Answers). In that virtual environment, users may create avatars similar to their real-selves because they may want to be recognized as an answer giver. Studies found that people may not like avatars with a cartoon-like design, and this could be systematically related to age, with older subjects preferring realistic virtual figures (e.g., Scwind, Wolf, Henze, & Corn, 2015). However, realistic avatar appearance is also not possible in many fantasy MMOs since the avatars are not always humans, although most are humanoids. *LotRO* allows players to create humanoid characters, but the choices are still limited for each customized part.

Studies also found that age may impact how players customize their avatars to represent themselves through these avatars (e.g., Villani et al., 2016). Older adolescents represented themselves with more facial details and with facial and body sexual features compared to younger adolescents. Future studies may investigate how adults differ from adolescents and younger children in the impact of customization behaviors on character identification and motivation.

This study did not manipulate different types of customization (see Turkay & Adinolf, 2010). When players create their characters, they don't only make choices about their avatar's appearance, but also about their characters' abilities (i.e., what they will do in the game). It is possible that these different type of customizations result in different behavioral, psychological and motivational outcomes. Future studies should differentiate the impact of different types of customization on players' identification with and empathy toward their characters.

This study was conducted with novice MMO players. The results may not be fully applicable to players of varying expertise. It is reasonable to think that experts may bring dramatically different expectations to their gameplay, their customization practices, and how these may impact their relationships with their avatars.

Related to expertise, a longer study may find different results. Although this study involved significant amounts of gameplay, it is likely that as players gain more expertise, the impact of certain type of customization may become more salient and others may become weaker for increasing player identification with and empathy toward their characters.

CONCLUSION

In conclusion, identification was a strong contributor to players' positive or negative game experiences. Avatar-based customization played an important role in players' identification with their characters by increasing their sense of autonomy and was also a significant predictor for players motivation. Future studies are needed to differentiate the effects of customizing character skills from customization of avatar appearance as these relate to identification, as well as to examine how differences in given customization choices constrain or enhance identification and identity exploration possibilities in multiple virtual environments.

REFERENCES

Ames, C. (1992). Classrooms: Goals, structures, and student motivation. *Journal of Educational Psychology, 84*(3), 261–271. doi:10.1037/0022-0663.84.3.261

Arnett, J. J. (2010). *Adolescence and emerging adulthood: A cultural approach* (4th ed.). Upper Saddle River, NJ: Pearson-Prentice Hall.

Bailey, R., Wise, K., & Bolls, P. (2009). How avatar customizability affects childrens arousal and subjective presence during junk food-sponsored online video games. *Cyberpsychology & Behavior, 12*(3), 277–283. doi:10.1089/cpb.2008.0292 PMID:19445632

Bers, M. (2001). Identity construction environments: Developing personal and moral values through the design of a virtual city. *Journal of the Learning Sciences, 10*(4), 365–415. doi:10.1207/S15327809JL-S1004new_1

Bessiere, K., Seay, A. F., & Kiesler, S. (2007). The ideal elf: Identity exploration in World of Warcraft. *Cyberpsychology & Behavior, 10*(4), 530–537. doi:10.1089/cpb.2007.9994 PMID:17711361

Birk, M. V., Atkins, C., Bowey, J. T., & Mandryk, R. L. (2016). *Fostering intrinsic motivation through avatar identification in digital games*. Paper presented at CHI 2016, San Jose, CA. http://doi.org/doi:10.1145/2858036.2858062

Chandler, D., & Griffiths, M. (2004). Who is the fairest of them all? Gendered readings of Big Brother 2 (UK). In E. Mathijs & J. Jones (Eds.), *Big Brother International: Format, Critics and Publics* (pp. 40–61). London, UK: Wallflower Press.

Christy, K. R., & Fox, J. (2016). Transportability and presence as predictors of avatar identification within narrative video games. *Cyberpsychology, Behavior, and Social Networking, 19*(4), 283–287. doi:10.1089/cyber.2015.0474 PMID:26919032

Cohen, J. (1999). Favorite characters of teenage viewers of Israeli serials. *Journal of Broadcasting & Electronic Media, 43*(3), 327–345. doi:10.1080/08838159909364495

Cohen, J. (2001). Defining identification: A theoretical look at the identification of audiences with media characters. *Mass Communication & Society, 4*(3), 245–264. doi:10.1207/S15327825MCS0403_01

Davis, M. H. (1983). Measuring individual differences in empathy: Evidence for a multidimensional approach. *Journal of Personality and Social Psychology, 44*(1), 113–126. doi:10.1037/0022-3514.44.1.113

Deci, E. L., & Ryan, R. M. (1985). *Intrinsic motivation and self-determination in human behavior*. New York, NY: Plenum Press. doi:10.1007/978-1-4899-2271-7

Dickey, M. D. (2007). Game design and learning: A conjectual analysis of how massively mutliple online role-playing games (MMORPGs) foster intrinsic motivation. *Educational Technology Research and Development, 55*(3), 253–273. doi:10.1007/s11423-006-9004-7

Dolgov, I., Graves, W. J., Nearents, M. R., Schwark, J. D., & Brooks Volkman, C. (2014). Effects of cooperative gaming and avatar customization on subsequent spontaneous helping behavior. *Computers in Human Behavior, 33*, 49–55. doi:10.1016/j.chb.2013.12.028

Dove, T. (2002). The Space between: Telepresence, re-animation and the re-casting of the invisible. In M. Reiser & A. Zapp (Eds.), *New screen media: cinema/art/narrative*. London: British Film Institute.

Ducheneaut, N., Wen, M. D., Yee, N., & Wadley, G. (2009). Body and mind: A study of avatar personalization in three virtual worlds. *ACM Conference on Human Factors in Computing Systems*. doi:10.1145/1518701.1518877

Ducheneaut, N., Yee, N., Nickell, E., & Moore, R. J. (2006). Alone together?: Exploring the social dynamics of massively multiplayer online games. *Proceedings of the SIGCHI Conference on Human Factors in Computing CHI '06* (pp. 407-416). ACM. doi:10.1145/1124772.1124834

Erikson, E. (1968). *Identity youth and crisis*. New York: Norton.

Fischer, P., Kastenmüller, A., & Greitemeyer, T. (2010). Media violence and the self: The impact of personalized gaming characters in aggressive video games in aggressive behavior. *Journal of Experimental Social Psychology, 46*(1), 192–195. doi:10.1016/j.jesp.2009.06.010

Flanagan, M. (1999). Mobile identities, digital stars, and post-cinematic selves. *Wide Angle., 21*(1), 77–93. doi:10.1353/wan.1999.0002

Fox, J., & Bailenson, J. N. (2009). Virtual self-modeling: The effects of vicarious reinforcement and identification on exercise behaviors. *Media Psychology, 12*(1), 1–25. doi:10.1080/15213260802669474

Fron, J., Fullerton, T., Ford Morie, J., & Pearce, C. (2007). *Playing dress-up: Costumes, role-play and imagination*. Philosophy of Computer Games Conference, Reggio Emilia, Italy.

Ganesh, S., van Schie, H. T., de Lange, F. P., Thompson, E., & Wigboldus, D. H. (2011). How the human brain goes virtual: Distinct cortical regions of the person-processing network are involved in self-identification with virtual agents. *Cereb Cortex.*, *22*(7), 1577–1585. doi:10.1093/cercor/bhr227 PMID:21917741

Giddings, S. (2007). I'm the one who makes the Lego Racers go: Virtual and actual space in videogame play. In S. Weber & S. Dixon (Eds.), *Growing Up Online: Young People and Digital Technologies* (pp. 35–48). New York: Palgrave Macmillan. doi:10.1057/9780230607019_3

Giddings, S., & Kennedy, H. (2008). Little jesuses and fuck-off robots: On aesthetics, cybernetics, and not being very good at Lego Star Wars. In M. Swalwell & J. Wilson (Eds.), *The Pleasures of Computer Gaming: Essays on Cultural History, Theory and Aesthetics* (pp. 13–32). Jefferson, NC: McFarland.

GoSupermodel [PC Game]. Copenhagen, Denmark: watAgame.

Hamilton, J. G. (2009). Identifying with an Avatar: A multidisciplinary perspective.*Proceedings of Cumulus Conference'09.*

Hefner, D., Klimmt, C., & Vorderer, P. (2007). Identification with the player character as determinant of video game enjoyment. In L. Ma, M. Rauterberg, & R. Nakatsu (Eds.), *Entertainment computing–International Conference of Entertainment Computing* (pp. 39–48). Berlin: Springer. doi:10.1007/978-3-540-74873-1_6

Higgins, E. T. (1987). Self-Discrepancy: A Theory Relating Self and Affect. *Psychological Review*, *94*(3), 319–341. doi:10.1037/0033-295X.94.3.319 PMID:3615707

Hitchens, M., Drachen, A., & Richards, D. (2012). An investigation of player to player character identification via personal pronouns.*Proceedings of The 8th Australasian Conference on Interactive Entertainment: Playing the System.* doi:10.1145/2336727.2336738

Hoffner, C., & Buchanan, M. (2005). Young adults wishful identification with television characters: The role of perceived similarity and character attributes. *Media Psychology*, *7*(4), 325–351. doi:10.1207/S1532785XMEP0704_2

Hoffner, C., & Cantor, J. (1991). Perceiving and responding to mass media characters. In J. Bryant & D. Zillmann (Eds.), *Responding to the screen: Reception and reaction processes* (pp. 63–101). Hillsdale, NJ: Lawrence Erlbaum Associates, Inc.

Hollingdale, J., & Greitemeyer, T. (2013). The changing face of aggression: The effect of personalized avatars in a violent video game on levels of aggressive behavior. *Journal of Applied Social Psychology*, *43*(9), 1862–1868. doi:10.1111/jasp.12148

Jansz, J. (2005). The emotional appeal of violent video games for adolescent males. *Communication Theory*, *15*(3), 219–241. doi:10.1111/j.1468-2885.2005.tb00334.x

Kafai, Y. B., Fields, D. A., & Cook, M. S. (2010). Your second selves: Player-designed avatars. *Games and Culture*, *5*(1), 23–42. doi:10.1177/1555412009351260

Kim, C., Lee, S., & Kang, M. (2012). I became and attractive person in the virtual world: Users identification with virtual communities and avatars. *Computers in Human Behavior, 28*(1), 1663–1669. doi:10.1016/j.chb.2012.04.004

Klimmt, C., Hefner, D., & Vorderer, P. (2009). The video game experience as true identification: A theory of enjoyable alterations of players self-perception. *Communication Theory, 19*(4), 351–373. doi:10.1111/j.1468-2885.2009.01347.x

Klimmt, C., Hefner, D., Vorderer, P., Roth, C., & Blake, C. (2010). Identification with video game characters as automatic shift of self-perceptions. *Media Psychology, 13*(4), 323–338. doi:10.1080/152 13269.2010.524911

Koehne, B., Bietz, M. J., & Redmiles, D. (2013). *Identity Design in Virtual Worlds.* Paper presented at the 4th International Symposium, IS-EUD 2013, Copenhagen, Denmark.

Kolb, A., & Kolb, D. (2009). The learning way: Meta-cognitive aspects of experiential learning. *Simulation & Gaming, 40*(3), 297–327. doi:10.1177/1046878108325713

Latham, G. P., & Locke, E. A. (1979). Goal setting: A motivational technique that works. *Organizational Dynamics, 8*(2), 6880. doi:10.1016/0090-2616(79)90032-9

Lim, S. (2006). *The effect of avatar choice and visual POV on game play experience* (Unpublished doctoral dissertation). Stanford University, Stanford, CA.

Lim, S., & Reeves, B. (2009). Being in the game: Effects of avatar choice and point of view on psychophysiological responses during play. *Media Psychology, 12*(4), 348–370. doi:10.1080/15213260903287242

Looy, J. V. (2015). Online games, characters, avatars, and identity. *The International Encyclopedia of Digital Communication and Society.* Retrieved from http://onlinelibrary.wiley.com/doi/10.1002/9781118767771. wbiedcs106/full

Looy, J. V., Courtois, C., & Vocht, M. D. (2010). *Player identification in online games: Validation of a scale for measuring identification in mmorpgs.* Paper presented at the 3rd International Conference on Fun and Games, Leuven, Belgium.

Looy, J. V., Courtois, C., Vocht, M. D., & De Marez, L. (2012). Player identification in online games: Validation of a scale for measuring identification in MMOGs. *Media Psychology, 15*(2), 197–221. doi :10.1080/15213269.2012.674917

Lord of the Rings Online [PC Game]. Warner Bros. Entertainment Inc.

Lozano, S. C., Hard, B. M., & Tversky, B. (2007). Putting action in perspective. *Cognition, 103*(3), 480–490. doi:10.1016/j.cognition.2006.04.010 PMID:16765339

Maccoby, E. E., & Wilson, W. C. (1957). Identification and observational learning from films. *Journal of Abnormal and Social Psychology, 55*(1), 76–87. doi:10.1037/h0043015 PMID:13462664

Mahmassani, H. S., Chen, R. B., Huang, Y., Williams, D., & Contractor, N. (2010). Time to play? Activity engagement in multiplayer online role-playing games. *Transportation Research Record, 2157*(2), 129–137. doi:10.3141/2157-16

Mantovani, F., & Castelnuovo, G. (2003). Sense of presence in virtual training: enhancing skills acquisition and transfer of knowledge through learning experience in virtual environments. In G. Riva, F. Davide, & W. A. IJsselsteijn (Eds.), *Being there: Concepts, effects and measurement of user presence in synthetic environments* (pp. 167–181). Amsterdam, The Netherlands: Ios Press.

Markus, H., & Nurius, P. (1986). Possible selves. *The American Psychologist, 41*(9), 954–969. doi:10.1037/0003-066X.41.9.954

McDonald, D., & Kim, H. (2001). When I die, I feel small: Electronic game characters and the social self. *Journal of Broadcasting & Electronic Media, 45*(2), 241–258. doi:10.1207/s15506878jobem4502_3

Murphy, S. D. (2004). Live in your world, play in ours: The spaces of video game identity. *Journal of Visual Culture, 3*(2), 223–238. doi:10.1177/1470412904044801

Newman, J. (2002). The myth of the ergodic videogame. *The International Journal of Computer Game Research., 2*(1), 1–8.

OBrien, H. L., & Toms, E. G. (2010). The development and evaluation of a survey to measure user engagement. *Journal of the American Society for Information Science and Technology, 61*(1), 50–69. doi:10.1002/asi.21229

Okita, S. Y., Turkay, S., Kim, M., & Murai, Y. (2013). When observation beats doing: Learning by teaching with virtual peers and the effects of technological design choices on learning. *Computers & Education, 63*, 176–196. doi:10.1016/j.compedu.2012.12.005

Park, B.-W., & Lee, K. C. (2011). Exploring the value of purchasing online game items. *Computers in Human Behavior, 27*(6), 2178–2185. doi:10.1016/j.chb.2011.06.013

Przybylski, A. K., Rigby, C. S., & Ryan, R. M. (2010). A motivational model of video game engagement. *Review of General Psychology, 14*(2), 154–166. doi:10.1037/a0019440

Ratan, R., Rikard, R., Wanek, C., McKinley, M., Johnson, L., & Sah, Y. J. (2016). *Introducing Avatarification: An Experimental Examination of How Avatars Influence Student Motivation* (pp. 51–59). IEEE; doi:10.1109/HICSS.2016.15

Reijmersdal, E. A. V., Jansz, J., Peters, O., & van Noort, G. (2013). Why girls go pink: Game character identification and game-players motivations. *Computers in Human Behavior, 29*(6), 2640–2649. doi:10.1016/j.chb.2013.06.046

Schmierbach, M., Limperos, A. M., & Woolley, J. K. (2012). Feeling the Need for (Personalized) Speed: How Natural Controls and Customization Contribute to Enjoyment of a Racing Game Through Enhanced Immersion. *Cyberpsychology, Behavior, and Social Networking, 15*(7), 364–369. doi:10.1089/cyber.2012.0025 PMID:22687145

Schneider, E. F., Lang, A., Shin, M., & Bradley, S. D. (2004). Death with a story: How story impacts emotional, motivational, and physiological responses to first-person shooter video games. *Human Communication Research, 30*(3), 361–375.

Schultheiss, D. (2007). Long-term motivations to play MMOGs: A longitudinal study on motivations, experience and behavior. In A. Baba (Ed.), *DiGRA 2007-Situated Play (Proceedings of Digital Games Research Association International Conference 2007)* (pp. 344–348).

Schwind, V., Wolf, K., Henze, N., & Korn, O. (2015). *Determining the characteristics of preferred virtual faces using an avatar generator.* Paper presented at ChiPlay 2015. doi:10.1145/2793107.2793116

Shaw, A. (2011). "He could be a bunny rabbit for all I care": Exploring identification in digital games. *Proceedings of DiGRA 2011: Think Design Play: The fifth international conference of the Digital Research Association* (DIGRA).

Soutter, A. R. B., & Hitchens, M. (2016). The relationship between character identification and flow state within video games. *Computers in Human Behavior, 55*(B), 1030–1038. http://doi.org/<ALIGNMENT. qj></ALIGNMENT>10.1016/j.chb.2015.11.012

Star Wars: *The Old Republic* [PC Game]. Bioware.

Taylor, N., Kampe, C., & Bell, K. (2015). Me and Lee: Identification and the play of attraction in The Walking Dead. *Game Studies, 15*(1). Retrieved from http://gamestudies.org/1501/articles/taylor

Taylor, T. L. (2002). Living digitally: Embodiment in virtual worlds. In R. Schroeder (Ed.), *The Social Life of Avatars: Presence and Interaction in Shared Virtual Environments*. London: Springer-Verlag. doi:10.1007/978-1-4471-0277-9_3

Teng, C.-I. (2010). Customization, immersion satisfaction, and online gamer loyalty. *Computers in Human Behavior, 26*(6), 1547–1554. doi:10.1016/j.chb.2010.05.029

Thomas, A. (2007). Blurring and breaking through the boundaries of narrative, literacy, and identity in adolescent fan fiction. *A New Literacies Sampler, 29*, 137.

Trepte, S., & Reinecke, L. (2010). Avatar creation and video game enjoyment: Effects of life-satisfaction, game competitiveness, and identification with the avatar. *Journal of Media Psychology: Theories, Methods, and Applications, 22*(4), 171–184. doi:10.1027/1864-1105/a000022

Turkay, S. (2012). User experiences with avatar customization in Second Life and Lord of the Rings Online.*Proceedings of Teachers College Educational Technology Conference*.

Turkay, S., & Adinolf, S. (2010). Free to be me: A survey study on customization with World of Warcraft and City of Heroes/Villains players. *Procedia: Social and Behavioral Sciences, 2*(2), 1840–1845. doi:10.1016/j.sbspro.2010.03.995

Turkle, S. (1994). Constructions and reconstructions of self in virtual reality. Playing in MUDs. *Mind, Culture, and Activity, 1*(3), 158–167. doi:10.1080/10749039409524667

Turkle, S. (1995). *Life on the screen: Identity in the age of Internet*. New York: Simon & Schuster.

Vasalou, A., & Joinson, A. (2009). Me, myself and I: The role of interactional context on self-presentation through avatars. *Computers in Human Behavior, 25*(2), 510–520. doi:10.1016/j.chb.2008.11.007

Villani, D., Gatti, E., Triberti, S., Confalonieri, E., & Riva, G. (2016). Exploration of virtual body-representation in adolescence: The role of age and sex in avatar customization. *SpringerPlus*, *5*(1), 740. doi:10.1186/s40064-016-2520-y PMID:27376008

von Feilitzen, C., & Linne, O. (1975). The effects of television on children and adolescents identifying with television characters. *Journal of Communication*, *4*(4), 31–55.

Waddell, T. F., Sundar, S. S., & Auriemma, J. (2015). Can customizing an avatar motivate exercise intentions and health behaviors among those with low health ideals? *Cyberpsychology, Behavior, and Social Networking*, *18*(11), 687–690. doi:10.1089/cyber.2014.0356 PMID:26406804

Waggoner, Z. (2009). *My avatar, my self: identity in video role-playing games*. Jefferson, NC: McFarland.

Watts, M. (2016). *Avatar self identification, self esteem, and perceived social capital in the real world: A study of World of Warcraft players and their avatars*. Graduate Thesis and Dissertations. Retrieved from http://scholarcommons.usf.edu/etd/6155

Weinreich, P., & Saunderson, W. (Eds.). (2003). *Analyzing identity: Cross-cultural, societal and clinical contexts*. London: Routledge.

Whyville [PC Game]. Numedeon.

Williams, K. D. (2011). The effects of homophily, identification, and violent video games on players. *Mass Communication & Society*, *14*(1), 3–24. doi:10.1080/15205430903359701

World of Warcraft [PC Game]. Blizzard entertainment Inc.

Worth, N. (2015). *Players and avatars: The connections between player personality, avatar personality, and behavior in video games*. Retrieved from https://dr.library.brocku.ca/handle/10464/6985

Yoon, G., & Vargas, P. T. (2014). Know thy avatar: The unintended effect of virtual-self representation on behavior. *Psychological Science*, *25*(4), 1043–1045. doi:10.1177/0956797613519271 PMID:24501111

Zhong, Z., & Yao, M. (2012). Gaming motivations, avatar-self-identification and symptoms of online game addiction. *Asian Journal of Communication*, *23*(5), 555–573. doi:10.1080/01292986.2012.748814

APPENDIX

Table 10. Correlations between variables in the regression model for Session 1

	1	2	3	4	5
1. Customization	1				
2. Motivation	.374**	1			
3. Perceived Similarity	.371**	.377***	1		
4. Embodied Presence	.236	.405***	.776***	1	
5. Wishful Identification	.259	.171	.793**	.623***	1

Note. Statistical significance: *p < .05; **p < .01; ***p < .001.

Table 11. Correlations between variables in the regression model for Session 2

	1	2	3	4	5
1. Customization	1				
2. Motivation	.344**	1			
3. Perceived Similarity	.407***	.450***	1		
4. Embodied Presence	.250*	.326**	.773***	1	
5. Wishful Identification	.377**	.238	.818***	.705***	1

Note. Statistical significance: *p < .05; **p < .01; ***p < .001.

Table 12. Correlations between variables in the regression model for Session 3

	1	2	3	4	5
1. Customization	1				
2. Motivation	.411**	1			
3. Perceived Similarity	.390***	.427***	1		
4. Embodied Presence	.309**	.425***	.794***	1	
5. Wishful Identification	.354**	.323**	.848***	.740***	1

Note. Statistical significance: *p < .05; **p < .01; ***p < .001.

Table 13. Correlations between variables in the regression model for Session 4

	1	2	3	4	5
1. Customization	1				
2. Motivation	.411**	1			
3. Perceived Similarity	.390***	.427***	1		
4. Embodied Presence	.309**	.425***	.794***	1	
5. Wishful Identification	.354**	.323**	.848***	.740***	1

Note. Statistical significance: *p < .05; **p < .01; ***p < .001.

Table 14. Summary of hierarchical regression analysis for variables predicting motivation at the end of Session 1

	B	SE	β	t	R²	Δ R²
Step 1					.14	
Constant	3.07	.64		4.83		
Customization	1.29	.40	.37**	3.20		
Step 2					.29	.24
Constant	2.64	.71		3.73		
Customization	.97	.41	.28*	2.34		
Perceived Similarity	.45	.39	.27	1.16		
Embodied Presence	.54	.29	.33	1.88		
Wishful Identification	-.62	.35	-.32	-1.75		

Note. Statistical significance: *p < .05; **p < .01; ***p < .001.

Table 15. Summary of hierarchical regression analysis for variables predicting motivation at the end of Session 2

	B	SE	β	t	R²	Δ R²
Step 1					.14	
Constant	3.07	.64		4.83		
Customization	1.29	.40	.37**	3.20		
Step 2					.29	.24
Constant	2.08	.60		3.50		
Customization	.63	.37	.21	1.70		
Perceived Similarity	1.09	.36	.68**	3.06		
Embodied Presence	.09	.27	.06	.39		
Wishful Identification	-.76	.34	-.43*	-2.23		

Note. Statistical significance: *p < .05; **p < .01; ***p < .001.

Table 16. Summary of Hierarchical regression analysis for variables predicting motivation at the end of Session 4

	B	SE	β	t	R²	Δ R²
Step 1					.14	
Constant	3.07	.64		4.83		
Customization	1.29	.40	.37**	3.20		
Step 2					.44	.40
Constant	.48	.59		.80		
Customization	1.15	.39	.32**	2.95		
Perceived Similarity	.71	.38	.40	1.86		
Embodied Presence	.53	.26	.33*	2.06		
Wishful Identification	-.51	.33	-.30	-1.54		

Note. Statistical significance: *p < .05; **p < .01; ***p < .001.

Chapter 4
An Experiment on Anonymity and Multi–User Virtual Environments:
Manipulating Identity to Increase Learning

Richard N. Landers
Old Dominion University, USA

Rachel C. Callan
Old Dominion University, USA

ABSTRACT

Little prior research has empirically examined anonymity in learning. In this study, we manipulated learner identity by experimentally assigning learners to participate in online discussion either anonymously or using their actual name, crossed with learning medium (OpenSim/Second Life vs. real-time chat), with the goal of determining if anonymous discussion in multi-user virtual environments (MUVE) provides unique value to learning (a 2x2 between-subjects design). Results from a quantitative hierarchical multiple regression analysis revealed both main effects: participants who were anonymous scored lower ($d = -0.46$) and participants discussing in a MUVE scored lower ($d = -0.47$) on the learning measure without interactive effect, suggesting that anonymizing participants during content-related discussion may reduce learning under certain circumstances. We suggest instructors encourage learners to represent themselves authentically in any VEs to maximize learning and also discourage instructors from adopting MUVEs if their only reason to do so is to host synchronous discussion.

INTRODUCTION

Multi-user virtual environments (MUVEs) provide an interactive 3D environment for learners to connect with each other through the Internet, representing themselves as avatars and interacting with each other through text and/or voice chat (Delwiche, 2006). Because MUVEs permit complete customization of the learning environment by the instructional designer, this technology provides several new opportuni-

DOI: 10.4018/978-1-5225-1817-4.ch004

ties to develop instructional content not possible or prohibitively expensive with traditional methods. For example, traditional emergency responder triage training requires the hiring of actors, the rental of space, the building of sets, and a tremendous expenditure of resources; such training is more feasible and less costly in a virtual environment, especially if the training will need to be reproduced regularly. Unfortunately, as MUVEs have increased in popularity, our scientific understanding of the potential benefits of MUVEs and their evaluation has not increased at the same rate (Landers & Callan, 2012). As a result, MUVEs have been deployed in many contexts without much rationale for doing so other than their novelty or media popularity, creating unproductive and confrontational debates about their value among stakeholders (Herold, 2012).

Some researchers have thus called for a change in focus in the study of MUVEs, "moving beyond the 'if' of virtual worlds to the 'when' and 'for what reason'" (Cormier, 2009, p. 543). We endorse this view. The barriers to entry for MUVEs (e.g., computing resources, software training) are too high to justify their deployment broadly across learning contexts. Instead, researchers must focus upon identifying the specific value added by the use of MUVEs in a scientific and systematic fashion, to determine where the use of MUVEs provides the most additional value over other instructional settings, especially through experimentation (Kim, Lee & Thomas, 2012). In doing so, a more consistent and practical research literature surrounding MUVEs can be developed. Although MUVEs have a great deal of potential, it will only be through cautious, systematic evaluation of that potential that we will increase our understanding of "when" and "for what reason." In a review of empirical research on this question, Wang and Lockee (2010) were able to identify only four unique empirical studies of MUVEs in distance education and called for a substantial increase in activity in this area. With this paper, we respond to these calls by empirically investigating a very practical question in this line of inquiry: "Is a MUVE a preferred setting for students holding online discussions?"

Virtual Environments for Learning-Related Communication

In a broad and comprehensive review of research conducted in the MUVE literature related to education, Kim, Lee and Thomas (2012) identified that 15 of the 65 papers in the interdisciplinary MUVE literature at that time focused upon its use as a communication space. This popularity can be largely attributed to two ideas. First, perception of social presence, which here refers to the degree to which a learner perceives himself to exist as fully present in the MUVE in the same way he or she feels present in a face-to-face interaction, is viewed as being a critical component to successful learning delivered at a distance (Lee, 2004; Wang & Lockee, 2010). Second, there is preliminary evidence to suggest MUVEs can be an effective medium by which to promote social presence through immersive simulation of real-life spaces and capabilities (van der Land, Schouten, van den Hooff, & Feldberg, 2011; Edirisingha, Nie, Pluciennik & Young, 2009). For example, feelings of presence are in part stimulated by non-verbal cues, which are more easily replicated with an avatar in a MUVE than in a chat room (Davis, Murphy, Owens, Khazanchi, & Zigurs, 2009).

In the communication context, MUVEs gain these properties through several technical capabilities. First, they provide a compelling illusion of 3D space, enabling either the simulation of spaces already existing in reality or the creation of unique spaces not possible with traditional classroom resources (Salmon, 2009). Second, they provide identity-building tools, such as avatar creation and customization (Dickey, 2005). Third, the environment is more media rich than other discussion environments, permitting immediate and more comprehensive communication between avatars than possible in other, less media-rich environments (Yap, 2011). These specific technical advantages are generally viewed as beneficial to identity development and thus learning through their ability to create immersion (Salmon, 2009; Wang & Burton, 2013). These capabilities have been proposed as reasons for MUVEs to produce superior learning outcomes when learner discussion takes place within them.

On the other hand, there are substantial barriers to successful use of MUVEs. Landers and Callan (2012) describe three major challenges to the adoption of MUVEs for learning. First, learners with little experience in MUVEs are likely to be more uncomfortable and face additional challenges when initially learning to interact with fellow learners. This is likely to redirect cognitive resources away from learning (Mania, Wooldridge, Coxon & Robinson, 2006). Second, as suggested in constructivist learning theories, learning is participative; if learners approach material to be learned with a negative attitude, they are likely to learn less. Third, the use of MUVEs in an organizational culture where MUVEs are not common (e.g., a typical college or university setting) is likely to be met with resistance and skepticism, which itself can undermine learning. For example, Liu (2006) noted reluctance from university faculty to view MUVEs as legitimate educational environments. If faculty communicated this disbelief to their students, either intentionally or unintentionally, those students would be likely to learn less in a MUVE learning environment to which they were later exposed. These problems would not be present in a MUVE-based college or university, but for instructional designers in most colleges and universities considering adoption of MUVEs, this is problematic.

Overall, few studies have empirically examined the effect of MUVEs on learning, and among those that have, most are qualitative and limited in the scope of conclusions that can be drawn from them (Wang & Lockee, 2010). While they provide an excellent starting point in this domain, triangulation between both qualitative and quantitative research is needed to provide compelling evidence for a particular theory or theoretical perspective (Jick, 1979), and quantitative evidence for the effectiveness of MUVEs is especially lacking. With the increasing use of technology-based learning (Paradise, 2008), this research is especially timely to provide much needed information regarding the comparative effectiveness of different platforms in producing learning.

We choose to contrast MUVEs with chat rooms in particular to represent a realistic choice instructional designers would face when picking synchronous learner discussion technologies. Additionally, Childress and Braswell (2006) noted that MUVEs and chat rooms are similar in that they provide the real-time discussion that is lacking in asynchronous media like email and online discussion boards but are also dissimilar in that MUVEs allow participants to showcase their personality and develop mood in an online discussion more easily than in a chat room. At the same time, students are likely already very familiar with chat-based messaging through instant-messaging and text-messaging whereas a MUVE is likely unfamiliar for most. The novelty of a MUVE could prove distracting for learners trying to participate in discussion while distracted by the interface, ultimately leading to poorer learning outcomes. Given theory suggesting that the use of MUVEs could be either helpful or harmful, and the lack of compelling prior empirical work demonstrating either, we propose investigating both possibilities in an empirical framework.

Research Question 1: How does participation in MUVE discussion groups affect performance on a learning outcome measures in comparison to chat-based discussion groups?

Anonymity in Learning

A major question faced by instructional designers implementing online discussion, whether in a MUVE or chat room, is the representation and identification of learners within that discussion. The designer must decide if learners will be represented authentically, with real names and developed identities, or anonymously, with assumed identities. In the context of MUVEs, anonymity is sometimes assumed by researchers. For example, van Deusen-Scholl, Frei and Dixon (2005) suggest that the use of a MUVE should increase feelings of security in social interactions by encouraging a feeling of anonymity. However, we contend that these two concepts – anonymity and participation in a MUVE – are artificially conflated in such researchers' conceptions. Just as a person can be anonymous or fully identified in any computer-mediated context, this is equally true within a MUVE. For example, a learner who has been given an undeveloped avatar (a generic male or female model, for example), uses text chat only, and has a nonspecific in-MUVE name is effectively anonymous. In contrast, a learner who is able to customize her avatar, communicate via voice chat, and is identified by her real name is authentically represented based upon her individual preferences (although perhaps with some liberties taken in avatar construction). Instructional designers often have complete control over this representation of their students by way of course policy.

Several researchers have suggested that anonymity contributes to stronger learning outcomes as produced by collaborative online discussion. When learners participate in collaborative discussion anonymously, the preexisting social barriers between students are missing, be they by age, race, gender, socioeconomic status, or any other characteristic (Steinkeuhler & Williams, 2006; von Der Emde, Schneider & Kotter, 2001). Observance of such characteristics can have a substantial effect on perceptions and judgments (King, Madera, Hebl, Knight & Mendoza, 2004), making this freedom potentially quite valuable. Thus, anonymity is likely to be most beneficial to learning when those social barriers would have been salient to the learner without anonymity. In the present study, to maximize the potential benefit of anonymity, we therefore chose a population and discussion topic to maximize this salience: American college students learning and discussing US affirmative action policies in the US Southeast at a university with a racially diverse student population.

Exploring the effects of anonymity on online interactions in general is mixed. When the goal is creative (e.g., idea generation), anonymity tends to produce greater and more critical participation (Jessup, Connolly, & Galegher, 1990), likely due to decreased inhibition (El-Shinnaway & Vinze, 1997). When anonymity is applied to decision-making tasks, outcomes are generally negative, with one meta-analysis of computer-mediated work teams finding an increase in time to make a decision and a decrease in member satisfaction with the team, yet an increase in perceptions of team effectiveness in comparison to non-anonymous computer-mediated teams (Baltes, Dickson, Sherman, Bauer & LaGanke, 2002). The presence of anonymity in group decision making may even increase group polarization (Sia, Tan & Wei, 2002), increasing the probability that a group will produce extreme opinions. Perhaps most critical, anonymity is linked with deviant and antisocial communications behaviors online, most notable "flaming" (Alonzo & Aiken, 2004). Research on the effect of anonymity on learning quality from discussion is limited, but because most discussion takes the form of decision making (e.g., to come to an agreement on an answer to a provide discussion question), it is expected that the influences on learner participation are similar.

Given the potential for anonymity to benefit learners in education despite the drawbacks identified in psychology, we again set out to examine both possibilities.

Research Question 2: How does anonymity affect performance on learning outcome measures in comparison to authenticity?

Medium-Anonymity Interaction

As can be seen above, we view the current theoretical literature regarding MUVEs and anonymity to contain support for contradictory viewpoints. Some researchers believe MUVEs elicit feelings of anonymity, claiming that this anonymity will increase comfort and sharing in the context of online discussion (van Deusen-Scholl, Frei and Dixon, 2005). In contrast, other researchers believe that the formation of strong online identities and feelings of belongingness are the primary benefits to MUVEs for learning (Lee, 2004). These two perspectives can be reconciled if it is the combination of anonymity and the use of MUVEs that result in uniquely beneficial outcomes. In particular, these two perspectives can both be true if the provision of anonymity within the MUVE context is uniquely beneficial to learning beyond what we would expect from the overall effects of MUVEs and anonymity. Thus we propose a hypothesis to test the interactive effect of both.

Hypothesis 1: Anonymity and discussion medium will interact such that learners anonymously representing themselves in MUVEs will perform better on a learning outcome measure than anonymous learners in chat rooms, authentic learners in chat rooms and authentic learners in MUVEs.

METHOD

Participants

Participants were 125 undergraduates at a large university in the US Southeast completing psychological research studies in order to either fulfill course requirements or to earn extra credit in their courses. On average, participants were female (68%) and 22.34 years old (SD = 5.82) with a 3.10 grade point average (SD = 0.56). They self-identified across a wide range of college experience (28% freshmen, 25% sophomores, 22% juniors, 19% seniors, 6% other). Overall, participants self-identified as a moderately racially diverse group, accurately representing the population of the university (1% American Indian or Native American, 3% Asian or Pacific Islander, 30% Black or African American, 5% White Hispanic, and 61% White Non-Hispanic).

Materials

Instructional Content

The instructional content used for this study consisted of two fifteen-minute lecture videos on the topic of US affirmative active policies created by a subject matter expert with experience teaching this topic. This topic was chosen to maximize the potential benefit of MUVEs; namely, that by discussing a topic that many American undergraduates feel uncomfortable discussing in-person, we hoped to maximize the importance of their ability to "equally communicate with other learners regardless of their social position, race, religion and personal background" (Kim, Lee & Thomas, 2012, p. 3). Each lecture video consisted of a series of images of PowerPoint slides with audio narration from the subject matter expert.

Virtual Environment

The virtual environment used for this study was OpenSim, an open source 3D application server. Open-Sim was chosen:

1. Because it was designed to mimic the functionality of the popular virtual world, Second Life, which is the most popular MUVE for educational research and use (Salmon, 2009; Kim, Lee & Thomas, 2012) and
2. Because the environment is more controllable than in Second Life (e.g., passers-by can interrupt participant sessions Second Life).

An installation of OpenSim was used within the first author's research laboratory intranet. Within this environment, a setting for group discussion was designed consisting of a 3D navigation training area, a building, and a circle of virtual chairs in a classroom within that building, along with various decorations throughout the environment intended to increase participant immersion.

Measures

Discussion Medium and Anonymity

Discussion medium was coded such that 1 represented discussion in a MUVE and 0 represented discussion in a chat room. Anonymity was dummy coded such that 1 represented anonymous discussion and 0 represented authentically represented discussion.

Learning Outcomes

To ensure content validity in the cognitive learning outcome measures used, the creator of the lecture videos drafted 10 short answer questions to assess learning. A second subject matter expert reviewed these items for content and additionally assessed the lecture video content to ensure it could be reasonably expected that learners would be able to provide high-quality answers to all questions. Two independent raters blind to experimental condition assessed the quality of all participant responses to the short answer measures on a Likert-type scale anchored between 1 and 7, and the mean score of these two raters was used in analyses. The inter-rater reliability of these two raters was very high, $ICC(2,2) = 0.928$. From this development process and evidence, we concluded that this measure reliably and validly assessed the target learning domain.

Procedure

Participants first completed an online demographics survey, which included a question asking if they knew anyone else participating in the study. Participants were asked to attend three training sessions across one week. Times were chosen to ensure all learning groups consisted of between three and five group members, and any participants that knew each other were assigned to distinct groups. On the first day, participants were introduced to their group members in person and completed an ice-breaker exercise to improve rapport with other group members. They were also instructed not to discuss the content of the study with anyone outside the laboratory, including their group members, until the experiment concluded (at the end of the week). On the second day, participants watched the first lecture video and participated in face-to-face group discussion. On the third day, participants watched the second lecture video, after which their group was assigned to one of four experimental conditions: anonymous chat, authentic chat, anonymous MUVE, or authentic MUVE. Thus, the design of this study can be considered a 2x2 between-subjects factorial. Subjects were exposed to each other face-to-face first to increase this study's external validity to settings where some face-to-face group discussion has occurred, followed by a shift to a virtual or partially virtual format (e.g., work teams transitioning to telework, hybrid courses in which students attend in-person but are supplemented by online content, etc.).

In the chat conditions, participants were physically isolated and briefly trained on how to participate in a chat room, followed by the discussion period within a chat room. In the MUVE conditions, participants were physically isolated from each other, and completed a 30-minute training exercise to ensure they could successfully navigate and participate in the MUVE, which includes instructions on avatar customization, followed by a discussion period within the MUVE. To eliminate a potential confound between the MUVE and chat conditions, voice chat was disabled in the MUVE, standardizing the communication format across technologies.

In anonymous conditions, participants were given false names consisting of everyday terms plus numbers (e.g., coffee43) which appeared immediately before their written discussion comments (e.g., "coffee43: So what do you think?"), consistent with anonymity manipulations in prior research (e.g., Reinig & Mejias, 2004). In authentic conditions, participants were represented with their first name and last initial. In MUVE conditions, names also appeared floating above participant avatars.

In all conditions, the discussion period was held at a maximum of 30 minutes and discussion questions were provided. After discussion, all participants completed the learning outcome measure.

RESULTS

To investigate the study research questions and hypothesis, a hierarchical multiple regression analysis was conducted. In this analysis, main effects (anonymity and virtual environment) were entered in Step 1, and their interaction was added in Step 2. Because these models were nested, this enables a statistical test of the difference in overall estimates of model fit provided by each multiple-R^2. These regressions appear in Table 1.

Table 1. Hierarchical multiple regressions of learning outcomes on experimental conditions

Model/Variable	b	SE	Beta	95% CI b	R^2	ΔR^2
Model 1					0.085	0.085**
Intercept	4.597					
MUVE	-0.341**	0.131	-0.231	[-0.600, -0.083]		
Anonymity	-0.333*	0.128	-0.229	[-0.587, -0.079]		
Model 2					0.094	0.009
Intercept	4.711					
MUVE	-0.505**	0.198	-0.341	[-0.896, -0.113]		
Anonymity	-0.511**	0.207	-0.352	[-0.920, -0.102]		
Interaction	0.290	0.263	0.176	[-0.232, 0.811]		

Note. 95% CI b indicates 95% confidence interval surrounding each regression weight b,
** $p < .01$, * $p < .05$

To interpret these regressions, we first examined Hypothesis 1, which asked if there would be an interaction between the two main effects. In the presence of an interaction that adds significantly to prediction of the outcome variable, Model 2 should be the focus of interpretation since it includes that interaction term. Without incremental variance explained by the interaction term, Model 1 should be the focus of interpretation. The increase in model fit (ΔR^2) contributed by the addition of the interaction term was small and statistically insignificant, with less than 1% incremental variance explained by inclusion of the interaction term. Thus Hypothesis 1 was not supported. Without an interaction, interpretation of research questions focused upon Model 1, which appears in Figure 1.

Figure 1. Illustration of study effects from Model 1

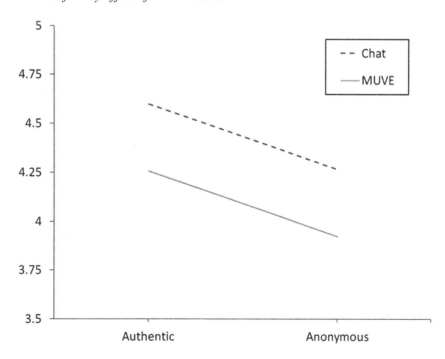

To examine Research Question 1, which explored the impact of MUVE vs. chat rooms as a discussion medium on learning outcomes, we examined the unstandardized regression coefficient associated with the use of the MUVE. The effect was negative and statistically significant; the use of a MUVE resulted in weaker learning outcomes. On average, short answer responses were rated 0.341 points lower ($d =$ -0.469), a moderate effect (Cohen, 1988).

To examine Research Question 2, which explored the impact of anonymity on learning outcomes, we examined the unstandardized regression coefficient associated with anonymity. The effect was negative and statistically significant; anonymity resulted in weaker learning outcomes. On average, short answer responses were rated 0.333 points lower ($d =$ -0.458), also a moderate effect.

Short answer responses from anonymous MUVE-based learners are predicted to be rated 0.674 points lower ($d =$ -0.927) than authentic chat-based learners, a large effect.

DISCUSSION

The study fills three major gaps in the literature. First, by finding that the use of MUVEs harmed learning outcomes, this is the first study to compare cognitive learning outcomes associated with the use of chat rooms and MUVEs directly. We believe this to be valuable because it represents a realistic choice by instructional designers; once it has been decided to add a discussion component in online instruction, a medium for that discussion must be chosen. If the choice is between chat-based or MUVE-based discussion groups, the results of this study indicate that chat groups are preferred when learning outcomes are prioritized. This also has some practical budgetary implications in that more money is being allocated to technology-based learning systems than in the past (Paradise, 2008). Both of the conditions in this study rely upon a computer-based learning system, but MUVEs are generally more costly to implement than a chat rooms. Naturally, institutions want the best and most advanced systems for their courses, but these results suggest this enthusiasm should be tempered not only by cost concerns but also effects on learning outcomes.

Second, by finding that anonymity harmed learning outcomes, we extend research on the use of anonymity to the context of virtual environments. Although researchers often assume anonymity of participants in virtual environments, this study demonstrated that anonymity in both chat room and MUVE discussion groups can be manipulated explicitly to help or harm learning outcomes within both technological contexts. More explicitly, researchers should not confound anonymity and instructional medium because these effects can exist independently; the use of a 3D virtual environment does not imply anonymity for all users, and given similar boundary conditions (e.g., use of authentic names), neither environment is likely experienced as more anonymous than the other. When designing a computer-based learning environment, the use of anonymity should be an explicit decision made based upon pedagogical needs, rather than a feature added casually or because of assumptions about its effects on participants. These results suggest that careless use of anonymity in a learning environment can have real, detrimental effects on learning outcomes. Future research should explore mediators to explain this effect.

Third, investigation of Hypothesis 1 did not provide support for an interaction between instructional medium and anonymity. This suggests that there are no substantial unique benefits to learning from the use of anonymity within the MUVE context in comparison to chat rooms. In contrast, we instead recommend future research to investigate the specific advantages brought to MUVEs through avatar customization and other identity- and immersion-enhancing approaches. Weakening identity does not appear valuable, but strengthening identity may be valuable if it ultimately enables learners to feel more engaged in the task or more immersed in the environment. To facilitate identity building, we recommend future researchers investigate customization of avatars by explicitly manipulating the types of customization options available to them, from body type, facial features, hair, and clothing to choice of species. Although we did not capture it explicitly, we noticed that participants in the anonymous condition were willing to switch the gender of their avatar whereas no participants in the authentic condition ever did. This additional affordance of anonymity might provide unique beneficial effects undetectable in the present study context.

Limitations

We identified four primary limitations to this study. First, because students were randomly assigned to discussion groups and discussion groups were randomly assigned to conditions, data were not truly independent; a systematic team composition effect may have influenced the ultimate effectiveness of the experimental manipulations. We chose not to investigate this effect explicitly because

1. This is an implicit assumption of most research in the area of technology-enhanced student discussion (e.g., Jong, Lai, Hsia & Lin, 2013) and
2. The statistical power to do so would be much greater than was available.

In this spirit, future research should investigate longitudinal and cross-level effects (i.e., the prediction of individual learning outcomes from discussion-group characteristics) using multilevel approaches.

Second, because this was a lab study, we have assumed that the learning processes engaged in by students in a lab study are generalizable to the learning processes engaged in by students in other contexts. We believe this to be justifiable given the increased experimental rigor in the present design and the effects observed. In order to meaningfully alter the conclusions drawn here with a different population of learners, the effect of both anonymity and discussion medium would need to not only be weaker, but to change the direction of their effect. This would suggest a quite complex interaction of main effects by study population, and such effects are highly unusual.

Third, learners inexperienced in MUVE navigation were used as the population here, which is both a strength and limitation. This is a limitation in that these results might not generalize to a population of learners who have established identities within a particular MUVE. For example, if a college opened inside Second Life whose primary student population was made up of current Second Life residents, we would not expect the present results to apply. The specific psychological processes by medium are also unclear; for example, we only provided 30 minutes of MUVE training. Although this was sufficient to permit participants to navigate and communicate in the MUVE, it is possible that expert MUVE users would not have experienced the decline in learning outcomes. Thus, these results may not generalize to expert MUVE users in general. However, for this reason, we do believe them to generalize well to common recipients of MUVE-based instruction: a wide variety of learners who, on average, have relatively little experience with MUVEs before being asked to participate in one.

Fourth, although we manipulated anonymity explicitly and experimentally, we cannot conclude from this alone what aspect of anonymity or instructional medium resulted in the observed differences. A test of psychological processes affected by anonymity, like identity, was not provided to learners. Thus, we have demonstrated a learning benefit, but the specific mechanism is unknown. We call researchers to measure these processes explicitly in future studies of anonymity and identity representation.

CONCLUSION

Although MUVEs produced poorer learning outcomes in comparison to chat rooms in this study, it should not be concluded that we suggest MUVEs are not a valuable setting for learning. Instead, we conclude that MUVEs should only be used when pedagogically appropriate. The need to implement online discussion is not by itself a compelling reason to use a MUVE over a chat room. The MUVE environment does not itself provide any learning advantages to typical students, and the idea that the unique affordances of anonymity brought by MUVEs provide additional motivation to share and participate have not been supported here. Instead, it is likely that a shift to a MUVE environment for discussion brings with it several immediate disadvantages resulting from learner inexperience with such environments even after training (Landers & Callan, 2012), ultimately harming learning.

We instead suggest that MUVEs are better suited for the creation of learning tasks that cannot be easily produced in non-virtual environments and the implementation of pedagogic approaches which could not easily be created without use of a MUVE. For example, Montoya, Massey and Lockwood (2011) describe the benefits to collaborative behavior experienced by learners working toward a group goal in a MUVE. In this context, the MUVE is actually being used to facilitate a team activity, in contrast to its use purely as a communication medium. If that activity could not be held otherwise (e.g., in a chat room), a MUVE might be a practical and effective choice. Ketelhut and Nelson (2010) describe the use of MUVEs to implement a scientific reasoning curriculum for seventh-grade student in order to decrease the costs and increase the safety of doing so, finding relatively minor differences between physical and virtual uses. In this context, such activities although beneficial to learning would not be possible due to outside constraints, like funding and risk of bodily harm.

The negative effect of anonymity allows a more direct recommendation: simply providing anonymity, regardless of online discussion format, appears harmful to learning outcomes. In both the chat and virtual world discussion groups, anonymous learners did not perform as strongly on the outcome measures. As we have now demonstrated that anonymity in discussion can affect learning, there is much greater promise for researchers to explore potential mechanisms for this effect. For example, anonymous learners may engage in more social loafing than authentically represented learners, resulting in a less rich discussion. Anonymous learners may be more inclined to share controversial opinions, but this may have a chilling effect on discussion. Future research should explore these possibilities explicitly.

There is much work to be done here to identify what specific learning situations are best suited for these technologies in order to provide the practical advice on which technology should be implemented and under what conditions so desperately needed in this literature. In general, we recommend a cautious, reasoned approach to the deployment of MUVEs for educational purposes, with careful attention paid to complete evaluative techniques (Landers & Callan, 2012). MUVEs are most valuable in settings where their use brings special value, especially foreign language education and science education involving simulation of real-life processes. But when faced with the everyday decision of whether to host online discussion groups in a MUVE or elsewhere, the present research suggests MUVEs are not a wise choice.

For researchers, we recommend a shift away from narrative reviews of the ability of MUVEs to effectively simulate real-world spaces and case studies reporting the ability of individual MUVE deployments to do just that. At this point, these are answered questions; essentially any physical space or scenario can be recreated in Second Life or any other MUVE at a fraction of the cost of conducting such a simulation in-person. There is no need for continued attempts to prove this point, and hyperbole suggesting the only limit to MUVEs is the imagination of the instructional designer is unhelpful. The compelling questions of MUVEs now are the practical ones: when instructional objectives permit the use of a MUVE or another technology to accomplish the same objective, which should be chosen? Are there unique uses or categories of uses of MUVEs that help people achieve their learning goals in ways not possible with other technologies? We hope this paper to serve as a compelling example of one such investigation in this desperately needed direction.

REFERENCES

Alonzo, M., & Aiken, M. (2004). Flaming in electronic communication. *Decision Support Systems*, *36*(3), 205–213. doi:10.1016/S0167-9236(02)00190-2

Baltes, B. B., Dickson, M. W., Sherman, M. P., Bauer, C. C., & LaGanke, J. S. (2002). Comptuer-mediated communication and group decision making: A meta-analysis. *Organizational Behavior and Human Decision Processes*, *87*(1), 156–179. doi:10.1006/obhd.2001.2961

Childress, M. D., & Braswell, R. (2006). Using massively multiplayer online role-playing games for online learning. *Distance Education*, *27*(2), 187–196. doi:10.1080/01587910600789522

Cohen, J. (1988). *Statistical power analysis for the behavioral sciences* (2nd ed.). Hillsdale, NJ: Lawrence Erlbaum Associates, Publishers.

Cormier, D. (2009). MUVE eventedness: An experience like any other. *British Journal of Educational Technology*, *40*(3), 543–546. doi:10.1111/j.1467-8535.2009.00956.x

Davis, A., Murphy, J., Owens, D., Khazanchi, D., & Zigurs, I. (2009). Avatars, people, and virtual worlds: Foundations for research in metaverses. *Journal of the Association for Information Systems*, *10*(2), 90–117.

Delwiche, A. (2006). Massively multiplayer online games (MMOs) in the new media classroom. *Journal of Educational Technology & Society*, *9*, 160–172.

Dickey, M. D. (2005). Three-dimensional virtual worlds and distance learning: Two case studies of Active Worlds as a medium for distance education. *British Journal of Educational Technology*, *36*(3), 439–451. doi:10.1111/j.1467-8535.2005.00477.x

El-Shinnawy, M., & Vinze, A. S. (1997). Technology, culture, and persuasiveness: A study of choiceshifts in group settings. *International Journal of Human-Computer Studies*, *47*(3), 473–496. doi:10.1006/ijhc.1997.0138

Herold, D. K. (2012). Second life and academia: Reframing the debate between supporters and critics. *Journal of Virtual Worlds Research*. Retrieved from http://journals.tdl.org/jvwr/index.php/jvwr/article/view/6156/5976

Jessup, L. M., Connolly, T., & Galegher, J. (1990). The effects of anonymity on GDSS group process with an idea-generating task. *Management Information Systems Quarterly*, *14*(3), 313–321. doi:10.2307/248893

Jick, T. D. (1979). Mixing qualitative and quantitative methods: Triangulation in action. *Administrative Science Quarterly*, *24*(4), 602–611. doi:10.2307/2392366

Jong, B.-S., Lai, C.-H., Hsia, Y.-T., & Lin, T.-W. (2013). Effects of anonymity in group discussion on peer interaction and learning achievement. *IEEE Transactions on Education*, *56*(3), 292–299. doi:10.1109/TE.2012.2217379

Ketelhut, D. J., & Nelson, B. C. (2010). Designing for real-world scientific inquiry in virtual environments. *Educational Research*, *52*(2), 151–167. doi:10.1080/00131881.2010.482741

Kim, S. H., Lee, J., & Thomas, M. K. (2012). Between purpose and method: A review of educational research on 3D virtual worlds. *Journal of Virtual Worlds Research*. Retrieved from http://jvwr-ojs-utexas.tdl.org/jvwr/index.php/jvwr/article/view/2151/5973

King, E. B., Madera, J. M., Hebl, M. K., Knight, J. L., & Mendoza, S. A. (2004). Career self-management: Its nature, causes and consequences. *Journal of Vocational Behavior*, *65*(1), 112–133. doi:10.1016/S0001-8791(03)00052-6

Landers, R. N., & Callan, R. C. (2012). Training evaluation in virtual worlds: Development of a model. *Journal of Virtual Worlds Research*. Retrieved from http://journals.tdl.org/jvwr/index.php/jvwr/article/view/6335/6300

Lee, K. M. (2004). Presence, explicated. *Communication Theory*, *14*(1), 27–50. doi:10.1111/j.1468-2885.2004.tb00302.x

Liu, C. (2009). Second life learning community: A peer-based approach to involving more faculty members in Second Life. *Proceedings of the Second Life Education Workshop at the Second Life Community Convention*, (pp. 6-10).

Mania, K., Wooldridge, D., Coxon, M., & Robinson, A. (2006). The effects of visual and interaction fidelity on spatial cognition in immersive virtual environments. *IEEE Transactions on Visualization and Computer Graphics*, *12*(3), 396–404. doi:10.1109/TVCG.2006.55 PMID:16640253

Montoya, M. M., Massey, A. P., & Lockwood, N. S. (2011). 3D collaborative virtual environments: Exploring the link between collaborative behaviors and team performance. *Decision Sciences*, *42*(2), 451–476. doi:10.1111/j.1540-5915.2011.00318.x

Paradise, A. (2008). *2008 state of the industry in leading enterprises: ASTD's annual review of trends in workplace learning and performance*. Alexandria, VA: American Society for Training & Development.

Reinig, B. A., & Mejias, R. J. (2004). The effects of national culture and anonymity on flaming and criticalness in GSS-supported discussions. *Small Group Research*, *35*(6), 698–723. doi:10.1177/1046496404266773

Salmon, G. (2009). The future for (second) life and learning. *British Journal of Educational Technology*, *40*(3), 526–538. doi:10.1111/j.1467-8535.2009.00967.x

Sia, C.-L., Tan, B. C. Y., & Wei, K.-K. (2002). Group polarization and computer-mediated communication: Effects of communication cues, social presence, and anonymity. *Information Systems Research*, *13*(1), 70–90. doi:10.1287/isre.13.1.70.92

Steinkuehler, C. A., & Williams, D. (2006). Where everybody knows your (screen) name: Online games as third places.. *Journal of Computer-Mediated Communication*, *11*(4), 885–909. doi:10.1111/j.1083-6101.2006.00300.x

van der Land, S., Schouten, A. P., van den Hooff, B., & Feldberg, F. (2011). Modelling the metaverse: A theoretical model of effective team collaboration in 3D virtual environments. *Journal of Virtual Worlds Research*, *4*. Retrieved from http://journals.tdl.org/jvwr/index.php/jvwr/article/view/6126

van Deusen-Scholl, N., Frei, C., & Dixon, E. (2005). Coconstructing learning: The dynamic nature of foreign language pedagogy in a CMC environment. *CALICO Journal*, *22*, 657–678.

von der Emde, S., Schneider, J., & Kotter, M. (2001). Technically speaking: Transforming language learning through virtual learning environments (MOOs). *Modern Language Journal*, *85*(2), 210–225. doi:10.1111/0026-7902.00105

Wang, F., & Burton, J. K. (2013). Second Life in education: A review of publications from its launch to 2011. *British Journal of Educational Technology*, *44*(3), 357–371. doi:10.1111/j.1467-8535.2012.01334.x

Wang, F., & Lockee, B. B. (2010). Virtual worlds in distance education: A content analysis study. *The Quarterly Review of Distance Education*, *11*, 183–186.

Yap, J. (2011). Virtual world labyrinth: An interactive maze that teaches computing. *Proceedings of the Defense Science Research Conference and Expo (DSR)*. doi:10.1109/DSR.2011.6026883

Chapter 5
Digital Divide:
Comparing the Impact of Digital and Non-Digital Platforms on Player Behaviors and Game Impact

Geoff Kaufman
Carnegie Mellon University, USA

Mary Flanagan
Dartmouth College, USA

ABSTRACT

With a growing body of work demonstrating the power of games to transform players' attitudes, behaviors, and cognitions, it is crucial to understand the potentially divergent experiences and outcomes afforded by digital and non-digital platforms. In a recent study, we found that transferring a public health game from a non-digital to a digital format profoundly impacted players' behaviors and the game's impact. Specifically, players of the digital version of the game, despite it being a nearly identical translation, exhibited a more rapid play pace and discussed strategies and consequences less frequently and with less depth. As a result of this discrepancy, players of the non-digital version of the game exhibited significantly higher post-game systems thinking performance and more positive valuations of vaccination, whereas players of the digital game did not. We propose several explanations for this finding, including follow-up work demonstrating the impact of platform on basic cognitive processes, that elucidate critical distinctions between digital and non-digital experiences.

INTRODUCTION: GAMES AS TOOLS FOR STIMULATING SIGNIFICANT LEARNING AND ATTITUDE CHANGE

There has been growing enthusiasm among members of both learning science and game studies communities surrounding the notion that games can encourage a significant shift in players' thinking and empower them with a plethora of new cognitive skills. One perspective that has gained particular traction in this regard is the argument that games can effectively facilitate a 'systems thinking' approach to

DOI: 10.4018/978-1-5225-1817-4.ch005

real-life issues: that is, games can equip players with a greater understanding of, and appreciation for, the interrelationships that exist between the individual elements of a system. To illustrate, Zimmerman (2007) has suggested that games have the capacity to instill a more advanced "systems literacy," one that "stresses the importance of dynamic relationships, not fixed facts." Similarly, Bogost (2007) claimed that games help players "learn to reflect on the natural or artificial design of systems in the material world," and Gee (2004) designated well-designed games as "learning machines," in part because they can facilitate systems thinking. Thus, in the games and learning literature, the argument that games can improve players' systems thinking aptitude has inspired noteworthy levels of consensus and empirical support.

Likewise, work done over the past decade has demonstrated that games can change players' attitudes and behaviors on important social issues. For example, Kato and colleagues' study of the video game *Re-Mission* showed that playing the game inspired higher levels of adherence to treatment plans among adolescent cancer patients (Kato, Cole, Bradlyn, & Pollock, 2008). Gustafsson and colleagues (2009) showed that a digital game that aimed to teach players about energy use inspired a significant long-term drop in household energy consumption among players of the game. In their meta-analysis of studies investigating the effects of playing games with pro-health content, Baranowski and colleagues (2008) showed that out of the 27 studies they reviewed, a majority demonstrated evidence of significant changes in players' pro-health attitudes and behaviors as a result of playing the focal games.

Prior work on the impact of games on cognition and behavior has been provocative, arguably even paradigm-shifting, but there is still much to learn about how designers can effectively model news ways of thinking or acting through their games or systems. One major unresolved issue is the basic distinction between digital and non-digital platforms – and the potentially divergent experiences and learning outcomes they offer players. As part of a recently completed empirical study testing the efficacy of a public health game, called *POX: Save the People*, created by our design laboratory (Kaufman & Flanagan, 2016a), we sought to answer the fundamental question: does translating the same game from a non-digital to digital format influence players' perceptions of the game and/or impact the effectiveness of the game as a tool for inspiring changes to attitudes and cognition? And, if such cross-platforms differences were to emerge, to what could we attribute them? In this paper, we present the design of the digital and non-digital versions of *POX* and an overview of the research approach we employed to address these provocative questions. We then offer a set of explanations (and empirical validation supporting one particular explanation) for the unexpected finding that the *digital* version of the game, despite being a nearly identical translation of the non-digital version, proved significantly less effective at facilitating learning and belief change.

The History and Design of *POX: Save the People*

In 2010, the Tiltfactor game design and research laboratory was asked by the Mascoma Valley Health Initiative, a New Hampshire public health organization, to create a board game demonstrating the role vaccines play in preventing the spread of disease, for use in classrooms and health fairs. The first game produced from this charge, *POX: Save the People* (2010), is played on a game board of 81 (9x9) spaces, with each space representing one person in a community in which disease has just begun to spread. At the start of the game, two people are infected with a disease; they are represented by red spaces near the center of the board. Six yellow spaces on the board represent people with susceptible immune systems (e.g. pregnant women, babies, individuals with HIV or AIDS, and people with cancer), who cannot be vaccinated and, thus, are especially vulnerable (see Figure 1).

Figure 1. Non-digital POX game board

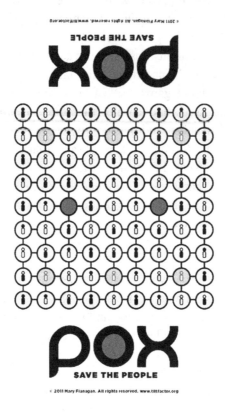

The game proceeds as players alternate drawing cards from the *POX* deck, which reveal either that the disease has spread in a particular direction or that a random outbreak has occurred. Each card also allows players to deploy public health resources either to vaccinate a particular number of uninfected people or to cure a number of infected people on the board. Deaths occur when an infected person is surrounded on all possible sides by all infected people, or when the infection spreads to a vulnerable person on the board. Infections, vaccinations/cures, and deaths are represented by the placement of red, blue, and black chips, respectively, on the spaces on the board. The game is won if infected people on the board are surrounded entirely by vaccinated people, and the disease can no longer spread in any direction, before a pre-specified number of deaths have occurred. *POX* aims to demonstrate the rapidity with which disease can spread and increase players' appreciation for the effectiveness of vaccination for increasing "herd immunity," the effect whereby unvaccinated people are protected by the immunity of others in their population (John & Samuel, 2000). Moreover, by modeling and reinforcing how each individual's decision to be vaccinated or not can impact the health of specific others in a particular population, the game's mechanic is intended to promote an increase in players' systems thinking aptitude.

Comparing the Digital and Non-Digital Versions of *POX*

As part of a multifaceted experimental study assessing the impact of *POX* (Kaufman & Flanagan, 2016a), we randomly assigned a sample of twenty-six middle school and high school students from New England to play, in pairs, the original non-digital version of *POX* or a new digital version of the game we created for the Apple iPad. In designing and implementing the digital version of *POX* to be used in the study, we took great care to minimize any differences between the digital and non-digital versions of the game beyond those necessitated by platform (see Figures 1 and 2 for a comparison). Specifically, in place of the card deck from the non-digital version of *POX*, the digital version featured a "Draw" button, which players tapped to reveal the next event card, and displayed the card text at the top of the screen. Likewise, in place of the physical chips used in the non-digital version of the game, the digital version featured color-coded circles, which players tapped to select a particular chip type; players were then required to tap a particular space on the game screen to place an infection, vaccination/cure, or death. In addition, tapping a gray circle allowed players to "undo" the placement of a chip (e.g., in cases when players made errors in placing infections or reconsidered the spaces on which they wished to place vaccinations or cures). All other elements of game play – including the scripted rules read to participants by the experimenter and the sequence of cards drawn by players – as well as the experimental procedure were held constant to allow a fair and unambiguous comparison between the physical, non-digital version of the game and the digital, tablet-based version.

The results revealed that the non-digital version of *POX* instilled in players a greater appreciation for the value of vaccination (as assessed by a subjective valuation measure requiring players to allocate as much or as little of a $10,000 fund to either vaccinating uninfected citizens or curing infected citizens) and significantly improved players' scores on a validated measure of systems thinking aptitude (Sterman, 2002), compared to the baseline scores reported by participants in a no-game control group. In contrast, there was *no* evidence of significant attitude change or increased systems thinking aptitude among players of the digital version of the game. Furthermore, players of the digital version of the game rated the game as significantly more "complicated" on a post-game questionnaire than did players of the non-digital version of the game. To reiterate: this strikingly divergent pattern of results emerged despite

Figure 2. Digital POX game screen

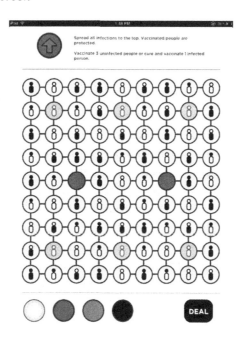

the fact that, apart from the cosmetic differences noted above, the digital and non-digital versions of the game were essentially identical to one another.

This curious finding was not one that we hypothesized would emerge, and it begs the obvious question: why would translating the same game to a digital format, carefully crafted to maintain the rules and mechanic to be as close as possible to the original non-digital game, so significantly impact players' perceptions – and, consequently, reduce the effectiveness of the game as a tool for stimulating attitude change and learning? Analysis of player's in-game behaviors and outcomes provided some valuable clarity in understanding the impact the game's platform was having on how players approached the game. For one, we found a clear difference in the success rate of players of the two versions of the game. Specifically, whereas all but one of the digital game players *lost* the game (i.e., they did not successfully contain the spread of the disease before 5 deaths had occurred), the majority of non-digital game players *won* the game (i.e., they successfully contained the spread of the disease). Moreover, the rate of play was significantly faster, and the length of play significantly shorter, among participants who played the game in the digital format. In turn, participants who played the game in its digital form appeared to make their game decisions with greater haste (in the interest of seeking more immediate consensus) and with less consideration of the reasons for, and the downstream consequences of, key decisions, such as the placement of chips for vaccinations and cures.

Next, we offer some alternative conjectures that might elucidate why the translation from non-digital to digital impacted players' subjective experience and perceptions of the game's complexity. These explanations center on the general notion that digital and non-digital games may mentally activate, or prime, different mindsets or emotional states. We present follow-up work demonstrating the profound impact of platform on cognitive processing. We then explore the notion that digital and non-digital games encourage typical play styles that differ in their pace of play as well as their levels of between-player collaboration, discussion, and reflection. Finally, we discuss the possibility that the digital game we used in the study may have defied players' expectations about the features and mechanics that a digital game *should* contain – particularly ones that serve to facilitate game play in a digital format.

Do Digital and Non-Digital Platforms Activate Different Cognitive or Affective States?

Reflecting on the divergent patterns of decision making and strategizing evoked by the digital and non-digital versions of the game led us to predict that digital technologies may, in fact, "prime" or activate differing default cognitive states in individuals. In particular, the finding that players of the digital game appeared to prioritize immediate, localized solutions rather than long-term, global solutions to the game's challenges led us to hypothesize that digital and non-digital platforms may impact the level of abstraction used to process or *construe* information. Construal-level theory (CLT), posited by psychologists Trope and Liberman (2010), posits that the more psychologically close versus distant individuals perceive themselves to be from a stimulus or event, the more likely they are to think of it in terms of concrete, lower-level details versus abstract, higher-level interpretations. According to CLT, the likelihood of utilizing more concrete versus abstract construal levels may shift depending on a number of factors (e.g., temporal or spatial distance between people and objects, hypotheticality of events, etc.) that are "primed" or activated by the current situation or one's current mindset. Might it have been the case that players of the digital version of *POX* utilized more short-term, local strategies because the platform itself had activated a more concrete (and less abstract) mindset?

To test this basic hypothesis, we conducted a series of studies investigating whether digital and non-digital platforms might trigger different default cognitive construal levels in individuals in general information processing contexts (Kaufman & Flanagan, 2016b). Two initial experiments revealed that individuals who completed the same task on a digital mobile device (a tablet or laptop computer) versus a non-digital platform (a physical print-out) exhibited a lower level of construal, exhibiting a higher emphasis on immediate, concrete details over abstract, decontextualized interpretations. This pattern emerged both in greater preference for concrete versus abstract descriptions of behaviors for participants randomly assigned to complete a standard measure of construal level preference on a digital versus non-digital platform as well as superior performance by digital platform participants on detail-oriented questions (and inferior performance on inference-focused questions) on a reading comprehension test. A pair of final studies found that the likelihood of correctly solving a problem-solving task requiring abstract "gist" processing was lower for participants who processed the information for task on a digital platform but, at the same time, heightened for digital platform participants who had first completed an activity activating an abstract mindset. These results provide strong evidence for a potential divide in the default level of construal activated by digital versus non-digital platforms.

In addition to activating a lower level of cognitive construal, it may also be possible that digital platforms prime concepts related to cognitive complexity. That is, most individuals may have formed a schematic representation of "digital" (or of "technology" more generally) that contains links to attributes such as "complex," "intricate," or, as our results suggest, "complicated." At the same time, perhaps most individuals' representation of "non-digital" contains links to such attributes as "uncomplicated" or "straightforward." Psychologists have shown that the traits or attributes that are incorporated in individuals' schematic representations of categories (such as "non-digital" versus "digital") can be automatically – and subconsciously – activated upon exposure to a general category or a specific exemplar from that category (Bargh & Chartrand, 1999; Mandler, 1984; Rumelhart, 1980) and subsequently influence perceptions, judgments, and behaviors (e.g., Bargh, Chen, & Burrows, 1996; Higgins, 1996; Jacoby & Kelley, 1987). If, indeed, people are more inclined to link "digital" with "complex" and/or "non-digital" with "simple," this divergent associative pattern could explain why participants in our study reported perceiving the digital version of the game as more complicated than the non-digital version, despite the uniformity in the game elements between the two platforms.

A second, and related, possibility is that players may enter into digital and non-digital play experiences with different affective or physiological states, which influence their judgments of game complexity. For instance, perhaps digital platforms stimulate heightened levels of arousal or an increased sense of urgency, whereas non-digital platforms, as a benefit of their greater familiarity and accessibility, may decrease player arousal and increase their level of relaxation and comfort. If so, one could argue that, particularly with a new game with a somewhat intricate set of rules and mechanics, the heightened arousal and urgency activated by a digital platform could serve to exacerbate the game's level of difficulty from players' points of view. Indeed, prior research in psychology has shown that increased arousal levels usually impair performance on novel or complex tasks (Lupien et al., 2007; Yerkes & Dodson, 1908). Given that the game of *POX* was both novel and subjectively complex in its rules and mechanics for our sample of participants, any additional arousal caused by the digital platform itself– and any lack of self-efficacy participants might have experienced in regard to their ability to navigate an unfamiliar form of technology – could explain both why players of the iPad version of the game perceived it to be more complicated as well as why they were less able to grasp the game's key concepts related to herd immunity and systems dynamics.

CONCLUSION AND FUTURE DIRECTIONS

Going forward, we will seek to disentangle the additional explanations we proposed above by subjecting them to systematic empirical tests. To measure individuals' schematic representations of "non-digital" versus "digital," for example, we can employ a *semantic priming* procedure, in which we subliminally expose participants to a particular word or image (such as the word "digital" or the image of a digital tool) and then, using a *lexical decision task*, measure their reaction time for judging a subsequent string of characters as words or non-words (Meyer & Schvaneveldt, 1971). To the extent that individuals implicitly associate "digital" with attributes such as "complicated," participants should be faster to respond to word strings that connote complexity than to neutral word strings after being primed with "digital" words or images (versus neutral words or images). Likewise, measuring participants' arousal and emotional states, as well as their perceived level of self-efficacy, upon learning that they will be playing a non-digital or digital game (or upon initial exposure to a non-digital or digital game) will allow us to determine the extent to which players go into a non-digital or digital game play experience in divergent physiological or emotional states. In addition, to assess the extent to which the significantly lower levels of attitude change and learning exhibited by players of the digital game in our study can be attributed to a play style marked by a faster pace and less between-player collaboration and discussion, we could instruct players of the digital game to adopt a slower, more deliberative style and determine the impact on players' beliefs and cognition. Taken together, this set of investigations will help elucidate what factors were "lost in translation" between the digital and non-digital versions of *POX* and, more broadly, provide valuable insights regarding the patterns of expectations, perceptions, experiences, and consequences evoked by digital and non-digital platforms.

REFERENCES

Baranowski, T., Buday, F., Thompson, D. I., & Baranowski, J. (2008). Playing for real: Video games and stories for health-related behavior change. *American Journal of Preventive Medicine, 34*(1), 74–82. doi:10.1016/j.amepre.2007.09.027 PMID:18083454

Bargh, J. A., & Chartrand, T. L. (1999). The unbearable automaticity of being. *The American Psychologist, 54*(7), 462–479. doi:10.1037/0003-066X.54.7.462

Bargh, J. A., Chen, M., & Burrows, L. (1996). Automaticity of social behavior: Direct effects of trait construct and stereotype activation on action. *Journal of Personality and Social Psychology, 71*(2), 230–244. doi:10.1037/0022-3514.71.2.230 PMID:8765481

Bogost, I. (2007). *Persuasive games: The expressive power of video games*. Cambridge, MA: MIT Press.

Gee, J. P. (2004). Learning by design: Games as learning machines. *Interactive Educational Multimedia, 8*, 15–23.

Gustafsson, A., Bång, M., & Svahn, M. (2009). Power explorer: A casual game style for encouraging long term behavior change among teenagers. In *Proceedings of the International Conference on Advances in Computer Entertainment Technology* (pp. 182-189. New York: ACM. doi:10.1145/1690388.1690419

Higgins, E. T. (1996). Knowledge activation: Accessibility, applicability, and salience. In E. T. Higgins & A. W. Kruglanski (Eds.), *Social psychology: Handbook of basic principles*. New York: Guilford Press.

Jacoby, L. L., & Kelley, C. M. (1987). Unconscious influences of memory for a prior event. *Personality and Social Psychology Bulletin, 13*(3), 314–336. doi:10.1177/0146167287133003

John, J. T., & Samuel, R. (2000). Herd immunity and herd effect: New insights and definitions. *European Journal of Epidemiology, 16*(7), 601–606. doi:10.1023/A:1007626510002 PMID:11078115

Kato, P. M., Cole, S. W., Bradlyn, A. S., & Pollock, B. H. (2008). A video game improves behavioral outcomes in. adolescents and young adults with cancer: A randomized trial. *Pediatrics, 122*(2), 305–317. doi:10.1542/peds.2007-3134 PMID:18676516

Kaufman, G., & Flanagan, M. (2016a). High-low split: Divergent cognitive construal levels triggered by digital and non-digital platforms. In *Proceedings of the 2016 CHI Conference on Human Factors in Computing Systems* (pp. 2773-2777). ACM. doi:10.1145/2858036.2858550

Kaufman, G., & Flanagan, M. (2016b). Playing the system: Comparing the efficacy and impact of digital and non-digital versions of a collaborative strategy game. In *Proceedings of the 2016 DiGRA/FDG Conference*.

Lupien, S. J., Maheu, F., Tu, M., Fiocco, A., & Schramek, T. E. (2007). The effects of stress and stress hormones on human cognition: Implications for the field of brain and cognition. *Brain and Cognition, 65*(3), 209–237. doi:10.1016/j.bandc.2007.02.007 PMID:17466428

Mandler, J. M. (1984). *Stories, scripts, and scenes: Aspects of schema theory*. Hillsdale, NJ: Lawrence Erlbaum Associates.

Meyer, D. E., & Schvaneveldt, R. W. (1971). Facilitation in recognizing pairs of words: Evidence of a dependence between retrieval operations. *Journal of Experimental Psychology, 90*(2), 227–234. doi:10.1037/h0031564 PMID:5134329

Rumelhart, D. E. (1980). Schemata: the building blocks of cognition. In R. J. Spiro et al. (Eds.), *Theoretical Issues in Reading Comprehension*. Hillsdale, NJ: Lawrence Erlbaum.

Sterman, J. (2002). All models are wrong: Reflections on becoming a systems scientist. *System Dynamics Review, 18*(4), 501–531. doi:10.1002/sdr.261

Trope, Y., & Liberman, N. (2010). Construal-level theory of psychological distance. *Psychological Review, 117*(2), 440–463. doi:10.1037/a0018963 PMID:20438233

Yerkes, R. M., & Dodson, J. D. (1908). The relation of strength of stimulus to rapidity of habit-formation. *The Journal of Comparative Neurology and Psychology, 18*(5), 459–482. doi:10.1002/cne.920180503

Zimmerman, E. (2007). Gaming literacy: Game design as a model for literacy in the 21st century. *Harvard Interactive Media Review, 1*, 30–35.

Section 2
Learning Applications

Chapter 6
Making Lifelike Medical Games in the Age of Virtual Reality:
An Update on "Playing Games with Biology" from 2013

Thomas B. Talbot
University of Southern California, USA

ABSTRACT

Medical simulations differ from other training modalities in that life processes must be simulated as part of the experience. Biological fidelity is the degree to which character anatomical appearance and physiology behavior are represented within a game or simulation. Methods to achieve physiological fidelity include physiology engines, complex state machines, simple state machines and kinetic models. Games health scores that can be used in medical sims. Selection of technique depends upon the goals of the simulation, expected user inputs, development budget and level of fidelity required. Trends include greater availability of physiology engines rapid advances in virtual reality (VR). In VR, the expectation for a naturalistic interface is much greater, resulting in technical challenges regarding natural language and gesture-based interaction. Regardless of the technical approach, the user's perception of biological fidelity, responsiveness to user inputs and the ability to correct mistakes is often more important than the underlying biological fidelity of the model.

INTRODUCTION

Videogames have been in the life or death business since their inception. Players 'die' or suffer injuries in games as a routine matter. Some of these approaches are very simple, such as when Mario is hit by Donkey Kong's barrel (Donkey Kong, Nintendo Corp.). Others are a bit more sophisticated, such as the progressively bloodied character depictions in Wolfenstein 3D and Doom (id Software). The medical education folks are constantly creating new simulation experiences with ever higher fidelity. The question is, can we adapt approaches from entertainment games to medical simulations or even better, create compelling and realistic medical games? Are there parts that are medically unique? If so, how do we

DOI: 10.4018/978-1-5225-1817-4.ch006

simulate this with an interactive experience? When it comes the biological parts, how much fidelity is optimal? This paper explores the question of simulating the biological processes that make something appear lifelike and medically convincing. The intent is to contrast approaches based upon type of training, development effort and impact on the learner. This is particularly relevant to consider given maturation of virtual patient technology in the last three years along with ongoing rapid advances in virtual reality. Even with new technology, the principles outlined in the original 2013 version of this article (Talbot, 2013a) remain as relevant now as they were then.

Physiological Fidelity

Many training scenarios involve demonstrations of physiological action with an expectation that the learner diagnose a condition based upon the demonstrated physiology, make interventions and receive a realistic physiological response as would be seen in a patient encounter. A variety of mechanisms exist that can do with tradeoffs in the fidelity, dynamism and effort involved in their creation.

Complex Fidelity: Physiology Engines

A sophisticated and scientifically valid experience with complex fidelity can be achieved through physiology engines. Physiology engines are computer coded mathematical models that simulate body systems. Basic physiology engines replicate the cardiovascular system and the effects of hemorrhage, fluids and medications on the model. Some manikins include such engines (Cooper & Taqueti, 2008). More complex physiology engines are multi-system with large pharmacology libraries and multi-drug interactions. An example of a multi-system model is BioGears [Figure 1], created by the Applied Research Associates and funded by the Defense Department. BioGears can readily simulate a wide variety of conditions such as hemorrhage, heart failure, ketoacidosis or hyperaldosteronism. The results of BioGears outputs are in

Figure 1. BioGears physiology engine capability set
Image courtesy Applied Research Associates.

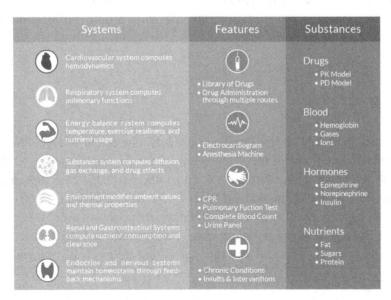

the form of graphs or data that will closely match results from physiology research studies and textbooks. Publically available, BioGears open-source (Apache 2.0 License) physiology includes common drugs and game engine plug-ins (Applied Research Associates, 2016). With such an engine, it is theoretically possible to have a combat game with numerous non-player characters, each running their own physiology engine instance so they will have accurate responses to injuries the player inflicts or attempts to treat.

Physiology models are a high end solution that can run in real or accelerated time. They have the capability to mimic realistic physiological activity and can gracefully manage unexpected user inputs. They can cope with the effects of multiple interventions even if those interventions are antagonistic to each other. One problem common to physiology engines is that realistic changes in physiology may be too gradual or subtle for the learner to notice unless on-screen indicators readily depict historical trends. Some physiology processes, such as sepsis or chemistry changes, unfold too slowly to be observed during an educational scenario. In these cases, the simulation will appear insufficiently responsive and fail to engage the learner. Ironically, realistic responses to user inputs can reduce the user's impression of biological fidelity if they are too gradual.

The need to closely observe monitor displays while tracking ongoing changes to physiology can and does distract the learner from observing the patient (Grant, McNiel & Luo, 2010). It is often difficult for a simulation to correlate virtual patient verbal behavior or appearance with the state of the physiology engine. Efforts to demonstrate changes in patient appearance in Virtual Reality (VR) simulations based upon physiological parameters have been attempted [Figure 2] and are maturing (Knight et al., 2010).

Visual patient representations can separate out physiological data like pulse, respiration, temperature and capillary refill and tie it to relevant animations for pallor, flushing, sweating, anxiety and distress. Image courtesy TruSim, a division of Blitz Game Studios.

Physiology engines are often present in high-end medical simulations. Higher end manikins such as the METI (CAE Healthcare) iStan and SimMan 3G (Laerdal Corp.) employ physiology models that focus on the respiratory and cardiovascular systems. With these systems, changes in pulse, blood pressure and respiratory rate are concretely accessible from the physical exam of the manikin as well as on a monitoring display. These engines will respond appropriately to artificial ventilation, chest compres-

Figure 2. Virtual patient "Dying Dave"

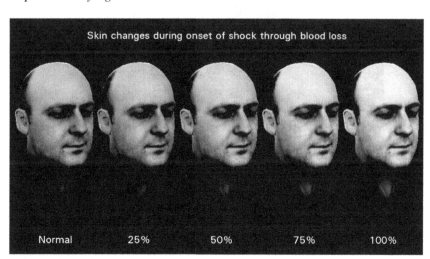

sions and cardiac medications, for example. The high interactivity and close linkage of the physiological response closely replicates an actual critical care encounter. A shortcoming of manikins is the limited behavioral repertoire and the presence of monitoring displays which are often watched over by learners who neglect the physical exam. They are also mostly static collections of plastic and are not always convincing interaction partners. Manikin features rated by medical students to be most useful include chest rise, palpable pulses, interactive voice and the vital signs display (Grant et al., 2010).

Anesthesia simulation is a common application for physiology engines. These can be conducted with manikins, on a computer screen using virtual patient avatars (Donoghue et al, 2008) or with a simulated patient monitor (Figure 3). The most sophisticated manikins can simulate gas exchange on real anesthesia equipment. Because anesthesia training is heavily biased towards pharmacological effects and subtle trends, physiology engines are ideal for anesthesia and other procedural simulations (Morgan & Cleave-Hogg, 2002).

Physiology engines are also strongly suited to detailed exploratory activities, especially for advanced learners. They are unique in that they permit repetitive explorations while attempting different approaches. This empowers the learner to discover relationships between interventions experimentally. The last few years has brought about a considerable rise in the use of physiology engines, spurred by the no-cost availability of BioGears and by the requirement to use BioGears in the Defense Department's upcoming Advanced Modular Manikin. With wider use, the limitations of this approach are becoming more well-known, such as lack of impactful, sudden changes and technical difficulties overriding engine parameters. BioGears and other engine development continues and future advances such as system variable overrides, integration with state machines, engine state-saving and approaches to reduce processor requirements will increase their practicality (Leathrum et al., 2015).

Figure 3. A VR high-fidelity medical trainer employs a physiology engine for precise determination of drug effects. Physiology engines permit combinations of user inputs that may be unexpected by the developer yet still produce reliably lifelike results.
HumanSim image courtesy Virtual Heroes division of Applied Research Associates.

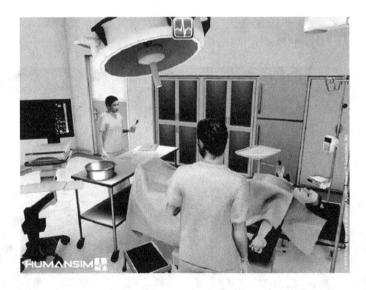

Atypical Fidelity: Kinetic Models

A different approach to simulated physiology is the SIMapse Nerve Agent Laboratory. SIMapse visually demonstrates cholinergic neurotransmission, the effects of nerve agents and actions of various nerve agent antidotes on different body systems. The approach of SIMapse is less mathematical and more kinematic; neurotransmitter molecules are graphically depicted in 3D space and interact with receptors, destructive enzymes and other agents. The physiology process is graphically demonstrated as actions and behaviors. The results (Figure 4) are a very close approximation to known science even though the simulation does not employ actual physiology data, yet it does deliver a high impact learning experience (Talbot, 2008).

The SIMapse approach is very game-like and the approach works well with interactive software and gaming technology. When it was being developed, the author's four-year old child would ask to "play the game with the green balls." The fact that people, even those unaware of the intended medical purpose, can interact with and successful complete challenges in the simulation, shows the promise of the exploratory features in games. SIMapse is not itself a game, but it has game-like features with immediate visual and auditory responsiveness coupled with the ability for the user to engage in consequence-free exploration.

There is potential, for instructional reasons, for many pharmacological and biological processes to be kinesthetically demonstrated. As long as the rules of the simulation approximate reality, little or no physiology data is needed. Examples where this may be useful for teaching includes mechanical and chemical processes like muscle contraction, digestion, mitosis, biochemistry or hearing. These areas are all low hanging fruit for STEM education.

Figure 4. The SIMapse Nerve Agent Laboratory v3 provides a realistic portrayal of nerve agent pharmacology through motion and sound for educational purposes. The program simulates physiological behavior without referring to actual physiological data. It teaches accurate physiology by demonstrating physiology mechanisms, relationships and pharmacology behavior. Trends over time are depicted as colored spark lines at the bottom of the display.

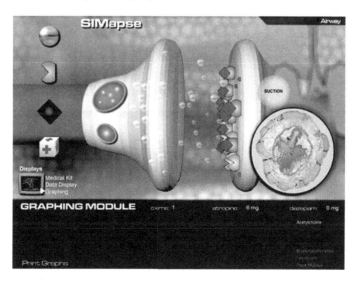

Moderate Fidelity: Complex State Machines

In practice, physiology engines are neither necessary nor desirable in a good number educational situations because simpler methods for depicting physiology states are often more practical. Moderate fidelity approaches to depicting physiology are often managed by complex state machines (CSMs) also known as hierarchical finite state machines (Ahlquist, 2007). Complex state machines are computer programs consisting of logical rules and decision tree based logic that responds to user activity. User actions, simulation timers and other events trigger different states that change the patient presentation and vital signs. This technology is very commonly implemented in a variety of videogame genres and should be familiar to most videogame developers.

CSMs are designed for scenario based training and respond to well defined, known possible interactions. A major advantage of state machines is that expression of different states is often a marked change that is readily noticed by the learner. It is also easy to indicate changes in patient behavior, vital signs or appearance because these changes can be concretely tied to a change in the state machine. The CSM approach is ideally suited for training scenarios with limited depth and scope. Simulations appear more responsive to the learner because they provide immediate and visible responses to learner interaction.

The patient status is pre-defined within blocks and rules or actions change the state until a final outcome is reached. Depending on the complexity of logic involved, a state-based patient may contain a *Simple* or *Complex* state machine. In an example from the *Vital Signs* simulator [Figure 5], the rules are based on a tally of actions; complex state models will add to this by evaluating dynamic variables and multiple variables to effect a state change.

Figure 5. Typical design of a state-based virtual patient. This example depicts expected emergency room treatment for an unstable pediatric appendicitis patient. States are depicted in boxes, with each state having physical signs or other patient characteristics altered. Text over lines depicts conditions required to change state. Outcomes, declared for evaluative purposes, are shown as circles.
Courtesy Todd Chang, MD, Children's Hospital Los Angeles and BreakAway games.

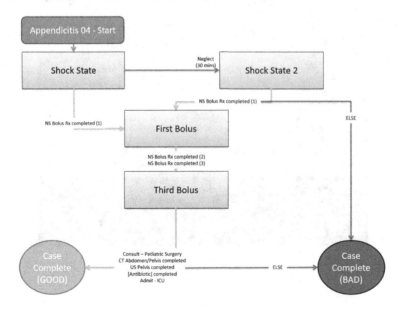

The major disadvantage of state machines is that they do not respond well to unexpected, complex or combinatorial inputs. Undesirable inputs and program complexity is addressed by limiting the variety of possible interventions. Recovery from user errors once a scenario has moved down a decision tree is difficult to program. Another disadvantage is that each branch point must be individually coded. Adding additional branch points or levels to the state machine can exponentially increase the development work necessary to build the scenario (Riedl & Young, 2006). Medium and high end manikins often feature this type of state machine and may be packaged with a scenario builder toolkit. In the practice of visiting dozens of simulation centers in the United States, it is the author's observation that few centers go through the effort to create custom scenarios with a toolkit. Instead, they tend to rely upon scenarios provided by the manufacturer. VR scenario and game-based training often employs the CSM model. CSMs are generally not easily authorable without a toolkit. Those that are programmed by developers are often limited by quality and availability of contact with a subject matter expert (SME) who can vet the rules and iteratively test a state machine system.

Another medium fidelity approach is to couple a state machine to some sort of physiology model (Leathrum et al., 2015). When the US Army Field Management of Chemical and Biological Casualties Course (FCBC) required a nerve agent pharmacology trainer targeting less advanced learners than would be appropriate for the SIMapse Nerve Agent Laboratory, the SIMapse engine was adapted for a multimedia application called Nerve Academy. Nerve Academy employs an on-screen lecturer who delivers mini-lessons coupled with pre-programmed use of the SIMapse engine. It also includes numerous interactive activities at the end of mini-lessons that trigger events in the engine. The result is a responsive learning experience with high fidelity that is very easy for the learner to use. It may be possible to mix multimedia and physiology with a game but special care must be taken so as not to impair gameplay mechanics.

The advantage of combining a limited set of inputs or a state machine to a physiology model is that it is possible to have high biological fidelity and visible trends in data while allowing for simplicity of use and well defined, responsive changes in the appearance of the model. Another advantage to coupling a limited interaction set to a physiology model is that doing so greatly simplifies the complexity and sophistication required of the model by limiting the parameters the model has to account for.

Low Fidelity: The Simple State Machine

Most educational scenarios and simulations in medicine employ low physiological fidelity to good effect. Low fidelity approaches require less technology, effort and sophistication to pull off and therefore are easier to author.

Patient simulations can employ simple state machines (SSMs) to great effect. Simple state machines consist of 3 or more fixed states that alter the appearance, communication and physiology data of the simulated patient. They lack branching and conditional features of the more complex CSMs yet still offer many of their benefits. They are especially useful in adding a dynamic appearance to a simple case presentation when creation of an in-depth simulation is too resource intensive. They can be created with simple technology, such as web pages, interactive animations or PowerPoint™.

An example familiar to the author is a simple animation-based application called the "Cyanide Exposure Simulator" (US Army USAMRICD). The simulation is usually deployed during large classroom sessions. It consists of seven possible states that demonstrate an inhalational exposure to cyanide and the effects on human physiology. States are selected with two buttons to traverse back and forth through a timeline. Each step down the timeline plays a 10-15 second video clip, changes signs and alters graphs

(Figure 6). The overall effect is that of a dynamic simulation that seems to portray a wealth of biological data. The video with the actor conveys the clinical picture. The rolling displays for the pneumograph, EKG and EEG are fixed lines that are progressively uncovered, producing the illusion of live monitoring. Vital signs of respiratory rate, heart rate, cardiac output and blood pH are represented by triangle indicators on linear gauges. The transition between states is a simple animation that moves the indicators over 3 seconds. The impression of this gradual transition is that of physiology that is changing with the timeline. In truth, the vital signs presented are generic as everything else. The cyanide simulator effectively portrays cyanide effects even though no detailed physiology data is ever conveyed to the learners. In fact, providing such level of fidelity that includes more detail would diminish educational effectiveness (Clark & Mayer, 2008). Based on user feedback as a developer, the author finds that most learners are unlikely to detect a difference between this simple state model and an expensive version that employs a physiology engine if the physiology changes seem logical.

SSMs can also be used for intervention based training. Virtual Nerve Agent Casualty (VNAC) pushes the envelope for a simple state model to simulate treatment of a severe nerve agent exposure. (US Army USAMRICD, 2005). Video of a patient is played while the learner interacts by dropping antidotes and interventions onto the patient display. The state model plays a new video with each intervention and counts up correct interventions until a required quantity is reached. At this point, the state is changed which alters data on the screen [Table 1]. The simulation requires persistence on part of the learner but results in a satisfactory simulated experience despite the fact that the biological fidelity is low. A drawback of this simple application is that it is very unforgiving of learner errors and does not allow for a corrective pathway if treatment errors are made.

Figure 6. The cyanide exposure simulator is a simple state machine consisting of seven frames. It employs simple animation effects to create the impression of live physiology. Numerous physiology displays are hand drawn graphics that are progressively revealed, offering the illusion of real-time monitoring. Except for button controls, the simulation required absolutely no programming. This example demonstrates that low fidelity approaches can convincingly convey a dynamic process to learners.

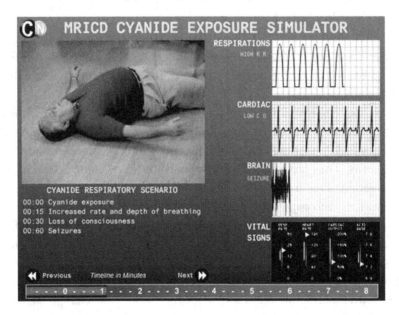

Table 1. Simple state model of Virtual Nerve Agent Casualty (VNAC). (States 4 & 5 are omitted for clarity.) VNAC is a product of the US Army Medical Research Institute of Chemical Defense Chemical Casualty Care Division

Initial State	State 2	State 3	State 6 Final State for Success	State 7 Final State for Failure
Conditions: Default	Activating Conditions: 3 Atropine 3 Oxime 1 Diazepam	Activating Conditions: 4 Atropine 3 Oxime 3 Diazepam	Activating Conditions: 15 Atropine 4 Oxime 4 Diazepam	Activating Conditions: 5 minute delay in treatment Seizures not controlled in 10 min An error is made
Vitals: Heart Rate 140 Respiration: 30 Blood Pressure: 40 systolic Secretion 4+ Bronchospasm 4+ Twitch + Seizure + "The patient is twitching and having difficulty breathing…"	Vitals: Heart Rate 120 Respiration: 24 Blood Pressure: 60 systolic Secretion 3+ Bronchospasm 3+ Twitch + Seizure +	Vitals: Heart Rate 130 Respiration: 20 Blood Pressure: 100 systolic Secretion 2+ Bronchospasm 2+ Twitch - Seizure -	Vitals: Heart Rate 160 Respiration: 13 Blood Pressure: 140 systolic Secretion - Bronchospasm - Twitch - Seizure - "Great job, the patient is stable for transport"	Vitals: Dead "You just didn't treat her well enough"

SSMs are very well suited to games and a number of mechanics can be employed to change the state machine. They can me implemented as primary branches in a game tree or as items that can be activated or changed within a game environment by the player (Talbot, Sagae, John, & Rizzo, 2012).

Low Fidelity with High Familiarity: Health Scores

The most game-based approach to depicting physiology is the health score. Health scores are simple numeric or bar graph representations of health. They consist of a point-based score or 100-point scale and are often called hit points. This very simple and low fidelity representation of health status is ubiquitous and is readily understood by game players. In games, the player's avatar loses hit points upon receiving damage. Losing all hit points results in death of the player. Hit points tend to gradually regenerate or are restored by activating plus-ups.

Medical games can also exploit health scores. One approach to health scores employs trend zones. For example, one can split the range of hit points with low, stable and high zones [Figure 7]. High health scores will improve until health is full. Scores in the stable zone will improve very slowly and scores in the low health zone will automatically decrease. Simply setting the health score based upon a virtual patient's disease or improvement after intervention will now be followed by automatic, ongoing action. This action can be enhanced further by adding non-linear response curves (Mark, 2009). With trend zones, the score will always be moving, encouraging the learner to intervene. This approach requires very little development effort (Talbot, 2013b).

A more sophisticated approach from the gaming world uses score modifiers. Score modifiers come in four basic forms: instant damage, instant healing, damage over time (DoT) and healing over time (HoT). Instant modifiers are a one-time reduction or improvement to the health score. DoT is a continu-

Figure 7. Health Scores represent total health by points or a percentage displayed on a bar graph. This type of display is not capable of showing historical values but the score can be observed to change if the learner watches it. The above sample includes a legend that depicts trend zones that would otherwise be invisible to the learner. Health scores in the low trend zone automatically decline and scores in the high zone automatically increase over time. The score does not change within the stable zone. A little additional math creates a surprisingly vibrant and useful indicator of patient health for game based learning.

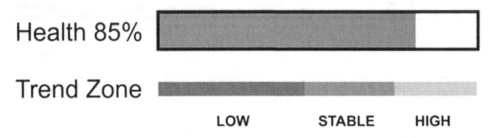

ous score reduction over a specified amount of time. In the example of a bleeding virtual patient, the health score will progressively decline on the screen as bleeding is a DoT effect. If the learner gives the patient a blood transfusion, perhaps some points will be added to the health score, but the score will continue to decline. If the learner intervenes and stops the bleeding (i.e. Tourniquet), then the DoT effect is cancelled out. Applying a blood transfusion (instant healing) will now permanently increase the score because the DoT effect is no longer present. Careful application of different score modifiers can mimic responsive and sophisticated physiology. The drawback is that health is being represented by a single moving bar; such a display typically does not show historical trends. Learners who grew up with video games are accustomed to this health scores even though it is not widely used for medical simulations. An additional benefit of this approach is that health score language is very familiar to game developers. Further research is needed to assess the impact of health scores on learner perception.

A practical example of how effective health scores are can be implemented with a very minimal software program written by the author. In the example described here [Figure 8], a program is created called "Exsanguitron 150". The program is coded in Flash Actionscript 2.0 and the only display outputs are a single bar graph along with a simple text box. The program states is features a "SUPER DYNA-MODEL" which is intended to give the false impression that some sophisticated set of algorithms is crunching away. The function "this.onEnterFrame" runs twelve times per second and updates the health variable, which is also associated with the width of the health bar graph on the screen. The entire model consists of the simple equation "health += healingOverTime + instantHealing – damageOverTime – instantDamage." Even without specific knowledge of the programming language, the simplicity of this approach is obvious.

When the health score-based simulator is started (start_btn.onRelease), the simulator states that a trauma patient has arrived and is bleeding from a gunshot wound. Damage over time (DoT) effect is applied followed by a rapid decrease in the size of the health bar. The player has three options at this point; one is to apply a bandage (bandage_btn.onRelease) by pressing BANDAGE which slows the DoT a bit. If the player selects IV placement (iv_btn.onRelease), then there is a small instant damage effect followed by enabling the transfusion button. The TRANSFUSION button's function simply adds an instant healing effect. The player can apply transfusions indefinitely but health will continue to decline. The OPERATE button causes a large instant damage, so that a low health 'patient' will require transfusions

Figure 8. Exsanguitron 150. This simple medical simulation employs a single bar graph, text output and health scores.

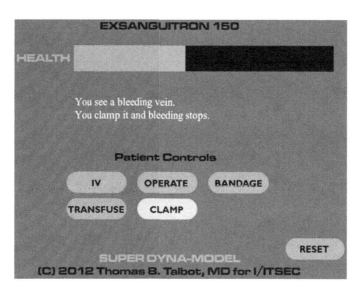

before they are stable enough for an operation. The operation exposes a bleeding vessel and activates the CLAMP button. Once operated on, the CLAMP button starts a function to turn off DoT and apply a healing over time (HoT) at a modest rate. The player can then transfuse blood that will permanently increase the patient's health. There is additional code in the transfuse function that accelerates HoT if the patient gets above 75% health.

Although the Exsanguitron 150 is a very simple demonstration of health score concepts, it is surprisingly playable and makes for a popular demonstration. Note that with each button pressed, the on-screen text box changes with a new message. These text messages create an interactive narrative for the player. Strangely enough, this combination of a single moving bar graph, health scores and interactive narrative makes for a lively and an engaging encounter for a short period of time. Although this simulation is very primitive, it is plausibly accurate. If this simple code base were to be buttressed with a vital sign monitor or an animated 3D character, the effect would appear sophisticated and expensive despite having the same underlying simplicity. A variety of decisions can be applied that will result in death or recovery of the simulated patient. The Exsanguitron 150 can be tried out online with any Flash-enabled browser (Talbot, 2012).

Health Score Code Sample (Actionscript 2.0)

```
this.onEnterFrame = function() { // control loop
        // The line below does all the computations for the 'physiology mod-
el'
        health += healingOverTime + instantHealing - damageOverTime - instant-
Damage;
        if (health < 0) {
```

```
                              health = 0;
                              this.debug_txt.text = "Patient has died.  RESET sce-
nario to start over"
                              eraseButtons();  }
          if (health > 400){
                              health = 400;
                              this.debug_txt.text = "Congratulations!  You saved
the patient." }
          health_mc._width = health;  // this animates the bar graph
          instantHealing = 0;     // need to reset instant healing back so it
just counts once
          instantDamage = 0;                  // same for damage
}
this.start_btn.onRelease = function() {
          debug_txt.text = "Trauma patient arrives.  \nHe is bleeding with a
gunshot wound to the gut."
          damageOverTime = 2;
          instantDamage = 75;
          this._visible = false
          start_txt._visible = false;
}
this.operate_btn.onRelease = function() {
          debug_txt.text = "You quickly operate, upon opening the abdomen,  \
nYou see a bleeding vessel. "
          clamp_btn._visible = true;
          clamp_txt._visible = true;
          instantDamage = 50;
}
this.clamp_btn.onRelease = function() {
          debug_txt.text = "You see a bleeding vein.  \nYou clamp it and bleed-
ing stops."
          damageOverTime = 0;
          healingOverTime = 0.1
}
this.iv_btn.onRelease = function() {
          debug_txt.text = "Your nurse places two large bore IVs. "
          transfuse_btn._visible = true;
          transfuse_txt._visible = true;
          instantDamage = 15;
}
this.transfuse_btn.onRelease = function() {
          transfusionsGiven ++;
          debug_txt.text = "Blood transfusion " + transfusionsGiven + " in prog-
ress."
```

```
        if (health < 300)
        {
                instantHealing = 40;
        } else {
                if (healingOverTime > 0) healingOverTime = 0.5;
        }
}
this.bandage_btn.onRelease = function() {
        debug_txt.text = "Applying a compression bandage. \nThis may slow
bleeding a little bit."
if (damageOverTime >= 1) damageOverTime = 0.75;
}
```

If, for example, one desired to create a simulation for coordinating a response to a very large number of casualties, the use of simple methods such as simple state machines and health scores allows for patients that change noticeably over the course of the exercise and act responsively to player intervention. The player will be busy prioritizing and selecting treatments and will likely not take notice that the fidelity is shallow. In fact, such simulation depends on the fact that fidelity is shallow so learners focus on "the big picture." The question of how the learner perceives fidelity in the simulation is a worthy topic for learning game research.

The Static Presentation Is the Most Common Medical Simulation Case

The most common method of depicting physiology is through a static presentation. Static presentations state vital signs and provide a case in written or verbal form. Static presentations can have as little or as much detail as desired with little effort required on the part of the author. This format is commonly employed in written tests, magazines, multimedia and web pages to effect and is well known to medical learners. While the advantages involve ease of authorship and distribution, the disadvantage is the lack of interaction. This format does a poor job of demonstrating progression and the effects of intervention. Static presentations have strictly right and wrong answers without consideration of creative possibilities. This format is the most common type of educational patient case. Static Presentations are a poor fit for game approaches.

Physiological Fidelity: Applications

Each approach to depicting physiology has its own best use [Table 2]. Advanced learner simulations and exploratory activities are well suited to physiology engines. Interactive case scenarios can be conducted with a physiology engine, but complex and simple state machines are usually preferred due to the relative simplicity of development and lower computing resource requirements. Since state machines consist of a few dozen calculations to perform versus thousands for a physiology engine, state machines require fewer computing resources to run. Although computers are always becoming more powerful, the resource requirements to run a physiology engine in real time become significant when attempting to run 100 simultaneous instances within a serious game. Another area where the logical simplicity of state machines is preferable includes low power and low computing resource environments such as

Table 2. Comparison of approaches to virtual patient physiology

	Physiology Engines	Complex State Models	Simple State Models	Health Scores	Static Presentations
Handling of unexpected & complex inputs	Easy	Difficult	Impossible	Moderate	N/A
Ease to correlate visualization with model	Difficult	Easy	Very Easy	Moderate	Very Easy
Response to user input	Gradual	Instant	Instant	Gradual / Instant	None
Graceful recovery from learner errors	Yes	Challenging	No	Yes	N/A
Suitability for lengthy scenarios	High	Effort to build increases w/ length	Low	High	Low
Biological Fidelity	High	Moderate	Low	Low	Low
Typical perception of biological fidelity	Moderate-High	High	Low	Moderate	None
Best Use Scenario	Advanced Simulations & Exploratory Learning	Interactive Case Scenarios & Game Based Training	Interactive Case Scenarios, Presentations & Mini-activities	Game Based Training	Case Studies
Development Effort	Moderately Difficult, but Improving	Moderate	Easy	Easy	Very Easy

mobile devices and tablets. Game based training is well suited to complex state machines and health scores. Presentations and mini-activities with few options are well suited to simple state machines. Case studies are most easily written as a static presentation, though adding a state machine can increase the interactive possibilities. The available number of quality medical training scenarios is limited by the effort required to develop them. Fortunately, the most medical scenarios do not require high physiological fidelity. Clever developers employ a number of tricks to create the impression of physiological fidelity. These techniques include visible responsiveness to user input and use of animation.

Gameplay, Interactivity, and Narrative

One of the most neglected aspects of medical games is the game itself. A medical game serves no purpose, no matter how realistic, if it lacks compelling gameplay and interaction. Fancy graphics, accurate anatomy and physiological fidelity are not the only, nor the most important features of a successful medical simulation. The quality of a simulation-based training experience depends on successful engagement with the learner. The need to create engagement for medical simulations is just as important as it is for the successful entertainment oriented game. Achieving engagement depends on a sense of immersion, successfully executing visuals, responsiveness and a good narrative. Creating the sense of immersion is more important than 3D or the level of visual detail in the simulation. It depends on having a consistent simulation world with things to do or see that are interesting to the learner (Alexander, Brunye, & Sidman, 2005). Medical games can achieve engagement with the learner more successfully if actions they perform in the scenario are followed by a visible or audible response (Kenny, Parsons, & Rizzo, 2009).

Responsiveness connects the learner to the scenario. In the case where virtual humans are encountered, responsiveness establishes likeability and rapport with the learner. Non-verbal cues and gestures, even random ones, increase this sensation of rapport with the scenario and virtual patient. For these reasons, factors such as "response to user input", "perception of biological fidelity" and other factors are listed in Table 2, which is a comparison of approaches to virtual patient physiology. This table is based upon the author's experience as a developer and interactions with hundreds of learners using various medical simulations. In addition to design choices such as the level of fidelity required and the amount of development effort one wishes to expend, one should not neglect the impact of old-fashioned storytelling; research strongly demonstrates that narrative is a successful tool to engage people (Tortell & Morie, 2006).

Virtual Reality Simulations

The capability and affordability of virtual reality technology has improved greatly since this paper was originally published in 2013. Virtual (VR) and Mixed Reality (MR) are obvious venues for virtual patient simulations, yet the principles behind creating effective and responsive appearing patients remains the same as it always has been. The primary challenge that virtual reality adds is the task of naturally interacting with the patient. Windows and Mouse Pointer (WIMP) interactions and menu systems are very clunky in VR. The MedVR laboratory at the USC Institute for Creative Technologies, the author's lab, is conducting multiple research efforts to address the interactivity through adding gestural and conversational interfaces. It is likely that VR users will desire to converse with and physically manipulate their virtual patients in a naturalistic manner.

The lab's Open Medical Gesture (OpenMG) project is developing a set of natural hand gesture interactions that are specific to medical interactions which will work with a variety of sensors that includes optical sensors such as Leap Motion, Microsoft Kinect 2.0, and Intel RealSense in addition to sensor-laden gloves. With regards to a conversational interface, we developed a virtual standardized patient (VSP) capability called USC Standard Patient (Talbot, Kalisch, Christoffersen, & Rizzo, 2016), which allows a learner to conduct complete medical interviews in a conversational manner, including embodied emotional performances by the patient (Talbot, Sagae, John & Rizzo, 2012). Although such technology currently is setup to run in one state (non-acute setting), it is easily possible to adapt state-based responses alterations that would simulate the effects of patient health changes during the simulation. In this manner, a patient experiencing respiratory distress may provide briefer or aggravated answers and may stop responding to questions as their health deteriorates. It is possible to construct such interactions where the user asks from a selection of available choices (John & Talbot, 2013) or a more complex system can respond to questions based on the user's whims (Talbot, 2016). Such complex VSPs are called Natural Language Random Access (NLRA) systems. Although these technologies are currently at the leading edge of interactive simulation research, their availability and development expense will improve as has been the case with 3D graphics and physiology engines.

CONCLUSION

The author recommends that those intending to create medical simulations employ the simplest technology possible that achieves the learning objectives. Each of the approaches described here has its best use case for use in medical games or simulations. Dealing with the issues around biology is a challenge for the game designer and game developer because of the need to have fidelity. Biological fidelity in medical simulation should never be an end in and of itself. Physiology, anatomy, interaction, narrative and the technology behind them represent an array of tools, just like the choice of game engine, art tools and physics package. The choice of these tools must be determined by educational objectives. More complex systems will require more time, effort and money to create. Recent advances in Virtual Reality will serve to increase expectations for naturalistic interactions with virtual patient simulations, yet the biologically-based principles described here continue to apply. Excessive fidelity results in the trade-off of less complete and compelling training content within a fixed budget. Although some applications rightly require exacting fidelity, many do not. Medical educators must choose the most appropriate level of technology that achieves their learning and assessment objectives. When doing so, they may often find that the level of fidelity required is lower than what they initially expected.

REFERENCES

Ahlquist, J. (2007). *Game Development Essentials: Game Artificial Intelligence*. New York: Thomson.

Alexander, A. L., Brunye, T., & Sidman, J. (2005). From gaming to training: A review of studies on fidelity, immersion, presence and buy-in and their effects on transfer in pc-based simulations and games. *DARWARS Conference Proceedings*. Accessed at http://www.aptima.com/publications/2005_Alexander_Brunye_Sidman_Weil.pdf

Applied Research Associates. (2016). *BioGears Physiology Engine*. Retrieved on June 26th, 2016 at www.biogearsengine.com

Clark, R. C., & Mayer, R. E. (2008). e-learning and the science of instruction: Proven guidelines for consumers and designers of multimedia learning. San Francisco: Pfeiffer.

Cooper, J., & Taqueti, V. (2008). A brief history of the development of mannequin simulators for clinical education and training. *Postgraduate Medical Journal*, *84*(997), 563–570. doi:10.1136/qshc.2004.009886 PMID:19103813

Donoghue, A. J., Durbin, D. R., Nadel, F. M., Stryjewski, G. R., Kost, S. I., & Nadkarny, V. (2008). Perception of Realism During Mock Resuscitations by Pediatric Housestaff: The Impact of simulated Physical Features. *J Soc Simulation in Healthcare*, *3*(3), 113–137.

Grant, T., McNeil, M. A., & Luo, X. (2010). Absolute and Relative Value of Patient Simulator Features as Perceived by Medical Undergraduates. *J Soc Simulation in Healthcare*, *5*(4), 213–218.

John, B., & Talbot, T. B. (2013). *Virtual Child Witness*. International Pediatric Simulation Society Proceedings.

Kenny, P. G., Parsons, T. D., & Rizzo, A. A. (2009). Human Computer Interaction in Virtual Standardized Patient Systems. In Human-Computer Interaction, Part IV, HCII, (LNCS), (vol. 5613, pp. 514-523). Berlin: Springer.

Knight J.F., Carlet S., Tregunna B., Jarvis S., Smithies R., de Freitas S., Dunwell I., & Mackway-Jones K. (2010). *Serious gaming technology in major incident triage training: A pragmatic controlled trial.* Academic Press.

Leathrum, J. F., Mielke, R. R., Audette, R., McKenzie, F., Armstrong, R. K., Miller, G. T., . . . Scerbo, M. W. (2015). An Architecture to Support Integrated Manikin-Based Simulations. *Society for Modeling & Simulation International Conference Proceedings.* SCSC.

Mark, D. (2009). *Behavioral Mathematics for Game AI.* Boston: Charles River Media.

Morgan, P. J., & Cleave-Hogg, D. (2002). A worldwide survey of the use of simulation in anesthesia. *Canadian Journal of Anaesthesia, 49*(7), 659–662. doi:10.1007/BF03017441 PMID:12193481

Riedl, M. O., & Young, R. M. (2006). From Linear Story Generation to Branching Story Graphs. *IEEE Computer Graphics and Applications, 26*(3), 23–31. doi:10.1109/MCG.2006.56 PMID:16711214

Talbot, T. B. (2008). *SIMapse Nerve Agent Laboratory 2.0 and Nerve Academy CD-ROM.* Referenced at https://ccc.apgea.army.mil/products/info/products.htm

Talbot, T. B. (2012). *Exanguitron 150 Health-Score based trauma simulator demonstration.* Accessed at http://www.doctortalbot.com/healthscore

Talbot, T. B. (2013). Playing with Biology: Making medical games that appear lifelike.[July-September.]. *International Journal of Gaming and Computer-Mediated Simulations, 5*(3), 83–96. doi:10.4018/jgcms.2013070106

Talbot, T. B. (2013). Balancing Physiology, Anatomy & Immersion: How Much Biological Fidelity is Necessary in a Medical Simulation? *Journal of Military Medicine., 178*(10S), 26–33. PMID:24084303

Talbot, T. B. (2016). *Natural Language Understanding Performance & Use Considerations in Virtual Medical Encounters.* Medicine Meets Virtual Reality Proceedings.

Talbot, T. B., Rizzo, A., Christofferson, K., & Kalish, N. (2016). *USC Standard Patient virtual standardized patient.* Accessed on June 26th, 2016 at http://www.standardpatient.org

Talbot, T. B., Sagae, K., John, B., & Rizzo, A. A. (2012a). Designing useful virtual standardized patient encounters. *Interservice/Industry Training,Simulation and Education Conference Proceedings.*

Talbot, T. B., Sagae, K., John, B., & Rizzo, A. A. (2012b). Sorting out the Virtual Patient: How to exploit artificial intelligence, game technology and sound educational practices to create engaging role-playing simulations. *International Journal of Gaming and Computer-Mediated Simulations, 4*(4).

Tortell, R., & Morie, F. J. (2006). Videogame play and the effectiveness of virtual environments for training. *Proceedings of the Interservice/Industry Training, Simulation, and Education Conference.*

Chapter 7
Using Serious Gaming to Improve the Safety of Central Venous Catheter Placement:
A Post–Mortem Analysis

Daniel Katz
Icahn School of Medicine at Mount Sinai, USA

Prabal Khanal
3D Systems Inc., USA

Andrew Goldberg
Icahn School of Medicine at Mount Sinai, USA

Kanav Kahol
Arizona State University, USA

Samuel DeMaria
Icahn School of Medicine at Mount Sinai, USA

ABSTRACT

Serious gaming a tool that can be used to train new physicians in a manner that keeps patients out of harm's way. This is especially true when teaching procedures, which in the medical community if often done in a "see one, do one, teach one" manner. Additionally, many teachers focus on technical aspects of the procedure and may leave out or de-emphasize non-technical portions of the procedure such as hand washing and patient positioning. This chapter per the authors investigates the utility of serious gaming in teaching physicians technical procedures. The chapter begins with game development and will end with a discussion of the results of the prospective randomized study.

INTRODUCTION TO THE CENTRAL VENOUS CATHETER

Approximately 5 million central venous catheters (CVCs) are placed by physicians annually in the United States.(Gould, 2003) These catheters are often placed in critically ill patients to infuse potent medications, blood products, and/or to provide high concentration total parenteral nutrition (TPN). CVC's are placed under sterile conditions, usually with ultrasound guidance, in a repetitive technical pattern. Regrettably, as with any medical procedure, complications occur; in this case at a rate of anywhere between 5%-26% of the time (Merrer, De Jonghe & Golliot, 2001; Raad, Darouiche & Dupuis, 1997). Common complications due to CVC placement include infection, pneumothorax (air trapped in the lung), arterial

DOI: 10.4018/978-1-5225-1817-4.ch007

puncture (carotid, subclavian, or femoral vessels), thrombosis (local blood clot) and embolism (mobile blood clot) with occurrence rates that are often inversely correlated with clinical experience.(Fares & Block PH, 1986; Sznajder, Zveibil, Bitterman & Weiner, 1986) The subsequent costs of catheter-related complications are high, with a single catheter-related infection, for example, costing between $4,000 - $56,000.(H. S. et Al, 2010) Guidelines and recommendations are continually being established and updated regarding CVC placement in an attempt to minimize these complications, including the use of principles such as aseptic technique and antibiotic-coated catheters.(Anesthesiology, 2010) While much has been done regarding training practitioners in the technical skills of CVC placement using part-task trainers (i.e., mannequins)(Dong, Suri, Cook, Kashani, Mullon, Enders, Rubin & Ziv, 2010; Rosen & Uddin, 2009), successfully locating and cannulating a central vein is but one part of the process. In fact, many key steps designed to prevent untoward effects involve non-technical skills such as proper hand hygiene technique, ergonomic kit set up, and manometry are learned by practitioners through an apprenticeship model (i.e., see one, do one, teach one) which can lead to non -standardized practices or even perpetuate poor practices.

Healthcare practitioners are increasingly being trained in realistic and highly interactive simulated environments so they can learn not only psychomotor skills (e.g., lumbar puncture, endotracheal intubation), but also key management and non-technical steps which make their tasks safer (Toff, 2010). Simulation, for example, has been proven an effective teaching tool in a variety of healthcare environments including laparoscopy (Aggarwal, Ward & Balasundaram, 2007; Fried, Feldman & Vassiliou, 2004), bronchoscopy (Blum & Powers, 2004), and in team-training exercises in areas such as ACLS (Fletcher, Flin, McGeorge, Glavi & Maran, 2003; Wayne, Didwania, Feinglass, Fudala & Barsuk, 2008). Additionally, it has been shown that skill retention when using simulators is often superior to standard practices and that the use of simulation reduces the learning curve of many standardized procedures. (Andreatta P, Chen Y, Marsh M, 2010; Stefanidis D, Korndorffer J, Sierra R, 2005) Likewise, it has been shown that not only can simulators improve outcomes, but they can improve efficiency of performing procedures as well (Aggarwal, Ward & Balasundaram, 2007; Barsuk, McGahie, Cohen, Balachandran, 4AD; Britt & Reed, 2007). One specific simulation modality that has yet to be fully utilized to improve performance is serious gaming.

Serious gaming as an instrument for learning is being increasingly utilized in health care fields and may lead to better skill-based outcomes.(C. C. et Al, 2009) Gaming as a training tool for physicians has not been widely available as it is relatively novel and game development can be expensive. However, more opportunities are becoming available as development becomes less expensive.("C Programming Tutorial," n.d.; "Java Made Easy," n.d.) The aim of this project was to create an interactive screen-based game for internal jugular venous cannulation and CVC placement that incorporates the non-technical aspects of the procedure. We then sought to test the hypothesis that simulation-based training with the CVC game would be superior to traditional clinical training received by junior anesthesia residents at a major academic center, as measured by a standardized rating tool.

What Went Right

Game Development

The CVC serious game was our department's first venture into the gaming world, and as such required partnering with an entity with some experience in developing serious games. Through a chance occurrence at a simulation meeting, we were put into touch with Dr. Kanav Kahol, who was a member of the Human Symbiosis Lab based at Arizona State University at that time. He was able to find a graduate student in need of a research project, with enough programming experience to help us make our game. Having such a small development team had some advantages. For instance, communication between members of the group was easy to organize, in spite of the large distance between New York and Arizona. We found it helpful to have regular meetings to discuss problems that arose during game development, as well as strategy sessions on proposed ideas for study design. We quickly found that one of the biggest gaps that we needed to bridge was that of getting our developer at ASU some practical experience with central venous catheters. Although he had been able to both read about the subject and watch a few videos on catheter placement, we found it incredibly challenging to discuss some of the clinical aspects of the game that we wanted to be highlighted. Our solution to this problem was to bring him on site to NY, where we put him with our hospital's "line service" (a dedicated team in the surgical intensive care unit who place central venous catheters for the majority of the patients in the hospital). While visiting he was able to observe several CVC placements while also interacting with the clinical team and gaining insight into some of the aspects of CVC placement that are often not found in books or videos. This experience was helpful when designing the game interface, as he could now arrange the medical tools on the game interface in a practical manner.

Another hurdle encountered while developing our game was choosing the proper platform for development. Several options were available to us, but we had to be sure to choose a medium for game play that would be readily available to our test subjects while having development tools that our graduate student was familiar with. Luckily, our department has a history of being early adopters of technology, and had already begun an initiative to give the residents in our department (our test subjects) iPads in lieu of an academic book stipend. As a gaming and research tool, the iPad was an excellent choice. Not only was there a great learning tool with a built-in store to distribute our game, but the team was able to use development tools that were compatible with IOS, namely the Unreal gaming engine, and Maya, our graphics design tool.

Once the platform and engine were picked, it came time to work out the finer details of the game design. Our initial idea was to have the participant be a member of the "line service" and encounter a number of virtual patients presenting for CVC placement. Based on each clinical scenario the patients would experience either easy line placement, or complications based on errors made (e.g., if the user did not wash their hands then the game would give the patient an infection). However, once development began, we found this type of comprehensive patient experience to be both extremely resource intensive and distracting from the perspective of the user. After all, the purpose of the game was to learn about and practice safe CVC placement, not the clinical management of critically ill patients or how best to cope with the consequences of improper CVC placement. We therefore broke the game down into its most basic elements. The user would start by introducing himself to the patient with a simple button push and would then proceed step by step through the placement of a CVC by clicking on the tools in the correct order as seen in Figure 1. We found this to be a better design that was less distracting and much easier to make than what we initially proposed.

Now that our basic design was completed, we wanted to incorporate a feedback mechanism that was both evidence based and validated. After a prolonged literature search, we were able to find a grading scheme that had been developed to evaluate central line performance that had been validated in other

Figure 1. Randomization scheme

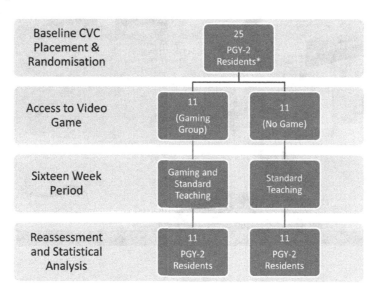

studies (Dong, Suri, Cook, Kashani, Mullon, Enders, Rubin & Ziv, 2010). This grading scheme, designed by Dong et al, was the basis for the scoring system in the game. The system itself was very simple. Each correct step gave the user points, while the user received no points for either missing steps, or performing steps in the wrong order. After the virtual line was placed, the user was directed to a screen summarizing their performance as seen in Figure 2. A tutorial mode was also added to guide the novice user through the correct steps of CVC placement as seen in Figure 3.

Figure 2. CVC game module title screen

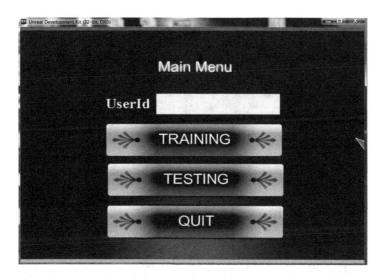

Figure 3. Screenshot of training mode in progress

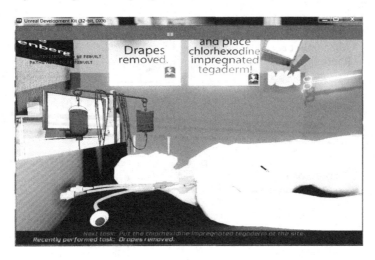

Study Design

Our overall study design was a prospective randomized control trial involving anesthesiology residents at a major academic tertiary care facility in New York as seen in Figure 4.

Every year in July, a new set of residents joins our department to begin their postgraduate medical training in anesthesiology. We felt as though these new residents were perfect test subjects for our study for a variety of reasons. First, they were mostly inexperienced as a group at placing CVCs. Second, each resident in the class starts new, negating any bias that comes from looking at the same population later in the year (i.e. after their line service rotation in the ICU). Additionally, for the first month of training the residents are covered by attending physicians in a one on one fashion, which made it easier to bring the residents to the lab to perform their baseline CVC measurements.

Figure 4. Screenshot of post-game "report card"

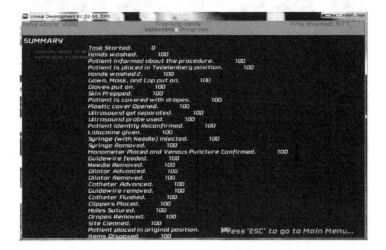

Each resident was brought to the Mount Sinai HELPS (Human Emulation, Education, and Evaluation Lab for Patient Safety) Center for baseline data collection. They filled out a brief survey asking about their baseline level of comfort with placing CVCs. We then had them place a CVC on a training mannequin and observed/timed their placement. Scores were based off of the same validated checklist mentioned earlier (Dong, Suri, Cook, Kashani, Mullon, Enders, Rubin & Ziv, 2010). Residents were then randomized by coin flip to either have access to the game, to play as often as they would like versus their control counterparts who would get the routine training available at the time. We asked that those with the game play it at least once per week.

After four months, which was deemed by the clinical team involved in the study design to be enough time to gain skills from both using the game as well as some clinical experience in the operating rooms, the residents were brought back to the HELPS Center to place another CVC on the mannequin. Those evaluating the residents did know which residents were assigned to which group, and no one had access to the pre-intervention data. As with the first line placement, the residents were graded and timed according to the checklist. We found that this study design was sufficient to adequately assess a difference between the two groups and was relatively free from bias. It also required little investment in resources, as the same kit could be recycled, and the HELPS Center had already acquired the part task trainer we were using for the CVC placement.

Our primary endpoints for evaluation were easily measurable, reproducible, and clinically relevant. We were able to find significant differences between the two groups in terms of time to catheter placement, overall score in catheter placement, a decrease in time per step (see Table 1), and most importantly, residents who played the game were less likely to skip "critical" steps of the procedure, such as proper hand hygiene, and confirmation of venous puncture by manometry (see Table 2). Secondary endpoints were also measured, along with a post study survey looking at the frequency of play as well as overall satisfaction of the game (see Table 3). We found that most subjects were happy with the quality of our game, but would have preferred better graphics and more than one level of catheter placement.

What Went Wrong

Game Development

While the development of our game ran smoothly, it was far from ideal. The large geographic distance between team members made a site visit logistically challenging and expensive. Likewise, since our study was otherwise unfunded there was a general lack of resources. Additionally, there was a very strict time constraint on game development, which put even greater stress on our team. If the game was not ready for the July group of residents, we would have had to wait another year to run our study. The combination of the resource and time constraints meant that some of the features of our game had to be

Table 1. Score and time changes: A decrease in time per step

Score and Time Changes	Control Group	Gaming Group	P Value
Mean Score Change (SE)	0 (0.64)	3.2 (0.51)	0.0004
Mean Total Time Decrement, sec (SE)	108 (33.5)	270 (53.8)	0.014
Mean Time Per Step, sec (SE)	61 (3.2)	49 (4.3)	0.0005

Table 2. Critical steps

Step of CVC Placement	Control Group (% Missed Step)	Gaming Group (% Missed Step)	Chi Square
Hands Washed Pre-Patient Introduction	81%	72%	0.61
Patient Introduction/Consent Verification*	54%	9%	0.02
Placement of Patient in Trendelenberg*	72%	9%	0.002
Primary Scrub*	81%	9%	0.003
Gown and Glove	9%	0%	0.3
Skin Preparation	0%	0%	-
Patient Draping	0%	0%	-
US Probe properly covered	0%	0%	-
Application of US gel	0%	0%	-
Verification of Compressibility of IJ Vein	0%	0%	-
Time Out Verification	100%	90%	0.3
Skin Localization	0%	9%	0.3
Insertion of syringe with back pressure*	81%	9%	0.0006
Confirmation of venipuncture via manometry*	72%	9%	0.002
Insertion of guidewire	0%	0%	-
Removal of puncture needle	0%	0%	-
Insertion/removal of dilator	0%	0%	-
Catheter insertion	0%	0%	-
Removal of guidewire	0%	0%	-
Catheter flush	9%	0%	0.3
Use of clipper to secure catheter	36%	9%	0.12
Sterile dressing placement	9%	0%	0.3
Pt. repositioned	81%	72%	0.61
Proper disposal of items	81%	90%	0.5
Hands washed after procedure	100%	100%	-

Table 3. Survey responses

Survey ResponsesStatement	% Responding with Rank of 3 or Greater (Likert 1-5 Scale)
Having access to the game increased my comfort with placing central lines.	100%
After using the game I would feel more comfortable teaching another clinician the procedure.	91%
I was satisfied with the CVC game.	81%
Having the game raised my awareness about the potential pitfalls of the procedure.	82%
Having the game made the process of placing central lines more safe.	100%

curtailed, or outright dropped. For example, we had wanted to include multiple levels in our game, but were only able to provide one. We had also wanted to include a leaderboard that would enable those playing the game to see their scores relative to their peers. We found this to be too difficult to organize given our constraints. We had also hoped for higher-end graphics as well as music, but did not have the resources to employ a graphic designer or sound engineer. Our post-doctoral student, who had limited experience with Maya, had to make all of the graphics.

The Unreal engine itself proved to be a good choice, but there were some technical issues such as game crashes that were encountered when sending builds between institutions. Likewise, it was challenging to move the game onto the iPads, mostly because those on the team had little experience with Apple development. Likewise, since we did not have the personnel to maintain the game once it was launched, as IOS updated we encountered game crashes on some of the iPads. Testing the game was a challenge as well, since all of our prospective users were test subjects and could therefore not be used to test the game to get real user feedback.

Study Design

Our study, while successful, had several design flaws. Many of the issues encountered dealt with our subjects themselves. Our sample size was very small, and although they were just beginning their training in anesthesiology, the clinical experience gained in their respective intern years may have confounded our data. Likewise, since our residents are only a small group at tertiary care facility, the generalizability of the data obtained may be questioned. It is also atypical for residents who operate under tight budgets to have iPads, although the pervasiveness of these devices is ever increasing. Finally, we found that some of the residents did not bring their iPads to work, which gave them fewer opportunities to play the game.

For a study on a limited budget, our modality for testing competence with CVC placement (i.e. on a mannequin) was resource intensive. The mannequin used for testing itself costs well over one thousand dollars, and if we had not already obtained the part task trainer for other uses we would not have been able to afford it. Likewise, taking the residents out of the operating rooms put a constraint on the rest of the anesthesiology staff, although it was mitigated by the timing of our project (still one on one coverage). Our resource constraint prevented us from using truly independent evaluators (outside of our department). Two study subjects were also lost secondary to the time constraint of our study as they were on vacation or at outside institutions during their follow up.

Another criticism which may have impacted our results was the design of our control group. While designing the study it had been decided that the control group would not undergo any additional training for CVC placement unless they would have outside of the study. One of the criticisms encountered from this design is that had the residents been supplied with a CVC checklist, or the game's grading scheme and not played the game, our results might have been different. Finally, we found that part of the time difference may have been due to some of the more technical aspects of the procedure that were not covered in the game. For example, the game generated the correct ultrasound view once the player clicked on the ultrasound, but in the lab the subjects had to obtain the correct view on their own.

CONCLUSION

Overall our serious gaming study was successful despite its shortcomings. We were able to show significant improvements in both technical skill and adherence to guidelines for CVC placement. While the study group did report that they would have preferred more variety in the game along with better graphics, on the whole the feedback we received was largely positive.

Given our positive pilot study we are going back to drawing board and rebuilding parts of the game to make it more stable and enjoyable to play. We plan on implementing new interface designs based on the user feedback we received. Additionally, our department is now amenable to beginning other gaming projects, two of which are currently under development. We strongly believe that gaming is an incredibly powerful learning tool, and when it comes to training the next generation of physicians in very underutilized.

REFERENCES

Aggarwal, R., Ward, J., Balasundaram, I., Sains, R., Athanasiou, T., & Darzi, A. (2007). Proving the Effectiveness of Virtual Reality Simulation for Training in Laparoscopic Surgery. *Annals of Surgery, 246*(5), 771–779. doi:10.1097/SLA.0b013e3180f61b09 PMID:17968168

Al, C. C. (2009). Relationships Between Gaming Attributes and Learning Outcomes. *Simulation & Gaming, 40*(2), 217–266.

Al, H. S. (2010). Prevention of Central Venous Catheter Bloodstream Infections. *Journal of Intensive Care Medicine, 25*(3), 131–138. doi:10.1177/0885066609358952 PMID:20089527

Andreatta, P., Chen, Y., & Marsh, M. C. K. (2010). *Simulation based training improves applied clinical placement of ultrasound-guided PICCs*. Supp Care Cancer.

Anesthesiology, A. S. of. (2010). *Central Venous Access Guidelines Draft*. Retrieved from www.asahq. org/clinical/CentralVenousAccessGuidelinesDraft06142010.pdf

Barsuk, J. H., McGahie, W. C., Cohen, E. R., & Balachandran, J. S. (2009). Use of simulation based mastery learning to improve the quality of central venous catheter placement in a medical intensive care unit. *Journal of Hospital Medicine, 7*(7), 397–403. doi:10.1002/jhm.468 PMID:19753568

Blum, M. G., Powers, T. W., & Sundaresan, S. (2004). Bronchoscopy simlulator effectively prepares junior residents to competently perform basic clinical bronchoscopy. *The Annals of Thoracic Surgery, 78*(1), 287–291. doi:10.1016/j.athoracsur.2003.11.058 PMID:15223446

Britt,, R.C., & Reed,, S.F. (2007). Central line simulation: A new training algorithm. *The American Surgeon, 73*(7), 682–683. PMID:17674940

C Programming Tutorial. (n.d.). Retrieved from http://www.cprogramming.com/tutorial.html

Dong, Y., Suri, H. S., Cook, D. A., Kashani, K. B., Mullon, J. J., Enders, F. T., & Ziv, A. D. W. et al. (2010). Simulation-based objective assessment discerns clinical proficiency in central line placement: A construct validation. *Chest, 137*(5), 1050–1056. doi:10.1378/chest.09-1451 PMID:20061397

Fares, L.G., II, & Block, P.H. (1986). House staff results with subclavian cannulation. *Am Surg, 52*(2), 108–111.

Fletcher, G., Flin, R., McGeorge, P., Glavin, R., & Maran, N. P. R. (2003). Non-technical skills (ANTS): Evaluation of a behavioural marker system. *British Journal of Anaesthesia, 90*(5), 580–588.

Fried, G. M., Feldman, L. S., Vassiliou, M. C., Fraser, S. A., Stanbridge, D., Ghitulescu, G., & Andrew, C. G. (2004). Proving the value of simulation in laparoscopic surgery. *Annals of Surgery, 240*(3), 518–525. doi:10.1097/01.sla.0000136941.46529.56 PMID:15319723

Gould, M. M. D. (2003). Preventing Complications of Central Venous Catheterization. *The New England Journal of Medicine, 348*(12), 1123–1131. doi:10.1056/NEJMra011883 PMID:12646670

Java Made Easy. (n.d.). Retrieved from http://www.java-made-easy.com/

Merrer, J., De Jonghe, B., & Golliot, F. (2001). French Catheter Study Group in Intensive Care. Complications of femoral and subclavian venous catheterization in critically ill patients: A randomized control trial. *Journal of the American Medical Association, 286*(6), 700–707. doi:10.1001/jama.286.6.700 PMID:11495620

Raad,, I., Darouiche,, R., & Dupuis,, J. (1997). Central venous catheters coated with minocycline and rifmapin for the prevention of catheter-related colonization and bloodstream infections. A randomized, double blind trial. *Annals of Internal Medicine, 127*(4), 267–274. doi:10.7326/0003-4819-127-4-199708150-00002 PMID:9265425

Rosen, B. T., Uddin, P. Q., Harrington, A. R., Ault, B. W., & Ault, M. J. (2009). Does personalized vascular access training on a nonhuman tissue model allow for learning and retention of central line placement skills? Phase II of the procedural patient safety initiative (PPSI-II). *Journal of Hospital Medicine, 4*(7), 423–429. doi:10.1002/jhm.571 PMID:19753570

Stefanidis, D., Korndorffer, J. Jr, Sierra, R., Touchard, C., Dunne, J. B., & Scott, D. J. (2005). Skill retention following proficiency-based laparoscopic simulator training. *Surgery, 138*(2), 165–170. doi:10.1016/j.surg.2005.06.002 PMID:16153423

Sznajder, J. I., Zveibil, F. R., Bitterman, H., & Weiner, P. B. S. (1986). Central vein catheterization. Failure and complication rates by three percutaneous approaches. *Archives of Internal Medicine, 146*(2), 259–261. doi:10.1001/archinte.1986.00360140065007 PMID:3947185

Toff, N. (2010). Human Factors in Anaesthesia: Lessons From Aviation. *BJA, 105*(1), 21–25. doi:10.1093/bja/aeq127 PMID:20507856

Wayne, D. B., Didwania, A., Feinglass, J., Fudala, M. J., Barsuk, J. H., & McGaghie, W. C. (2008). Simulation-based education improves quality of care during cardiac arrest team responses at an academic teaching hospital: A case-control study. *Chest, 133*(1), 56–61. doi:10.1378/chest.07-0131 PMID:17573509

Chapter 8
Making Learning Fun:
An Investigation of Using a Ludic Simulation for Middle School Space Science

Min Liu
The University of Texas at Austin, USA

Jina Kang
The University of Texas at Austin, USA

Lucas Horton
The University of Texas at Austin, USA

Royce M. Kimmons
Brigham Young University, USA

Jaejin Lee
The University of Seoul, South Korea

ABSTRACT

We examine the use of a ludic simulation designed for middle school space science to support students' learning and motivation. A total of 383 sixth graders and 447 seventh graders participated in this study. The findings showed that sixth- and seventh-graders perceived the simulation as having substantial ludic characteristics and educational value. The results indicated that having a playful experience is important for this age group and that participating in a ludic simulation can help motivate students to learn school subjects. Results also indicated that incorporating ludus into the learning experience can improve students' attitudes toward the subject matter. Implications of policy, research, and practice with regard to using ludic simulations to support classroom-based learning were discussed.

INTRODUCTION

Increasing interest in digital games within popular culture has led many to consider the effects that playful or ludic simulations can have on learning. With the advent of mobile devices with gameplay functionality, children also play games for longer periods of time, with mobile phone gamers now playing over two hours per day, an increase of 57% in two years (NPD Group, 2015). With such an explosion of interest in the ludic value of digital media, in this chapter we describe a ludic simulation designed for middle school space science and highlight previous and emergent research findings that can help us better understand the value of ludic simulations in education. To this end, we will proceed by first

DOI: 10.4018/978-1-5225-1817-4.ch008

presenting a brief overview of previous research studies conducted on the simulation and then explore some intricacies of students' ludic experiences within it. In so doing, we hope to provide valuable insights to educators interested in the topic.

THEORETICAL FRAMEWORK

Considerations of the pedagogical value of *ludus,* or play, dates back at least two thousand years to Platonic and Aristotelian aesthetics (Mosca, 2013) and also feature prominently within constructivist metatheory, having been of interest to both cognitive constructivists (Piaget, 1951) and social constructivists (Vygotsky, 1978). In recent years, the topic has received renewed attention (cf. Singer, Golinkoff, & Hirsh-Pasek, 2006), and ludic elements have been utilized to teach everything from training first responders in explosive blast incidents (Waddington et al., 2013) to critically examining historical causes of war (Iglesia & Luis, 2016) to reminding family members to complete chores (McGonigal, 2011). Even without explicit learning objectives or immersion in unfamiliar experiences, ludic play may also serve as a means for reimagining and re-envisioning the mundane by introducing pleasure into the ordinary (Iversen, 2014). At early stages of development, children engage with the world and people around them through playful interactions that allow them to learn by imitation, symbolic interaction, and cognitive representation, thereby constructing experiential knowledge about the world (Piaget, 1951) or mimetically replicating it (Mosca, 2013). As a result, play for children is "an engaging and deliberate activity to which they devote great effort and commitment" (Rieber, 1996, p. 44), and out of such play, children can develop deep and important understandings. Current research in a variety of fields suggests that "play is an important mediator for learning and socialization throughout life" (Rieber, 1996, p. 44; see also Csikszentmihalyi & Bennett, 1971) and that the principles of play can be effectively used to teach learners of all ages.

With the introduction of digital technologies, researchers were empowered to think about play in new and innovative ways, and digital games as a method of play have become commonplace amongst consumers on computers, game consoles, and mobile devices. In 2009, it was reported that 42 percent of U.S. homes had a game console (Ivan, 2009), and it has been recently estimated that 78% of teens own a cell phone and that most own a portable gaming device or music player (Pew Research Center, 2013). With the ubiquity of these devices, Internet-based social networking technologies and new content distribution platforms such as Valve Corporation's Steam (2003) and Apple's App Store (2008) have enabled the growth of new popular methods of digital gaming like massively multiplayer online games (MOOG's), casual games, mobile games, and social gaming.

This rapid growth and the prevalence of digital games in our culture have led many to consider the questions we might answer and the problems we might solve through play. McGonigal (2011), for instance, argues that games in today's society "are fulfilling *genuine human needs* that the real world is currently unable to satisfy" and that games, if properly harnessed, have the potential to address real-world problems. Current gamification or ludification movements agree with this stance and hold that a "new ludic system" is arising in conjunction with a variety of ludic social phenomena (e.g., the video game industry, theme parks, etc.). Ortoleva (2012) explains that this "new ludic system would not exist without thinking machines, to which we owe a great variety of playful practices, from video games to casual games, to those peculiar games that are social networking websites," and in the words of Fuchs (2012), "we have a society with a 'high lusory attitude' ... in using these ludic interfaces [e.g., digital games], we increasingly turn work, war, sport and health into gamified processes." Focusing on specific problems in education, Squire (2003) has argued that digital games can "elicit powerful emotional reactions in their players, such as fear, power, aggression, wonder, or joy" (p. 2) and that designers of educational products have much to learn from game developers with regard to designing "interface, aesthetic, and interactivity" (p. 11) to support learning, and Gee (2003) has further argued that good commercial games incorporate "learning principles that … are all strongly supported by contemporary research in cognitive science" (p. 1). Regarding the educational value of games, Gee even goes so far as to argue that "games may be better sites for preparing workers for modern workplaces than traditional schools" (p. 3).

From these perspectives, games and the play that people engage in through them have the potential for serving important and transformative roles in education and society, and many have attempted to harness this predicted power of games for educational pursuits (e.g., Barab, Pettyjohn, Gresalfi, Volk, & Solomou, 2012; Barab, Thomas, Dodge, Cartequx, & Tuzun, 2005; Clarke, Dede, Ketelhut, & Nelson, 2006; Ketelhut, 2007; Nelson, 2007; Nelson, Ketelhut, Clarke, Bowman, & Dede, 2005; Zech et al., 1994). Throughout these endeavors, however, there has been a great deal of confusion and lack of clarity with regard to what types of games might have the most impact for education, what aspects of games are valuable, and what we even mean when we use the word "game." As a result, in modern vernacular, the terms *computer, digital,* and *video game* are used inclusively to refer to a variety of types of programs that do a variety of things. Although a clear, universal definition of *games* has yet to emerge, researchers continue to consider the diverse range of game-like environments in an inclusive manner to better understand their potential impact on teaching and learning. This inclusive approach seems more appropriate than creating contentious categories of game-like media, which may overemphasize differences between media types rather than focusing research efforts on commonalities (e.g., *ludus*). Nevertheless, some clarification is needed in the field if we are to understand the value of ludic experiences and their components in an analytic manner.

In a strict sense, any digital game may be considered a ludic simulation, because it constitutes a playful representation of reality (Parker & Becker, 2013), but not all ludic simulations may be classified as games, because they may lack traditional gameplay elements, such as game mechanics or narrative. Lindley (2003) attempts to capture some of the complexity of "what is a game" by offering a "high level framework for game analysis and design." According to Lindley's framework, games can be classified in accordance with how heavily they emphasize four factors: gambling (or chance), ludology (or playfulness), simulation (or representation of a system), and narratology (or story). Lindley places these four factors in a three-dimensional tetrahedron (see Figure 1) and explains that different genres of games may be effectively mapped to different locations within the tetrahedron. Lindley's framework is important for game and educational researchers, because it empowers us to talk about games in ways that are more intentional, meaningful, and directed while simultaneously allowing us to escape the confines of restrictive game definitions.

Within education in particular, Lindley's framework is valuable, because it allows us to focus upon certain aspects of games that are educationally valuable for a given context (e.g. play, real-world fidelity, etc.) without having to address other elements that may not be as relevant (e.g. chance, etc.). This framework also gives us flexibility to talk about a diversity of educational media that in cultural vernacular might be called "games" without fitting a strict definition of the word.

Within this tetrahedron, simulations are of particular interest to educators for their emphasis on skill development. In Lindley's words: "Simulations … are not interesting as games or stories, but for understanding how a particular system functions in different circumstances" (p. 1). For this reason, simulations have been used in a variety of fields to support educational goals, and many popular commercial games

Figure 1. Lindley's (2003) three-dimensional classification model for game analysis and design (p. 2)

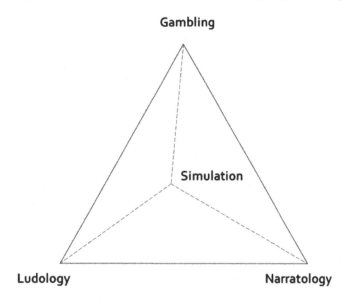

could be considered simulations, since they provide representations of systems that can be tweaked and manipulated by players. For example, *Flight Sim X* (2006) simulates airplane flight, *Garry's Mod* (2004) simulates laws of physics, *Grand Theft Auto* (2008) simulates many aspects of city and criminal life, and *Civilization* titles (1991) simulate aspects of economics, warfare, and diplomacy.

However, rather than being pure simulations, these commercial products incorporate other aspects of game design (e.g. ludology) to make the simulated experience motivational and meaningful to players. *Grand Theft Auto* ignores certain aspects of the criminal justice system, like authentic jail time, and allows players to freely explore the world and to interact with it, and *Civilization* provides players with animations, musical tracks, missions, a variety of scenarios, and even the ability to artificially introduce novel factors into a running scenario (like an attack helicopter in the Stone Age). By so doing, these *ludic simulations* offer an interesting and engaging blend of skill development and playfulness that would be lost in a simulation that did not incorporate ludic elements or a game that did not simulate interactive systems. Unlike true simulations, which would replicate a system with absolute fidelity and realism, ludic simulations hold ludicity to be as important as fidelity or realism.

The term *ludic simulation* is becoming used more frequently in educational game research, and many research projects have utilized games and virtual environments that might be meaningfully classified as ludic simulations, even though they may not adopt the term (Angehrn, 2006; DeNeve & Heppner, 1997; Ketelhut, Dede, Clarke, Nelson, & Bowman, 2007; Kimmons, Liu, Kang, & Santana, 2012; Linser, Ree-Lindstad, & Vold, 2007; Roberts, 1976). For example, much research involving the development and use of virtual worlds, multiuser virtual environments (MUVEs), and multimedia enhanced learning environments might be meaningfully discussed from the perspective of their ludicity and simulation properties, but have not been, largely due to divergent research emphases and lack of a common theoretical framework. However, current interest in ludic simulations reflects a larger ludification movement in society (Fuchs & Strouhal, 2008; Raessens, 2006), and current research into educational games should consider the ways in which ludic simulations can support learning by focusing on two specific elements of gamification: *ludus* and simulation.

RESEARCH CONTEXT

The research context for this study is a ludic simulation called *Alien Rescue*. *Alien Rescue* (AR) is a problem-based educational ludic simulation for sixth-grade space science (Liu, Horton, Lee, Kang, Rosenblum, O'Hair, & Lu, 2014; Liu, Horton, Olmanson, & Toprac, 2011; see also http://alienrescue. edb.utexas.edu). The goal of AR is to engage students in solving a complex problem that requires them to use the tools, procedures, and knowledge of space science and to apply processes of scientific inquiry while learning about our solar system.

Acting in the role of a space scientist, the learner's goal is to find suitable homes within the solar system for six different alien species, each with different habitat requirements, who have been displaced from their home planets. The experience challenges students to learn how scientists work, plan, and conduct scientific inquiry and to develop well-justified problem solutions. The inquiry process presents an authentic context in which students must exercise high-level thinking skills, such as goal setting, hypothesis generation, problem solving, self-regulation, evaluation of various possible solutions, and the presentation of evidence. AR is designed as a sixth grade science curriculum unit to be completed over the course of approximately fifteen 50-minute class sessions and aligns with National Science Education Standards and Texas Essential Knowledge and Skills (TEKS). To support students in this endeavor, AR's design centers on a collection of tools, each of which is intended to support various aspects of the learner's thinking and problem solving process.

AR engages learners in roleplaying, as they take on the role of a space scientist aboard the fictional *International Space Station Paloma*. Roleplaying directly engages learners in the problem context of the simulation and allows learners to participate in its narrative structure. Students are first situated in the narrative through a video introduction that features a variety of audio and video elements. In this opening video, a series of breaking news segments, delivered by professional news anchors, relays the news that aliens have entered Earth's orbit and have broadcasted a plea for help. Subsequent reports depict Earth's response to the plea and shifting public consensus, which lead to the eventual formation of a special United Nations task force to address the crisis. Through the introductory video, students are introduced to the goals and context of the simulation and are oriented to their role as scientists tasked with saving the alien species.

After watching the introductory video, students are free to roam the 3D environment of *ISS Paloma*, which includes five independent rooms that are connected to one another via a central area. These rooms include the Alien Database, Probe Design Center, Probe Launch Center, Mission Control Center, and Communication Center, and each room provides access to a specific scientific tool. Additionally, a simulated augmented reality interface presents students with a toolbar that can be used to access persistent tools (e.g. Solar System Database, Concept Database, Notebook etc; see Figure 2) while navigating the space station. These tools are available for information gathering, data recording and analysis, experimentation, and reporting (See Figures 2 & 3) and are designed to support complex thinking and problem solving processes. A brief description of each major tool follows:

- The Alien Database provides information on the six alien species, their journey to our solar system, and their home planets.
- The Solar System Database provides students with information on the solar system and features high quality images and meaningfully designed hypertexts. Selected planets and their moons are presented with relevant images and text.

Figure 2. Screenshots of various tools provided in Alien Rescue to support the process of scientific inquiry

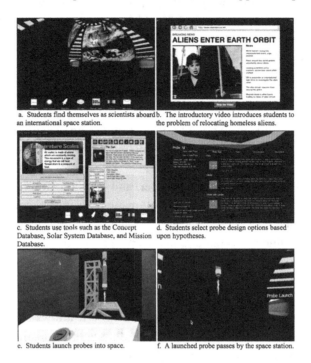

a. Students find themselves as scientists aboard an international space station.

b. The introductory video introduces students to the problem of relocating homeless aliens.

c. Students use tools such as the Concept Database, Solar System Database, and Mission Database.

d. Students select probe design options based upon hypotheses.

e. Students launch probes into space.

f. A launched probe passes by the space station.

Figure 3. Screenshots of some tools, including the Alien Database, Probe Launch Center, and Communication Center

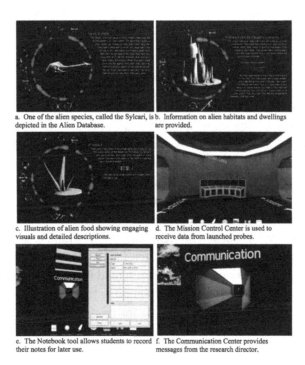

a. One of the alien species, called the Sylcari, is depicted in the Alien Database.

b. Information on alien habitats and dwellings are provided.

c. Illustration of alien food showing engaging visuals and detailed descriptions.

d. The Mission Control Center is used to receive data from launched probes.

e. The Notebook tool allows students to record their notes for later use.

f. The Communication Center provides messages from the research director.

- The Mission Database provides information on past space missions, helping students understand processes of research in space science and providing exemplars of possible probe designs.
- The Concept Database provides just-in-time instruction on a variety of scientific concepts, such as gravity, temperature, and atmosphere, and is available to help students address knowledge gaps as they are encountered within the simulation. Each concept is presented in an interactive format that supports the acquisition of conceptual knowledge through animations, simulation, and informal knowledge checks.
- A Notebook tool allows students to record information during the simulation, subsequently reducing the cognitive load required to manage information while mirroring the tools and processes of practicing scientists.
- The Probe Design Center, Probe Launch Center, and Mission Control Center allow students to build, launch, and receive data from probes. Following their investigation of the solar system and the habitat requirements of the aliens and the formation of initial hypotheses around appropriate solutions, students are able to design and launch probes to gather additional information from a specific planet or moon. Their work in this phase can be used to confirm or disconfirm hypotheses or help address information gaps in order to further inform the students' work.

The Probe Design Center is of particular interest, because it allows students to design their own probes by selecting a probe type and equipping it with the scientific instrumentation required to test a given hypothesis. The process of designing and launching probes simulates the actual process of scientific investigation in space science, and a budget system simulates a real-world constraint that requires students to be strategic in the configuration of their probes. An incorrectly designed probe can malfunction, thus wasting crucial funds. As a gamification element, the Probe Design Center aims to help students identify efficient methods of scientific investigation and recognize realistic constraints that impact scientific inquiry. After designing a probe, students have the opportunity to launch it from within the Probe Launch Center, a process that includes a simulated rocket launch. Data from each probe are available from the Mission Control Center and are presented using a variety of images. Invalid probe configurations and randomization result in error messages, further supporting the authenticity of the simulation and encouraging students to refine their approach to designing probes.

Apart from these authentic design elements built in the simulation, equally important are the built-in fantasy components to provide an imaginative narrative of the simulation in order to maximize the authenticity of the learning experience such as the story of the distressed aliens, the shifts in public opinion, the urgency of the situation, and the fantasy of saving alien species. More specifically, the playful learning experience is stimulated through fantasy components in the tool called Alien Database, which provides a rich source of information about the home planets of aliens, their journey, characteristics, appearance and habitat requirements through fantastic 3D graphics and text. The 3D models and artifacts were designed by the principles of educational fantasy (Lee, 2015; Kim, 2009; see Figure 3). Although the alien narratives are fictional, they are presented in a realistic way to promote the fantasy of the simulation, thereby encouraging students to respond to the aliens with empathy and emotion. To solve the central problem (i.e. finding a suitable home for an alien species), conducting research in the Alien Database and understanding essential components for the survival of the alien species are important steps in order to perform further scientific investigation and use other tools such as Probe Design and Probe Launch Centers.

PREVIOUS RESEARCH

As designers and developers of this ludic simulation, we are interested in determining if its use has an impact on student learning. Two recent research studies investigating this topic were conducted (Kimmons et al., 2012; Liu et al., 2011).

In the first study, we examined the effects of AR on learning and the relationship between learning and motivation (Liu et al., 2011) among sixth graders ($n = 220$). ANOVA results indicated significant increases in students' scientific knowledge following use of the simulation, as measured by a domain-specific science knowledge test. This finding was supported qualitatively through student responses to open-ended questions in which they described specific concepts learned. In investigating the relationship between learning and motivation, the study found a significant positive correlation between student knowledge scores and overall motivation. Of particular importance to this current study, qualitative analysis of student open-ended responses indicated significant use of the word "fun" as a descriptor of the simulation.

In the second study, we further examined the relationship between learning and attitudes (Kimmons et al., 2012) among participating sixth graders ($n = 478$). Results using ANOVAs and regression analyses showed that use of the simulation had a significant effect on student achievement, female students averaged higher science knowledge gain scores than male students, and students with a better attitude toward the simulation had a significantly higher post-test achievement score. Qualitative analyses supported these findings.

Findings from our previous research have indicated that sixth graders' science knowledge improved after using the simulation and students with more positive attitudes toward the simulation had higher achievement scores. Both studies employed a mixed-methods design, using both quantitative and qualitative data. When students were asked to respond to open-ended questions such as "How would you describe *Alien Rescue* to a friend?" or "What do you think of *Alien Rescue*?," responses included ludic explanations like the following: "freaking awesome!!!" "soooooooooooooooooooooooooooooo FUN!!!!!!!!!!!!!!!!!" Throughout these studies, students often referred to this ludic simulation as a game and expressed that it was fun to use.

This leads us to consider the following: What aspects of AR do students consider to be fun and why? The current study continued this line of inquiry and built upon our previous research by further examining the ludic aspect of the simulation from two perspectives. First, we asked participating sixth graders from two schools (in different school districts) to provide their thoughts on the simulation. In the first study described above, our participants were from 'regular education' (RegEd) classes, and in the second study, participants included talented and gifted (TAG), RegEd, and students with limited English proficiency or learning disabilities. In this follow-up study, we again included sixth graders from all ability groups in the analysis, because we wanted to further investigate sixth graders' experiences using the simulation. Second, we surveyed a group of seventh graders from four schools (different from the two sixth-grade participating schools), who had used the simulation in the previous year, in an attempt to find out how they compared their use of AR to other science activities they had experienced. Our rationale was that if the students truly enjoyed the simulation, then they probably would remember it one year later and that the experience of these participants should allow us to further investigate the topic. To direct our inquiry, we asked the following research questions:

- What do middle school students think of Alien Rescue as a tool to learn science?
- Is AR fun for them to use it? If so, in what way? If not, why not?
- What features do middle school students consider fun?

METHOD

In this section, we will explain the methods used for collecting and analyzing data related to the ludic simulation under investigation. We will begin by exploring the participants, setting, and data sources utilized and then proceed to a discussion of our analysis techniques.

Participants, Setting, and Data Sources

Six Graders

Sixth graders ($n = 383$) from two public middle schools in a mid-sized southwestern city in the United States participated in this follow-up study (see their demographic information in Figures 4 and 5). These sixth graders used AR as their curriculum for space science in place of regular textbooks for three weeks in their daily 50-minute science classes. Each student had his or her own computer for use but also worked in a small group, which is a recommended instructional strategy for implementing AR. After they completed AR, students were asked to respond to the following open-ended questions:

Figure 4. Demographics of two six-grade participating schools: Ethnic grouping breakdown

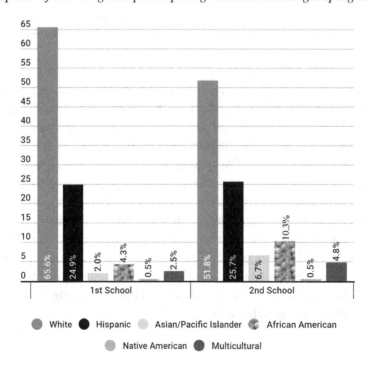

Figure 5. Demographics of two six-grade participating schools: % of economically disadvantaged/at-risk/limited English proficiency)

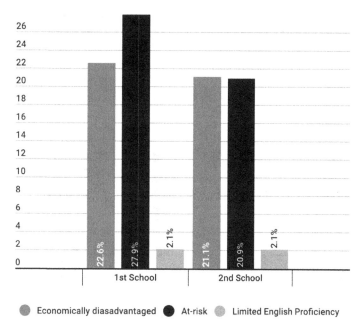

1. How would you describe Alien Rescue to a friend? Or what do you think of Alien Rescue?
2. What did you learn from Alien Rescue?
3. What did you like about Alien Rescue? Or what is your favorite part of Alien Rescue? Why?
4. What did you dislike about Alien Rescue? What is your least favorite part of Alien Rescue? Why?

Seventh Graders

Seventh graders ($n = 447$) from four different public schools (see demographic information in Figure 6) were given a survey one year after they used AR. Survey questions included: "Of all the activities you have done in science since 6th grade, what would you like to have a chance to do again?," "Do you remember *Alien Rescue*?" and "List 3 or more things you remember about *Alien Rescue*." Several Likert scale questions were also utilized and will be presented below.

Analysis

Students' responses were first cleaned, removing meaningless words or sentences and empty responses, leaving a total of 358 responses from sixth graders (female=46%; male =53%) and 439 from seventh graders (female=53.7%; male =46.3%). Not all students responded to all questions and the n in each table below reflects the actual response rate for each question. To analyze the open-ended responses, we followed the constant comparative method of analysis practice (Lincoln & Guba, 1985; Strauss & Corbin, 1990). In examining sixth graders' responses to the first question, our intent was to learn how the students described their experience in using the simulation. Before creating a frequency count of the words the students used, we removed words such as "to," "the," "a," "an," "that," and "and" to increase

Figure 6. Demographics of four seventh-grade participating schools

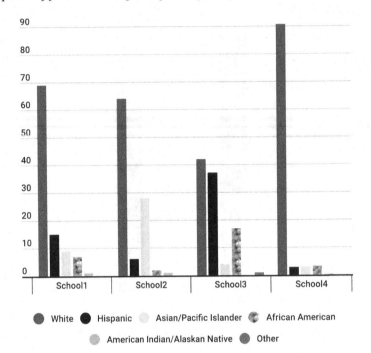

the prominence of relevant adjectives, nouns, and verbs. The reference to the program name, *"Alien Rescue"* or "program" or "I think" as the start of the sentence were also removed. Typos were eliminated or replaced with correct spelling, and variations and misspelled words, such as alieb/alien/aliens, gets/ got/get, and probes/probe, were combined. For example, in this statement "I think alien rescue was a lot of fun. I learned a lot. And I got to help aliens," "I think," "alien rescue," "was," and "a" were removed. After the data were cleaned, a word cloud was generated using wordle.net from students' responses to question one, which was produced by coupling word frequency with font size (the bigger the font size, the higher the frequency).

Sixth graders' responses for questions two to four were read and chunked from a line-by-line analysis of the data. Relevant information was extracted through a systematic and iterative examination of the raw data. These extracted units were coded to describe what the students said about their experience through "focused coding" (Charmaz, 2006). As the codes were compared with each other, similar codes were combined, different ones were separated, and various categories emerged at the next level (Creswell, 2005). Such analyses continued until an "emergence of regularities" (Lincoln & Guba, 1985) was reached. We then examined and re-examined the codes, categories, and emergent themes in light of our research questions. Two researchers were involved in the process of coding, checking, and verifying the codes, categories, and themes until 100% inter-rater reliability was reached on their interpretations.

The quantitative data in the seventh graders' responses of the survey questions were analyzed descriptively. Their responses to the open-ended questions were analyzed following the same practice as described above.

FINDINGS

Sixth Graders' Responses

For the question: "How would you describe *Alien Rescue* to a friend?" Or "What do you think of *Alien Rescue*?," a total of 1,072 words were extracted out of the 358 statements. Words used by the students to describe their experience included: fun, learn, solar-system, aliens, find, helpful, home, information, interesting, probe, game, computer, and so on (see Table 1). The word "fun" has the highest frequency.

We then further examined 183 statements in which the word "fun" is positively used. Students' responses ranged from simple answers such as "fun" and "very fun" to more elaborate statements such as "it was really FUN and could help a lot of people! especially for the people who would like to go to space someday," "it is very FUN. it help[ed] you learn. i want to do it again," "i think was really FUN and enjoyable. i think was a good source to learn more about space." Reasons cited by the students ranged from more generic statements such as "a FUN way to learn," "it was very very FUN!!!!!!!!!!!," to more specific statements indicating the aspects of the program they considered fun. For example, students stated, "I think was very FUN and interesting. It was cool to see the alien and launch probe and get to learn about planet," "Its FUN. You can work with a group. Its a problem solving game," "It was FUN to do because you get to figure out what alien which to what planet and their needs," and "A FUN activity that get you to enjoy science and not just read out of the textbook. You get to help aliens find home in our solar system. But you also learn A LOT!!!" Table 2 provides the main reasons students considered AR to be a fun experience.

So what have students learned from using AR? Out of a total 515 coding units, approximately 51% of the responses were related to learning knowledge about our solar system (the planets, moons, and their characteristics) and about 16% were about learning the scientific instruments (creating and launching

Table 1. Word Cloud of students' responses to "How would you describe Alien Rescue to a friend?" Or "What do you think of Alien Rescue?"

Word Cloud		Word	Frequency (%)
		fun	183 (17%)
		learn	108 (10%)
		solar-system	93 (8.7%)
		aliens	74 (6.9%)
		find	46 (4.3%)
		helpful	41 (3.8%)
		home	38 (2.7%)
		information	30 (2.5%)
		interesting	29 (2.7%)
		probe	27 (2.5%)
		game	24 (2.2%)
		computer	20 (1.9%)

Note. Word count below 20 is not listed.

Table 2. Main reasons revealed in student statements in which the word 'fun" was used positively

Why Students Considered Fun	Sample Quotes
a fun way to learn about solar system, space science, science	i think it is FUN. and that it is a good learn[ing] activity. that it was cool to learn about alien, planet and moon. It is FUN an. It is a perfect way to learn. it is the best way to learn about the solar-system
An educational or a learning experience	I would describe as FUN. It can help you learn and has surprises on the way. I would say while most of it was awesome, I would describe alien [rescue] to a friend to be really FUN. It is informational and valuable to a student's education. I would also say that it is creative.
a game	[It] was a FUN learn experience. The type of game like this should be more widely used among school districts. This was a healthy way for kids to learn about the planet. A FUN computer game that you go around to different plants try to find home for alien in our solar-system.
Learn to collaborate, work in groups	its FUN and help us learn. teaches teamwork. super FUN. I think that it was FUN because we had partners that we chose on our own and it was very delightful to be on the computers with a person we trust and know and we could communicate. Except i would like to do it more often.
Get to help aliens, learn about aliens, design/launch probes	i think [it] was FUN because we could buy things. because we could roam around the space station and see what the space station looks like. finally i think was FUN because we could send probe around the galaxy and see what the world look like. I think that [it] is very educational and is cool how you get to help alien. I like when you get you send probe to moon and planet. I think alien rescue was FUN over all.
Fun but challenging	its FUN learning about different planet and i love a challenge and this was a big one FUN and challenging, a worthwhile goal
Problem solving, scientific process	it is a FUN activity that lets you interact and make your own probe. It is also educational because you can learn about different planet. You also have a budget, just like in real life. [It] is a FUN way to study planet. It also can tell you a lot of information about planet. You also get to learn about alien and figure out where each alien goes.
Feel good, want to do again	I think that was a very FUN interesting thing to do. It was one of my favorite projects all year. I hope to do something like this again this year. It was very nice. it was enjoyable and i think i did a good job. it was FUN.

probes and various instruments needed for each type of probe). Other concepts or processes students stated they had learned include alien species (8%), scientific concepts such as magnetic fields, gravity and temperature scales (7%), problem solving (4%), conducting research (4%), managing a budget (2%), and working with others (2%). "Nothing" comprised about 4% of the responses. Below are a few sample statements:

- I learned many different facts about the moons and planets in our solar system that I haven't known before, and some were quite interesting. I enjoy learning about outer space, therefore I thought that Alien Rescue was a neat game that could help us learn about the solar system. (Student 1).
- I learned mostly about magnetic fields, gravity, elements and the solar system. I also learned how the different instruments work for probes. (Student 2).
- From alien Rescue how to really research and find information using tools and problem solving hard questions. (Student 3).

Of various aspects the students liked the most, the top five were probe-related (33.84%), alien-related (22.28%), exploring the 3D environment (9.86%), learning about the solar system (9.52%), and problem solving or doing research (8.67%). Other aspects the students liked included: working with peers and managing the budget. 2% of the responses indicated that they did not like anything (see Table 3).

In answering "I wish there were more activities like *Alien Rescue* and why?" 38% ($n = 149$) of the students responded "strongly agree," 19.6% ($n = 77$) responded "agree," 15.1% ($n = 59$) responded "somewhat," 9.9% ($n = 39$) responded "disagree," and 17.3% ($n = 68$) responded "strongly disagree." We further examined those responses of strongly agree and strongly disagree to understand students' rationale. The reasons the students strongly agreed included because it was "fun," "cool, entertaining or

Table 3. Student responses to "What did you like about Alien Rescue?" Or "What is your favorite part of Alien Rescue?"

Category	%	Sample Quotes
Probes related	33.84%	Launching probes because we got design our own probe and try to see if our ideas would work. My favorite part was probe launching. I loved how the probes would send back info so quickly. It really boggles my mind how a probe could go off so quickly and give back so much information!!!!!!!!!!!!!!!!!!
Aliens related	22.28%	My favorite parts were learning about the aliens. They have very different needs than humans. I also liked the time when you sent the aliens to the specific planet. Getting to learn about the aliens because I liked to look at the different pictures that the alien had. That included the habitat and the food.:)
Exploring 3D environment	9.86%	Exploring Paloma. It was cool to see all the different rooms. Also looking at the aliens.... Great job an designer(s) part!! It was a cool 3D environment, and I enjoyed exploring it. The Pictures because they actually showed what they look like. I also liked how you got to see the probe go into space.
Learning about Solar system	9.52%	I thought being able to look at all the planets gave me a new view on them. When we did research on the planets. Because we learned a lot of new things.
Problem solving/Research	8.67%	Figuring out what type of aliens some planets have and what they do, and what they eat and breath to live on that planet. My favorite part was doing the research. I liked this best because it gave me an opportunity to learn about different worlds and moons.
Working in groups	3.06%	I love Alien Rescue because we got to work with friends and think on our own about how to get answers versus reading in a textbook to get answers. Working with collaborations because it would have been difficult if we were working alone.
Managing budget	2.04%	That there is a budget. Also that you get to send probes into space. I liked these because it gives people challenges. Our favorite part of Alien rescue was building the probes. Because you can tell how much money is an average probe.
Game	2.04%	It is fun and creative. I like it because no one never wants to play a game that's boring and just learn from it. It was a very kid-like gaming world, which made me feel free to do whatever I needed to win the game. This game is very fun and I liked being able to learn about the world we live in. It's very entertaining.
Other (including a sense of accomplishment, multimedia features, computer-based etc.)	6.63%	Getting to the end because I felt happy and confident. It gave me a reason to be happy with myself. The reason is because at first I did not understand what to do. The video the aliens sent. Because everybody thought it was real. I enjoyed how they added extra stuff like a note pad, the table of elements and other tools because it was very useful.
Nothing	2.04%	Nothing

Note. Total units= 588.

interactive," "educational or learning about solar system or problem solving," and "using computers." The reasons the students strongly disagreed included because it was "boring or not fun," "[activity] took too long," "confusing," "not helpful or educational." Below are a few sample responses:

- In alien Rescue you got to play a game that helped you with science. (Positive response).
- Because we get to move around and figure things out. It's also like a puzzle. (Positive response).
- Because we learned things while we were having fun playing games. (Positive response).
- Well because it wasn't fun and it was a lot of work. (Negative response).
- Because it was confusing and i didn't like it. (Negative response).

Seventh graders were also asked to list 3 or more things they remembered about AR. Of a total of 888 coding units, what the students remembered the most are various aspects about helping aliens (30%), designing and launching probes (14%), learning about planets in our solar system (14%), exploring the 3D space station (8%), and doing research (5%). Other items students mentioned they remembered include: managing time and a budget, a challenging/difficult project, various multimedia features (i.e. graphics, video), working in groups, and nothing (2%).

DISCUSSION AND IMPLICATIONS

The Role of Fun in Learning

With multiple data sources, it is clear that the sixth graders generally considered their use of AR to be a fun experience. The word "fun" has the highest frequency in their responses to an open-ended question as shown in the word cloud in Table 1. Seventh graders' responses confirmed this finding in that over 50% of the seventh graders rated their experience as a 4 or 5 (toward the positive end) on several Likert scale questions asking if using the ludic simulation was fun or enjoyable (see Figures 7 and 8 and Table 4). This finding is consistent with our previous studies (Kimmons, et al., 2012; Liu, et al., 2011) and supports the idea of gamified processes as described by Fuchs (2012) and the manner through which ludic simulations support a sense of playfulness, as suggested by Ortoleva (2012).

Both sixth- and seventh-graders indicated that they learned both the content (i.e. our solar system, various science concepts and scientific instruments) and thinking skills such as problem solving and researching. Students also learned about working in groups, managing a budget, and how to engage in problem solving. One student responded that AR "taught us useful skills such as time management, working in a group, computer skills, working independently too." Our qualitative data analysis supports previous quantitative findings on the positive relationship between use of the ludic simulation and student learning. The finding that students had fun while learning supports the literature emphasizing the value of play and playfulness (Barab et al., 2005; Garris, Ahlers, & Driskell, 2002; Rieber, 1996; Squire, 2003), and illustrates the possibility of creating playful and fun interactions for purposeful and intentional contexts such as school learning. That is, our findings support the idea that games can be contexts in which significant learning can occur, as suggested by Gee (2003).

Many students expressed their desire to use AR again: "It was FUN. You should do this every 6 weeks! Thanks!," and "It did teach me a lot of things I did not know! I would probably LOVE to do it

Figure 7. 7ᵗʰ Graders' Responses on the question about "Compared to other Science activities you have done since 6th grade, Alien Rescue was fun"

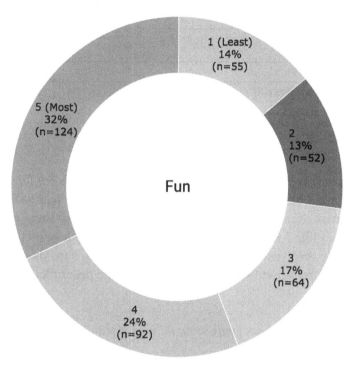

Figure 8. 7ᵗʰ Graders' Responses on the question about "Compared to other Science activities you have done since 6th grade, Alien Rescue was interesting"

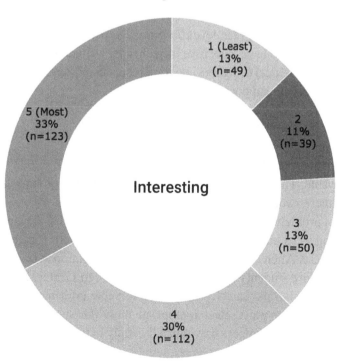

Table 4. Seventh graders' responses to several Likert scale questions

	Very True (5)	(4)	(3)	(2)	Not True at All (1)
I enjoyed doing Alien Rescue very much.	28.1% (n=110)	22.2% (n =87)	22.2% (n =87)	12% (n =47)	15.6% (n =61)
Alien Rescue was fun to do.	34.5% (n =135)	20.7% (n =81)	17.9% (n =70)	12.3% (n =48)	14.6% (n =57)
I would describe Alien Rescue as very interesting.	27.9% (n =109)	23.3% (n =91)	20.3% (n =79)	11% (n =43)	17.4% (n =68)
Alien Rescue was enjoyable.	30.5% (n=117)	21.9% (n=84)	19% (n=73)	10.2% (n=39)	18.5% (n=71)

again." Without indicating project or activity names, AR was the top choice for seventh graders across all the activities completed within their sixth grade science course. One year later, over 90% of students remembered the simulation. Nearly 60% of the seventh graders agreed or strongly agreed that they wish there were more activities like AR. Such findings provided a clear indication that these middle school students would like to use this type of program in the future. Perhaps the most encouraging finding is that that some students expressed self-confidence and motivation toward learning science as shown in such statements as:

It was FUN. I learn a lot and now I am going to do this [be a scientist] when I get older.

I did very well and I see that I am good at space science.

Ample research has shown that motivation and self-efficacy play important roles in influencing learning and achievement (Ames, 1990; Bandura, 1986, 1997; Lane & Lane, 2001; Lepper, Iyengar, & Corpus, 2005; Schunk, 1995). However, research has also shown a general reduction in students' interest in science beginning at the sixth grade level (Osborne, Simon, & Collins, 2003). Our finding that students' use of AR was shown to have a positive influence on attitude towards science should provide an additional impetus for educational designers and researchers to explore, design, and research technology enriched ludic simulations to support learning.

Attributes of a Fun Experience

Of particular interest to this study are those aspects of the ludic simulation that middle school students considered fun or enjoyable. The findings centered on two aspects (i.e. probe-related and alien-related) and features related to these two.

In solving the central problem of finding relocation sites for the aliens, the students must engage in a series of problem-solving steps including gathering information from the databases (e.g. Solar System Database, Mission Database, Alien Database). However, the information in those databases is intentionally incomplete and therefore students must use the Probe Design Center, Probe Launch Center, and Mission Control Center to design and launch probes to gather more information and test their hypothesis. In designing each probe, students must select appropriate tools. These probe related tools simulate the tools scientists use and the inquiry process they typically apply in their work. Students are given opportunities to experiment and establish for themselves a suitable problem-solving path. The design intention of AR is to provide an authentic learning context where students can apply various thinking skills to find a solution. Students' responses related to the probe tools specifically demonstrated the importance of realism and the role of being a scientist:

Making probes were fun. I felt like an astronaut!

Sending probes was cool, because you got to pick what probe you wanted to send and all the stuff for it. You kind got the feeling of being one of those people that work for NASA and other places.

This sense of realism is a significant motivating factor for these young scientists.

While the probe related tools were designed to provide a sense of fidelity and realism, the design of Alien Database is intended to create a sense of imagination and fantasy. The essential information about the aliens (i.e. their body, food, habitat, communication symbols, and their home planets) is presented through rich, colorful, and interactive 3D. Each species has its own distinct look and feel. The results suggest that this visual and playful interface elicits a strong sense of fantasy among these students aged 11-13; the aliens are one of the top features students liked about AR. In addition, the fantasy element is also embedded in the narrative of the simulation as presented by the introductory video. This approach of blending more realistic representation with fictional and imaginative elements apparently prompted strong empathy from this age group, a finding consistent with Squire's (2003) belief that games can evoke strong emotional responses in the player. Among those features that students indicated as their favorites (see Table 3), 22.28% are alien related, the second highest. Of this category, 42% are about helping or saving aliens, as shown in sample quotes:

Finding homes for the aliens, because when you find one you just feel so excited.

Sending an alien to their planet because it just makes you feel good to know that you worked hard for that moment.

In addition, the narrative of the young scientists tasked with saving the aliens is situated in an open-ended problem-based context where there are multiple built-in challenges. Once the students are presented with the central problem, there are no instructions within the simulation that direct their work. Students are encouraged to explore and discover in a self-directed way while negotiating one of many possible solution paths. There are also six different species, each of which can have more than one solution. Some habitats are more optimal than others, requiring students to weigh a diverse range of possibilities and develop well-articulated justifications. Additionally, the budgetary constrains present in designing and launching probes prompt students to make careful decisions so as not to be wasteful. While this problem-solving process is challenging, it represents an authentic level of real-world complexity and provides another motivational element that promotes joy and self-confidence in these students: "It was very FUN and help me learn more about science. Thank you for making this. I love it so much.:)"

In addition, working in groups is shown to be a feature many students liked. Group work encourages collaboration within and between the groups, as well as competition, a feature the students considered entertaining and enjoyable.

The findings validate the design of the simulation and highlight several attributes that made AR a fun learning experience for these middle school students: exploratory, interactive, immersive, playful, media-rich, roleplay, engaging narrative, and a challenging problem scenario. Addressing the three factors in Lindley's tetrahedron (2003), AR places equal importance on simulation and ludology and delivers a playful experience in an intentional problem-based narrative. With these attributes, it is also necessary to point out designs of technology enhanced environments must be solidly grounded in learning principles and designed with social responsibilities.

Students' responses also indicated three aspects that they did not like: they perceived it as too difficult, wanted to see more interactive features, and experienced some technical glitches. As discussed above, this problem-based ludic simulation presents a complex problem over a period of 15 days. For some sixth graders, this self-directed approach is difficult and time-consuming, highlighting the need to implement additional technology-based scaffolds to support students in acquiring the expertise necessary to fully engage with the problem.

Summary and Implications for Policy, Research, and Practice

In summary, the findings of this study confirmed our previous research and provided further evidence to show that sixth- and seventh-graders perceived AR as having substantial ludic characteristics and educational value. The results indicated that having a playful experience is important for this age group and that participating in a ludic simulation can help motivate students to learn school subjects. Results also indicated that incorporating *ludus* into the learning experience can improve students' attitudes toward the subject matter, which is a valuable finding for STEM-related fields in particular, due to current low interest and poor performance in these fields in the US.

Given the results of our research on the potential impact of ludic simulations in supporting classroom-based learning, there are a number of issues to consider related to policy, research, and practice. In particular, we are interested in exploring potential pathways for further conceptualizing ludic simulations as a legitimate form of instructional practice, better understanding how students learn through ludic learning experiences, and supporting the development of new pedagogies that guide the use of ludic simulations in teaching and learning.

School policies governing the availability of technology resources, access to technology support, curricular alignment, and the use of game-like learning environments within classroom all converge to influence the extent and manner in which ludic simulations are diffused into educational contexts. Ongoing research is essential in evaluating the efficacy of ludic simulations to advance learning within and across multiple disciplines, promoting increased interest and adoption of these simulations within schools, and facilitating necessary shifts in policy that acknowledge the role of ludic simulations in supporting curricular objectives and help ensure student access to these learning environments.

Our research further highlights the need for more research on the use of ludic simulations, particularly as they relate to more established areas of instructional practice, including their role in supporting inquiry and problem-based learning and their effectiveness in facilitating productive collaborative learning experiences among students. Further research on instructional design methodologies related to the design and development of ludic simulations will promote development of strategies to support students in achieving learning outcomes through play. Our research revealed several attributes are of critical importance in designing ludic simulations for middle school students. Just as the name denotes, ludic simulations rely upon a blend of reality and fantasy, and fun in Alien Rescue was achieved by striking a balance between the fidelity of a realistic simulation and the fantasy of imaginative narratives and interactions. Future research into ludic simulations should continue to seek to understand this balance and how to optimally support learning and engagement through effective juxtaposition of realism and fantasy via game mechanics, narrative, and other game elements. Our research has also shown that making the ludic simulation too complex can lead to student confusion and frustration, so future research should also seek to identify appropriate levels of game complexity for different groups of learners. In addition, the creation of robust assessment and evaluation methodologies around ludic simulations will allow researchers and practitioners alike to evaluate student success within these learning environments and understand the specific ways through which ludic simulations can support learning.

Finally, additional research is required in order to identify the types of instructional strategies and methods that will enable teachers to facilitate student learning within game-like learning environments. Our work borrows significantly from research on constructivist learning environments and the application of instructional approaches -- such as problem-based learning -- that historically have not explicitly considered the ludic characteristics of student learning experiences. While the existing body of research undoubtedly provides a substantial basis for the design and application of ludic simulations, there also exists a space for new pedagogies and strategies to be developed that guide the effective application of these simulations.

REFERENCES

Ames, C. A. (1990). Motivation: What teachers need to know. *Teachers College Record*, *90*(3), 409–421.

Angehrn, A. A. (2006). L2C: Designing simulation-based learning experiences for collaboration competencies development. Association for Learning Technology, 31.

App Store [computer software]. Cupertino, CA: Apple, Inc.

Bandura, A. (1986). *Social foundations of thought and action: A social cognitive theory*. Englewood Cliffs, NJ: Prentice-Hall.

Bandura, A. (1997). *Self-efficacy: The exercise of control*. New York: W.H. Freeman.

Barab, S., Thomas, M., Dodge, T., Carteaux, R., & Tuzun, H. (2005). Making learning fun: Quest Atlantis, a game without guns. *Educational Technology Research and Development*, *53*(1), 86–107. doi:10.1007/BF02504859

Barab, S. A., Pettyjohn, P., Gresalfi, M., Volk, C., & Solomou, M. (2012). Game-based curriculum and transformational play: Designing to meaningfully positioning person, content, and context. *Computers & Education*, *58*(1), 518–533. doi:10.1016/j.compedu.2011.08.001

Charmaz, K. (2006). *Constructing Grounded Theory: A Practical Guide through Qualitative Analysis*. Thousand Oaks, NJ: Sage Publications.

Civilization [computer software]. Alameda, CA: MicroProse.

Clarke, J., Dede, C., Ketelhut, D. J., & Nelson, B. (2006). A design-based research strategy to promote scalability for educational innovations. *Educational Technology*, *46*(3), 27–36.

Creswell, J. W. (2005). *Educational Research: planning, conducting, and evaluating quantitative and qualitative research* (2nd ed.). Merrill.

Csikszentmihalyi, M., & Bennett, S. (1971). An exploratory model of play. *American Anthropologist, 73*(1), 45–58. doi:10.1525/aa.1971.73.1.02a00040

DeNeve, K. M., & Heppner, M. J. (1997). Role play simulations: The assessment of an active learning technique and comparisons with traditional lectures. *Innovative Higher Education, 21*(3), 231–246. doi:10.1007/BF01243718

Flight Sim X [computer software]. Redmond, WA: Microsoft Corporation.

Fuchs, M. (2012). Ludic interfaces. Driver and product of gamification. *GAME*. Retrieved July 12, 2012, from http://www.gamejournal.it/ludic-interfaces-driver-and-product-of-gamification/

Fuchs, M., & Strouhal, E. (2008). *Games. Kunst und Politik der Spiele*. Wien, Austria: Sonderzahl Verlag.

Garris, R., Ahlers, R., & Driskell, J. E. (2002). Games, motivation, and learning: A research and practice model. *Simulation & Gaming, 33*(4), 441–467. doi:10.1177/1046878102238607

Garry's Mod [computer software]. Walsall, UK: Facepunch Studios LTD.

Gee, J. P. (2003). What video games have to teach us about learning and literacy. *Computers in Entertainment, 1*(1), 20–20. doi:10.1145/950566.950595

Grand Theft Auto IV [computer software]. New York: Rockstar Games.

Ivan, T. (2009). NPD: 26 Percent Of Kids Own A Game Console. *EDGE*. Retrieved from http://www.edge-online.com/news/npd-26-percent-kids-own-game-console

Ketelhut, D. J. (2007). The impact of student self-efficacy on scientific inquiry skills: An exploratory investigation in River City, a multi-user virtual environment. *Journal of Science Education and Technology, 16*(1), 99–111. doi:10.1007/s10956-006-9038-y

Ketelhut, D. J., Dede, C., Clarke, J., Nelson, B., & Bowman, C. (2007). Studying situated learning in a multi-user virtual environment. In R. E. Mayer (Ed.), *Assessment of problem solving using simulations* (pp. 37–58). Mahwah, NJ: Lawrence Erlbaum Associates.

Kim, I. (2009). *A Study on the Factors and the Principles of the Fantasy in the Educational Context* (Doctoral Dissertation). Seoul National University.

Kimmons, R., Liu, M., Kang, J., & Santana, L. (2012). Attitude, Achievement, and Gender in a Middle School Science-based Ludic Simulation for Learning. *Journal of Educational Technology Systems, 40*(4), 341–370. doi:10.2190/ET.40.4.b

Lane, J., & Lane, A. (2001). Self-efficacy and academic performance. *Social Behavior and Personality, 29*(7), 687–694. doi:10.2224/sbp.2001.29.7.687

Lepper, M. R., Iyengar, S. S., & Corpus, J. H. (2005). Intrinsic and extrinsic motivational orientations in the classroom: Age differences and academic correlates. *Journal of Educational Psychology, 97*(2), 184–196. doi:10.1037/0022-0663.97.2.184

Lincoln, Y. S., & Guba, E. D. (1985). *Naturalistic Inquiry*. Thousand Oaks, CA: Sage Publications, Inc.

Lindley. (2003). *Game taxonomies: A high level framework for game analysis and design*. Retrieved June 18, 2012, from http://www.gamasutra.com/view/feature/2796/game_taxonomies_a_high_level_.php

Linser, R., Ree-Lindstad, N., & Vold, T. (2007). *Black Blizzard: Designing role-play simulations for education*. Retrieved from http://www.eric.ed.gov/ERICWebPortal/contentdelivery/servlet/ERICServlet?accno=ED500156

Liu, M., Horton, L., Lee, J., Kang, J., Rosenblum, J., O'Hair, M., & Lu, C. W. (2014). *Creating a Multimedia Enhanced Problem-Based Learning Environment for Middle School Science: Voices from the Developers. Interdisciplinary Journal of Problem-Based Learning, 8(1)*. doi:10.7771/1541-5015.1422

Liu, M., Horton, L., Olmanson, J., & Toprac, P. (2011). A study of learning and motivation in a new media enriched environment for middle school science. *Educational Technology Research and Development, 59*(2), 249–265. doi:10.1007/s11423-011-9192-7

McGonigal, J. (2011). *Reality is broken: Why games make us better and how they can change the world*. Penguin Press HC.

Nelson, B. (2007). Exploring the use of individualized, reflective guidance in an educational multi-user virtual environment. *Journal of Science Education and Technology, 16*(1), 83–97. doi:10.1007/s10956-006-9039-x

Nelson, B., Ketelhut, D. J., Clarke, J., Bowman, C., & Dede, C. (2005). Design-based research strategies for developing a scientific inquiry curriculum in a multi-user virtual environment. *Educational Technology, 45*(1), 21–27.

Ortoleva, P. (2012). Homo ludicus. The ubiquity of play and its roles in present society. *GAME*. Retrieved from http://www.gamejournal.it/homo-ludicus-the-ubiquity-and-roles-of-play-in-present-society/

Osborne, J., Simon, S., & Collins, S. (2003). Attitudes towards science: A review of the literature and its implication. *International Journal of Science Education, 25*(9), 1049–1079. doi:10.1080/0950069032000032199

Piaget, J. (1951). *Play, dreams, and imitation in childhood*. New York: W. W. Norton & Company.

Raessens, J. (2006). Playful identities, or the ludification of culture. *Games and Culture, 1*(1), 52–57. doi:10.1177/1555412005281779

Rideout, V. J., Foehr, U. G., & Roberts, D. F. (2010). *Generation M2: Media in the lives of 8- to 18-year-olds*. Kaiser Family Foundation. Retrieved from http://www.kff.org/ entmedia/upload/8010.pdf

Rieber, L. P. (1996). Seriously considering play: Designing interactive learning environments based on the blending of microworlds, simulations, and games. *Educational Technology Research and Development, 44*(2), 43–58. doi:10.1007/BF02300540

Roberts, N. (1976). *Simulation gaming: A critical review*. Retrieved July 12, 2012, from http://www.eric.ed.gov/ERICWebPortal/contentdelivery/servlet/ERICServlet?accno=ED137165

Schunk, D. H. (1995). Self-efficacy and education and instruction. In J. E. Maddux (Ed.), *Theory, research, and application* (pp. 281–303). New York: Plenum Press.

Singer, D. G., Golinkoff, R. M., & Hirsh-Pasek, K. (2006). *Play = learning: How play motivates and enhances children's cognitive and social-emotional growth* (1st ed.). Oxford University Press. doi:10.1093/acprof:oso/9780195304381.001.0001

Squire, K. (2003). Video games in education. *International Journal of Intelligent Games & Simulation*, *2*(1), 49–62.

Steam [computer software]. Bellvue, WA: Valve Corporation. Retrieved from http://store.steampowered.com

Strauss, A., & Corbin, J. (1990). *Basics of qualitative research: Grounded theory procedures and techniques*. Thousand Oaks, CA: Sage Publications.

Vygotsky, L. S. (1978). *Mind and Society: The Development of Higher Mental Processes*. Cambridge, MA: Harvard University Press.

Zech, L., Vye, N. J., Bransford, J.D., Swink, J., Mayfield-Stewart, C., & Goldman, S.R., & Cognition and Technology Group at Vanderbilt. (1994). Bringing geometry into the classroom with videodisc technology. *Mathematics Teaching in the Middle School Journal*, *1*(3), 228–233.

Section 3
Health Enhancement and Clinical Intervention

Chapter 9

Teaching Childbirth Support Techniques Using the Prepared Partner and Digital Birth:
The Design and Development of Games for Dads-To-Be

Alexandra Holloway
University of California – Santa Cruz, USA

ABSTRACT

In today's California, a mother's primary social support person in childbirth is her partner, guiding her through a multidimensional experience, helping her make sense of unforgettable emotions and sensations. Preparing the partner is an integral step to making sure that the mother is well-supported in her birth. Because the mother's experience is influenced by the support she receives, and because birth partners need more support than is recognized, we target birth partners with a learning intervention. We investigate video games as a vehicle for knowledge transfer to the birth partner, both as currently available and as a positive learning tool. To address the problem of limited access to childbirth preparation methods, we investigated, designed, and evaluated two games: The Prepared Partner, an online Flash game, and Digital Birth, an iPhone application. Both games allow the user to practice various supportive actions in the realm of childbirth support for a mother in labor. We found that players of The Prepared Partner met learning goals while enjoying the game.

INTRODUCTION

Childbirth support – supporting a mother throughout labor and the birth of a child or children – is a complex task, as evidenced by the number of books, websites, and articles available for expectant parents. Most women and their partners receiving prenatal care consider attending childbirth preparation classes, which may include a unit on labor support or comfort measures during labor. Unfortunately,

DOI: 10.4018/978-1-5225-1817-4.ch009

access to printed and online media and in-person childbirth preparation can be limited due to working hours, distance to the classes, economic hardships, and many other reasons.

We present the iterative human-centered, interdisciplinary design and evaluation of two games about childbirth support, The Prepared Partner and Digital Birth, and the surrounding domain research that informed the designs. We applied mixed ethnographic methods of gathering requirements to inform the tools. Our over-arching goal was to reach a large number of women and their birth partners, and to increase satisfaction with the birth experience and the feelings of preparedness among first-time parents.

We began by investigating the practice of childbirth preparation by administering an online survey. Participants generally prepared by taking childbirth preparation classes, though not in such large numbers as we expected.

Given our results from the survey, we gathered information about childbirth support from various sources. We developed The Prepared Partner as a pilot or proof-of-concept application, and evaluated it for learning and enjoyment.

This early success led us to continue considering how games might be a good medium for deploying information about childbirth support. Prior to proceeding, we performed a thorough search for childbirth scenes in commercially-available games in order to investigate the landscape surrounding birth in video games.

We conducted further targeted investigation about childbirth support using ethnographic interviews, and observation of childbirth classes. In the interviews, we focused on birth partners' preparation methods, goals and experiences of import when providing childbirth support, and partners' perceived utility as support-providers. For the childbirth education classes, we collected information about the curriculum as it pertained to childbirth support.

Using this information, we developed a second game, Digital Birth, using the feedback from The Prepared Partner together with the interview data. Digital Birth uses the same artificial intelligence engine as The Prepared Partner, but is founded on techniques and user goals from the ethnographic investigations.

CHILDBIRTH PREPARATION

The first stage of our research into a tool to help women have a positive birth experience was to investigate how women and their birth partners prepare for birth. We examine the relationship between the childbirth preparation, feelings of preparedness, learning in childbirth, and overall satisfaction with the birth experience.

Our literature review revealed that childbirth preparation is related to satisfaction regarding childbirth or the choice of childbirth method. However, many of these studies have a limited user base and focus on a few types of childbirth preparation methods.

The Listening to Mothers II survey (LTM) (Declercq, Sakala, Corry, & Applebaum, 2007) summarizes the habits of American women in preparing to conceive, preparing for labor and birth, the birth outcomes and statistics, and postpartum demographics, including breastfeeding incidence and duration. The survey found that the most important source of information about pregnancy and childbirth for first-time mothers (33%, N=146) was books, followed by friends and/or relatives (19%), and the Internet (16%). Childbirth education classes were cited as important only 10% of the time, although most (56%) first-time mothers enrolled and attended such classes.

There has been a significant amount of research about the benefits of childbirth preparation. Lumley and Brown showed that attenders of childbirth education classes did not show increased satisfaction with their birth experience compared to the non-attenders (Lumley & Brown, 1993). Nichols came to the same conclusion: attending childbirth class did not have an effect on childbirth satisfaction (Nichols, 1995). Fabian, et al. found that although there were no statistical differences between attenders and non-attenders of childbirth class in terms of birth experience, those that attended classes were more likely to opt for an epidural during labor (Fabian, Rådestad, & Waldenstro¨m, 2005).

Goodman, et al. showed childbirth satisfaction was influenced by whether the expectations for labor and delivery were met (Goodman, Mackey, & Tavakoli, 2004). Morgan, et al. described that effective pharmacological pain relief was insufficient for determining maternal satisfaction with labor (Morgan, Bulpitt, Clifton, & Lewis, 1982).

We conducted a survey in May 2010 to attempt to answer the following research questions.

R1: How do expectant parents prepare for childbirth, and how do these choices affect the birth experience they will ultimately attain?

R2: What is lacking in childbirth preparation?

R3: Is "just doing it" really the best preparation?

R4: What preparation methods generate the best results?

R5: How do we measure the "best" outcome of childbirth preparation?

Participants were recruited as part of coursework in an undergraduate human-computer interaction class, open to all majors. Eligible participants had experienced vaginal or Caesarean childbirth, or had assisted their partner in having a child, in the role of main support person. Only one participant per family was eligible to complete the survey. Of the 125 individuals that started the survey, 120 eligible participants completed it in its entirety. Survey responses were collected in the last weeks of May, 2010. The only participants excluded from the study were minors under age 18, and participants that did not fit the eligibility criteria yet still completed the survey. The study received exemption from the Institutional Review Board (IRB) as part of the coursework (HS1308). Data were analyzed using IBM SPSS 18.0.

Most of the participants (70%) were women that gave birth to at least one baby. The remaining 30% replied that their partner or spouse had given birth to at least one baby. This demographic differentiates our survey from surveys specifically for mothers, such as LTM; it differs from those specifically for fathers, such as Chan's (Chan & Paterson-Brown, 2002), Hallgren's (Hallgren, Kilhgren, Forslin, & Norberg, 1999), Odent's (Odent, 1999), Steen's (Steen, Downe, Bamford, & Edozien, 2011) experiences with following fathers; and it differs from work with birth partners, e.g. Somers-Smith's work (Somers-Smith, 1999).

The mean number of births per participant was 2.2, with the mode of 2. The births occurred between 1934 and 2009 (with an average birth year 1990, and mode 1988) in the United States and abroad, including Argentina, Canada, China, France, Philippines, Russia, Singapore, and Taiwan.

The self-reported instrumental delivery rate, deliveries in which forceps or vacuum extraction were used, was 24%. The Caesarean section rate was 45% across all participants, and 39% across all births (i.e., normalized), which included first-time and subsequent births. Twenty percent of first-time mothers had Caesarean sections. The Caesarean section rate in this study was significantly higher than the US average, reported to be 30% of all births (Althabe & Belizan, 2006), and higher than the 32% average rate reported in LTM. It is interesting to note that Caesarean section rates of over 10% are considered detrimental to maternal and infant health (Belizan, Althabe, & Cafferata, 2007). Participants reported that 62% used a pharmacological method of pain relief (e.g., narcotic, epidural, spinal). This is lower than the average reported by LTM (76%), possibly indicating a rise in the use of pharmacological pain relief as most participants in our survey had birthed in the 1980s–1990s; however, without specific geographic data, the effects of geography cannot be discounted. The average birth mass of first babies in our study was 3.33kg.

The remainder of the survey focused on the participants' first birth experience.

Preparing for Childbirth

Experts in the field of childbirth were consulted to compile a list of the most common ways to prepare for childbirth. The experts were childbirth educators, doulas, and doula trainers. The finalized list included talking to a woman who has given birth (e.g., mother, sister, friend); talking to a man whose partner has given birth (e.g., father, brother, friend); taking childbirth preparation classes; reading books, watching videos, and reading Internet sites; talking to a doctor; and talking to another professional (e.g., doula, midwife).

We asked participants four questions about their methods of preparing for childbirth.

1. **Preparation:** How did you prepare for labor and childbirth?
2. **Usefulness:** Which method of preparation did you find to be most helpful?
3. **Repeat Preparation:** If you were to go back in time and have your baby again, how would you learn about the labor and childbirth process?
4. **Recommendation:** If your good friend were going to have a baby, how would you recommend that she learn about the childbirth process?

Multiple answers were allowed only for the preparation, repeat preparation, and recommendation questions. Write-in answers were coded and counted.

One-sample χ^2 tests showed $p < 0.01$ for all items. Figures 1, 2, 3 and 4 summarize the findings described below.

We found that the overwhelming majority of participants (81%) prepared by talking to other women that had given birth, and 26% of participants found this to be the most useful method of preparation, making talking to other women the second most useful method of preparation cited by participants. However, less than half of participants (48%) would recommend preparing by talking to other women. Our results confirmed the LTM results, in which friends were cited as the second most useful method of childbirth preparation by 19% of first-time mothers.

The second-most popular way to prepare for childbirth was through books, videos, and other media (77%) and 20% of participants thought this was the most useful method. Listening to Mothers found 33% of first-time moms found books, and 16% cited the Internet, to be the most important source of information. In our survey, 63% of participants would recommend books and other media to their friends. Not surprisingly, the Internet is gaining popularity, and is ranked among the most influential methods of gaining information about pregnancy and childbirth (Handfield, Turnbull, et al., 2006).

Most (63%) of participants reported preparing for childbirth by taking childbirth preparation classes. Childbirth education classes were seen as the most helpful method of preparation, marked as most useful by 35% of participants. This was a marked difference from the Listening to Mothers survey, in which

Figure 1. Preparation methods for labor and childbirth

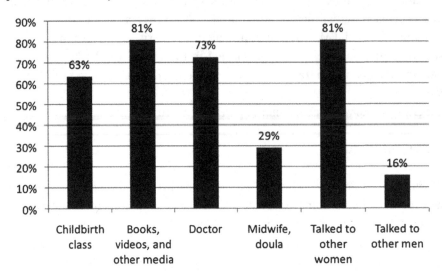

Figure 2. Preparation methods: What was most useful?

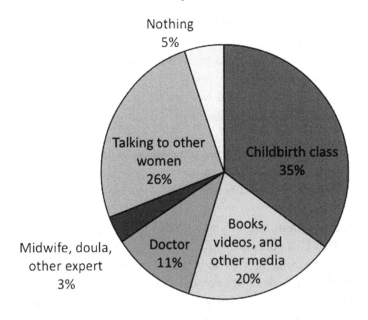

only 10% of first-time moms found childbirth education classes as the most important source of information about being pregnant and giving birth. In our survey, most participants (71%) would choose to take childbirth classes if they could repeat their preparation, and 82% of participants would recommend childbirth classes to their friends. That is, we found that participants that did not prepare by childbirth class wish they had. Discussing the coming birth with a doctor was a method 56% of participants used to prepare. About a tenth (11%) of participants marked this as the most useful method of preparation. However, only 43% would prepare this way again, indicating that 13% of those that prepared by talking to a doctor would not choose to do this again. More than half (56%) of participants would recommend

Figure 3. Preparation methods: What would you do again?

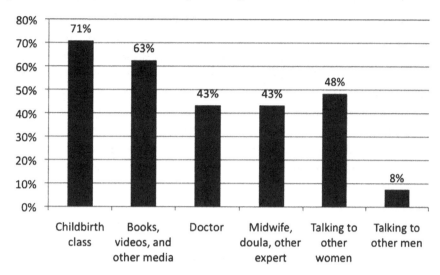

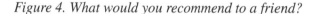

Figure 4. What would you recommend to a friend?

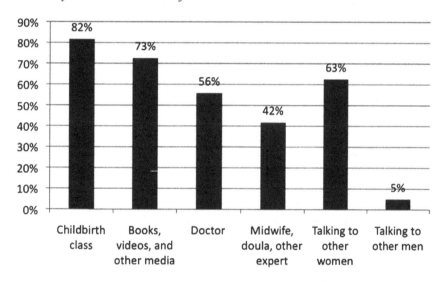

to a friend to prepare by talking to a doctor. Talking to another professional, such as a doula or midwife, was a method 29% of participants used (although only one participant used a doula in the birth). Only low 3% of participants thought this was the most useful method of preparation, although research suggests that this is the most overall beneficial way to feel supported in childbirth (Van Zandt, Edwards, & Jordan, 2005; Klaus, Kennell, & Klaus, 1993, 2002). Only 10% of participants said that a midwife was present at the birth for continuous labor support, indicating that some participants either spoke with midwives and doulas to prepare, and subsequently chose medical care through family doctors and obstetricians, or some midwives were not present for the entire labor and childbirth process for continuous support. Regardless, 43% would recommend this method of preparation to friends, indicating that new parents recognize the positive influence a midwife or doula can have on a birth experience and birth outcome.

Talking to men whose partner had given birth was not as popular, but present (16%), and few partici-pants said they were likely to prepare by talking to other men again (8%). Not one participant thought this was the most useful method of preparation, and only 5% of participants would recommend talking to men, presumably birth partners, to prepare for birth. We hypothesize that this is a cultural paradigm that is shifting; indeed, men as birth partners in the labor room did not become a norm until the late 1980s (Leavitt, 2009). As of 2003, 93–98% of fathers in the UK attend their partners' births (Kiernan & Smith, 2003), and their presence has tangible benefits to the mothers' birth experience, engagement with the infant, and parental attachment to the baby and to the partner (Fatherhood Institute, 2007).

There was a relationship between preparing by childbirth class with the first child, and choosing to prepare by childbirth class again ($p = 0.006$). There was no similar relationship, however, for any other preparation method.

Support in Childbirth

We asked participants who participated in supporting the mother during childbirth. All answers were significant ($p < 0.001$, one-sample binomial test). The mean number of non-medical personnel present to offer support to the mother was 1.50 ($p < 0.001$, one-sample Kolmogorov-Smirnov test). Most (92%) participants had (or provided) some continuous support during labor (see Figure 5).

Most mothers (78%) had spousal support during labor and childbirth. Some (28%) had parents sup-porting them. Some were accompanied by a sister or brother (15%), a friend (13%), and/or a midwife (10%). Nine participants (8%) reported having no continuous labor support, aside from the intermittent hospital staff visits from doctors and nurses. Only one participant reported having a doula, or profes-sional childbirth assistant, present at the birth.

We found a significant relationship between the total number of support persons with the participant during labor and childbirth and the total number of different ways the participant prepared for the birth ($p < 0.001$). The more different ways participants prepared for their birth, the more people were present for continuous support during the birth. Participants that had spousal support prepared by reading books

Figure 5. Support during labor: Who was there for continuous labor support?

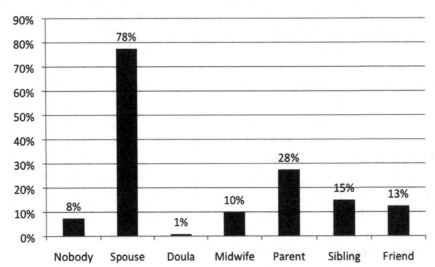

($p = 0.001$), taking childbirth class ($p = 0.001$), and talking to their doctor ($p = 0.001$). As a couple, the woman and her partner were likely to prepare for childbirth together. Participants that had nobody with them during labor and childbirth for support were likely to prepare for childbirth by reading books ($p < 0.001$); however, there was a negative correlation between having no support person present during the birth and the number of books read.

Pain Relief in Labor

The majority (62%) of participants reported using pharmacological methods of pain relief, such as morphine, Demerol, narcotics, or epidural analgesia during the birth of their first child. Only 22% reported using a non-pharmacological techniques, such as water therapy, aromatherapy, massage, acupuncture, a TENS machine, or another natural method. Further correlations are discussed below.

Satisfaction with Support in Childbirth

DONA International, an organization of birth and postpartum doulas, defines the role of a birth doula as a woman that provides "continuous physical, emotional and informational support to the mother before, during and just after childbirth." We asked participants to rate satisfaction with the different support components during labor, which we defined as emotional support, physical support (e.g., helping the mother move around), cognitive support (i.e., presence and company), and informational support (e.g., telling the mother what is happening). We also asked participants to score their satisfaction with pharmacological pain relief and non-pharmacological, or natural, pain relief. We used a four-point Likert scale (very unsatisfied, unsatisfied, satisfied, very satisfied). The findings are statistically significant ($p < 0.001$, one-sample χ^2) and are summarized in Figure 6.

- **Emotional:** 80% of participants replied they were satisfied with the emotional support received, compared to 15% of participants unsatisfied.
- **Physical:** For physical support (e.g., helping the woman in labor move around) 75% were satisfied with the support received; 18% were unsatisfied.
- **Cognitive:** We define cognitive, or mental, support as presence and company. 76% of participants reported being satisfied with the cognitive support they received in labor, and 18% were unsatisfied with it.
- **Informational:** Informational support, being told what was happening during the stages of labor and during childbirth, was found to be satisfactory by 77% of participants, and unsatisfactory by 19%.
- **Pain Relief Options:** Most (57%) of the participants were satisfied by the pharmacological pain relief (e.g., narcotics or epidural); however, 20% were unsatisfied with it (and 21% answered that this question did not apply to them). Finally, natural, non-pharmacological pain relief was found to be satisfactory by 46% of participants, and unsatisfactory by 18% (and 33% answered that this question did not apply to them).

Figure 6. Satisfaction with support in labor

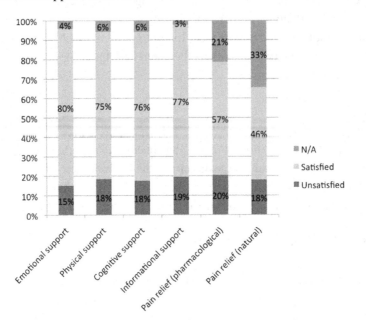

Total

We found a significant relationship between the total number of people supporting the mother and the satisfaction rating with respect to emotional support ($\chi2$, $p < 0.05$), physical support ($p < 0.05$), and cognitive support ($p < 0.05$). The total number of people was also related to the total number of ways the participants prepared for labor and childbirth ($p < 0.01$).

Learning in Labor

Is "just doing it" the best preparation for labor and childbirth? Five percent of participants said there is no best, most useful preparation: "Nothing really prepares you for childbirth except doing it; then you are prepared for the next one." To investigate this phenomenon, we asked participants to rate, on a four-point Likert scale, their feelings about their knowledge level before the birth and after the birth of their first child.

First, we asked: "How much did you know about the labor and childbirth process before your or your partner's first birth?" The options were nothing, a little / I had studied it a long time ago, some / I had studied it recently, and people sought my advice on this. Then, we asked: "How much did you know about the labor and childbirth process after your or your partner's first birth?" The options were nothing, a little / as if I had studied it a long time ago, some / as if I had studied it recently, and people seek my advice on this.

We found that the rating of what participants felt they knew before the labor increased dramatically after the labor. Significance was measured with Wilcoxon Signed Ranks Test, and p < 0.001 for all of the following items.

Before the labor, participants' answers were largely split. About half of the participants replied that they knew "some" or a significant amount about the topic. That is, they replied "Some / I had studied it recently" or "people sought my advice on this." These statements were chosen for their concrete, direct interpretations. The other half of participants answered that they knew a little or nothing about the topic, marking "A little / I had studied it a long time ago" or "Nothing" on the survey form.

After the labor, the answers very highly polarized. The majority of participants answered that they had a good or excellent understanding of all items. In particular, very few participants (11% or less) responded that they still knew "nothing" about an aspect of labor and childbirth after the birth. The statistical breakdown is described below:

- **Labor Process (Stages of Labor, etc.):** Participants' responses were an average of 27% higher for the post-birth question than the pre-birth question. After the birth, only 6% of participants replied that they knew only a little or nothing about the labor process. The mode of birth was not a factor — there was no difference between participants that delivered vaginally and participants that delivered by Caesarean section. Figure 7 shows the distribution of answers.

- **Comfort Techniques:** The mean rating for comfort techniques was 19% higher in the post-birth question. However, 20% of participants marked that they still knew a little or nothing about comfort techniques. One possible reason that 20% of participants knew a little or nothing about natural comfort techniques and pain relief options is because of the high first-time Caesarean section rate. There was no correlation between knowledge about comfort techniques and pain relief method or mode of birth (see Figure 7).

- **Non-Pharmacological Pain Relief Options:** Knowledge about non-pharmacological, or natural, pain relief options before the birth was split: nearly half knew "some" or more. After the birth, the number increased by 19%. Unfortunately, a quarter (25%) of participants still knew a little or nothing about natural pain relief, despite having delivered a baby. As with comfort techniques, one possible reason so few mothers and their partners knew about natural pain relief options is because 20% of these mothers delivered via Caesarean section. Figure 8 shows a summary of this finding.

- **Pharmacological Pain Relief Options:** Twenty-two percent more participants responded that they knew "some" or a significant amount about pharmacological pain relief options after their birth experience than before. However, 16% said they knew a little or nothing (see Figure 8). Because 38% of participants did not use pharmacological pain relief in labor, this number is not surprising.

- **Labor and Birth Positions:** Participants' ratings of their knowledge of labor and birth positions rose by 19% in the post-birth question compared to the pre-birth question. Figure 9 summarizes the participants' answers.

- **Tools and Props for Helping Laboring Women:** Although participants' responses were evenly split before the birth, after the birth, participants' scores for their knowledge of tools and props for helping laboring women rose by 22%. Figure 9 shows a summary graph.

- **Delivery Process:** Twenty-two percent more participants answered that they knew "some" or a significant amount about the delivery process after their birth experience. See Figure 10.

- **Postpartum:** Responses about the early postpartum period on the pre-birth question were split: half of participants said they knew "some" or a significant amount; half said they knew a little or nothing. On the post-birth question, 32% more participants said they knew "some" or a significant amount.

Figure 7. Before and after: how much did you know about the labor process and comfort techniques?

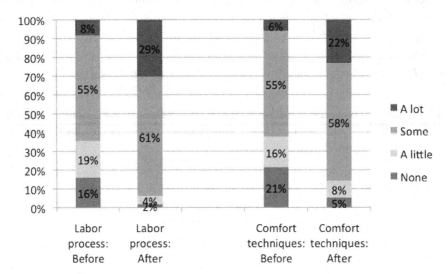

Figure 8. Before and after: how much did you know about pain relief options?

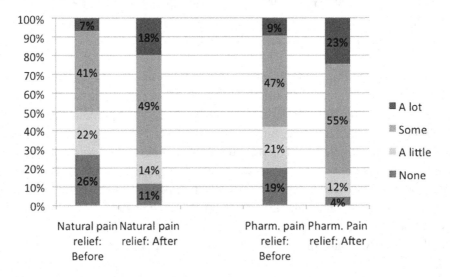

Prepared and Ready

We asked participants if they had felt prepared for labor and childbirth. Answers were provided on a four-point Likert scale (very unprepared, unprepared, prepared, very prepared). In retrospect, most (76%) participants felt some degree of preparation, feeling very prepared (18%) or prepared (58%). The remaining quarter of the participants (24%) felt unprepared (19%) or very unprepared (5%). See Figure 11 for a visual representation of this data. Our survey results are similar to the Listening to Mothers survey, in which 71% of mothers "reported feeling confident as they approached labor" and 24% felt unprepared.

Figure 9. Before and after: how much did you know about labor and birth positions and the tools and props for helping laboring women

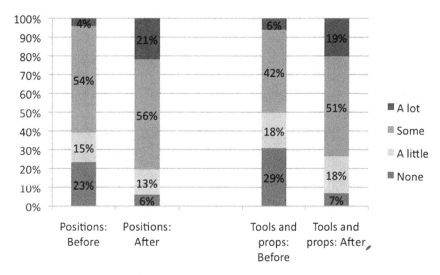

Figure 10. Before and after: how much did you know about the delivery process?

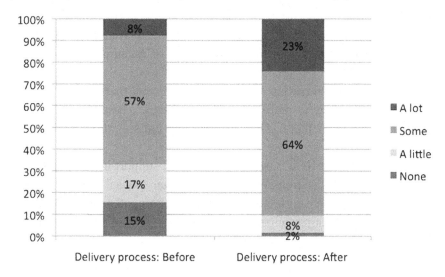

Correlations

Spearman's rho bivariate correlation was used to test non-parametric values. For each correlation table, we note significances at the 0.01 level (2-tailed) with two asterisks (**). Significant correlations at the 0.05 level (2-tailed) are noted with a single asterisk (*):

- **Preparation Methods and Labor Outcome:** We compared the preparation methods participants used and the outcome of the childbirth. Participants that prepared by taking childbirth classes, talking to other men, and talking to professionals (e.g., midwife, doula) were more likely to use

Figure 11. Did you feel prepared for labor and childbirth?

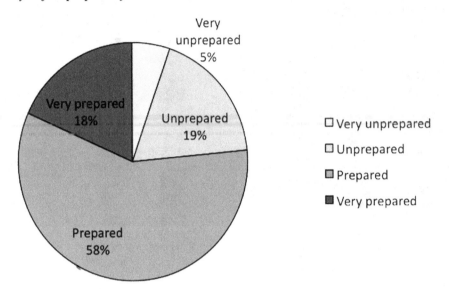

non-pharmacological methods of pain management during labor. Using natural techniques was also correlated with the number of books the participants read in preparation. We found that participants that prepared by talking with a doctor (73% of participants said they did this) were also likely to have an instrumental birth (i.e., by forceps or vacuum extraction). These results are summarized in Table 1.

- **Support in Labor and Preparation Methods:** Participants that reported being supported by their spouse were more likely to prepare by taking classes, reading books, and talking to their doctor. However, participants that had no support were unlikely to take classes and read books (see Table 2).

- **Support in Labor and Pain Relief:** Next, we examined support in labor and pain relief options used in labor. Table 3 shows a strong correlation between spousal support and pharmacological methods of pain relief. No such correlation was found for any other support person, including no support. Figure 12 shows that participants supported by a spouse were five times more likely to

Table 1. Childbirth preparation method versus instrumental birth and whether non-pharmacological methods of pain relief were used in labor

	Instrumental Birth	Used Non-Pharm.
Talking to men	—	.272**
Taking classes	—	.194*
Talking to doctor	.220*	—
Talking to professional	—	.421**
Number of books read	—	.251**

Table 2. Preparation method and support in labor

	Supported by...	
	Spouse	Nobody
Taking classes	.308**	−.204*
Reading books	.335**	−.394**
Talking to doctor	.311**	—
Number of books	.316**	−.302**

use pharmacological methods of pain relief than participants without a spouse present (10% vs. 50% — see Figure 12). We also found that participants supported by a midwife were both less likely to use pharmacological methods of pain relief and more likely to use natural pain relief options. Again, no such correlation was found for any other support person.

- **Satisfaction:** Participants that rated highly their satisfaction with any of emotional, physical, cognitive, and informational support during the birth of their first child were likely to rate all of these aspects highly (correlation coefficients all greater than 0.670, $p < 0.01$, two-tailed).

Satisfaction with pharmacological support was also correlated positively with all of the other aspects of labor (correlation coefficients greater than .240, $p < 0.01$, two-tailed). Satisfaction with non-pharmacological support was an exception: it was correlated only with satisfaction with emotional support (correlation coefficient 0.233, $p < 0.05$), and informational support (correlation coefficient 0.231, $p < 0.05$).

There was no correlation between the mode of birth (vaginal or Caesarean section) and satisfaction with the level of support.

Table 3. Support in labor and whether pharmacological or non-pharmacological methods were used

	Used Non-Pharm.	**Used Pharm.**
Spouse support	—	.206*
Midwife support	.365**	−.303**

Figure 12. Pharmacological methods of pain relief and whether a spouse was present during labor

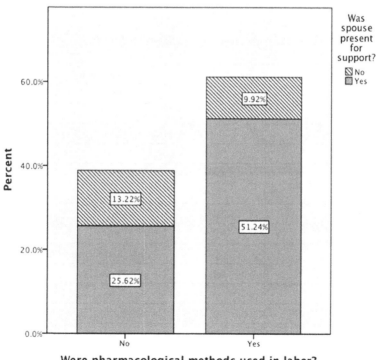

- **Satisfaction with Support and Support Person:** We found that both the total number of people supporting the mother during labor and childbirth — spouse, sister, mother, etc. — and the total number of methods used to prepare for childbirth were positively correlated to emotional, physical, and cognitive support satisfaction (see Table 4).

Table 5 shows that we found participants that had no support person(s) with them during their labor were unhappy with the level of emotional, physical, and cognitive support. Although unsurprising, this finding corroborates existing research about the importance of continuous support for a woman throughout her labor and birth. Further, participants with a friend supporting them in labor were more likely to be satisfied with emotional, physical, and cognitive support.

- **Satisfaction and Preparation Methods:** We compared participants' satisfaction with the support types in labor with the methods of labor preparation. Table 6 contains the correlation coefficients for these figures.

Table 4. Correlation between number of support persons present, the number of preparation methods used, and the satisfaction rating with emotional, physical, and cognitive support in labor

	Satisfaction with...		
	Emotional	**Physical**	**Cognitive**
No. persons	.349**	.278**	.295**
No. of methods	.342**	.358**	.292**

Table 5. Correlation between no support person or having a friend as a support person and satisfaction with emotional, physical, and cognitive support in labor

	Satisfaction with...		
	Emotional	**Physical**	**Cognitive**
Nobody	−.219*	−.227*	−.221*
Friend	—	.192*	.198

Table 6. Preparation methods and satisfaction with support in labor

	Satisfaction with...		
	Emot.	**Phys.**	**Cog.**
Talking to women	—	—	.184*
Talking to men	—	.204*	—
Taking classes	.214*	—	—
Reading books	.276**	.258**	—
No. of books	.287**	.223*	.219*
Talking to doctor	.236**	.291**	.192*
Talking to pro.	.305**	.268**	.282**
	Satisfaction with...		
	Info.	**Pharm.**	**Non-Pharm.**
Talking to men	—	—	.310**
Taking classes	—	.214*	—
Reading books	.238**	—	—
Talking to doctor	.357**	.184*	—
Talking to pro.	.355**	.188*	.277**

Talking to a doctor was positively correlated with satisfaction with all but non-pharmacological support. Doctors rarely prepare their patients by discussing natural pain relief options, as a doctor's specialty is with pharmacological methods of relieving pain.

Reading books, one of the most popular methods of preparation (81% of participants marked this option), was positively correlated with satisfaction with emotional, physical, and informational support in labor. me." Another participant wrote: "Class [was most useful to me], because we took it together." However, our results suggest that there was no correlation between taking a childbirth class and feeling supported on a cognitive level through presence and company. Preparing by taking classes was positively correlated only with satisfaction with emotional support and pharmacological pain relief support. That is, participants felt supported emotionally, and were satisfied with the medications they were given (if they chose to use them) to manage labor pain.

Talking to women, the other most popular method of preparation for childbirth (chosen by 81% of participants), was correlated only with satisfaction with cognitive support — that is, the sense of presence and company. However, participants found talking to women to be critical in preparing for childbirth, as one-quarter (26%) of participants cited talking to other women as the single most useful method of preparing for childbirth. One participant explained: "Talking to other mothers [was the most useful method of preparation]. They've been through it and were the most honest about what to expect."

- **Feelings of Preparedness and Support:** Participants that had a midwife or a friend present for support were more likely to respond that they felt prepared for the birth of their first child. No other such correlations were found for any other support person. Participants that used non-pharmacological methods of pain relief were more likely to say they had felt prepared. Feelings of preparedness were positively correlated with attending childbirth class. Table 7 summarizes these findings.

DISCUSSION

In this study, we asked participants to recall their first birth experience. The most common birth year was 1988, and the average was 1990 — most births occurred 22 to 24 years prior to taking this survey. We posit that the memory of the birth does not fade with time. Githens, et al., have found that mothers can remember the details of their births for four to six years (Githens, Glass, Sloan, & Entman, 1993); Tomeo and others saw that this memory can extend much longer: mothers can recall details of their pregnancies and birth weights of their infants 30 years after the birth of their child (Tomeo et al., 1999).

Table 7. Feelings of preparedness and midwife support, friend support, preparation by childbirth class, and whether non-pharmacological methods were used in labor

	Feelings of Preparedness
Midwife support	.204*
Friend support	.196*
Used non-pharm.	.211*
Childbirth class	.271**

Simkin found that women can recall particular details about their birth experience even 20 years later (Simkin, 1992). Because childbirth is a very significant event, we consider the retrospective survey approach a valid way to assess satisfaction with labor support, knowledge, and feelings of preparedness.

Participants were unlikely to prepare for childbirth using just one method. A combination of methods — childbirth class, talking to men, talking to women, and reading a number of books — were positively correlated.

Most (63%) of participants attended organized childbirth preparation classes. This is higher than the Listening to Mothers survey (56% of first-time mothers).

We found that respondents with no labor support also did not prepare for labor and childbirth by other methods, such as taking classes and reading books about childbirth. They were also less likely to have a positive birth experience, with less perceived emotional, physical, and cognitive support in labor than those that had labor support.

We found that participants value the experience of having a child as a method of childbirth preparation. Going through the experience of childbirth was found to be the best way to learn about the subject: participants replied that they knew significantly more about every aspect of childbirth after the fact.

The methods of preparing for childbirth have an effect later, with parents' satisfaction with the labor process. The most popular methods of preparing for childbirth were talking to other women and reading books, watching movies, and browsing the Internet for information. The former was not shown to have a positive correlation with any aspect of the labor and childbirth process other than cognitive support. Talking with other women may contribute to feelings of kinship – feeling a part of a larger whole; feeling connected to all women that have undergone the experience of childbirth (Davis-Floyd, 2004) – and make them feel supported on a mental level by the thought of these women. Participants that prepared with books and other media showed higher scores for emotional, physical, and informational support satisfaction in the birth process. The number of books participants read in preparation for labor was correlated not only with informational satisfaction (that is, how much information the participants received in labor), but also with emotional, physical, and cognitive satisfaction. This indicates that the number of books does not contribute to information alone. Mothers and their partners are preparing on a deeper level with each new book read. They are more likely to imagine a great number of birth outcomes, and prepare both mentally and emotionally for different possibilities. However, because those that prepared with books also prepared with other methods, including talking to other women, taking childbirth classes, and talking to their doctor, and because these same participants were likely to be supported in labor and childbirth by their spouse, it is difficult to draw a conclusion.

Although "just doing it" was found to be the best preparation for childbirth – that is, having a child is the best way to learn about childbirth and prepare for a subsequent birth – parents should have access to preparation methods for their first birth experiences. The most popular method of preparation was talking with other women who had given birth; however, it is an unstructured and anecdotal method. Other most common ways of preparing for a first child were reading books, watching videos, and browsing Internet sites for information. Although taking childbirth classes is the fourth most popular method of preparation, it is seen as the most useful, and is most likely to be recommended to friends – although individual impressions of the utility of childbirth education classes is mixed.

THE PREPARED PARTNER: A PROOF OF CONCEPT

The growing ubiquity of the Internet and other always-on media, such as games, informed our decision to try to incorporate common themes in childbirth education into a game. Because participants considered childbirth education to be important, yet did not necessarily find attending childbirth education classes as a valuable source of information for their own birth experience, we decided to distill the concepts found in childbirth education into a medium that can be easily consumed by a majority of people. We intended to leverage the Internet as a distribution medium, and games as a vehicle for content, in designing and implementing what became The Prepared Partner.

The Prepared Partner was designed to be an educational video game about labor and childbirth. Because literature suggests that fathers and birth partners need more support in labor and childbirth than was previously assumed (Hallgren et al., 1999), the target audience included anyone with an interest in childbirth, including future mothers and birth partners.

We started The Prepared Partner with five main goals for the system. They were as follows (Holloway & Kurniawan, 2010; Holloway, 2010; Holloway & Kurniawan, 2011).

1. To introduce natural coping mechanisms and their effects on labor,
2. To introduce the mechanics of labor and childbirth,
3. To train birth partners to help women in childbirth,
4. To practice interacting with a woman in labor, and
5. To simulate the stages of labor.

We used human-centered design, influenced by the childbirth preparation survey, in designing the game prototype.

Before designing and developing The Prepared Partner, we conducted thorough domain background research – an integral part of usability engineering as research must be completed before prototyping (Holzinger, 2005). We read accounts of childbirth, or birth stories, in popular books suggested to expectant parents, and paid particular attention to information about the stages of labor, relaxation to reduce anxiety, natural techniques to deal with pain and discomfort associated with childbirth, and information about pharmacological options available to mothers in a hospital or birth center (England & Horowitz, 1998; Gaskin, 2003; Goer, 1999; Simkin, 2008). We attended a class for training doulas for their work in continuous support of women throughout labor, birth, and breastfeeding initiation. This class was a thorough introduction to the mechanics of labor, the emotional implications and effects on the woman in labor and her partner, the options available to the parents, and involved hands-on practice of dozens of natural coping mechanisms. We experienced childbirth first-hand and assisted one other woman in the birth of her child, and used these experiences to fuel our research.

The game consisted of a user interface allowing the user to perform supportive actions for Amanda, the mother in labor, and an artificial intelligence unit which reacted to environmental and circumstantial cues (i.e., the progress of labor and the user's interactions with the mother). The game was implemented in Flash. Figure 13 shows a screenshot of the game.

Comfort measures, aggregated from the domain research mentioned above, were converted into a card-game mechanic. In speaking with several doulas, we found that professional childbirth support persons sometimes have a "deck" of support methods written out on index cards and kept in a box as a source of inspiration. The mother and her partner frequently find the "box of tricks" useful, and cite it as

Figure 13. Amanda is using chant, mantra, song, or prayer as way to vocalize her experience in active labor. Available actions are affirmation, counter-pressure to her back, and eat a sandwich

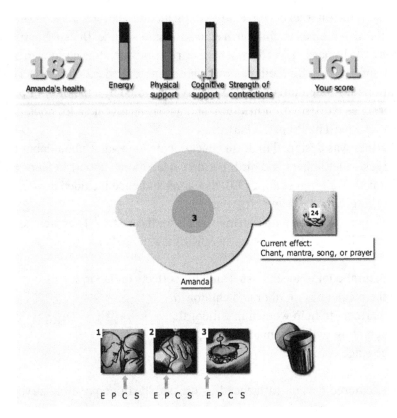

an inspiring way to helping them get through a kind of mental block in labor. We adopted this mechanic, creating a deck of about 50 comfort measures that would be randomized at the beginning of the game and then dealt to the player three cards at a time. When all cards had been in play, the deck would be reshuffled and dealt again.

The mother's overall well-being consisted of four traits: energy, emotional support, cognitive support, and the strength of her contractions. The traits were affected by a mathematical formula with a feedback loop, which required player intervention for a successful outcome. The player's selection of comfort measures affected the mother's traits, allowing her to have stronger contractions that would eventually lead to the birth of the child. How each comfort measure affected the mother was determined by her stage in labor, the empirical effectiveness of each comfort measure (Simkin & Bolding, 2004), and a small component of random chance.

We launched the game as part of a research study using a pre-test, intervention, and post-test (within-subjects) study design. A total of 51 participants completed all portions of the study; about half (47%) had no prior experience with childbirth and most (80%) of the participants were male.

The results of the study (Holloway & Kurniawan, 2011) showed that participants playing The Prepared Partner learned about the mechanics of labor and birth, and answered with more breadth and confidence when asked how to speed up labor naturally. Answers included more concrete actions such as "intimacy," "take a bath," "apply pressure to the lower back," and "acupressure." Before playing The

Prepared Partner, the answers were generally more vague and several participants included question marks in their answers, indicating uncertainty. Moreover, participants answered with a broader range of cognitive support methods on the post-test than the pre-test, most of which were presented in the game.

A few months after the study was conducted, one participant contacted the researcher to write that during his recent birth support experience, in the moment, he felt he had forgotten everything except the interactions he saw in The Prepared Partner.

These results indicated that a game was an effective way to transfer knowledge to the birth partner, and prompted further investigation into the nature of childbirth in games, and how to make a more accessible game for knowledge transfer.

VIDEO GAME DEPICTIONS OF LABOR AND CHILDBIRTH

In order to better understand the role of childbirth in commercially-available video games, we first had to determine which games had birth as a part of the story or player interaction. With help from online communities such as Quarter to Three we compiled a list of 34 games with birth as a major or minor game element. It should be noted that childbirth in games is not a common theme.

We found that video games generally paint an incomplete or incorrect picture of the human experience of childbirth from a theoretical standpoint (Holloway, Rubin, & Kurniawan, 2012). Moreover, these incomplete or incorrect ideas expressed by games teach the players these same incorrect notions, often reinforcing negative gender stereotypes, similarly to media effects in other domains.

It is well known that people are negatively influenced by inappropriate, over-sexualized depictions of women in video games (Behm-Morawitz & Mastro, 2009; Downs & Smith, 2010). Hence, though video games do not teach how to have a child, they do suggest the underlying theory of childbirth and childbirth support. Unfortunately, current, commercial video games are lacking in both respects.

Other media depicting childbirth are not without faults. As situational comedies use childbirth for comic relief both in television and in movies (Elson, 1997) the impact of optical media on notions of pregnancy and childbirth are both nontrivial and well documented, affecting perceptions of women's bodies, breastfeeding, and the childbirth process (Morris & McInerney, 2010; Ward, Merriwether, & Caruthers, 2006).

Video games fail to capture the whole gamut of childbirth experiences. There is a wide range of births not captured: women are never shown birthing upright, changing position; they are never shown eating or using comfort techniques in labor. Births are shown as speedy events of pushing out a baby, and only one game half-heartedly models active labor. No game models the third stage of labor (delivery of the placenta), though the mother in one game suggests a few healing spells for herself after the birth. Some games suggest that mothers have to endure some discomfort or pain in the process of birth.

One of the more realistic depictions of the pushing stage of labor, *Assassin's Creed 2* (2009) (Part 1: Birth of the Assassin) shows how Lucy pushes out her baby boy in a semi-sitting position on a table, assisted by two midwives. The midwives coax Lucy to push, and she bears down with all her might in the final pushes necessary to birth the child. In role-playing games such as *Dragon Quest V: Hand of the Heavenly Bride* (2009) and *Harvest Moon DS Cute* (2005) the father waits outside the birthing room, from which pained sounds emanate, and is told in a dialog message that the baby was born in a thematic nod to typical American maternity wards of the 1950s and 1960s.

Having understood the cultural landscape surrounding childbirth in video games, which was largely under-informed and misleading, we investigated the interaction modes. Most games did not allow the player to interact with the birth scene; however, some games allow the player to control the baby's point of view (*Fallout 3* (2008)) or limbs (*Assassin's Creed 2* (2009)) to some extent. In *Sims 3* (2009), the player is allowed to interact with the mother in labor; however, the interaction is limited to involuntary panic, or taking her to the hospital. This form of interaction, in which the player clicks on the mother and selects the only available option through a bubble menu, was fairly intuitive, if lacking in content. *Second Life* (2003) is a simulation game in which the player can purchase a birth package from an online vendor, and participate in the birth of the child. Due to its game-authoring tools, this game has the most diverse representations of birth of any of the games we surveyed. These games are shown in Figure 14.

BIRTH PARTNERS' GOALS FOR CHILDBIRTH SUPPORT

We set out to explore the partners experiences of the mothers birth, including attitudes for labor and birth, preparation strategies, labor support goals, birth preferences, and whether the experience unfolded in the way s/he expected. The purpose of the research was to inform a mobile video game about labor and childbirth support as an educational intervention for birth partners.

We wrote an analysis tool that scraped a Website hosting birth stories2. All of these birth stories were authored by women/mothers in the previous year, 2010–2011. In our preliminary analysis, we considered the common themes arising in 100 randomly-selected birth stories. The resulting Wordle is shown in Figure 15. A Wordle is useful for showing graphically common words and themes in a specific body of text. From this image, we determined that it is of high import to model contractions in our system.

Next, we conducted interviews lasting 20 minutes to an hour with 23 birth partners. Some birth partners were recruited before the birth; for them, we asked questions regarding preparation and what they hope to experience in their upcoming role of birth support. For the birth partners that had attended a birth, we asked questions pertaining to their role in the birth support and what they found to be useful (in terms of support strategies) and meaningful (in terms of emotional satisfaction) in the birth experience.

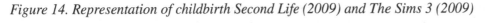

Figure 14. Representation of childbirth Second Life (2009) and The Sims 3 (2009)

Figure 15. Wordle, a graphical representation of common topics in 100 random birth stories

The interviews with birth partners revealed a significant need to feel a connection to the mother and the birth process. Affinity diagrams revealed two main categories of support strategies: emotional support, and physical support.

The main goal of emotional support is to calm the mother throughout the discomfort and fear that many mothers experience. Birth partners' stated and implied goals of emotional support were as follows.

- **Physical Presence:** Stay in the room with the mother such that she feels she is never alone.
- **Verbal Care:** Encourage the mother with words and explain that what she is feeling is normal.
- Listen and Respond to the mother's needs promptly and efficiently.
- **Mediate:** Interact with the nursing staff on the mother's behalf, relaying information and normalizing the experience for the mother.
- **Birth Plan Management:** Ensure that a birth plan prepared in advance is followed as closely as possible, and warn and explain to the mother any deviations.

Birth partners placed great import on their role in physical support. While emotional support is different for every person, and is difficult to teach effectively, physical support can be taught in childbirth preparation classes and described in textbooks and other media. The goal of physical support was to make the mothers' bodies more comfortable. The most common types of physical support discussed were rubbing, pushing on, or massaging the mothers back (especially lower back), and holding her hand. Sometimes birth partners would guide and assist the mother in using props such as a birthing (or yoga) ball, or support the mother as she squat, sit, bend over, or stand together to ease labor pain.

Birth partners expressed a desire to know they were needed in the course of the birth. In some cases, mothers become so inwardly-focused as the labor progressed that some birth partners felt that they did not receive the feedback they needed. Birth parters felt that physical support gave the best feedback: in supporting a mother physically, they were really doing something, and actively participating in the mother's birth. Emotional support, especially physical presence, was described as a much more passive method of support, and lacking feedback from the mother as she became more inwardly-focused in the course of the birth, and thus more difficult to know how the support was working for the mother.

Our results included that immediate feedback about whether specific action, physical or emotional, was welcome by the mother was key in making birth partners feel necessary and appreciated as support persons.

DIGITAL BIRTH: AN IPHONE SIMULATION OF LABOR

With the knowledge gleaned from our first prototype success, The Prepared Partner; together with the domain knowledge within the fields of childbirth, video games, and user interaction and experience; and added to that the 20+ hours of interview data from expectant and experienced birth partners, prototyped an iPhone game called Digital Birth.

We intended for Digital Birth to be available for free from prenatal clinics and low-cost maternity centers. The game would be distributed at these centers free of charge to any mother or birth partner that wished to obtain a copy of it. Specifically, we built an iPhone game which we targeted for lower-income Latino families from California, who are more likely to surpass whites in their use of data apps from handheld devices such as the iPhone (Smith, 2010).

The mother, Carmen, was the main focus of the game. Carmen was based on our interview data, designed under strict supervision of our anthropology collaborator, and was intended to be age- and race-neutral to appeal to many women or types of women within California. Preliminary inquiries with the target population confirmed that the model of Carmen was acceptable.

Digital Birth is set in a labor and delivery (L&D) room of a hospital-based birth center. The room was designed following visits to L&D wards of California hospitals, including Dominican Hospital of Santa Cruz, University of San Francisco, San Francisco General Hospital, Kaiser Permanente of San Francisco, Redwood City Sequoia Hospital, Good Samaritan Hospital San Jose, Sutter Maternity and Surgery Center of Santa Cruz, and Community Hospital of the Monterey Peninsula. Great import was placed on the use of hydrotherapy (e.g., using the bathtub or shower for pain management) in the visits to the hospitals and from the discussions with the L&D nurses during the tour(s). Thus, we chose to make prominent the large birth tub and the shower in the birth scene in Digital Birth. Other room features include an adjustable hospital bed, large window with window-seat, rocking chair (behind the bed), recessed lighting, hidden compartments for instruments and medical devices, a toilet/shower room with frosted glass, and art on the wall – all designed to create a cozy birthing atmosphere. The room design underwent several iterations, soliciting feedback from our midwifery collaborators until the appropriate level of realism was reached. The game interface can be seen in Figure 16.

Carmen can occupy a variety of positions within the environment, including standing near the bed, sitting up in bed, relaxing in the rocking chair, squatting against the side of the bed, on all fours, slow-dancing with her partner (the player), sitting backwards on a chair, kneeling, lunging, sitting on a birth ball, leaning against the shower wall, walking, sitting on the toilet, and resting against the side of the birth tub while immersed in the tub. Carmen can select one of these positions for herself based on her well-being (for example, if she is tired, she will select a lying-down position for herself and will be unable to change to a more vertical position until her energy is replenished), or these positions can be suggested to her by the player. The art used for Carmen's positions is shown in Figure 17.

In any position, Carmen's body glows gold during contractions, and a pull-out contraction monitor can verify the start, end, or peak of a contraction. In our initial interviews, as well as in our birth stories analyses, we found that birth partners typically turn to contraction timing as a supportive activity.

Figure 16. Carmen in Digital Birth starts the game by lying on her side in the hospital bed

Figure 17. Carmen's position art, by Phillip Vaughan, in Digital Birth

Moreover, many of the pregnancy- and birth-related applications we investigated included a contraction timer feature. Thus, we wanted to emphasize the mother's contractions in labor.

The supportive actions available in the game are grouped into six categories: relaxation, breathing, being together (i.e., partner support), position change, and verbal care (e.g., affirmation, tell her how strong she is, etc.). The categories came naturally from affinity diagramming interview responses and comparing them to categories of care in The Birth Partner (Simkin, 2008).

Rather than using "health" or maternal well-being as the main feedback metric about the mother for the player as we did in The Prepared Partner, we decided to use the amount of perceived support a mother feels. From our vast preliminary investigation, it became clear that all mothers are different and all births are different – that is, some mothers want plenty of hands-on support while other mothers just want to feel the presence of their partner. Thus, at the beginning of the game, we auto-generate certain traits for Carmen which we translate into a spectrum of the amount of desired support. The player must then stay within a window of that amount by performing actions, or just by being active in the game. If the player is too supportive (i.e., by performing too many actions or suggesting comfort measures too often for Carmen's liking), the results are detrimental to Carmen's labor coping, measured on Simkin's coping scale (Simkin & Bolding, 2004; Simkin, 2011). A visual representation of the spectrum of Carmen's support is shown in Figure 18.

Carmen's overall feelings of support, derived from the amount of support the player provides conflated with her desire for support (and support type aversion multiplier), are translated in realtime into a Simkin-style coping icon (see Figure 19).

We kept the support methods as playing cards metaphor from The Prepared Partner, but instead of dealing three random cards at a time, we decided to make all comfort measures available to the player at all times. In The Prepared Partner, one of our game goals was to show the player as many varied support methods as possible over the course of a play through. For Digital Birth, we wanted to mimic the "tool chest" that doulas describe possessing and accessing during the course of labor support. Thus, all supportive actions were available at all times, when they logistically made sense.

Figure 18. Carmen's desire for support is shown as a green window in this spectrum. The spectrum ranges from a small amount of support (i.e., presence) (A) to a lot of support (i.e., constantly supporting the mother with hands-on actions) (B). The actual amount of support the player is providing is shown as a superscript triangle (C). Carmen's ideal amount of support is shown with the brackets (lower bound D; upper bound E)

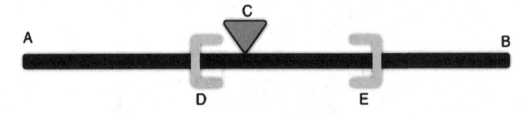

Figure 19. Penny Simkin's pain coping scale for labor and childbirth
Source: Simkin, 2011.

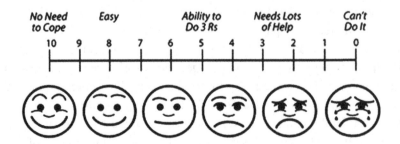

The core component of the way the mother, the non-player character in the game with whom the player interacts, experiences labor is the contraction heartbeat. This is a periodic oscillation that generates uterine contractions in the game, and it is currently implemented with variable contraction durations that correspond to the stages and substages of labor (early labor, active labor, transition, and pushing). The contraction heartbeat is available to the front-end for display via an API call.

The events of the game are not scripted, but are derived from a mathematical formula with a feedback loop that incorporates the stage of labor, the mother's well-being, and the amount of support the player offers the mother. That is, the game elements are procedurally-generated. As in The Prepared Partner, the player's interactions influence Carmen's well-being, and her well-being in turn influences how her labor progresses. At the end of the game, the player is shown a score screen showing a letter-grade corresponding to how well the player supported Carmen – i.e., how well the player stayed within Carmen's desired labor support throughout the birth.

FUTURE WORK

Digital Birth is a prototype game. It is currently undergoing a round of testing with students of nursing-midwifery as a part of their labor support curriculum. We will incorporate the students' feedback into the game. Afterwards, we plan to deploy the game to our intended audience using a within-subjects study design, looking for differences in perceived readiness for childbirth support, understanding of the mechanics of labor and birth and birth support, and childbirth support self-efficacy.

ACKNOWLEDGMENT

The author wishes to thank the following individuals for their contribution to this project at the various stages of work. Rebecca Emrick for her role in Latch Master, a game about teaching breastfeeding; Said Achmiz for his excellent work on the user interface of Digital Birth; Phillip Vaughan for his art design and assets used in Digital Birth; Alaric Holloway for his art used in The Prepared Partner and Digital Birth; Nina Shapiro, Greer Montgomery, and Salvador Contreras for their role in interviewing birth partners; and the author's mentors and advisor, Dr. Megan Moodie, Dr. Jenna Shaw-Battista, and Dr. Sri Kurniawan. The author also wishes to thank the many anonymous individuals that contributed their time to interviews, video game and user interface discussions, and survey data. Specifically, the author acknowledges the participation of the Quarter to Three and Mothering communities.

REFERENCES

Althabe, F., & Belizán, J. (2006). Caesarean section: The paradox. *Lancet*, *368*(9546), 1472–1473. doi:10.1016/S0140-6736(06)69616-5 PMID:17071266

Behm-Morawitz, E., & Mastro, D. (2009). The Effects of the Sexualization of Female Video Game Characters on Gender Stereotyping and Female Self-Concept. *Sex Roles*, *61*(11), 808–823. doi:10.1007/s11199-009-9683-8

Belizán, J., Althabe, F., & Carrerata, M. (2007). Health consequences of the increasing caesarean section rates. *Epidemiology (Cambridge, Mass.), 18*(4), 485–486. doi:10.1097/EDE.0b013e318068646a PMID:17568221

Chan, K., & Paterson-Brown, S. (2002). How do fathers feel after accompanying their partners in labour and delivery? *Journal of Obstetrics & Gynaecology, 22*(1), 11–15. doi:10.1080/01443610120101628 PMID:12521719

Davis-Floyd, R. E. (2004). *Birth as an american rite of passage: With a new preface*. University of California Press. doi:10.1525/california/9780520229327.001.0001

Declercq, E., Sakala, C., Corry, M., & Applebaum, S. (2007). Listening to mothers II: Report of the second national US survey of womens childbearing experiences. *Journal of Perinatal Education, 16*(4), 9–14. doi:10.1624/105812407X244769 PMID:18769512

Downs, E., & Smith, S. (2010). Keeping abreast of hypersexuality: A video game character content analysis. *Sex Roles*, 1–13.

Elson, V. L. (1997). *Childbirth in American movies and television: Patterns of portrayal and audience impact* (Unpublished doctoral dissertation). University of Massachusetts at Amherst.

England, P., & Horowitz, R. (1998). *Birthing From Within: An Extra-Ordinary Guide to Childbirth Preparation*. Albuquerque, NM: Partera Press.

Fabian, H., Rådestad, I., & Waldenström, U. (2005). Childbirth and parenthood education classes in Sweden. Womens opinion and possible outcomes. *Acta Obstetricia et Gynecologica Scandinavica, 84*(5), 436–443. doi:10.1111/j.0001-6349.2005.00732.x PMID:15842207

Fatherhood Institute. (2007). Fathers at the birth and after: Impact on mothers. In *Fatherhood Institute Research Summary: Fathers Attending Births*. Author.

Gaskin, I. (2003). *Ina May's Guide to Childbirth*. Bantam Books.

Githens, P., Glass, C., Sloan, F., & Entman, S. (1993). Maternal recall and medical records: An examination of events during pregnancy, childbirth, and early infancy. *Birth (Berkeley, Calif.), 20*(3), 136–141. doi:10.1111/j.1523-536X.1993.tb00438.x PMID:8240621

Goer, H. (1999). *The Thinking Woman's Guide to a Better Birth*. Perigee.

Goodman, P., Mackey, M., & Tavakoli, A. (2004). Factors related to childbirth satisfaction. *Journal of Advanced Nursing, 46*(2), 212–219. doi:10.1111/j.1365-2648.2003.02981.x PMID:15056335

Hallgren, A., Kilhgren, M., Forslin, L., & Norberg, A. (1999). Swedish fathers involvement in and experiences of childbirth preparation and childbirth. *Midwifery, 15*(1), 6–15. doi:10.1016/S0266-6138(99)90032-3 PMID:10373868

Handfield, B., Turnbull, S., & Bell, R. J. (2006). What do obstetricians think about media influences on their patients? *Australian and New Zealand Journal of Obstetrics and Gynaecology, 46*(5), 379–383. doi:10.1111/j.1479-828X.2006.00621.x PMID:16953850

Holloway, A. (2010). *System design and evaluation of The Prepared Partner: a labor and childbirth game* (Unpublished master's thesis). University of California, Santa Cruz, CA.

Holloway, A., & Kurniawan, S. (2010). System design evolution of The Prepared Partner: How a labor and childbirth game came to term. In Meaningful play. Academic Press.

Holloway, A., & Kurniawan, S. (2011). The Prepared Partner: Can a video game teach labor and childbirth support techniques? In Information quality in ehealth. Graz, Austria: Academic Press.

Holloway, A., Rubin, Z., & Kurniawan, S. (2012). What video games have to teach us about childbirth and childbirth support. In *Proceedings of the first workshop on design patterns in games* (p. 4). doi:10.1145/2427116.2427120

Holzinger, A. (2005). Usability engineering methods for software developers. *Communications of the ACM, 48*(1), 71–74. doi:10.1145/1039539.1039541

Kiernan, K., & Smith, K. (2003). Unmarried parenthood: new insights from the millennium cohort study. *Population Trends - London*, 26–33.

Klaus, M., Kennell, J., & Klaus, P. (1993). *Mothering the Mother: How a Doula Can Help You Have a Shorter.* Perseus Books.

Klaus, M., Kennell, J., & Klaus, P. (2002). *The Doula Book.* Da Capo Press.

Leavitt, J. W. (2009). *How did men end up in the delivery room?* George Mason University's History News Network. Retrieved May 13, 2013, from http://www.hnn.us/articles/116291.html

Lumley, J., & Brown, S. (1993). Attenders and nonattenders at childbirth education classes in Australia: How do they and their births differ? *Birth (Berkeley, Calif.), 20*(3), 123–130. doi:10.1111/j.1523-536X.1993.tb00435.x PMID:8240618

Morgan, B., Bulpitt, C., Clifton, P., & Lewis, P. (1982). Analgesia and satisfaction in childbirth (the Queen Charlottes 1000 mother survey). *Lancet, 320*(8302), 808–810. doi:10.1016/S0140-6736(82)92691-5 PMID:6126674

Morris, T., & McInerney, K. (2010). Media representations of pregnancy and childbirth: An analysis of reality television programs in the United States. *Birth (Berkeley, Calif.), 37*(2), 134–140. doi:10.1111/j.1523-536X.2010.00393.x PMID:20557536

Nichols, M. (1995). Adjustment to new parenthood: Attenders versus nonattenders at prenatal education classes. *Birth (Berkeley, Calif.), 22*(1), 21–26. doi:10.1111/j.1523-536X.1995.tb00549.x PMID:7741947

Odent, M. (1999). Is the participation of the father at birth dangerous? *Midwifery Today*, (51), 23.

Simkin, P. (1992). Just Another Day in a Womans Life? Part II: Nature and Consistency of Womens Long-Term Memories of Their First Birth Experiences. *Birth (Berkeley, Calif.), 19*(2), 64–81. doi:10.1111/j.1523-536X.1992.tb00382.x PMID:1388434

Simkin, P. (2008). The Birth Partner: A Complete Guide To Childbirth For Dads, Doulas, and All Other Labor Companions (3rd ed.). Harvard Common Press.

Simkin, P. (2011, February 28). Part 2: Pain, suffering, and trauma in labor and subsequent post-traumatic stress disorder: Practical suggestions to prevent PTSD after childbirth. *Science & Sensibility*.

Simkin, P., & Bolding, A. (2004). Update on nonpharmacologic approaches to relieve labor pain and prevent suffering. *Journal of Midwifery & Womens Health*, *49*(6), 489–504. doi:10.1016/S1526-9523(04)00355-1 PMID:15544978

Smith, A. (2010). *Mobile Access 2010*. Pew Research Center. Available at http://pewinternet.org/Reports/2010/Mobile-Access-2010/Summary-of-Findings.aspx

Somers-Smith, M. (1999). A place for the partner? Expectations and experiences of support during childbirth. *Midwifery*, *15*(2), 101–108. doi:10.1016/S0266-6138(99)90006-2 PMID:10703413

Steen, M., Downe, S., Bamford, N., & Edozien, L. (2011). Not-patient and and not-visitor: A meta-synthesis of fathers' encounters with pregnancy, birth and maternity care. *Midwifery*. PMID:21820778

Tomeo, C., Rich-Edwards, J., Michels, K., Berkey, C., Hunter, D., Frazier, A., & Buka, S. L. et al. (1999). Reproducibility and validity of maternal recall of pregnancy-related events. *Epidemiology (Cambridge, Mass.)*, *10*(6), 774–777. doi:10.1097/00001648-199911000-00022 PMID:10535796

Van Zandt, S., Edwards, L., & Jordan, E. (2005). Lower epidural anesthesia use associated with labor support by student nurse doulas: Implications for intrapartal nursing practice. *Complementary Therapies in Clinical Practice*, *11*(3), 153–160. doi:10.1016/j.ctcp.2005.02.003 PMID:16005832

Ward, L., Merriwether, A., & Caruthers, A. (2006). Breasts are for men: Media, masculinity ideologies, and men's beliefs about women's bodies. *Sex Roles*, *55*(9), 703–714.

Chapter 10
Beyond Gaming:
The Utility of Video Games for Sports Performance

Roma P. Patel
UC Davis Eye Center, USA

Jerry Lin
USC, USA

S. Khizer R. Khaderi
University of Utah Moran Eye Center, USA

ABSTRACT

The interest around the utilization of video games as a component of rehabilitative therapy has dramatically increased over the past decade. Research efforts have confirmed the positive effects of repetitive gaming in improving visual outcomes; however, there is limited knowledge on the mechanism of action delivered by repetitive gaming. Utilizing knowledge of the visual system, including targeting specific cells in the retina with visual stimuli, the authors captured the training effects of gaming to augment pre-selected skills. Specifically, the authors embedded a homerun derby style baseball game with a contrast threshold test, to stimulate parvocellular retinal ganglion cells. Parvocellular cells are the first line of the ventral, or "what" pathway of visual processing. Repetitive stimulation of the parvocellular system shows promising preliminary results in improving batting performance.

INTRODUCTION

With the current push to gamify health care, researchers have focused their attention to the role of video games. Emerging data now supports the potential benefits of video games in areas including physical and visual rehabilitation, visual development and vision training. Research over the last 15 years has highlighted direct benefits from video game play in visual processing speed, and the ability to process multiple visual inputs. For example, in 2003, a series of experiments conducted by Green et al. illustrated that one hour a day for 10 days of action video game play by non-gamers improved visual attention

DOI: 10.4018/978-1-5225-1817-4.ch010

abilities such as information processing and apprehending more information at a glance, while simultaneously improving the speed of stimulus-response.(Green & Bavelier, 2003). A more recent study showed that playing 5.5 hours of action video games over 9 weeks resulted in a 43% improvement in gray-scale contrast sensitivity versus non-action video gameplay.(Lietal., 2009). Furthermore, action video game play enhances the spatial and temporal resolution of vision, allowing the players to discern the stimulus despite being crowded with distractors both in physical space and in temporal sequence. (Green, Pouget, & Bavelier, 2010). Currently, other health-specific innovative applications of gaming are being explored including its use in the rehabilitation of visual skills after stroke, physical therapy, improved disease self-management, health education, and skills training for clinicians. Video games are currently being studied in the treatment of amblyopia with limited data showing at least a 5-fold faster visual acuity recovery compared to occlusion therapy (Fricker et al., 1981; Li et al., 2011).

Although the benefits of video games are being explored as stated above, the specific mechanisms for how video games enhance certain visual skill sets have not. In this era of developing specialized skills, this type of study is important to isolate methods of improvements and enhancement. We studied the visual mechanisms involved in baseball batting performance. By focusing on a specific visual skill set, the ability to hit a baseball at a high speed, we were able to deconstruct both the visual physiology involved, visual processing patterns and the type of visual stimulus needed to train this skill set. We embedded a home run derby style baseball video game with an algorithm designed to enhance batting performance based on the visual processing pattern noted in baseball players with batting averages above 0.300 (generally considered to be a good to very good batting average).

DEFINING THE RELATIONSHIP BETWEEN VISUAL PROCESSING AND SPORTS PERFORMANCE

To better study the visual function of an athlete, one must first understand the basics of visual processing. The visual processing model described by Ungerleider and Mishkin in 1982 consists of two anatomically and functionally distinct information pathways – a dorsal "where" pathway and a ventral"what" pathway. The dorsal pathway is the Magnocellular (M- cell/Parasol) system consisting of large soma with large dendritic fields and increased axon density in the periphery. Associated neurons have a fast response time with rapid decay, resulting in more transient vision. Although this system has less spatial resolution, it is more sensitive to subtle contrast, movement, location, and onset of stimuli. The ventral pathway is the Parvocellular (P-cell/Midget) system of small soma with small dendritic fields and slow conduction velocity (See Figure 1). This system is sensitive to shape, color, and detail resulting in higher spatial resolution. Thus, the ventral P cell pathway serves for object recognition and form representation while the dorsal M cell pathway provides spatial awareness and action guidance. Jaekl et al. have shown that the visual detection enhancement from multisensory integration (such as auditory input) is mainly articulated by the magnocellular system, which is most sensitive at low spatial frequencies (Jaekl & Soto-Faraco, 2010) Further investigation into the magnocellular pathways in athletes could elicit more knowledge on how their visual processing functions.

One such investigation conducted by Khaderi and colleagues evaluated whether the magnocellular pathway was heightened in athletes compared to the general population.[12] Using Frequency Doubling Technology(FDT), the M cells of the studied baseball players were stimulated to assess their relative sensitivity to the sensitivity of non-athletes. The central 20 degrees of each player's visual field under-

Figure 1. Parvocellular cells in the human visual processing system
Source: McGill University, used under copyright license.

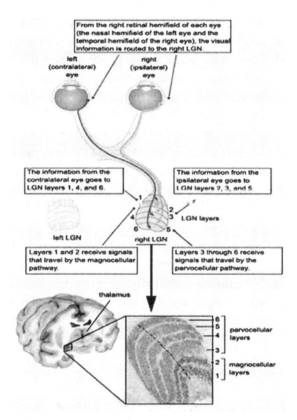

went threshold testing of M cell function, with higher FDT scores indicative of poor M cell function and low FDT scores indicative of good M cell function. Early analysis indicates that the athletes demonstrated higher FDT scores, cor- relating to greater central visual depression and poor M-cell response. Central visual depression is defined as the inability to detect visual stimuli in the central 20 degrees of the visual field during M cell threshold testing. Greater number of hours of organized sports play was statistically significant on multiple regression analyses to be correlated with higher FDT scores. These unexpected preliminary findings of greater central depression, indicative of decreased M cell sensitivity with increased hours of organized sports play, were then used as the basis for the development of a baseball simulation video game. This video game, the focus of this study, was designed to help answer the question – does focused training using algorithms directed at ganglion cell function in the central visual field measurably impact specific sports performance?

Pilot Study

Baseball Trainer Game System

The Baseball Trainer game is built on the Unity 4 engine, written entirely in the C# programming language. The system was configured to be played and deployed on standard PC computers using a mouse and 24" LCD monitors. It was designed to simulate batting practice session with a pitcher. The player view is actually in the perspective of the catcher to give a clear view of the baseball pitch and to control stimulus area. As seen in Figure 2, players are given the ability to configure the play setting to reflect their skill level, play style, and desired environment. This includes selecting between 9 different pitches the pitcher can throw and 9 different target areas for the pitches. The 9 different pitches include a four-seam fastball, two- seam fastball, the changeup, the curveball, the cutter, the forkball, the knuckleball, the slider, and the split-finger. The skill level changes the pitch types, speeds, and strikezones. All pitches target the strike zones and the pitcher will not throw a ball (pitch outside strike zone).

Of important note are the two different modes of the batting game. One is the standard batting practice game, shown in Figure 3, which is noted as the "Arcade" mode in the settings. A player is given a series of pitches and the player must click to swing and select the correct strike zone. The click must be timed within the time the ball is within the batting range and on the correct strike zone for the player to register a hit.

In the "Eye Trainer" mode, the baseball becomes a red stimulus for game players trying to train their parvocellular retinal ganglion cells, as shown in Figure 4. Using an approach based on static automated perimetry methodology, a binary staircase bracketing is used to vary luminance of the baseball against a blue or green background with focus on the central 10 degrees of the visual field while all other aspects of the game remain the same. After completing play, the player is given a batting practice breakdown, shown in Figure 5.

Figure 2. Game settings players can set

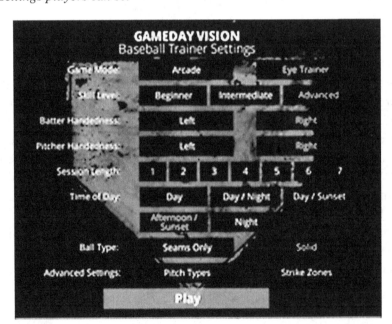

Figure 3. Control version of the baseball batting game

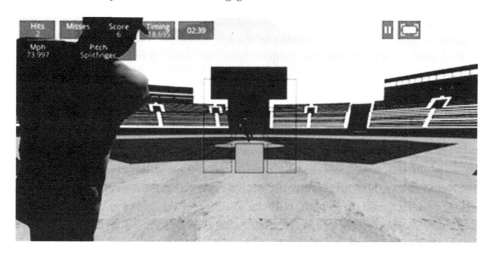

Figure 4. Eye training version of the baseball batting game

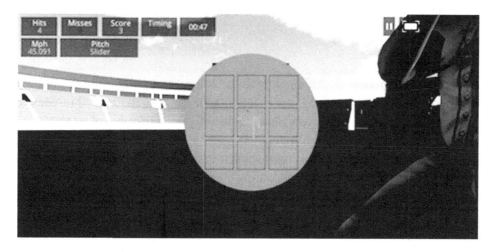

Figure 5. Batting Trainer session breakdown

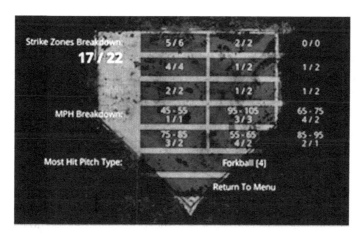

METHODS

A small test group of 20 high school baseball players aged 15 to 17 years old from a local high school volunteered to participate in the study. The subjects were randomized to play either a control version of the game or the test video game, which was the same video game with the contrast algorithm embedded into the video game. The test baseball game parameters were identical to the control version of the game except the test baseball game was run in eye-trainer mode as described above. Both video games simulated pitch speeds between 45-75 mph. Both the control and test groups played the baseball game for 7 minutes. The 7 minute time length is based on the standard luminance threshold testing time for parvocellular test function, which is typically used in glaucoma visual field testing. After 7 minutes of playing the video game, the batting performance of both groups was evaluated using an automated pitching machine at a set speed of 75 mph, with each subject receiving twenty pitches. This speed was selected based on the typical pitch speeds encountered at the high school level and was verified by the coaching staff of the team. There was up to a thirty-minute lag time between game play and batting, due to limitation in the number of automated pitching machines. The batting performances of the control and test groups, prior and after training with the two baseball batting video games were analyzed using paired sample T-tests performed in Microsoft Excel 2007.

Results

The raw data is presented in Table 1. Although both the control and test groups showed improvement in their batting performance, 0.650 to 0.675 (p-value of 0.708) and 0.630 to 0.770 respectively, the test group had a statistically significant change with a p-value of <0.01, (p-value of 0.006).

Also shown in Figure 6 and 7 is each individual batter's change in batting average. Side by side comparison shows a clear general trend of improvement in the test group versus variable outcomes in the control group. Figure 8 displays the overall batting average improvement following video game play between the control and test groups. The standard deviation for the control group was 0.1633 at start, and 0.13591 after 7 minutes. For the test group, the standard deviation was 0.167 at start, and 0.15129 after 7 minutes.

DISCUSSION

The improvement seen in both groups shows that video gaming targeting a specific part of the visual processing pathway can potentially result in a more significant improvement in sports performance, in a very short period of time. Although this was a small study, these results indicate the need for and potential promise of further research in evaluating the specific roles of retinal ganglion cell expression and visual processing in different types of visual tasks. By eliciting and isolating these roles, we can hope to develop training tools to enhance specific visual demands and overall sports performance in athletes.

The implications on game design and play also still requires further investigation, but from this report, we may be able to lay the framework for hypotheses. In the design of our game, we tried to keep the fidelity of the physics of the environment intact but greatly altered the visuals in terms of the angle of view, color, and definition of objects. Even with such relaxations, we were able to achieve some desired results, and it is questionable whether improvement in these game factors would increase visual training.

Table 1. Changes in batting averages before and after playing a video game with and without varied luminance of the central field

Age of Test Subject	Before	After
Control Subjects		
17	0.5	0.65
17	0.7	0.7
18	0.95	0.75
16	0.7	0.65
16	0.4	0.7
15	0.65	0.35
15	0.45	0.8
16	0.75	0.7
15	0.65	0.6
15	0.75	0.85
Test Subjects		
17	0.85	0.95
15	0.65	0.7
17	0.65	0.8
17	0.6	0.75
15	0.4	0.4
16	0.65	0.85
16	0.3	0.75
16	0.7	0.85
15	0.7	0.75
15	0.8	0.9

Figure 6. Change in control group batter average

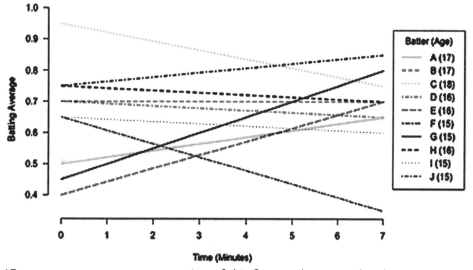

For a more accurate representation of this figure, please see the electronic version.

Figure 7. Change in test group batter average

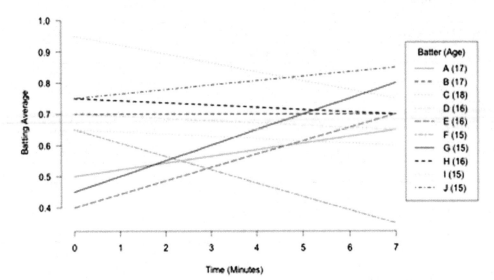

*For a more accurate representation of this figure, please see the electronic version.

Figure 8. Average change and standard deviations as part of t-test analysis

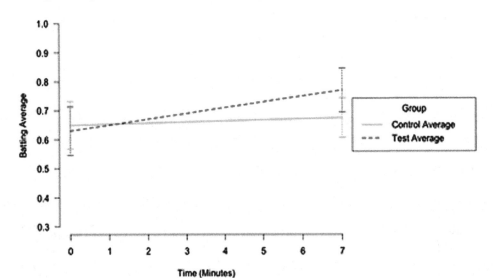

This could be true in many other game applications. We were also able to achieve these results using a standard computer with a flat video display, even with the game being heavily dependent on depth perception. It is also believed that this may be sufficient for some results in other game applications, but it is yet to be seen if more realistic game simulations yield better results.

The game design was also centered on the concept of incremental contrast challenge (bracketing) to the visual system while keeping most other factors constant. We did not use any other schemes such as bracketing other visual elements in tandem with contrast. Investigating the effectiveness of games employing other schemes by design is still warranted.

CONCLUSION

Due to the limited understanding of athletes' visual advantages, lack of precise methodologies to assess and train specific aspects of the visual processing pathways, the beneficial effect of video gaming on sports performance remains unclear. As further studies in the aforementioned arenas are performed, there is potential for the development of technology to incorporate video gaming into sports performance vision training programs.

REFERENCES

Fricker, S. J., Kuperwaser, M. C., & Stromberg, A. E. (1981). Use of a video-game/stripe presentation for amblyopia therapy. *Journal of Pediatric Ophthalmology and Strabismus, 18*(2), 11–16.

Green, C. S., & Bavelier, D. (2003). Action video game modifies visual attention. *Nature, 423*(6939), 534–537. doi:10.1038/nature01647 PMID:12774121

Green, C. S., Pouget, A., & Bavelier, D. (2010). Improved probabilistic inference as a general learning mechanism with action video games. *Current Biology, 20*(17), 1573–1579. doi:.cub.2010.07.04010.1016/j

Li, R., Polat, U., Makous, W., & Bavelier, D. (2009, May). Enhancing the contrast sensitivity function through action video game training. *Nature Neuroscience, 12*(5), 549–551. doi:10.1038/nn.2296 PMID:19330003

Li, R. W., Ngo, C., Nguyen, J., & Levi, D. M. (2011, August). Video-game play induces plasticity in the visual system of adults with amblyopia. *PLoS Biology, 9*(8). doi:10.1371/journal.pbio.1001135 PMID:21912514

Primack, B. A., Carroll, M. V., & McNamara, M. (2012, June). Role of video games in improv- ing health-related outcomes: A systematic review. *American Journal of Preventive Medicine, 42*(6), 630–638. doi:10.1016/j.amepre.2012.02.023 PMID:22608382

Chapter 11
Games and Other Training Interventions to Improve Cognition in Healthy Older Adults

Elizabeth M. Zelinski
University of Southern California, USA

ABSTRACT

Many of the cognitive declines in healthy aging are moderated by experience, suggesting that interventions may be beneficial. Goals for aging outcomes include improving performance on untrained tasks, remediating observed cognitive declines, and ensuring preservation of functional ability. This selective review evaluates current progress towards these goals. Most research focuses on untrained tasks. Interventions associated with this outcome include games and exercises practicing specific cognitive skills, as well as aerobic exercise, and modestly benefit a relatively narrow range of cognitive tasks. Few studies have directly tested improvements in tasks on which individuals have been shown to experience longitudinal decline, so this goal has not been realized, though remediation can be examined rather easily. Little work has been done to develop psychometrically strong functional outcomes that could be used to test preservation of independence in everyday activities. Virtual reality approaches to functional assessment show promise for achieving the third goal.

INTRODUCTION

A very wide range of cognitive processes, including speed, working memory, executive functions, memory, linguistic abilities, and knowledge are affected in old age. However, longitudinal age declines in cognition tend to be gradual but typically not statistically significant until about age 60 (see Schaie, 2005). The relative amount of decline varies by cognitive domain, with a correlation of about -.33 for age and episodic memory, and -.50 for age and speed (e.g., Verhaeghen & Salthouse, 1997). A few domains like language, remain stable until after the 70s (McGinnis & Zelinski, 2000), though declines in sensory

DOI: 10.4018/978-1-5225-1817-4.ch011

and perceptual processes may create functional impairments such as difficulties in communication (e.g., Schneider & Pichora-Fuller, 2000).

Although many of the declines associated with age may be due to degenerative physiological processes, recent evidence also points to the effects of certain moderators of performance that affect the extent to which age changes may be observed. These inform the basis of interventions to enhance cognitive processes in healthy older adults, that is, the majority of older persons, who do not develop dementing diseases or cognitive impairment, but who experience "normal" aging declines.

Cohort Differences

Substantial increases in reasoning and related abilities in people of different generations when compared at the same ages (e.g., Schaie, 2005), suggest that changes in the cognitive environment may affect some abilities that have been observed to decline with age. Zelinski & Kennison (2007) evaluated two birth cohorts of people aged 56-82, one born on average in 1908 and the other born on average in 1924 on reasoning, spatial ability, list recall, text recall, and vocabulary. The more recently born cohort had better scores at age 74 on all tests except for vocabulary, even though that group did show declines on all tests with age. The explanation for the observed cohort differences was that the skills associated with better performance are reinforced by the broader social culture and these affect scores into old age (Zelinski & Kennison, 2007).

Education

In samples representing the population of older American adults, education is a better predictor of performance on cognitive tasks than either health or depression, even though these are both important covariates of performance (Zelinski & Gilewski, 2003). Education is used as an index of cognitive reserve, the capacity for maintaining high levels of cognitive performance in the face of negative brain changes associated with medical conditions or normal aging, due to compensatory processes. Cognitive reserve is protective of decline even in dementia, whereby highly educated individuals reach the threshold of functional deficit for diagnosis with much more brain damage than those with low levels of education (Stern, 2006).

Cognitive Engagement

Recent policy statements from the scientific community indicate that cognitive engagement is important for protection against cognitive decline in aging. The NIH Consensus Development Conference Statement on Preventing Alzheimer's Disease and Cognitive Decline (Davidglus, et al., 2010) suggested that "increased involvement in cognitive activities in later life may be associated with slower cognitive decline and lower risk for mild cognitive impairment" (p.10). A review of modifiable risk factors for cognitive decline and dementia from the World Dementia Association suggested that a healthy diet and lifelong learning/cognitive training may be protective (Baumgart, et al., 2015). Finally, the Institute of Medicine, in its report on cognitive aging (IOM, 2015), suggested that individuals should take actions that "promote cognitive health, including be socially and intellectually engaged, and engage in lifelong learning."

Nevertheless, there is little current evidence that the benefits of cohort, education, or cognitive engagement do much more in healthy older individuals than to raise the baseline of performance. Age declines still occur for both those born more recently, and with high levels of education and of cognitive engagement (Zelinski, in press). This is where the potential to further reduce effects of decline in aging through interventions comes into play.

Malleability of Cognitive Functions

The findings of cohort differences, education, and cognitive engagement in explaining individual differences in older adults' cognitive performance suggest that it is possible to protect brain function in older adults through targeted experiences. The processes affected by cognitive aging are strongly related to each other (e.g., Zelinski & Lewis, 2003), and are observed in basic processes of perception, speed, working memory, and executive control, as well as in more complex cognitive domains. This suggests that improvement of cognitive skills in older adults can be supported by training programs that reflect this complexity.

Neuroplasticity

In parallel with the work on factors associated with cognitive outcomes in older adults, research over the past 40 years suggests that experiences constantly remodel the adult brain. Michael Merzenich and colleagues, for example, found that changes in stimulation as well as the effects of top-down processes such as attentional focus affect neuroplastic responses.

Changes in enervation of sensory inputs affect cortical responses so that they reorganize according to the available stimulation; for example, transection of nerves in the fingers of monkeys resulted in changes over time to somatosensory cortex response patterns so that representations of tactile stimulation reflected enervation from areas surrounding the lesion rather than the lesioned area (see, e.g., Buono-mano and Merzenich, 1998). Polley, et al. (2006) showed that rats trained to respond to specific stimulus features, such as the frequency or intensity of sound, produced cortical responses based on the training focus, even though their experimental stimuli included both feature sets. This suggests that attentional/ reward system plays an important roles in cortical reorganization. This leads to the observation that neuroplasticity is both positive and negative; practice in discrimination produces gains in the quality of representations that underlie neural responses, whereas disuse produces reductions in differentiation of representations (e.g., Draganski & May, 2008).

Merzenich and colleagues (e.g. Mahncke et al., 2006) suggested that cognitive aging effects represent negative plasticity. Cognitive declines arise from reductions in the schedules of brain activity associated with less cognitively demanding activities in old age, from declines in the brain's ability to detect signals against spontaneous neural network noise, from reduced neuromodulation of attention, and from negative learning. Reversing these processes by introducing intense, frequent, and extensive adaptive practice in perceptual discrimination, attention, and memory should, according to their model, improve cognitive performance in older people. They argued that engagement in reward systems is a critical feature of the model, which we will allude to in discussion of the relevance of games to cognitive training later.

It is important to note that it is not only the cognitive skills that are trained that should benefit from increasing the experiences that produce positive plasticity; these skills should extend to tasks that are not trained but share functions with the trained tasks arising from similar brain substrates (e.g ., Dahlin, et al.,

2008). Thus, the point of interventions for cognitive training of older adults involves a set of hierarchical goals: to produce transfer to untrained tasks, to rehabilitate and improve declining skills, and to ensure preservation of functional ability so that older adults may remain independent longer (see, e.g., Jobe, et al., 2001). The purpose of this chapter is to report on the relative success of current interventions to improve cognition in older adults with respect to the goals suggested here.

IMPROVEMENT OF UNTRAINED TASKS

Cognitive intervention studies demonstrate that, with training, older and younger adults can improve performance relative to control groups (Zelinski, 2009). Studies training general cognitive strategies such as mnemonics show benefits that are often quite narrow and specific, with positive effects typically confined to the particular task that was trained (Ball et al., 2002; Park et al., 2007). Studies that use the principles of positive plasticity suggested by Mahncke et al. (2006): adaptive, extensive practice of basic cognitive tasks involving perceptual discrimination and speed and executive control processes, and modulation of attention and reward systems have successfully demonstrated transfer to untrained activities (Zelinski, 2009; see Zelinski, Dalton, and Smith, 2011, for details). The types of training examined include working memory updating, multimodal training through real time strategy video games, attentional switch tasks and speeded perceptual discrimination (see Hindin & Zelinski, 2012 for details).

Physical fitness is associated with better cognitive performance (see Etnier et al., 1997). Randomized controlled aerobic exercise interventions with sedentary older adults have demonstrated cognitive enhancement in older adults for executive abilities, controlled processes such as choice RT, spatial, and simple RT tasks (e.g., Colcombe & Kramer, 2003). Animal models indicate that aerobic exercise produces neurogenesis, whereas studies with middle aged and older adults show that it increases hippocampal volume (Pereira, et al., 2007). Neuroimaging of older adults who engage in aerobic exercise has also established increased neural activity in the brain regions associated with executive control, as well as increases in the plasticity of brain networks as a result of cardiovascular training (see Hertzog, Kramer, Wilson, & Lindenberger, 2009).

The level of improvement with training interventions for older adults was investigated in a meta-analysis of the relative untrained cognitive task improvements in older adults from 25 cognitive and 17 aerobic exercise interventions (Hindin & Zelinski, 2012). It compared the effect sizes associated with improvements in performance after accounting for practice effects; previous work for aerobic interventions (Colcombe & Kramer, 2003) had only assessed effects in those in the training group. Results indicated that estimated average effect sizes were modest but roughly equivalent for aerobic and for cognitive training studies (with $d = .33$ or an equivalent $r = .16$ for both kinds of interventions). To compare the effect sizes from the meta-analyzed studies with that of a pharmacological intervention, Hindin and Zelinski (2012) estimated the effect size over 28 cognitive outcomes for young adult male volunteers in a study (Turner, et al., 2003) evaluating modafinil, a narcolepsy drug used off-label for cognitive enhancement compared to placebo. Using the same multilevel analysis methodology as for the meta-analysis of the aerobic and cognitive training studies, they found that benefits of modafinil with an estimated average $d = .23$, equivalent to an $r = .11$, compared to placebo, were rather similar to those of the nonpharmacological interventions.

Despite the similarity of the effect sizes for the untrained outcomes of both cognitive and aerobic interventions, it is likely that they may involve different mechanisms for the training benefit. Nevertheless, the goal of determining whether cognitive training is associated with improvements in untrained outcomes has, in a preliminary way, been met. Yet many questions remain. There are few peer-reviewed randomized controlled trials of training interventions. It is unclear whether interventions generalize to broad abilities. It is not clear whether the cognitive improvements are due to the specific training methods used or to other confounding factors, such as possible benefits of interacting with project staff (Lövdén, et al., 2010). The long-term benefits to performance of either type of training in are unknown. That is, few studies have followed participants for more than a year after training ends; discontinuing either aerobic or cognitive training programs may be associated with fading of the effectiveness of their cognitive benefits. There is evidence that the neuroplasticity training tested in the study by Smith and colleagues (2009) effects were reduced three months after the training ended (Zelinski, et al., 2011).

Rehabilitation and Improvement of Declining Cognitive Skills

There is very little work at the current time on interventions conducted on populations of older adults where it can be established that abilities that have declined in those individuals have been improved. Although the aerobic and cognitive training studies clearly improve performance on untrained tasks, all of the studies are essentially cross-sectional in nature. No longitudinal study of healthy cognitive aging has used aerobic or brain plasticity interventions to improve performance in individuals showing declines from previously measured levels of ability that we are aware of.

However, there may be a dynamic relationship between changes in cognitive and physical activities thought to improve cognitive performance and objective cognitive performance changes. As already indicated, cognitive reserve has been thought to be protective of functional performance so that individuals who develop dementia in the face of high levels of reserve experience a later onset and steeper declines after onset (Stern, 2009). Most individuals do not develop dementia, however, so it is has been proposed that healthy older adults could experience smaller longitudinal declines in cognition assuming that reserve builds during adulthood because of beneficial lifestyle factors (Stern, 2009).

A series of harmonized analyses of four longitudinal datasets of people aged 55 and over from the US, Canada, and Sweden, with 9 – 21 years of follow-up, examined the relationships between engagement in positive lifestyle activities and cognitive change. Mitchell et al. (2012) examined the association between changes in everyday cognitively stimulating activities and in performance on semantic knowledge, memory, fluency, and reasoning. Positive relationships, controlling for education and baseline activity and test performance were observed for all measures except for reasoning. Lindwall, et al., (2012) investigated the relationship of changes in physical activity engagement with cognitive change and found a positive relationship for changes in reasoning but not the other tests. Brown et al., (2012) found no relationship between social activity engagement changes and cognitive changes. However, in other work, James, Wilson, Barnes, and Bennett (2011) did find that those who engaged in more social activities longitudinally declined less on episodic memory, semantic memory, working memory, speed, and visuospatial ability over five years.

These studies may suggest that the dynamics of cognitive and physical engagement with cognitive outcomes from the observational studies cited here can be harnessed to reverse previous decline patterns, but until interventions have been done on individuals with longitudinally observed decline patterns in otherwise healthy old age, the goal of rehabilitating and reversing declining skills has not yet been met.

Critically, there is no current evidence that *any* intervention can delay or prevent Alzheimer's disease or dementia (US Department of Health and Human Services, 2010). At best, aerobic exercise and cognitive engagement interventions have modest effects on relatively narrow outcomes. Exploratory work into the cognitive benefit of interventions in group cognitive activities, and civic engagement in several laboratories in the US is ongoing. Other pathways to cognitive improvement that involve combining approaches, for example aerobic and cognitive training, are also being tested. However, none of these studies are evaluating rehabilitation of observed declines in healthy older adults.

Ensure Preservation of Functional Ability

The point of most interventions for cognition is that interventions should help older adults to remain independent. However, there has been very little movement towards that lofty and increasingly urgent goal. Only a few attempts have been made to develop outcome measures that readily simulate the cognitive demands of everyday activities. Those few measures that currently exist, however, do not appear to either actually or validly reflect either psychometric function or everyday functional abilities. Measures of subjective performance, for example, of whether users think that they have difficulties in everyday remembering tend to be very modestly to poorly correlated with actual performance on psychometric tests (see, e.g. Zelinski & Gilewski, 2004). Subjective improvement in everyday functioning was associated in one study with participation in a neuroplasticity-based intervention (Smith, et al., 2009) but effects were not significant three months after the intervention was discontinued (Zelinski, et al., 2011).

Only a few measures in training studies assess objective functional performance of older adults. These include the Timed Instrumental Activities of Daily Living (TIADL; Owsley, Sloane, McGwin, & Ball, 2002) and Observed Tasks of Daily Living (OTDL; Diehl, Willis, & Schaie, 1995). The TIADL measures how long it takes older adults to complete tasks that they can do accurately such as making change and reading instructions on a can of food. Performance on the TIADL has been validated with processing speed but is not correlated with OTDL (Owsley, et al, 2002). The OTDL is correlated with memory and fluid intelligence (Diehl, et al., 1995). However, neither the TIADL nor the OTDL showed training-related improvement immediately after training (e.g. Ball et al., 2002; McArdle and Prindle, 2008) or up to 10 years later (Rebok et al., 2014).

Laboratory-based assessments thought to have high face validity with daily activities, include the Cooking Breakfast (Craik & Bialystok, 2006) and the Virtual Week (Rendell & Craik, 2000) tasks, which use different amounts of information to be multitasked or to be remembered prospectively during simulated everyday activities. Cooking Breakfast is associated with performance on neuropsychological executive and working memory tests (Rose, et al., 2015). It and the Virtual Week were used for assessment of transfer in a trial of aerobic exercise crossed with retrospective and prospective memory training (McDaniel, et al., 2014). Despite no no training-related improvement on Cooking Breakfast, prospective memory tasks within Virtual Week showed training-related improvements. Participants may have had sufficient practice in applying the cognitive skills learned to the Virtual Week tasks relative to the Cooking Breakfast game.

The Assessment of Motor and Process Skills (AMPS; Fisher, 2006) assesses ability to complete participant-chosen personal and instrumental activities of daily living (ADL). The AMPS produces a motor index that measures clumsiness and physical difficulty in task performance that likely reflects physical components of an ADL, and a process measure that likely reflects executive functioning components. A study of multimodal cognitive training in older adults (Pieramico et al., 2012), showed improvements in AMPS process scores.

There is little assessment of other important activities associated with independence such as driving. Yet driving safely is an example of a behavior that is malleable and potentially can benefit from interventions. The overall rates for both fatal and nonfatal crashes for drivers age 70 and over declined substantially between 1995 and 2008, despite increases in the population of older drivers. Declines in crash rates have been significantly larger for drivers over age 70, and even greater for drivers over age 80, compared to the declines for drivers aged 35-54 (Cheung & McCartt, 2010). Although some of the change is attributed to safer cars and increasingly stringent rules for older adults' driver licensing in many states, improved general health, including better vision and cognition in the older population, is a critical factor (Cheung & McCartt, 2010). A pilot study of an intervention of computerized training of different aspects of attention in older drivers used driving performance on a simulator as an outcome. Results indicated suggested that the training reduced errors (Cassavaugh & Kramer, 2009). Simulator performance is not precisely the same as that of actual driving, so these results are suggestive, though encouraging.

Self-regulation of driving in older adults is another source of reduced crash risk. Adults over the age of 65 are more likely to use seat belts, to drive when conditions are safest, and are less likely to drive impaired, for example, to drink and drive, than other age groups (Centers for Disease Control, 2011). A substantial percentage of older adults self-regulate their driving because of concerns about visual and cognitive impairments (Braitman & McCartt, 2008). People whose processing speed is very slow have a relatively high rate of driving cessation. An intervention involving speeded visual perception training did not show improvements on untrained cognitive tasks, but, paradoxically, those individuals deficient in speeded visual perception who received the training were less likely to report cessation of driving 3 years after the intervention than those not receiving the training (Edwards, Delahunt, & Mahncke, 2009). The intervention, however, does not benefit individuals with normal processing speed for their age, (Edwards, et al., 2009) so it has limited benefit for the larger population of older adults.

In summary, the few efforts to use psychometrically sound and objective functional outcome measures in training studies have produced limited success. There is clearly a need for more real life functional outcome assessment to test whether interventions do help healthy older adults maintain independence. Relatively little is known about how normal age declines in cognition contribute to daily functioning problems, and whether interventions will reverse such declines. Recent innovations in virtual reality approaches to assessment of everyday functioning, and the development of computer driven health games to improve daily functioning can play an important role in meeting this goal. Much remains to be done, but continued work in developing everyday outcome measures that can be used to evaluate the role of cognitive interventions in old age is critical for the future.

THE ROLE OF GAMES IN MEETING THE GOALS OF INTERVENTIONS

Very few of the cognitive intervention studies, including the ones cited here, use a complex game approach to cognitive training. Yet games may be an important platform for encouraging sustained practice of cognitive skills. There has been no systematic evaluation of the role of long-term practice of cognitive interventions in outcomes; in the Hindin and Zelinski (2012) meta-analysis, the duration of cognitive training was approximately 6 weeks, with a range of 2 to 12 weeks during which there were an average of 17 sessions with a range of 3 - 45 sessions. In addition, it is likely that the discontinuation of direct cognitive training is associated with declines over time in the relative effect of the training on untrained outcomes (Hindin & Zelinski, 2012), though this has not been carefully evaluated. One large trial of interventions to improve memory, reasoning, and processing speed indicated that booster sessions 12 months after the primary intervention was helpful in maintaining training gains (Ball et al., 2002). It is not known how long older adults would continue to participate in a typical intervention; however, even after engaging in a physical fitness intervention, such as a walking program, older adults are likely to be less active several years after the intervention has ended (McAuley, et al., 2007). This, of course, does not bode well for continued performance of repetitive and presumably, boring, cognitive exercises.

We have elsewhere suggested that digital games that implicitly encourage practice of cognitive skills might be an avenue to sustained commitment to practice because games are fun (Zelinski & Reyes, 2009; see also Baniqued, et al, 2013). Though this has not been directly tested in older adults to our knowledge, it was reported that five months after an action game play intervention that involved young men with no prior game experience, many of those participants spontaneously continued to play such games (Feng, Spence, & Pratt, 2007).

One model of why people enjoy games is the Presence-Involvement-Flow Framework (Takatalo, Nyman, & Laaksonen, 2008). It suggests that presence, which includes perceptual-attentive and spatial-cognitive processes that create the space of game play, involvement as the user's roles and attitudes towards the game space, and flow as the experience of the ability-challenge tension that motivates continuation of play. It has been suggested that motivation deepens attention and this is crucial to neuroplastic processes (e.g., Mahncke et al., 2006), and games may therefore provide an important platform for older adults to sustain practice of neurocognitive skills while being enjoyable. In addition, digital action games follow many of the principles of neuroplasticity; they involve extended practice of certain skills and actions, they require sensory discrimination, are adaptive to the player's level of competence and therefore maintain an appropriate level of challenge (Zelinski & Reyes, 2009).

Toril et al. (2014) meta-analyzed effects of video game engagement in studies evaluating cognitive benefits to older adults and found significant transfer to other tasks, but comparisons were against no-contact control groups and not traditional training programs. Belchior et al. (2013) found that older adults playing a first-person shooter game and those playing a puzzle game gained as much in cognitive task improvements as those receiving visual speed of processing training. These positive effects may be related to immersion and involvement with the games (Zelinski & Reyes, 2009). Belchior, Marsiske, Sisco, Yam, & Mann (2012) found that older adults rated engagement high if they were using an off-the-shelf video game condition and that engagement increased with game experience.

However, even games have some limitations. Toril et al. (2014) reported that shorter training periods were associated with better transfer than for longer ones, suggesting fading of novelty. Another issue is the level of challenge within the training. A study that allowed participants to select training tasks and difficulty level showed that most selected modestly difficult games and they did not engage in the most difficult (and potentially most beneficial) working memory game available (Bozoki, Radovanovic, Winn, Heeter, & Anthony, 2013). Bozoki et al. suggest that providing game software is insufficient to maintain motivation, interest, and gain.

Despite the challenges associated with increasing engagement with games and other approaches to increase intellectual engagement for protection against cognitive decline and dementia risk seem to have made their mark. A recent study reported that 61% of a representative sample of American adults over age 50 considered keeping mentally active "very important" for protection against Alzheimer's (Roberts, McLaughlin, & Connell, 2014). This message seems to have been successfully conveyed, as there were no differences in response patterns related to age, gender, race, or education. The findings suggest that the public may be receptive to training. Because attribution of disability due to aging contributes longitudinally to the development of cognitive deficit and frailty in older adults (Robertson & Kenny, 2015), it may also be important to emphasize to the public the considerable potential for intervention benefits.

Interest in developing commercial games to engage older adults as well as others in cognitive training has been burgeoning. Posit Science (positscience.com, San Francisco, CA) was the first company to test an intervention, its Brain Fitness program, in a large randomized controlled multisite clinical trial of people aged 65-93 (Smith et al., 2009; Zelinski et al., 2011), and showed successful improvement on untrained tasks . Posit Science has expanded its programs from the original auditory training program to visual training and executive function training in an online package called Brain HQ with testing extended to a wide range of users, including those with mild traumatic brain injury and cancer survivors. Another company, Lumos Labs (lumosity.com, San Francisco, CA), has created a substantial database and is involved in supporting research on its online training program's efficacy. More broadly, Sharp-Brains (sharpbrains.com, San Francisco, CA) provides independent marketing and product information to companies, clinicians, and consumers about advances in applied neuroscience products, including games, to improve cognitive and emotional functioning across the life span. A professional society, the Entertainment Software and Cognitive Neurotherapeutics Society (ESCONS, escons.org), was recently organized to create collaborations and develop scientific guidance for the development of digital games to assist in diagnosis and treatment of mental health problems and to support cognitive functioning. It now holds annual meetings to showcase recent research in this area. Other organizations such as the Games for Health (gamesforhealth.org) society, supported by the Robert Wood Johnson Foundation, encourage research in a number of health related applications such as digital games to enhance cognition.

At this point in time, these developments are clearly exciting. Yet the evaluation of the progress towards the goals of cognitive interventions for aging remains similar for both the research-based and commercially-based arenas. Both standard interventions and some games have been shown to improve performance on untrained tasks. Limited work thus far has been done to improve performance in those with measurable previous declines, or on functional outcomes related to maintaining independence. There is much work ahead; the field is in its infancy, but there is reason to be optimistic about the role of games to improve cognition in older adults.

REFERENCES

Ball, K., Berch, D. B., Helmers, K. F., Jobe, J. B., Leveck, M. D., Marsiske, M., & Willis, S. L et al.. (2002). Effects of cognitive training interventions with older adults: A randomized controlled trial. *Journal of the American Medical Association*, *288*(18), 2271–2281. doi:10.1001/jama.288.18.2271 PMID:12425704

Baniqued, P. L., Lee, H., Voss, M. W., Basak, C., Cosman, J. D., DeSouza, S., & Kramer, A. F. et al. (2013). Selling points: What cognitive abilities are tapped by casual video games? *Acta Psychologica*, *142*(1), 74–86. doi:10.1016/j.actpsy.2012.11.009 PMID:23246789

Baumgart, M., Snyder, H. M., Carrillo, M. C., Fazio, S., Kim, H., & Johns, H. (2015). Summary of the evidence on modifiable risk factors for cognitive decline and dementia: A population –based perspective. *Alzheimers & Dementia*, *11*(6), 718–726. doi:10.1016/j.jalz.2015.05.016 PMID:26045020

Belchior, P., Marsiske, M., Sisco, S., Yam, A., Bavelier, D., Ball, K., & Mann, W. C. (2013). Video game training to improve selective visual attention in older adults. *Computers in Human Behavior*, *29*(4), 1318–1324. doi:10.1016/j.chb.2013.01.034 PMID:24003265

Belchior, P., Marsiske, M., Sisco, S., Yam, A., & Mann, W. (2012). Older adults engagement with a video game training program. *Activities, Adaptation and Aging*, *36*(4), 269–279. doi:10.1080/0192478 8.2012.702307 PMID:23504652

Bozoki, A., Radovanovic, M., Winn, B., Heeter, C., & Anthony, J. C. (2013). Effects of a computer-based cognitive exercise program on age-related cognitive decline. *Archives of Gerontology and Geriatrics*, *57*(1), 1–7. doi:10.1016/j.archger.2013.02.009 PMID:23542053

Braitman, K. A., & McCartt, A. T. (2008). Characteristics of older drivers who self-limit their driving. *Annals of Advances in Automotive Medicine*, *52*, 254–254. PMID:19026241

Brown, C. L., Gibbons, L. E., Kennison, R. F., Robitalle, A., Lindwall, M., Mitchell, M. B., & Mungas, D. et al. (2012). Social Activity and Cognitive Functioning Over Time. *Journal of Aging Research*, *2012*, 287438. doi:10.1155/2012/287438 PMID:22991665

Buonomano, D. V., & Merzenich, M. M. (1998). Cortical plasticity: From synapses to maps. *Annual Review of Neuroscience*, *21*(1), 149–186. doi:10.1146/annurev.neuro.21.1.149 PMID:9530495

Cassavaugh, N. D., & Kramer, A. F. (2009). Transfer of computer-based training to simulated driving in older adults. *Applied Ergonomics*, *40*(5), 943–952. doi:10.1016/j.apergo.2009.02.001 PMID:19268912

Centers for Disease Control Data and Statistics. (2011). *New data on older drivers*. Retrieved from http://www.cdc.gov/Features/dsOlderDrivers/

Cheung, I., & McCartt, A. T. (2010). *Declines in fatal crashes of older drivers: Changes in crash risk & survivability*. Arlington, VA: Insurance Institute for Highway Safety.

Colcombe, S. J., & Kramer, A. F. (2003). Fitness effects on the cognitive function of older adults: A meta-analytic study. *Psychological Science*, *14*(2), 125–130. doi:10.1111/1467-9280.t01-1-01430 PMID:12661673

Craik, F. I. M., & Bialystok, E. (2006). Planning and task management in older adults: Cooking breakfast. *Memory & Cognition*, *34*(6), 1236–1249. doi:10.3758/BF03193268 PMID:17225505

Dahlin, E., Stigsdotter-Neely, A., Larsson, A., Backman, L., & Nyberg, L. (2008). Transfer of learning after updating mediated by the striatum. *Science*, *320*(5882), 1510–1512. doi:10.1126/science.1155466 PMID:18556560

Daviglus, M. L., Bell, C. C., Berrettini, W., Bowen, P. E., Connolly, E. S., & Cox, N. J. (2010, April26–28). … Trevisan, M. (2010). *National Institutes of Health State-of-the-Science Conference Statement: Preventing Alzheimer's Disease and Cognitive Decline. NIH Consensus and State-of-the-Science Statements*, *27*(4), 1–30. doi:10.7326/0003-4819-153-3-201008030-00260 PMID:20445638

Diehl, M., Willis, S., & Schaie, K. W. (1995). Everyday problem solving in older adults: Observational assessment and cognitive correlates. *Psychology and Aging*, *10*(3), 478–491. doi:10.1037/0882-7974.10.3.478 PMID:8527068

Draganski, B., & May, A. (2008). Training-induced structural changes in the adult human brain. *Behavioural Brain Research, 192*(1), 137–142. doi:10.1016/j.bbr.2008.02.015 PMID:18378330

Edwards, J. D., Delahunt, P. B., & Mahncke, H. W. (2009). Cognitive speed of processing training delays driving cessation. *The Journals of Gerontology. Series A, Biological Sciences and Medical Sciences, 64*(12), 1262–1267. doi:10.1093/gerona/glp131 PMID:19726665

Etnier, J. L., Salazar, W., Landers, D. M., Petruzzello, S. J., Han, M., & Nowell, P. (1997). The influence of physical fitness and exercise upon cognitive functioning: A meta-analysis. *Journal of Sport & Exercise Psychology, 19*(3), 249–277. doi:10.1123/jsep.19.3.249

Feng, J., Spence, I., & Pratt, J. (2007). Playing an action video game reduces gender differences in spatial cognition. *Psychological Science, 18*(10), 850–855. doi:10.1111/j.1467-9280.2007.01990.x PMID:17894600

Fisher, A. G. (2006). Assessment of Motor and Process Skills: Vol. 1. *Development, standardization, and administration manual* (6th ed.). Fort Collins, CO: Three Star Press.

Hertzog, C., Kramer, A. F., Wilson, R. S., & Lindenberger, U. (2009). Enrichment effects on adult cognitive development: Can the functional capacity of older adults be preserved or enhanced? *Psychological Science in the Public Interest, 9*, 1–65. PMID:26162004

Hindin, S., & Zelinski, E. M. (2012). Extended practice and aerobic exercise interventions benefit untrained cognitive outcomes in older adults: A meta-analysis. *Journal of the American Geriatrics Society, 60*(1), 136–141. doi:10.1111/j.1532-5415.2011.03761.x PMID:22150209

IOM (Institute of Medicine). 2015. *Cognitive aging: Progress in understanding and opportunities for action.* Washington, DC: The National Academies Press. Retrieved from http://search.proquest.com/docview/1712600597?accountid=14749

James, B. D., Wilson, R. S., Barnes, L. L., & Bennett, D. A. (2011). Late-life social activity and cognitive decline in old age. *Journal of the International Neuropsychological Society, 17*(06), 998–1005. doi:10.1017/S1355617711000531 PMID:22040898

Jobe, J. B., Smith, D. M., Ball, K., Tennstedt, S. L., Marsiske, M., Willis, S. L., & Kleinman, K. et al. (2001). ACTIVE: A cognitive intervention trial to promote independence in older adults. *Controlled Clinical Trials, 22*(4), 453–479. doi:10.1016/S0197-2456(01)00139-8 PMID:11514044

Kennison, R. F., Petway, K. T II, & Zelinski, E. M. (under review). *Cognitive reserve and cohort effects interact in psychometric measures of the Long Beach Longitudinal Study.*

Lindwall, M., Cimino, C. R., Gibbons, L. E., Mitchell, M. B., Benitez, A., Brown, C. L., & Piccinin, A. M. et al. (2012). Dynamic associations of change in physical activity and change in cognitive function: Coordinated and integrated analyses of four longitudinal studies. *Journal of Aging Research, 2012*, 493598. doi:10.1155/2012/493598 PMID:23029615

Lövdén, M., Bodammer, N. C., Kühn, S., Kaufmann, J., Schütze, H., Tempelmann, C., & Lindenberger, U. et al. (2010). Experience-dependent plasticity of white-matter microstructure extends into old age. *Neuropsychologia, 48*(13), 3878–3883. doi:10.1016/j.neuropsychologia.2010.08.026 PMID:20816877

Mahncke, H. W., Bronstone, A., & Merzenich, M. M. (2006). Brain plasticity and functional losses in the aged: Scientific bases for a novel intervention. *Reprogramming the Brain, 157*, 81–109. doi:10.1016/S0079-6123(06)57006-2 PMID:17046669

McArdle, J. J., & Prindle, J. J. (2008). A latent change score analysis of a randomized clinical trial in reasoning training. *Psychology and Aging, 23*(4), 702–719. doi:10.1037/a0014349 PMID:19140642

McAuley, E., Morris, K. S., Motl, R. W., Hu, L., Konopak, J. F., & Elavsky, S. (2007). Long-term follow-up of physical activity behavior in older adults. *Health Psychology, 25*(3), 375–380. doi:10.1037/0278-6133.26.3.375 PMID:17500625

McDaniel, M. A., Binder, E. F., Bugg, J. M., Waldum, E. R., Dufault, C., Meyer, A., & Kudelka, C. et al. (2014). Effects of cognitive training with and without aerobic exercise on cognitively demanding everyday activities. *Psychology and Aging, 29*(3), 717–730. doi:10.1037/a0037363 PMID:25244489

McGinnis, D., & Zelinski, E. M. (2000). Understanding unfamiliar words: The influence of processing resources, vocabulary knowledge, and age. *Psychology and Aging, 15*(2), 335–350. doi:10.1037/0882-7974.15.2.335 PMID:10879587

Mitchell, M. B., Cimino, C. R., Benitez, A., Brown, C. L., Gibbons, L. E., Kennison, R. F., & Piccinin, A. M. et al. (2012). Cognitively stimulating activities: Effects on cognition across four studies with up to 21 years of longitudinal data. *Journal of Aging Research, 2012*, 461592. doi:10.1155/2012/461592 PMID:23024862

Moore, D. J., Palmer, B. W., Patterson, T. L., & Jesre, D. V. (2007). A review of performance-based measures of functional living skills. *Journal of Psychiatric Research, 41*(1-2), 97–117. doi:10.1016/j.jpsychires.2005.10.008 PMID:16360706

Owsley, C., Sloane, M., McGwin, G. Jr, & Ball, K. (2002). Timed instrumental activities of daily living tasks: Relationship to cognitive function and everyday performance assessments in older adults. *Gerontology, 48*(4), 254–265. doi:10.1159/000058360 PMID:12053117

Park, D. C., Gutchess, A. H., Meade, M. L., & Stine-Morrow, E. A. L. (2007). Improving cognitive function in older adults: Nontraditional approaches. *Journals of Gerontology, Series B, 62B*(Special Issue 1SI1), 45–52. doi:10.1093/geronb/62.special_issue_1.45 PMID:17565164

Pereira, A. C., Huddleston, D. E., Brickman, A. M., Sosunov, A. A., Hen, R., McKhann, G. M., …Small, S. A. (2007). An in vivo correlate of exercise-induced neurogenesis in the adult dentate gyrus. *Proceedings of the National Academy of Sciences, 104*, 5638-5643. doi:10.1073/pnas.0611721104

Pieramico, V., Esposito, R., Sensi, F., Cilli, F., Mantini, D., Mattei, P. A., & Sensi, S. L. et al. (2012). Combination training in aging individuals modifies functional connectivity and cognition, and is potentially affected by dopamine-related genes. *PLoS ONE, 7*(8), e43901. doi:10.1371/journal.pone.0043901 PMID:22937122

Polley, D. B., Steinberg, E. E., & Merzenich, M. M. (2006). Perceptual learning directs auditory cortical map reorganization through top-down influences. *The Journal of Neuroscience, 26*(18), 4970–4982. doi:10.1523/JNEUROSCI.3771-05.2006 PMID:16672673

Rebok, G. W., Ball, K., Guey, L. T., Jones, R. N., Kim, H.-Y., King, J. W., & Willis, S. L. et al. (2014). Ten-year effects of the Advanced Cognitive Training for Independent and Vital Elderly cognitive training trial on cognition and everyday functioning in older adults. *Journal of the American Geriatrics Association*, *62*(1), 16–24. doi:10.1111/jgs.12607 PMID:24417410

Roberts, J. S., McLaughlin, S. J., & Connell, C. M. (2014). Public beliefs and knowledge about risk and protective factors for Alzheimers disease. *Alzheimers & Dementia*, *10*(5Supplement), S381–S389. doi:10.1016/j.jalz.2013.07.001 PMID:24630852

Robertson, D. A., & Kenny, R. A. (2015). Negative perceptions of aging modify the association between frailty and cognitive function in older adults. *Personality and Individual Differences*. doi:10.1016/j.paid.2015.12.010

Rose, N. S., Luo, L., Bialystock, E., Hering, A., Lau, K., & Craik, F. I. M. (2015). Cognitive processes in the Breakfast Task: Planning and monitoring. *Canadian Journal of Experimental Psychology*, *69*(3), 252–263. doi:10.1037/cep0000054 PMID:25938251

Salthouse, T. A. (2004). What and when of cognitive aging. *Current Directions in Psychological Science*, *13*(4), 140–144. doi:10.1111/j.0963-7214.2004.00293.x

Schaie, K. W. (2005). *Developmental influences on adult intelligence*. Oxford, UK: Oxford University Press. doi:10.1093/acprof:oso/9780195156737.001.0001

Schneider, B. A., & Pichora-Fuller, M. K. (2000). Implications of perceptual deterioration for cognitive aging research. In F. I. M. Craik & T. A. Salthouse (Eds.), *The handbook of aging and cognition* (pp. 155–219). Mahwah, NJ: Erlbaum.

Smith, G. E., Housen, P., Yaffe, K., Ruff, R., Kennison, R. F., Mahncke, H. W., & Zelinski, E. M. (2009). A cognitive training program based on principles of brain plasticity: Results from the Improvement in Memory with Plasticity-based Adaptive Cognitive Training (IMPACT) study. *Journal of the American Geriatrics Society*, *57*(4), 594–603. doi:10.1111/j.1532-5415.2008.02167.x PMID:19220558

Stern, Y. (2006). Cognitive reserve and Alzheimer disease. *Alzheimer Disease and Associated Disorders*, *20*(Supplement 2), S69–S74. doi:10.1097/00002093-200607001-00010 PMID:16917199

Stern, Y. (2009). Cognitive reserve. *Neuropsychologia*, *47*(10), 2015–2028. doi:10.1016/j.neuropsychologia.2009.03.004 PMID:19467352

Takatalo, J., Nyman, G., & Laakosonen, L. (2008). Components of human experience in virtual environments. *Computers in Human Behavior*, *24*(1), 1–15. doi:10.1016/j.chb.2006.11.003

Toril, P., Reales, J. M., & Ballesteros, S. (2014). Video game training enhances cognition of older adults: A meta-analytic study. *Psychology and Aging*, *29*(3), 706–716. doi:10.1037/a0037507 PMID:25244488

Turner, D. C., Robbins, T. W., Clark, L., Aron, A. R., Dowson, J., & Sahakian, B. J. (2003). Cognitive enhancing effects of modafinil in healthy volunteers. *Psychopharmacology*, *165*, 260–269. PMID:12417966

U.S. Department of Health and Human Services, National Institutes of Health, NIH Consensus Development Program. (2010). *Preventing Alzheimer's disease and cognitive decline.* Retrieved from http://consensus.nih.gov/2010/docs/alz/ALZ_Final_Statement.pdf

Verhaeghen, P., & Salthouse, T. A. (1997). Meta-analyses of age-cognition relations in adulthood: Estimates of linear and nonlinear age effects and structural models. *Psychological Bulletin, 122*(3), 231–249. doi:10.1037/0033-2909.122.3.231 PMID:9354147

Zahodne, L. B., Manly, J. J., MacKay-Brandt, A., & Stern, Y. (2013). Cognitive declines precede and predict functional declines in aging and Alzheimers disease. *PLoS ONE, 8*(9), e73645. doi:10.1371/journal.pone.0073645 PMID:24023894

Zelinski, E. M. (2009). Far transfer in cognitive training of older adults. *Restorative Neurology and Neuroscience, 27*, 455–471. PMID:19847070

Zelinski, E. M. (in press). Does cognitive training reduce risk for dementia? In G. E. Smith & S. Farias (Eds.), *Handbook of Dementia.* Washington, DC: American Psychological Association.

Zelinski, E. M., Dalton, S. E., & Smith, G. E. (2011). Consumer-based brain fitness programs. In A. Larue & P. Hartman-Stein (Eds.), *Enhancing Cognitive Fitness in Adults: A Guide to the Use and Development of Community Programs* (pp. 45–66). New York: Springer. doi:10.1007/978-1-4419-0636-6_3

Zelinski, E. M., & Gilewski, M. J. (2003). Effects of demographic and health variables on Rasch scaled cognitive sores. *Journal of Aging and Health, 15*(3), 435–464. doi:10.1177/0898264303253499 PMID:12914012

Zelinski, E. M., & Gilewski, M. J. (2004). A 10-Item Rasch Modeled Memory Self Efficacy Scale. *Aging & Mental Health, 8*(4), 293–306. doi:10.1080/13607860410001709665 PMID:15370046

Zelinski, E. M., & Kennison, R. F. (2007). Not your parents test scores: Cohort reduces psychometric aging effects. *Psychology and Aging, 22*(3), 546–557. doi:10.1037/0882-7974.22.3.546 PMID:17874953

Zelinski, E. M., & Lewis, K. L. (2003). Adult age differences in multiple cognitive functions: Differentiation, dedifferentiation or process-specific change? *Psychology and Aging, 18*(4), 727–745. doi:10.1037/0882-7974.18.4.727 PMID:14692860

Zelinski, E. M., & Reyes, R. (2009). Cognitive benefits of computer games for older adults. *Gerontechnology (Valkenswaard), 8*(4), 220–235. doi:10.4017/gt.2009.08.04.004.00 PMID:25126043

Zelinski, E. M., Spina, L. M., Yaffe, K., Ruff, R., Kennison, R. F., Mahncke, H. W., & Smith, G. E. (2011). Improvement in Memory with Plasticity-based Adaptive Cognitive Training (IMPACT): Results of the 3-Month Follow-up. *Journal of the American Geriatrics Society, 59*(2), 258–265. doi:10.1111/j.1532-5415.2010.03277.x PMID:21314646

Chapter 12

Computer–Presented and Physical Brain–Training Exercises for School Children:
Improving Executive Functions and Learning

Bruce E. Wexler
Yale University, USA

ABSTRACT

This chapter reviews the neuroscience foundation for understanding and harnessing neuroplastic processes that shape the structure and function of the human brain after birth, describes a newly developed, integrated series of computer presented and physical exercises to promote activity-related development of neurocognitive systems of attention and executive function in elementary school children, and reviews evidence of the efficacy of the program. The computer-presented brain exercises have new functionalities that more fully shape the training to each user's individual profile of cognitive strengths and weaknesses than was previously possible. The programs also provide assessments of each child's cognitive strengths and weaknesses based on built in formal tests of cognition and error analytic algorithms applied to 15-20,000 responses from each child while using the brain training program.

INTRODUCTION

The Problem

A recently completed study assessed attention skills in 2,000 elementary school children and followed them for 16 years (Pingault et al, 2011). Children with attention problems when they were six years old were 7.6 times more likely than their classmates to never graduate from high school. This poor attention group included 17% of the study population. Failure to graduate from high school is associated with underemployment, unemployment, drug use and jail time. Current estimates are that approximately

DOI: 10.4018/978-1-5225-1817-4.ch012

7-10% of elementary-aged children have been diagnosed with ADHD. Childhood ADHD is similarly associated with many of the same undesirable long term outcomes. In some schools, attention problems are even more common. In all schools, children with attention problems require disproportionate teacher time and can affect the learning environment for all children in the classroom.

Neuroplasticity and the Scientific Foundation for Brain Training to Improve Attention

The neural basis of all cognitive functions are networks of hundreds of thousands of neurons distributed widely throughout the brain. The interconnections among nerve cells that create these functional systems are not determined by our genes, but instead are heavily influenced by stimulation and experience after birth. Hubel and Weisel (1970; 1988) were awarded the Nobel Prize for demonstrating the great extent to which early sensory experience shapes brain structure and function in mammals. Meaney and colleagues at McGill extended this work to show the particular importance of maternal stimulation in shaping life-long features of the brain and behavior(Champagne et al, 2008). They further demonstrated that these effects are produced in part by altering methylation of DNA and thus turning specific genes on (Weaver et al, 2004). In an experimental tour de force, Sur and colleagues at MIT converted normal auditory cortex into visual cortex by replacing auditory with visual input in new born ferrets (Sharma et al, 2000), suggesting that neuroplastic potential may have even fewer limits than previously thought. Merzenich and others have now conducted numerous experiments in animals elucidating training and stimulation parameters that maximize neuroplastic reshaping of structure and function (e.g., Jenkins et al, 1990).

The structure and function of the human brain are shaped after birth by stimulation from the environment to a much greater extent than are the brains of any other animal. Moreover, only human beings shape the environment that in turn shapes their brains, a transgenerational process called cultural evolution (Wexler, 2006). Education is an important component of these processes. Figure one shows basic sensory plasticity in humans; the white areas in the brain are activation during functional magnetic imaging (fMRI) of the "visual" cortex by auditory stimulation in people who were blind since birth or soon thereafter (Weaver and Stevens, 2007). Figure two shows the effects on brain structure of practicing a musical instrument for many hours as a child (Schlaug, 2001). Violin players make simple repetitive movements of their right hand with the bow, and the sensorimotor cortex in the left hemisphere (circled) which controls the right hand serves as a reference. The left hand, in contrast, makes rapid and complex movements controlling the strings. The volume expansion in the right hemisphere compared to the left is evident to the naked eye – it results from activity-dependent recruitment of neural resources, and increased connections among the neurons. Piano players make complex movements with the fingers of both hands and have "buffed up" motor cortices in both hemispheres. The human brain remains highly plastic for a much longer time after birth than do the brains of any other animals and parts of the brain associated with attention control and other cognitive executive functions continue to develop throughout childhood and adolescence.

Figure 1. Activation of normal visual cortex by auditory stimulation in early blind individuals; fMRI study with white indicating areas of activation
Source: Image provided by the author A. Stevens and reprinted with permission.

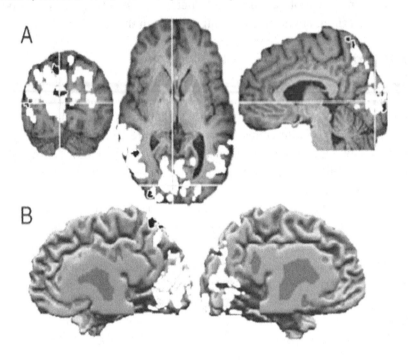

Figure 2. Upper: volume expansion of sensorimotor cortex in string players; left hand panel is from adults who had practiced the violin for many hours as a child. The left sensorimotor cortex (circled) controls the right hand that makes simple repetitive movements with the bow. The right side of the brain controls the left hand which makes rapid, complex movements while fingering the strings. Volume expansion on the right compared to the left is clear to the naked eye, presumably from activity dependent recruitment of neural resources and increased inter-neuronal connections. Right panel shows bilateral expansion of the sensorimotor cortex in piano players
Source: Image from Schlaug, 2001 and reprinted with permission from the publisher.

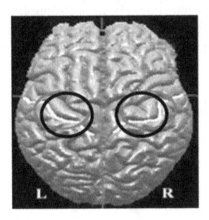 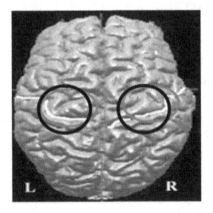

Harnessing Neuroplasticity to Improve Cognition

In the past decade medical scientists have begun to develop new treatments based on the new basic science research on neuroplasticity. Norman Doidge's book "The Brain That Changes Itself" provides examples of what he calls "neuroplasticians" from multiple branches of medicine (Doidge, 2007). Our research group has been a leader in development of plasticity-based treatments for adult psychiatric disorders, publishing what is probably the first paper to use plasticity-based computer-presented exercises to treat cognitive dysfunction in people with schizophrenia (computerized cognitive remediation or CCRT, Wexler et al, 1997), and the first paper showing normalization of task-related regional brain activation in patients after treatment, using in that study computerized training of working memory and fMRI (Figure 3, Wexler et al, 2000). More recent work has shown that the benefits of CCRT generalized to cognitive tasks not part of the training itself, persisted at least one year after training ended, and translated to the work place -- patients with schizophrenia randomly assigned to CCRT plus work therapy worked more hours and earned more money during the year after treatment ended than did patients who received only work therapy (Wexler and Bell, 2005). There have now been over40 published studies of CCRT in schizophrenia and several meta-analyses showing significant benefits of treatment with average effect size of 0.4 (Wykes et al, 2011).

Success using brain exercises to improve cognition in adults with illnesses affecting their brains provides strong empirical support for the possibility of creating brain exercises to improve cognition

Figure 3. Normalization of task-related regional brain activation after working memory training in a 52-year-old man with Schizophrenia. The robust left inferior frontal activation seen in healthy subjects was absent before training in the patient but normal after 16 weeks of training
Source: Image provided by the author.

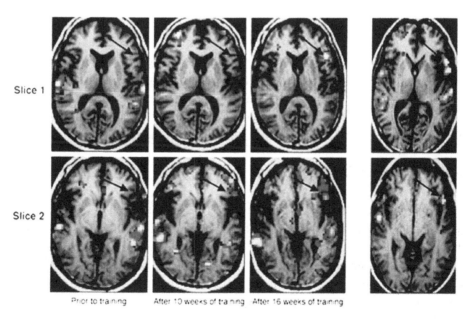

Slice 1

Slice 2

Prior to training   After 10 weeks of training   After 16 weeks of training

Patient Subject   Healthy Subject

during childhood when neural systems supporting these functions are very actively developing and neuroplasticity is high. Further support comes from appreciation of how dependent brain development is on stimulation from the environment. Too many children come to school without having had the stimulation necessary to promote development of neural systems and cognitive functions essential for success in school. When they enter school demands are made of them for which, through no fault of their own, they are not neurocognitively prepared to meet. This sets off a deviant developmental trajectory of great cost to the child, the family, the school and society. For these children, brain training can be a "school lunch program for the brain." It provides intensive stimulation ("food for the brain") of the under-developed neurocognitive systems, allowing the children to catch up in their neurodevelopment and cognitive skills. Other children come to school with a diagnosis of Attention Deficit Hyperactivity Disorder (ADHD), and have compromised executive function and poor school performance. Brain imaging research has shown that the neural systems that support executive function are slow and incomplete in development in many children with ADHD. Targeted stimulation by brain training programs is designed to accelerate the development of these systems, and provide a non-pharmacologic treatment for ADHD. Finally, ELL children fail to get the full stimulation from school until they acquire sufficient English competency. Many have also had limited stimulation prior to coming to school because of the circumstances associated with their immigration. For these children, non-verbal brain training provides essential stimulation of developing brain systems while they develop English competency.

Physical Activity, Neuroplasticity, and Cognition

Multiply replicated studies in animals show that non-specific physical activity of wheel running increases neuroplasticity, hippocampal volumes and performance on hippocampal-related learning and memory tasks. Recent studies in children have shown that children who are physically more fit have: superior performance on multiple aspects of attention, executive control and memory; elevated event-related brain potential indices of executive function; and greater volumes of the hippocampus and dorsal striatum which are thought to be important for the cognitive operations (Davis and Cooper, 2011). Recent randomized controlled-trials have shown that simple aerobic exercise after school increases academic performance (Davis et al, 2011). We took this research one step further by designing a series of physical exercises that all include a cognitive component. The physical exercises engage the same neurocognitive systems as do the computer exercises but in the context of whole body movement and social interaction. The computer and physical exercises together constitute an integrated program to promote development of brain systems and associated attention sustaining and executive functions. It is called Activate.

The Computer Exercise Component of *Activate*

The computer component itself has three components. The original version of the first game,"Catch the Ball" requires children to follow one or more balls bouncing randomly across the screen and click on them with the mouse when the ball turns a color that matches current target criterion. At the most basic level it is a simple continuous performance task and the child has to click on the ball whenever it changes from the default color of yellow to the target color of red. At successive levels of greater difficulty: blue balls are introduced first as foils to be always ignored and then as targets when the target switches randomly between red and blue as indicated on the side of the screen; green balls are added but are never targets; and working memory based target criterion are introduced such as it is a target only when the ball is the same color as the one before. After the child progresses through all variations with one ball bouncing across the screen, the variations are all repeated with two balls and then three balls. With multiple balls on the screen, the memory-based criterion applies to the history of each ball separately; thus the current target may be red for one of the bouncing balls and blue for another. Within each level there are multiple sublevels of increasing difficulty based on progressively shorter duration of the color change indicating possible targets (the response window to register correct clicks on target remains fixed and is considerably longer than the duration of the color change, but the more fleeting color changes requires more focused attention and rapid and sensitive processing of sensory input). At each of these sublevels, the speed with which the ball(s) move across the screen becomes faster or slower as the child's errors decrease or increase (adaptive tracking). When a child reaches preset graduation criteria of speed and accuracy, he or she is moved onto to the next sublevel, and when they graduate from all sublevels they move to the next level (levels are defined by different target criterion and sublevels by duration of the color changes that define targets). Since some children can never function at the faster speeds necessary to challenge other children, the programs also have built in "plateau criteria" to detect performance asymptotes or individual ceilings. Children are moved to the next sublevel and level when plateau or graduation criteria are met. The different levels of "Catch the Ball" require among them sustained attention, response inhibition, cognitive flexibility, working memory directed attention, and divided and switching attention. New user interfaces were created to increase student engagement. In the current program there are two different user games with the same underlying computer code and sequence of cognitive challenges (Figure 4). In one, the yellow ball is now a moving light or "orb" that turns into red of blue jewels to click on and collect. In the other, a magic lens moves over wooden crates going across the screen to reveal whether or not there is a monkey inside. If the child clicks in the right kind ("target") monkey, the monkey is freed from the crate and runs across the screen.

Figure 4. Two computer-presented brain training exercises in Activate; Screen shots of Treasure Trunk and Magic Lense
Source: Images printed with the permission of C8Sciences.

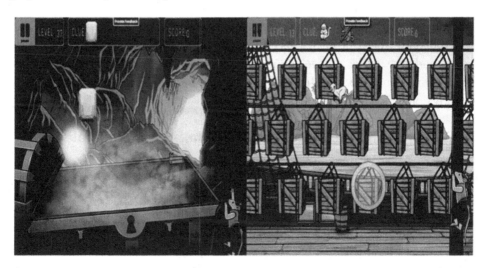

In the second computer component, called "Butterflies", butterflies enter the screen from the bottom and fly to the top carrying signs with pictures, words or number on them. Children must click on the butterflies carrying things that are members of a target category before the butterfly carries the sign off the screen. The first and easiest category is "Numbers"; the child must click on every butterfly carrying a number. Other categories are what philosophers refer to as "natural" and "basic" categories such as animals, plants or furniture. Others are lower level categories like small animals. Still others are "functional" or "temporary" categories like things found in a house, things that you take a vacation or modes of transportation. Others involve finding two things on the screen at the same time that go to together in some way such as "two things where one is used to make the other." Within each of these levels there are sublevels based on the number of butterflies on the screen at the same time. Within each of the sublevels, performance is tracked and the speed at which the butterflies fly is adjusted accordingly. Again there are graduation and plateau criteria that govern movement from one level to the next. This exercise requires sustained attention, response inhibition, visual searching and executive rule based direction of attention. In addition, it continuously exercises different aspects of category formation and use. Category formation is a core aspect of all thought and a higher level executive function. In the latest version of the game, a pirate throws things up in the area from a big chest and the child has to click on ones from the target category to help the pirate move them to another chest.

The third component is called "What Comes Next/What Came Before?" In this exercise there are four boxes for stimuli on one row and three more on a second row beneath the first. Stimuli are presented in three of the four boxes on the first row and in all three boxes on the second row. The child has to figure out the relationship among the stimuli in the first row and select the stimulus on the second row that fits the empty spot in the sequence evident on the first row. For example, if all three stimuli in the first row are green circles, then the correct choice from the second row is the green circle. If the first row shows a green circle, red triangle and another green circle, the correct choice is a red triangle. If the first row contains the numbers 9-7-5, the correct choice from the second row is "3." In different levels in this exercise, different types of rules define the relationships among the items in the first row. These include category principles like color and shape, numeric sequencing rules and visual rotations. Performance is tracked and within each level stimuli are presented for progressively shorter periods of time to require faster information processing and increase difficulty. Graduation and plateau criteria are again used to move children from one level to the next. This exercise requires sustained attention, response inhibition, use of categories and very active storage and manipulation of information in working memory. In the latest version, the boxes with the stimuli are on the chests of a row of ducks that happily fly off if the pattern is properly completed.

Game Like Features and the "Meet the Child Half-Way" Principle

Activate has a game-like visual environment called built around the theme of a Pirate Island (Figure 5). However, the training games require attention and effort –they are still "school." They are designed to "Meet the Child Halfway"; they are engaging and fun but require effort. This distinguishes them from commercial computer gains designed for entertainment. Many children who cannot sustain willful and effortful attention necessary for school and many jobs, can play these commercial gains for hours. This is because the commercial entertainment games they play actually "hijack" the child's attention through activation of lower brain reward centers, and bypass the frontal executive systems that are under devel-

Figure 5. Game like environment to "Meet the Child Half-Way"
Source: Image printed with the permission of C8Sciences.

oped and in need of strengthening. In the study cited above of the effects of inattention on high school graduation rates, key elements of the initial assessment of attentional competence were abilities to sustain attention, resist distraction and sustain effort (Pingault et al, 2011).

Innovations in Activate

1. **Automatic Individualization of Treatment:** The category of executive function includes a variety of cognitive operations and evidence is accumulating that there is little generalization of benefit if only one operation (e.g., working memory) is exercised (Melby-Levang and Hume, 2013). As soon as a training program includes multiple components to exercise different aspects of cognition, however, the problem is created of knowing when to move the user from one component to another. It is not possible to simply use a performance or graduation criterion because if it is set too low it will fail to challenge some users and if it is set too high some users will never move on. Most programs therefore just keep every one on any specific component for the same fixed amount of time or number of trials. Where there is an option to repeat a component, there is no data-driven guidance. In the C8 programs, graduation criteria are paired with plateau criteria. The graduation criteria are set high enough to provide appropriate challenge for all levels of users. The plateau functions monitor performance over a long enough period to identify if performance has stopped improving short of graduation criteria, and if so moves the user to the next type of cognitive exercise. By use of graduation and plateau criteria, ACTIVATE moves children through exercises quickly in areas of their strength, keeps them working longer in areas of their weaknesses, and avoids keeping them working on exercises for too long after their maximum gain has been reached (at least for the moment, the program brings them back later for another try). In this way, the treatment shapes itself to the needs of the individual user.

2. **Online Error Diagnostics:** C8 programs recognize 40 different types of errors and use this information in two different ways. First, when a child makes a specific type of error above a criterion frequency, the CCRT automatically provides a corrective strategy message and an example of how to do the problem correctly. In addition, for some errors, the program also makes a temporary change in the way the stimulus or problem is presented so as to make it easier to see, understand or do correctly. When the child responds correctly to the same type of problems over a few trials after the corrective strategy message, the program provides special rewards. A teacher in a classroom cannot provide this sort of specific and immediate corrective feedback regularly to individual children. Secondly, C8 error analytic algorithms analyze the approximately 20,000 responses users make while doing the training exercises to create a profile of each child's areas of relative cognitive strengths and weaknesses, similar to a neuropsychological assessment. Teachers are using these reports to help personalize instruction.

The Physical Exercise Component (PE)

There are 100 individual and group exercises that begin with more basic physical and cognitive demands and become progressively more complex as the class moves through the structured curriculum. Video examples of all exercises prepare teachers and all exercises are diagrammed (e.g., Figure 6). Lesson plans for each day instruct teachers how to organize the class and move from one exercise to the next in an orderly way that itself requires attention and self-regulation. Early exercises emphasize sustained attention and self-regulation. Later ones require working memory, cognitive flexibility and multiple simultaneous attention. In Figure 6, for example, children have to remember a distinct sequence of movement of each ball from child to child in the circle. Later exercises include sequences of Tai Chi movements or dance steps.

Figure 6. Two cognition-rich physical exercises
Source: Images printed with the permission of C8Sciences.

Methods for Evaluating Outcomes with Activate

C8 scientists have collected several types of evaluations of the effectiveness of Activate. Initial studies invited parents at two elementary schools to apply for their children to be enrolled in a free after school Activate program, indicating that half would be accepted and half assigned to a control or comparison group that simply received education as usual. Teachers unfamiliar with the specific children created the two groups, matching them for age and gender. Subsequently at other schools, outcomes were evaluated in children participating in programs implemented as enrichment initiatives, looking at dose response curves and comparisons to previous school outcomes. Outcomes were evaluated by formal tests of cognition automatically administered by the Activate program at the start and end of training, by student improvement on standardized tests of reading and arithmetic administered by the schools, and by educational outcomes of students with special education accommodations.

Three tests from the NIH Toolbox of tests to assess executive function and a Go/No-go test of response inhibition were built in to Activate. The Toolbox tests were the Flanker Test of sustained and focused attention, the Dimensional Change Card Sorting Test (DCCS) of sustained attention and cognitive flexibility, and the List Sorting Test of Working Memory (WM). In the Flanker Test, students see five arrows in a row pointing to the left or right. The students identify which way the middle arrow is pointing. On congruent trials, all arrows point in the same direction. On more difficult incongruent trials, the middle arrow points in a direction opposite to the other four. The Toolbox committee identifies reaction time (RT) on correct incongruent trials as the primary dependent measure, assuming celing effects on accuracy measures, but in some ages and populations accuracy is also of interest. In the DCCS, students match test pictures to one of two other pictures according either to similarity in color (80% of trials) or shape (20% of trials). Again, the Toolbox identifies RT on the correct less common (nondominant) trials as the primary dependent measure, but accuracy is also of interest. In the WM test, students have to remember a sequence of pictures of animals or household items, re-order the pictures in their minds from smallest to largest and then report the sequence in its new order. In the second part they see a series of animals and household objects intermixed, have to separate them into two sets, report the one set from smallest to largest, and then the other set from smallest to largest. The Go/No-go test has three sections. In the first, students are instructed to tap the space bar when they see the letter P - but to refrain from tapping when they see the letter R. In the second part, they switch and tap when they see R - but not P. In the final section, they tap when they see household items but not when they see pictures of attractive things to eat. The primary dependent measure is "No-go" trials correctly skipped. For some children the simple task of clicking on "Go" trials is also of interest. The measure of "No-go" trials skipped is only valid of at least 90% of "Go" trials are clicked.

Change within groups from before to after training were evaluated with paired t-tests. Differences between groups were evaluated by independent t-tests or Chi-Square. Predictions were directional and one-way p values were used.

RESULTS COMPARING ACTIVATE TO CONTROL GROUPS

School 1

The first school was in a largely white, socioeconomically working and middle class suburban neighborhood. Kindergarten, first and second grade children in the intervention group participated in 45 minute computer sessions followed by 45 minute PE sessions three afternoons per week for 12 weeks. This was the very first implementation of Activate and do to logistical reasons not all children successfully completed both pre and post testing. Among those with both and pre and post measures, children in the Activate group showed greater decreases in RT than those in the control group on their correct Flanker Incongruent trials (1046 msec vs. 358 msec), and were more likely to show a decrease in RT on correct DCCS non-dominant trials (11 of 12 vs. 7 of 13, chi-square, p=.035). Children in the Activate group showed a 132% increase in overall score in the WM test and 148% increase on the more difficult second part of the test, compared to 26% and 14% increases in the control group. Neither group showed notable improvement in WM. The school administered the NWEA standardized tests of reading and arithmetic in September before the Activate program began and again in March as the C8 program was ending. Children in the Activate group showed greater gains in reading going from 170.75 to 180.25 than children in the control group who went from 171.3 to 177.6. Activate were almost twice as likely to show a gain of 10 or more points (58% vs. 33%, p=.05 by Chi-Square). Gains in arithmetic were minimally higher in the Activate (9.6 points vs. 8.6 points).

School 2

The student body at the second school was 45% African American, 23% white and 23% Hispanic. More than 50% of the students were receiving free or reduced-price lunch, a marker of poverty. It was one of the lowest performing schools in its city. Second and third grade students participated in the program after school three times per week in 45 minute computer and 45 minute PE classes. The Activate showed greater improvement than those in the control group on the same NIH measures as in school #1, but the group differences were not statistically significant. This school administered the Blue Ribbon standardized tests of reading and mathematics. Three subtests were apriori identified as most closed linked to executive function: "Integrated Understandings" from the mathematics test and "Forming a General Impression" and "Developing an Interpretation" from the reading test. Children in the Activate program were 2.5 times as likely to show 50 points or greater gains on these subtests than were children in the control group, a difference significant by Chi-Square at p=.03). Moreover, when the C8 group was divided in half based on the total progress they made through the hundreds of progressive difficulty levels in the Activate computer training exercises, children who made more progress were more likely to show at least a 50 point gain in these subtests than were children who made less progress (Chi Square significant at p=.034). The high progress group actually began with lower scores on the three subtests but went to higher levels than did the children who progressed less through the C8 games (Figure 7). Lower initial scores on the standardized tests indicates that the children who progressed more in the exercises and gained more on the standardized tests were not just better learners than the other children, because if they were they would have had higher baseline scores on the standardized tests.

Figure 7. Children who progressed through difficulty levels gained more on standardized tests reflective of executive function

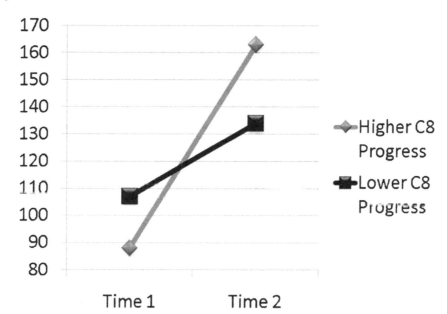

School 3

School #3 was an inner city school where 95% of children participated in the free/reduced price lunch program, 88% were African American and 7% Hispanic. In 2011, only 26% of 3rd grade students scored in the proficient range in state-wide tests of language arts and 42% were sufficient in math. In March of 2012, Activate was implemented in part during the school day and in part after school. Because of starting late in the school year and variation in the schedules of different children, only 20 of the 125 children completed more than 25 computer training sessions. Figure 8 shows a statistically significant (p=.03) dose response curve in gains in reading level on a state-wide test of reading level. Similar analyses identified statistically significant dose effect in gains in WM (p<.007). When children took the state proficiency exams again in the Fall of the next year, language proficiency had risen to 52% and math to 76%. The school moved from the bottom third to the top third in the city in one year. The principal and teachers attributed a large part of the improvement to Activate, explaining that in addition to improving attention and learning in individual children, improved self-regulation in children with attention problems led to improved classroom learning environments for all children. When the school began the Activate program again in that Fall, C8 obtained a third administration of the standardized tests of executive function on a subset of XX children. Figure 9 shows that in this A/B design, gains in cognition were greater over the 2.5 months of participating in Activate than they were in the following 5 months without Activate, providing evidence that the original gains were associated with Activate rather than normal development.

Figure 8. Gains in state reading levels are greater with more brain training

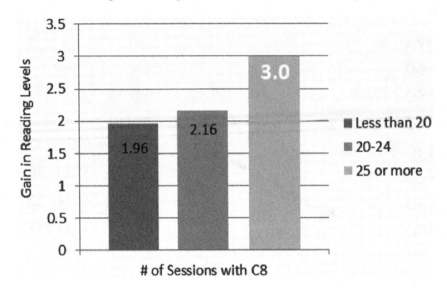

Figure 9. Gains on tests of cognition were greater during a 2.5-month period of brain training than during the subsequent 5 months

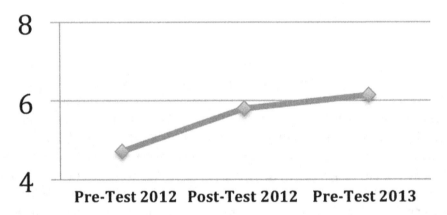

School 4

We recently completed an NIH-funded evaluation of Activate as a school-based treatment for children with ADHD. Attention-Deficit/Hyperactivity Disorder (ADHD) like other symptom-based diagnoses includes patients with different underlying disorders, confounding efforts to develop new treatments effective for only some patients. In some children with ADHD, brain regions supporting Executive Function (EF) are slow to develop. We used a two-step analytic process to determine whether doing the Activate exercises would decrease symptoms and improve EF in a subgroup of children with ADHD. Children (n = 73, mean age 7.3 +/- 1.1 years) with or sub-threshold for ADHD did the Activate exercises for approximately 36 hours over 15 weeks. Children constituted treatment-as-usual comparison groups during another 15-week period. Improvement or treatment response was defined as at least 30% reduction in parent ratings of symptoms. Tests of focused attention, response inhibition and working memory were administered by computer in the classroom at the start and end of training.

- **Results:** Children were more likely to improve following Activate than treatment-as-usual (27/66 vs. 13/66, McNemar p = .02). Responders also improved on the Flanker test of focused attention, the Go/No-Go test of response inhibition, the List Sorting test of Working Memory and clinician ratings (p = .009 - .01) while Non-Responders improved on none (p = .39 -.81). Response rate was higher in Inattentive and Combined Subtypes than in Hyperactive-Impulsive subtype.
- **Conclusion:** These findings suggest that a subset of children with ADHD may respond to brain-training with benefit generalized to both symptoms and cognitive function, and add to evidence of clinically relevant pathophysiological heterogeneity within ADHD.

School 5

School 5 was an inner city school where 80% of students qualified for free/reduced lunch, 45% were African American, 40% Hispanic, 5% Asian and 4% Caucasian. Just 33% of 3rd graders scored proficient in language arts on state-wide tests, and 44% were proficient in math. Activate was implemented late in the year and most students had only 14-18 computer sessions. The special education kindergarten at this school, however, was of particular interest. On the first day the children immediately proved unable to do the NIH tests of cognition, could not stick with the Activate exercises for more than a few minutes, and were frustrated and upset. C8 immediately adjusted the schedule for this class, removing the NIH and Go/No-go tests and reducing the duration of the C8 exercises to 3 minutes. The schedule was also set to automatically increase the duration of the exercises by 30 seconds/day. Four weeks later the C8 Field Director got a call from the school. "The K-SPED kids and their teachers want more." The children were coming in and logging on, completing two C8 exercises and saying they wanted the exercises to last longer. The Field Director moved the K-SPED to the same schedule as the rest of the school. Soon they were doing each exercise for 17 minutes continuously. Before the school year ended they were given the opportunity to do the NIH tests again. This time, 8 of the 10 children present were able to complete the Flanker test, and 4 of the 10 scored 89% to 100% correct on the congruent trials index of sustained attention. The school's vice-principal wrote a year later: "I just wanted you to know that those four students; A, An, Ad and K who were in a 12:1:1 with Ms. P's K/1-103 when you started with us Jan '12 really flourished and are in Gen Ed CTT/ LRE(least restrictive environment). Truly unheard of! Some of the things I noticed about these four students were that they were more focused (as opposed to easily distracted), more persistent (as opposed to giving up) and improved academically! In addition, there was an attitude switch."

Schools 6 and 7

Teachers in two urban elementary schools used Activate in their classes and compared gains on school-administered standardized tests of math and reading achievement (from Fall to Spring) to improvement on the same tests city-wide. Test results (Figure 10) are presented as proportion of children who meet proficiency levels (green), proportion who are just below (yellow) and children who are way below (red). In a first grade class from a very high poverty area (95% of children qualified for free or reduced lunch), 92% met proficiency in the Spring tests after using Activate during the school year while district wide only 63% met proficiency (Figure 10). In a third grade class using Activate, 83% met proficiency compared to 58% city-wide (Figure 11).

Figure 10. Comparisons of gains in school-administered Pearson standardized test of math achievement in a first grade class that used activate to gains in another class in the same school that did not use activate and to the city overall

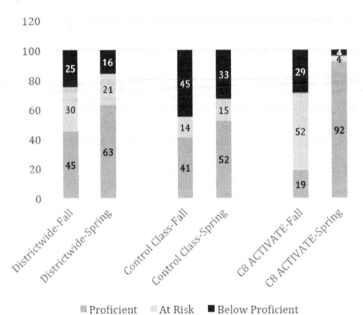

For a more accurate representation of this figure, please see the electronic version.

Figure 11. Comparisons of gains in school-administered Pearson standardized test of reading achievement in a third grade class that used activate to gains in the city overall

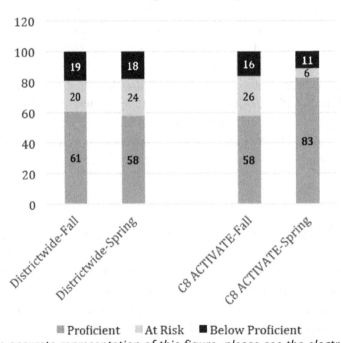

For a more accurate representation of this figure, please see the electronic version.

Nationwide Improvements in Focused Attention and Working Memory

The Activate program has now been used by thousands of children in schools across the USA. As part of the program evaluation, C8 Sciences automatically administers the tests of EF at several time points during the training. Figure 12 shows that there is little change in the Flanker test of focused attention or the working memory test when the tests are re-administered with two weeks without much training. There are highly significant improvements after 800 minutes of Activate training. Data are from over 1200 children grades kindergarten to third grade.

Children Enjoy the Activate Computer Games

Children typically do the computer games two or three times per week in 20-minute sessions that include four 5-minute games. They are randomly asked how much they like playing the games, approximately once every 5 days they play. Figure 13 shows responses from over 1,200 elementary school children indicating that most or the children most of the time enjoy playing the games.

DISCUSSION

Activate is a brain-based content independent pedagogy that integrates computer-presented and physical exercises to directly improve thinking abilities essential for academic success in elementary school children. The computer exercises incorporate new functionalities that powerfully individualize the user experience. The physical exercises produce a general increase in neuroplasticity, but beyond that are designed to include cognitive components that engage the same brain systems as do the computer exercises in the context of whole body activity and social interaction. Activate is also an assessment tool,

Figure 12. Improvements in Focused attention and working memory after 800 minutes of activate. 1200 children in elementary schools across the USA. No practice effects when simply retaking the test within a 2 weeks.

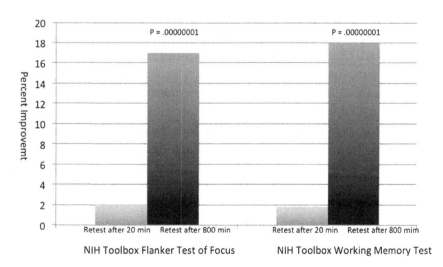

Figure 13.

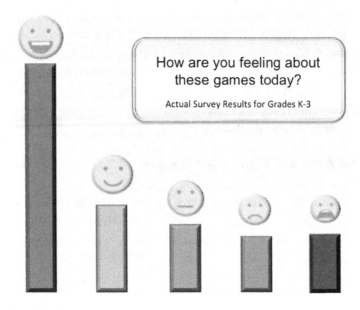

How are you feeling about these games today?

Actual Survey Results for Grades K-3

providing information about each child's areas of cognitive strength and weakness not previously available to most schools and families. The assessment functions include built-in tests of executive function from the NIH Toolbox and reports based on C8 error-analytic algorithms applied to 15,000 to 20,000 responses from each child as they do the computer brain training exercises.

Basic neuroscience research, studies of normal brain development in human beings, and studies of brain training to improve cognition in adults with major psychiatric illnesses all suggest that a program like Activate should positively impact cognitive development in young children. Much of the data evaluating effectiveness of the C8 brain training exercises comes from real world settings with limitations in scientific design and variations in implementation. The consistency of findings across these implementations, however, provides evidence that Activate has beneficial effects for many children. There is highly consistent evidence of increased performance on all aspects of the Flanker test of sustained and focused attention and some improvements in working memory. Changes in response inhibition have been less consistent.

Evidence from three schools suggests the program may be of value for children with learning challenges. Children with ADHD and children assigned to special education classes both showed robust improvements on multiple measures of cognition. Some of these changes were in areas of clear cognitive deficits, and after Activate many of them achieved scores comparable to other children of their age. A vice-principal noted that four of ten children in a special education kindergarten were moved to least restrictive mainstream classrooms after Activate where she said they showed good attention and good ability to sustain effort. She volunteered that such improvements and success were "unheard of." Neuroscience research has established without doubt that our brains develop after birth in response to stimulation from and activity induced by the human-made environment. It is not surprising then, that targeted stimulation and activation of neurocognitive systems could enhance function in neural systems that have been slow and incomplete in development. Many children come to school without having had enough cognitive stimulation to promote full age-appropriate development of cognitive abilities, even if they are not diagnosed with ADHD or designated as special education. For these children there is also a clear neuroscience rationale for expecting benefit. Moreover, if their cognitive abilities improve, they become better able to engage with the benefit from stimulation provided by the school curriculum. Activate has 100s of difficulty levels that will also challenge and stimulate the highest performing students in very efficient ways. Summary statistics on all elementary school users show large and highly statistically significant improvements in focused attention and response inhibition. Data on school administered standardized tests show that use of Activate for all children in general classrooms leads to very large gains in math and reading achievement.

Basic neuroscience studies of neuroplasticity in animals use reward paradigms to produce thousands of training trials daily. The remediation of cognitive deficits in psychiatric patients has shown to be most effective when done at least three times per week, and some successful studies have had patients participate in training four or five days week. In many schools and busy, stressed families, it is difficult to make time for three 40-minute computer training periods and two 40-minute physical exercise periods per week. It is unrealistic to expect benefit from any brain training program without devoting sufficient time and resources to it. However, it is done with enough intensity for a period of 6 to 12 months, it has the potential to have lasting benefit in years after; enhanced cognition and school performance often leads to more successful engagement with curricular learning opportunities which themselves can then potentially sustain and enhance the initial cognitive gains necessary to allow successful engagement with the curriculum. We have now repeatedly shown that children can significantly improve both executive functions important for learning and scores on math and reading achievement tests after 800 minutes of Activate computer game exercises done in 40 20-minute sessions over three to five months. Although the technical requirements of Activate and other brain training programs are quite limited, in some schools they also present implementation challenges. In some communities large numbers of teachers are unfamiliar and uncomfortable with computers and the internet. In general teachers have not been taught how to make optimal use of education technology as a teaching too. Many think that when you put the children in front of the computer, the program and computer do all that is required. Finally, in surprising numbers of schools, equipment is lacking –headphones don't work, computer mice are unreliable. Going from neuroscience to effective education intervention requires more than science.

REFERENCES

Champagne, D. L., Bagot, R. C., van Hasselt, F., Ramakers, G., Meaney, M. J., de Kloet, E. R., & Krugers, H. (2008). Maternal care and hippocampal plasticity: Evidence for experience-dependent structural plasticity, altered synaptic functioning, and differential responsiveness to glucocorticoids and stress. *The Journal of Neuroscience, 28*(23), 6037–6045. doi:10.1523/JNEUROSCI.0526-08.2008 PMID:18524909

Doidge, N. (2007). *The Brain That Changes Itself: Stories of personal triumph from the frontiers of brain science*. New York, NY: Penguin Group.

Hubel, D. H. (1988). Deprivation and development. In *Eye, Brain and Vision* (pp. 191–217). New York: Scientific American Library.

Hubel, D. H., & Wiesel, T. N. (1970). The period of susceptibility to the physiological effects of unilateral eye closure in kittens. *The Journal of Physiology, 206*(2), 419–436. doi:10.1113/jphysiol.1970. sp009022 PMID:5498493

Jenkins, W. M., Merzenich, M. M., Ochs, M. T., Allard, T., & Guic-robles, E. (1990). Functional reorganization of primary somatosensory cortex in adult owl monkeys after controlled tactile stimulation. *Journal of Neurophysiology, 63,* 82–104. PMID:2299388

Mclby-Lervag, M., & Hulme, C. (2013). Is working memory training effective? A meta-analytic review. *Developmental Psychology, 49*(2), 270–291. doi:10.1037/a0028228 PMID:22612437

Pingault, , Tremblay, R. E., Vitaro, F., Carbonneau, R., Genolini, C., Falissard, B., & Côté, S. M. (2011). Childhood Trajectories of Inattention and Hyperactivity and Prediction of Educational Attainment in Early Adulthood: A 16-Year Longitudinal Population-Based Study. *The American Journal of Psychiatry, 168*(11), 1164–1170. doi:10.1176/appi.ajp.2011.10121732 PMID:21799065

Schlaug, G. (2001). The brain of musicians: Structural and functional adaptation. *Annals of the New York Academy of Sciences,* 281–289. PMID:11458836

Sharma, J., Angelucci, A., & Sur, M. (2000). Induction of visual orientation modules in aud cortex. *Nature, 404*(6780), 841–847. doi:10.1038/35009043 PMID:10786784

Weaver, I. C. G., Cervoni, N., Champagne, F. A., DAlessio, A. C., Sharma, S., Seckl, J. R., & Meaney, M. J. et al. (2004). Epigenetic programming by maternal behavior. *Nature Neuroscience, 7*(8), 847–854. doi:10.1038/nn1276 PMID:15220929

Weaver, K. E., & Stevens, A. A. (2007). Attention and sensory interactions within the occipital cortex in the early blind: An fMRI study. *Journal of Cognitive Neuroscience, 19*(2), 315–330. doi:10.1162/jocn.2007.19.2.315 PMID:17280519

Wexler, B. E. (2006). *Brain and Culture: Neurobiology, ideology and Social Change.* Cambridge, MA: MIT Press.

Wexler, B. E., Anderson, M., Fulbright, R. K., & Gore, J. C. (2000). Improved verbal working memory performance and normalization of task-related frontal lobe activation in schizophrenia following cognitive exercises. *The American Journal of Psychology, 157,* 1094–1097. PMID:11007730

Wexler, B. E., & Bell, M. D. (2005). Cog Remedi and Voc Rehabilitation for Schizophrenia. *Schizophrenia Bulletin,* 931–941. doi:10.1093/schbul/sbi038 PMID:16079390

Wexler, B. E., Hawkins, K. A., Rounsaville, B., Anderson, M., Sernyak, M. J., & Green, M. F. (1997). Normal neurocognitive performance after extended practice in patients with schizophrenia. *Schizophrenia Research, 26*(2-3), 173–180. doi:10.1016/S0920-9964(97)00053-4 PMID:9323348

Wykes, T., Huddy, V., Cellard, C., McGurk, S. R., & Czobor, P. (2011). A meta-analysis of cognitive remediation for schizophrenia: Methodology and effect sizes. *The American Journal of Psychiatry, 168*(5), 472–485. doi:10.1176/appi.ajp.2010.10060855 PMID:21406461

Chapter 13
Promoting Physical Activity and Fitness with Exergames:
Updated Systematic Review of Systematic Reviews

Tuomas Kari
University of Jyvaskyla, Finland

ABSTRACT

This updated systematic review of systematic reviews evaluates the effectiveness of exergaming on physical fitness and physical activity. A systematic literature search was conducted on 10 databases, first in 2014 and then repeated in 2016. In total, 1040 and 287 articles were identified. 68 and 31 articles were found potentially relevant and selected for closer screening. The quality of all relevant articles was evaluated using the AMSTAR tool. After the duplicates were removed and inclusion, exclusion, and quality criteria were implemented, six and three articles remained for review. The results indicate that exergaming is generally enjoyed and can evoke some benefits for physical fitness and physical activity, but the current evidence does not support the ability of exergaming to increase physical fitness or physical activity levels sufficiently for significant health benefits. This systematic review also revealed gaps in previous research. Additional high-quality research and systematic reviews concerning exergaming are needed.

INTRODUCTION

Changes in society have led to a significant decrease in the level of physical activity of people during the past decades. One of the major changes has been the growing popularity of leisure time sedentary activities brought about by new media solutions such as television viewing, computer use, and video gaming (Matthews et al., 2008; Matthews et al., 2012). Sedentary activities have been shown to be a distinct risk factor for several adverse health outcomes among both adults (e.g. Matthews et al., 2012; Thorp, Owen, Neuhaus, & Dunstan, 2011) and children (e.g. Saunders, Chaput, & Tremblay, 2014; Tremblay et al., 2011).

DOI: 10.4018/978-1-5225-1817-4.ch013

The health consequences of physical inactivity as well as the health benefits of physical activity are well established (e.g. Lee et al., 2012; Warburton, Nicol, & Bredin, 2006; World Health Organisation [WHO], 2010, p. 10). Physical inactivity is a severe public health problem. It has been identified as the fourth most significant risk factor for global mortality (WHO, 2010, p. 10), and several studies have presented evidence on the increasing healthcare costs caused by physical inactivity (e.g. Kohl et al., 2012; Lee et al., 2012). Thus, physical inactivity is not just an individual problem but also a societal one, and due to its importance from the perspective of both public health and finance, finding new ways to promote physical activity and prevent physical inactivity is vital.

At the same time, the popularity of video gaming is on the rise. It has already become one of the most popular entertainment mediums in the world (Maddison et al., 2013), and market research firm Newzoo (2015) estimates that the worldwide market for video games will increase from US$83,6bn (2014) and US$91,5bn (2015 estimate) to US$113,3bn by 2018. This raises an interesting question about whether video games could be utilised as a medium to promote physical activity.

BACKGROUND

In recent years, a new form of video gaming that combines exercise and games has emerged. This type of gaming has been called by different terms such as 'exergaming', 'active gaming', or 'active video gaming' (AVG). They all refer to digital gaming that requires physical effort from the player in order to play the game, with the outcome of the game being mainly determined by these physical efforts (Mueller et al., 2011). Kari and Makkonen (2014, p. 2) provide a definition of exergaming as follows: "a form of digital gaming requiring aerobic physical effort – exceeding sedentary activity level and including strength-, balance-, or flexibility-related activity – from the player that determines the outcome of the game". Exergames are played in all age groups, but it seems that playing is more common among the younger age groups than the older (Kari, Makkonen, Moilanen, & Frank, 2013). The popularity of exergaming seems to be equal between men and women (Kari, Makkonen, Moilanen & Frank, 2012; Kari, 2015) and also between different physical activity background groups (Kari, 2015). However, the more active a person is in playing any digital games the more active he or she is also in exergaming (Kari, 2015).

The widespread familiarity and allure of video games makes exergaming an interesting research area, for example, in terms of promoting a more active and healthier lifestyle (Maddison et al., 2013). During the recent years, researchers have become increasingly interested in exergaming and especially in its effects on physical fitness and physical activity levels.

This study is an updated systematic review of systematic reviews and meta-analyses of exergaming published in the fields of information systems and healthcare. The first version of this study was published in 2014 (Kari, 2014). This updated study covers the additional literature published since the original version. The objective is to form a wide range view of the effects that exergaming activities have on physical fitness (PF) and physical activity (PA) levels and also to identify gaps in previous research. More precisely, the aim is to answer the following research questions:

1. What levels of exertion are typical for exergaming?
2. Can exergaming contribute to increasing physical activity?
3. Can exergaming be used to increase physical fitness?

This study also identifies relevant gaps in previous research and gives recommendations for future studies.

METHODOLOGY

The methodology followed the guidelines given by Smith, Devane, Begley, and Clarke (2011). The research design was determined *a priori*: the research questions, search strategy, and inclusion/exclusion criteria were established before the actual search and review. Flow of information through the different phases of this systematic review is presented in Figure 1, as guided by the PRISMA statement (Liberati et al., 2009; Moher, Liberati, Tetzlaff, & Altman, 2009).

Search Strategy

The original search took place in January-February 2014. It was conducted twice to ensure that no relevant articles were left unnoticed. For this updated version, the search was repeated in similar approach in June 2016 covering the articles published after the original search. The searches were conducted in the following 10 databases: Thomson Reuters Web of Science, ACM Digital library, IEEE Xplore Digital library, Health Games Research Database, AISeL, SPORTDiscuss, PubMed, The Cochrane Database of Systematic Reviews, The Database of Abstracts of Reviews of Effects, and Google Scholar.

The following keywords or their different forms were used alone or in combination in the search: 'exergame', 'exergam*', 'exertainment', 'active video game', 'console game', 'mobile game', 'computer

Figure 1. Flow diagram of study selection (2014 search + 2016 search)

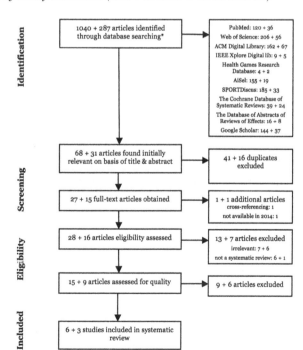

game', 'video game', 'serious game', 'persuasive game', 'active video gam*', 'console gam*', 'mobile gam*', 'computer gam*', 'video gam*', 'serious gam*', 'persuasive gam*' and 'physical activit*', 'fitness', 'motor activit*', 'exercis*', 'physical effect*', 'physical*', 'motivation', 'heart rate', 'energy expenditure', 'muscle activity', 'oxygen consumption', 'MVC', 'systematic review', 'review', 'meta-analysis', and 'meta*'. The actual keywords used varied a bit between different databases, depending on how the database treated search operators, but in every instance, the keywords used aimed for maximal coverage of the studies under search. At this stage, the articles were searched regardless of publication type (grey literature). In addition to the conducted database searches, the retrieved reviews were cross-referenced to find other potentially suitable systematic reviews and meta-analyses.

The original 2014 search revealed a total of 1040 articles. Through reading of the titles and abstracts, 68 articles were found to be initially relevant and were selected for closer screening. After removing duplicates, 27 articles remained. Cross-referencing revealed one additional new relevant article. This brought the total number of articles to 28, which dropped down to 15 after all the inclusion and exclusion criteria were introduced and down to six after quality assessment.

For this updated review, the search was repeated in June 2016 in similar systematic approach covering the articles published after the original search. This new search revealed a total of 287 new articles, out of which 31 were found initially relevant and selected for closer screening. After removing duplicates 15 remained. Also, one potentially relevant article from earlier years (Hall, Chavarria, Maneeratana, Chaney, & Bernhardt, 2012) that had to be excluded from the original review because no full text was available, was now included in this update. This brought the total number of new articles to 16. After implementing the inclusion and exclusion criteria, the number of new articles dropped down to nine and down to three after quality assessment. Thus, in total this updated systematic review included nine articles (six + three).

Inclusion and Exclusion Criteria

To be included in this review, the study needed to fulfil the following criteria:

1. It had to be a systematic review.
2. Because of the advances in the technology used in exergames, new game types, and novel physical measurement technology, this review only consisted of reviews published after 01/2010. However, these reviews could also include studies from earlier years.
3. Only published peer-reviewed journal and conference publications were included.
4. For feasibility reasons, only reviews in the English language were selected for closer screening. However, this only excluded three reviews in the initial search phase in 2014 and one review in 2016.
5. The main focus of the review was on exergames (not, for example, on eHealth interventions in general) and on PA or PF.

Reviews were excluded if they were found to be either:

1. Irrelevant (seven studies in 2014 and six studies in 2016) (2014: Cushing & Steele, 2010; Hieftje, Edelman, Camenga, & Fiellin, 2013; Ickes, Erwin, & Beighle, 2013; Maitland, Stratton, Foster, Braham, & Rosenberg, 2013; Parrish, Okely, Stanley, & Ridgers, 2013; Primack et al., 2012; Van

Camp & Hayes, 2012) (2016: Chao, Scherer, & Montgomery, 2015; Chen & Wilkosz, 2014; DeSmet et al., 2014; Laufer, Dar, & Kodesh, 2014; Molina, Ricci, Moraes, & Perracini, 2014; Velazquez et al., 2014) or

2. Not systematic (six studies in 2014 and one study in 2016) (2014: Best, 2013; Brox, Fernandez-Luque, & Tøllefsen, 2011; Foley & Maddison, 2010; Osorio, Moffat, & Sykes, 2012; Sween et al., 2013; Van Diest, Lamoth, Stegenga, Verkerke, & Postema, 2013) (2016: Sween et al., 2014).

If a review was both irrelevant and not systematic, it was categorised as irrelevant. Irrelevant studies included, for example, those whose main focus was on something other than exergaming and those which focused mainly on rehabilitation, learning, cognitive abilities, or something other than PF or PA. Studies that were low or medium in research design quality, assessed by the AMSTAR tool, were also excluded (nine studies in 2014 and six studies in 2016) (2014: Bleakley et al., 2013; Connolly, Boyle, MacArthur, Hainey, & Boyle, 2012; do Carmo, Goncalves, Batalau, & Palmeira, 2013; Guy, Ratzki-Leewing, & Gwadry-Sridhar, 2011; Lamboglia et al., 2013; Peng, Lin, & Crouse, 2011; Rahmani & Boren, 2012; Ruivo, 2014; Taylor, McCormick, Impson, Shawis, & Griffin, 2011) (2016: Bleakley et al., 2015; Dutta & Pereira, 2015; Gao & Chen, 2014; Hall et al., 2012; Norris, Hamer, & Stamatakis, 2016; Taylor, Kerse, Frakking, & Maddison, 2016).

Quality Assessment of the Reviews

To estimate the research design quality and risk of bias of the reviews, the AMSTAR tool (Shea et al., 2007; Shea et al., 2009) was used. All the articles that were identified as relevant after the implementation of all the inclusion and exclusion criteria were evaluated. AMSTAR was chosen because of its reliability (high interobserver agreement of the individual items with mean kappa = 0.70) and construct validity (intraclass correlation coefficients = 0.84) (Shea et al., 2009). AMSTAR is an 11-item instrument for evaluating the methodological quality of systematic reviews. The AMSTAR items are scored as 'yes', 'no', 'can't answer', or 'not applicable'. 'Can't answer' is chosen when the item is relevant but not described by the authors, whereas 'not applicable' is used when the item is not relevant. Every 'yes' answer affords one point for the study. The AMSTAR criterion consists of the following items:

1. 'Was an "a priori" design provided?'
2. 'Was there duplicate study selection and data extraction?'
3. 'Was a comprehensive literature search performed?'
4. 'Was the status of publication (i.e. grey literature) used as an inclusion criterion?'
5. 'Was a list of studies (included and excluded) provided?'
6. 'Were the characteristics of the included studies provided?'
7. 'Was the scientific quality of the included studies assessed and documented?'
8. 'Was the scientific quality of the included studies used appropriately in formulating conclusions?'
9. 'Were the methods used to combine the findings of studies appropriate?'
10. 'Was the likelihood of publication bias assessed?'
11. 'Was the conflict of interest included?' (Shea et al., 2009).

The studies were rated as being of low, medium, or good quality. The same rating has also been used in several previous studies (e.g. Fleming, Koletsi, Seehra, & Pandis, 2014; Jaspers, Smeulers, Vermeulen, & Peute, 2011; Płaszewski & Bettany-Saltikov, 2014; Prior, Guerin, & Grimmer-Somers, 2008; Seo & Kim, 2012). Item 11, 'Was the conflict of interest included?' differed from Shea et al. (2009) in that a score point was given if the conflict of interest was included for the systematic review itself—not needing to be included for each of the included studies. Only reviews that were scored as good (≥9 AMSTAR score) were included. Studies that were scored as low (≤4 AMSTAR score) or medium quality (5–8 AMSTAR score) were excluded. This was to ensure that possible false conclusions based on low quality research would be avoided (Shea et al., 2007). Also, Smith et al. (2011) point out that the strength of conclusions depends on the quality of included articles. Therefore, it is important that the included articles are of sufficient quality. AMSTAR item scores and total scores of the included articles are presented in Table 1.

Data Extraction and Synthesis

The included reviews were examined twice to authenticate the data extraction. Data extracted from each article included:

1. Methodological details (e.g. focus, aim, sample characteristics, number of included studies, game types, main outcome measures);
2. Key characteristics of the studies included in the reviews (e.g. publication years, number of participants, platforms);
3. Key findings pertaining to effects of exergaming on PF and PA and perceptions of exergaming (e.g. perception, adherence, barriers, facilitators);
4. Conclusions;
5. Reported limitations; and
6. Sources of funding.

Table 1. AMSTAR quality assessment scores of included articles

Reference	AMSTAR Scoring Items 1–11 (Shea et al., 2009)											AMSTAR Score
	1	2	3	4	5	6	7	8	9	10	11	
Barnett et al., 2011	+	?	+	+	+	+	+	+	+	−	−**	9
Biddiss & Irwin, 2010	+	+	+	+	−*	+	+	+	+	−	−**	9
Larsen et al., 2013	+	+	+	−	−*	+	+	+	+	+	−**	9
LeBlanc et al., 2013	+	+	+	+	−*	+	+	+	+	−	−**	9
Lu et al., 2013	+	+	+	+	−*	+	+	+	+	−	−**	9
Peng et al., 2013	+	+	+	+	+	+	+	+	−	−	−**	9
Bochner et al., 2015	+	+	+	+	−*	+	+	+	+	−	−**	9
Gao et al., 2015	+	+	+	?	−*	+	+	+	+	+	−**	9
Höchsmann et al., 2016	+	+	+	+	+	+	+	+	NA	+	−**	10

Scoring coded as: +: Yes, −: No, ?: Can't answer, −**: yes, but not for included studies = eligible for score point, −*: yes for included studies, but no list/reference of excluded studies

The quality of the included studies was also evaluated using the AMSTAR tool (Shea et al., 2007; Shea et al., 2009).

The data extracted from the included reviews was tabulated and summarised for further analysis. The effects of exergaming on physical fitness and physical activity are examined separately in the results section. Results concerning exergaming perceptions are also reported. Because of the target of this systematic review (systematic reviews), the included articles possessed heterogeneity, and therefore, a meta-analysis (pooling of results) was not performed. Instead, a qualitative narrative synthesis was conducted. The included articles from the 2014 search and 2016 search were analysed together.

RESULTS

The final number of included articles was nine (six and three). The key characteristics and methodological details of the included articles are presented in Table 2, and the key findings and conclusions in Table 3. Reported limitations and funding are presented in the Appendix. Out of the nine articles, three focused mainly on PF and six on both PF and PA. Six articles targeted children and youth, one targeted children and adults, one targeted adults, and one targeted the elderly. As the majority of video gamers are age 18 or older, e.g. 71% in the USA (Entertainment Software Association [ESA], 2014, p. 3), there is a need for more exergaming research targeting adults and the elderly. All articles were mainly focused on console-based exergaming and none mainly on mobile-based exergaming. This is most probably due to the fact that, as mobile-based exergames are a rather novel concept, so far the majority of studies regarding exergaming have focused on console-based exergames. However, it was surprising that even the new search did not reveal any research where the focus would have been mobile-based exergames, as their popularity has increased tremendously during the past two years. This demonstrates the need for more research on mobile-based exergaming. In some articles the division of included studies between interventions and laboratory studies was ambiguous. The final nine systematic reviews and meta-analysis articles had reviewed a total of 201 studies published between 2002 and 2014. The publication years of the included reviews and the studies in them are presented in the Appendix. Some studies were reviewed in more than one systematic review. The number of distinct studies reviewed in the included systematic reviews was 108.

Physical Fitness

The articles presenting the results of the effects of exergaming on PF provide a fairly consistent finding that the most typical level of exertion in exergaming is light-to-moderate for children and youth (Barnett, Cerin, & Baranowski, 2011; Biddiss & Irwin, 2010; Gao, Chen, Pasco, & Pope, 2015; LeBlanc et al., 2013; Peng, Crouse, & Lin, 2013), with the average metabolic equivalent (MET) values being just over the moderate threshold of 3 METs (Barnett et al., 2011; Biddiss & Irwin, 2010; Peng et al., 2013). Two articles (Höchsmann, Schüpbach, & Schmidt-Trucksäss, 2016; Peng et al., 2013) reported on the exertion level of exergaming among adults. Peng et al. (2013) concluded that the typical level of exertion is light-to-moderate also among adults, but lesser among older adults. Höchsmann et al. (2016) had focus on overweight adults, and they reported that most exergames do not provide moderate (>3 MET) intensity exercise for overweight individuals.

Table 2. Key characteristics and methodological details of the included articles

Reference	Focus	Studies	Participants and Data	Game Types	Main Outcome Measures
Barnett et al., 2011	PF + PA Youth	N = 13 (9 PF + 4 PA) 9 laboratory + 4 INT (3 RCT) 2006–2009	PF: N = 13–25 PA: N = 16–60 Age: 6–18 (6+) Weight: not pre-set Sex: both	Not pre-set Upper body, lower body, full body	PF: resting EE, video game EE, (relative) METs PA: play, PA, other outcome, facilitators of maintenance and barriers to maintenance of play
Biddiss & Irwin, 2010	PF + PA Children and youth	N = 18 (12 PF + 6 PA) 12 laboratory + 6 INT (2 RCT) 2002–2010	PF: N = 11–51 PA: N = 12–60 Age: 6–19 (≤21) Weight: not pre-set Sex: both	Mainstream Upper body, lower body, full body	PF: increase in EE & HR from resting values, MET PA: PA promotion, sedentary screen time, dropout rate (in studies)
Larsen et al., 2013	PF Healthy elderly	N = 7 (7 PF) 7 INT (7 RCT) 2011–2012	PF: N = 25–79 Age: N = 82–86 Weight: not pre-set Sex: both	Not pre-set Lower body, full body	PF: aerobic fitness, muscle strength, balance, body composition
LeBlanc et al., 2013	PF + PA Children and youth	N = 52 (52 PF + 22 PA)[a] 20 laboratory 35 INT (20 RCT) 2006–2012	PF & PA: N = 1-322 Age: 3–17 Weight: not pre-set Sex: both	Not pre-set Lower body, upper body, full body	PF: acute EE, PA: increased PA, decreased sedentary behaviour, change in fitness
Lu et al., 2013	PF Childhood	N = 14 (14 PF) 14 INT (10 RCT) 2005–2013	PF: N = 20–473 Age: 7–18 (≤18) Weight: not pre-set Sex: both	Not pre-set Lower body, upper body, full body	PF: BMI, BMI z-score / percentile / SD-score, waist circumference, waist-to-hip/height ratio, BI analysis
Peng et al., 2013	PF + PA Children and adults	N = 41 (28 PF + 13 PA) 28 laboratory + 13 INT (8 RCT) 2002–2011	PF: N = 8–100 PA: N = 12–60 Age: all age Weight: not pre-set Sex: both	Off-the-shelf & home use Lower body, upper body, full body	PF: MET, BMI, change in sedentary behaviour and physical activity pattern PA: adherence, motivation for play, enjoyment, rating of perceived exertion
Bochner et al., 2015	PF Children and youth	N = 7 (7 PF) 7 INT (7 RCT) 2008–2013	PF: N = 20-322 Age: 7–19 (<19) Weight: not pre-set Sex: both	Not pre-set Lower body, upper body, full body	PF: standardized mean difference (SMD) of weight change in kilograms between the intervention and control groups
Gao et al., 2015	PF + PA Children and youth	N = 35 (29 PF + 22 PA)[a] 7 laboratory 35 INT (7 RCT) 2006–2015	PF & PA: N = 11–1112 Age: 6–15 Weight: not pre-set Sex: both	Not pre-set Lower body, upper body, full body	PF: EE, HR, VO$_2$ max, MET, body composition and cardiovascular fitness PA: PA intensity, self-efficacy, enjoyment, motivation, rate of perceived exertion, attitudes, intention
Höchsmann et al., 2016	PF + PA Adults	N = 14 (14 PF + 13 PA)[a] 14 laboratory 1 INT (1 RCT) 2007–2014	PF: N = 12–100 PA: N = 12–100 Age: 19–71 (>18) Weight: overweight Sex: both	Not pre-set Lower body, upper body, full body	PF: changes in VO$_2$, EE, HR, body composition, blood parameters PA: activity counts, enjoyment, adherence, rating of perceived exertion

PF: physical fitness, PA: physical activity, INT: interventions, RCT: randomised controlled trial, EE: energy expenditure, HR: heart rate, MET: metabolic equivalent, BMI: body mass index, BI: bioelectrical impedance. [a] some had focus on both.

Table 3. Key findings and conclusions of the included articles

Reference	Effects of EG on PF	Effects of EG on PA	EG Perceptions
Barnett et al., 2011	The average intensity level of PA during EG play was approximately 3.2 METs (95% CI: 2.7, 3.7). EG can elicit PA of recommended intensity.	Sustainable EG play has yet to be demonstrated. No strong support for EG enabling engagement in play over periods of time necessary to make a contribution to health.	Most studies reported EG use declined over time. Barriers to maintenance: boredom, technical problems. Facilitators to maintenance: peer and family support, competition.
Biddiss & Irwin, 2010	Variable activity levels during EG play (game type), with mean (SD) percentage increases (from rest) of 222% (100%) in EE and 64% (20%) in heart rate. EG enables light-to-moderate-intensity physical activity.	Home EG play may provide some moderate increase in physical activity or decrease in sedentary screen time. Limited evidence of the long-term efficacy of EG for PA promotion.	Several studies noted a decrease in EG play during the study. Barriers: technical difficulties, changes in living arrangements, spatial, auditory. Facilitators: enjoyment, avoiding typical PA barriers, group play.
Larsen et al., 2013	6/7 studies found a positive effect of EG on the health of the elderly, but not superior when compared to traditional exercise.	–	Support for the beneficial effect of EG on motivation and EG being an enjoyable form of exercise.
LeBlanc et al., 2013	Controlled studies show that EG acutely increases light-to-moderate-intensity PA. The majority of the RCTs reported that an EG intervention had no effect on PF.	No clear findings about if or how EG increases habitual PA or decreases sedentary behaviour. No sufficient evidence to recommend EG as a means of increasing daily PA.	The appeal of EG is high for some children, but there is a lack of evidence suggesting long-term adherence. In general, children seem to enjoy EG.
Lu et al., 2013	Positive outcomes related to obesity were observed in 40% of the studies, all of which targeted overweight or obese children.	All but one study found significant change in proximate measures such as the duration of vigorous PA.	–
Peng et al., 2013	EG capable of providing light-to-moderate-intensity (game type) PA for both children and adults. EE of EG among older adults was found to be lesser. Relying only on EG for weight loss is not realistic.	3/13 studies demonstrated that EG resulted in increased PA. Little support regarding the long-term efficacy of using EG for self-managed PA promotion. Relying only on EG as a PA tool among children is not enough.	EG was better liked than traditional exercises. EG usage was low after the initial period among children. Adults had positive attitude to EG and found EG to be enjoyable. Perceived exertion varied (age).
Bochner et al., 2015	No difference in pre–post intervention weight change (in kilograms) between the exergaming and no-intervention group.	–	–
Gao et al., 2015	Physiological responses induced by EG are higher than those of sedentary behaviours. Effect sizes of HR favoured EG and had small effect for EE and MET, but not for VO_2 max over laboratory-based exercises.	EG increases PA from resting. EG can be used to replace sedentary behaviours. EG produced equivalent effects on moderate PA, and vigorous PA as field-based PA. EG can be used as an addition to, but not as a replacement for, traditional PA.	EG demonstrated large effect sizes for enjoyment/liking as compared to sedentary behaviours and small effect sizes as compared to laboratory-based exercise and field-based setting. EG demonstrated moderate effect sizes on self-efficacy as compared to field-based setting.
Höchsmann et al., 2016	All studies found significant increase in VO_2, EE, MET, or HR compared to rest and sedentary video game play, but the degree varied between game types. In most studies 3 METs not exceeded: EG not suitable to meet PA guidelines with overweight individuals.	Activity counts (of hip worn accelerometers) showed vast differences depending on the different game modes. Exercise adherence increased by 30% when EG compared with traditional exercise: potential to motivate overweight individuals to more PA.	Game-like game modes perceived more enjoyable than fitness-themed game modes. Significant correlation between enjoyment and EE.

PF: physical fitness, PA: physical activity, EG: exergaming, EE: energy expenditure, MET: metabolic equivalent, HR: heart rate.

Biddiss and Irwin (2010) also reported on the percentage increase in energy expenditure and heart rate from resting values. The values varied between game types. The mean percentage (SD) increases were 222% (100%) in energy expenditure and 64% (20%) in heart rate. They found percentage increases in heart rate (difference, −29%; 95% confidence interval, −47 to −11; P=.03) and energy expenditure (difference, −148%; −231% to −66%; P=.001) to be significantly lower for games that require primarily upper body movements compared with those that require lower body movements or those that engage the whole body (Biddiss & Irwin, 2010.) Gao et al. (2015) and Höchsmann et al. (2016) also reported that exergaming increased energy expenditure, METs, heart rate, and VO_2 from resting and sedentary behaviours. In addition, Gao et al. (2015) compared exergaming with laboratory- and field-based exercises and found that the effect sizes favoured exergaming over laboratory-based exercises on heart rate, energy expenditure, and MET, but not on VO_2 max.

As such, exergaming can, in most cases, provide exertion that surpasses the minimum intensity level recommended by the U.S. Department of Health and Human Services (2008, p. vii). However, the level of exertion seems to be dependent on the ability of the game to provide exertion of adequate intensity (Barnett et al., 2011; Biddiss & Irwin, 2010; Höchsmann et al., 2016) and on the player him or herself (Barnett et al., 2011; Biddiss & Irwin, 2010; Peng et al., 2013). Games that require lower body movement are more effective than games requiring only upper body movement, while games that require both are the most effective (Biddiss & Irwin, 2010; Bochner, Sorensen, & Belamarich, 2015; Gao et al., 2015; Höchsmann et al., 2016; Peng et al., 2013). Also, the intensity with which the player chooses to play the game (Barnett et al., 2011), skill level and gaming experience (Barnett et al., 2011; Peng et al., 2013), multiplayer participation (Biddiss & Irwin, 2010), length of the exergaming session (Höchsmann et al., 2016), as well as gender, age, and weight (Peng et al., 2013) may all have their impact.

When looking at longer-term effects of exergaming on PF among children and youth, the evidence of beneficial effects is limited. Biddiss and Irwin (2010) reported that exergaming did not result in changes in physiological measures at a statistically significant level. The concluding results in LeBlanc et al. (2013) were similar, as they reported that exergaming interventions in general had no effect on PF, with the evidence for the effect of interventions on cardio-metabolic health indicators being inconclusive. Bochner et al. (2015) reported that exergaming interventions did not have a significant effect on weight in youth. Lu, Kharrazi, Gharghabi, and Thompson (2013) reported, however, that around 40% of the studies they had reviewed observed positive obesity-related outcomes, mostly with overweight or obese children. Peng et al. (2013) concluded that only relying on exergaming for weight loss is not sufficient. Bochner et al. (2015) suggested that if exergaming replaces regular PA, it may increase the risk of obesity, but when exergaming replaces sedentary behaviours, it may have a positive effect on energy expenditure. Gao et al. (2015) provided a similar suggestion. LeBlanc et al. (2013) and Peng et al. (2013) added that the typical exertion level of exergaming is not sufficient to meet the guidelines of daily 60-minute moderate-to-vigorous intensity of PA for children.

Focusing on the elderly, Larsen, Schou, Lund, and Langberg (2013) found exergaming to have a positive effect on health. However, the effect was not superior compared to that from traditional exercise. Peng et al. (2013) pointed out that the typical light-to-moderate intensity of exergaming matches the PA recommendations for older adults.

Physical Activity

Five of the six articles focusing on the effects of exergaming on PA present a consistent result, which is that the evidence of exergaming contributing to increased PA is limited or inconclusive (Barnett et al., 2011; Biddiss & Irwin, 2010; Gao et al., 2015; LeBlanc et al., 2013; Peng et al., 2013). Regarding children and youth, the reported positive effects of exergaming on PA were short-term (Barnett et al., 2011; Biddiss & Irwin, 2010), and five of the articles either stated that there is little support for exergaming increasing long-term PA or did not provide reasonable evidence on this (Barnett et al., 2011; Biddiss & Irwin, 2010; Gao et al., 2015; LeBlanc et al., 2013; Peng et al., 2013). However, Höchsmann et al. (2016) reported that exercise adherence of overweight adults increased by 30% with exergaming compared to traditional exercise, and they suggested – with certain caution – that overweight people could increase their PA with exergaming. The other of the two articles that focused on PA among adults (Peng et al., 2013) stated that exergaming increased the PA attendance among adults but not among older adults. However, the evidence was limited and should be regarded with caution. Four articles suggested that exergaming has the potential to replace some sedentary behaviour (Biddiss & Irwin, 2010; Gao et al., 2015; LeBlanc et al., 2013; Peng et al., 2013). As such, it would seem that exergaming may increase PA and decrease sedentary behaviour in the short term, but in general, there is very limited evidence to support the ability of exergaming to increase long-term PA.

Perceptions

Seven of the articles also discussed the perceptions of exergaming. In general, children and youth (Biddiss & Irwin, 2010; Gao et al., 2015; LeBlanc et al., 2013), adults (Höchsmann et al., 2016; Peng et al., 2013), and the elderly (Larsen et al., 2013) were reported to enjoy exergaming. Beneficial effects on PA motivation among the elderly (Larsen et al., 2013) and overweight adults (Höchsmann et al., 2016) were also reported. Older adults also seem to enjoy lower intensity exergaming more than younger people do (Peng et al., 2013). Höchsmann et al. (2016), LeBlanc et al. (2013), and Peng et al. (2013) also reported that exergaming was generally better liked than traditional exercises. Still, four of the five articles focusing on PA and children and youth reported a decrease in exergaming play over time or during the interventions (Barnett et al., 2011; Biddiss & Irwin, 2010; LeBlanc et al., 2013; Peng et al., 2013). Barnett et al. (2013), Biddiss and Irwin (2010), and LeBlanc et al. (2013) all concluded that there is a lack of evidence supporting the long-term use and adherence to exergaming. Thus, it would seem that use continuance (or discontinuance) is a pertinent issue with exergaming.

Peng et al. (2013) reported on the perceived exertion of exergaming. Children perceived exergaming to be similar to lower intensity activities, while adults perceived exergaming to be similar to activities requiring higher metabolic exertion. Older adults' perception of the exertion level of exergaming was relatively low. When compared to actual measured exertion levels, children found exergaming to be less physically demanding than it actually was (Peng et al., 2013). Gao et al. (2015) reported that the perceived exertion of exergaming had large effect sizes over sedentary activities, but were not different with laboratory-based exercise.

Two studies suggested that multiplayer features such as interaction with others or competitive play with peers might increase the participation in and maintenance of exergaming, at least among children and youth (Barnett et al., 2011; Biddiss & Irwin, 2010). These studies also reported on facilitators and barriers to exergaming maintenance. Mentioned facilitators included competition, peer and family support, greater variety of music in a dance exergame (Barnett et al., 2011), enjoyment, and exergaming not being constrained by typical barriers to participation such as lack of transportation, seasonal conditions, or unsafe neighbourhoods (Biddiss & Irwin, 2010). Barriers included boredom, technical problems (Barnett et al., 2011) and difficulties, changes in living arrangements, and auditory nuisance (Biddiss & Irwin, 2010). Höchsmann et al. (2016) reported that game modes that were game-like were perceived more enjoyable than fitness-themed game modes. They also found a significant correlation between exergame enjoyment and energy expenditure. Gao et al. (2015) suggested the need for exergames to be constantly updated or upgraded to keep children interested enough to sustain behaviour.

FUTURE RESEARCH DIRECTIONS

This study also identified gaps in previous research. The biggest gap would seem to be the lack of research on mobile-based exergaming. Therefore, it is recommended that in the future, more studies should focus on this form of exergaming. There is also a need for more studies including adults and the elderly. In general, long-term effects should also be addressed more frequently. As many of the relevant systematic reviews were of not high quality, future systematic reviews on exergaming should pay attention to conducting high quality research from the outset. Also as the use of exergames seems to decrease or end in rather early stages, it suggests that use continuance of exergaming is something that researchers should focus on. These issues demonstrate the need for more research on exergaming to reach its potential benefits.

CONCLUSION

Evidence from the highest quality systematic reviews indicates that exergaming can provide exertion of the recommended intensity set by the U.S. Department of Health and Human Services (2008, p. vii). The typical levels of exertion for exergaming are light-to-moderate among children and youth as well as among adults, but less among the elderly and overweight adults. The exertion levels vary between different game types (upper body, lower body, full body) and between players, depending for example on demographics, chosen gaming intensity, and skill level. Current evidence does not support long-term benefits for PF. Evidence regarding PA suggests that exergaming might be able to contribute to PA on a short-term basis, but little support is found for long-term PA promotion. Use continuance with exergames seems to be a relevant problem, as the evidence does not support long-term adherence to exergaming, although it was found to be an enjoyable activity.

Implications for Practice

Even though exergaming is generally enjoyed and can evoke some benefits for PF and PA, the current evidence does not support the ability of exergaming to increase the PF or PA levels sufficiently for significant health benefits, partly due to use decreasing over time. Therefore, exergaming cannot be recommended as the only method for PF and PA promotion, and other means of physical activity should be used alongside exergaming for significant PF benefits. However, even if exergaming activity does not provide a sufficient level of physical activity, it can reduce the time spent on sedentary video gaming and other sedentary activities, such as sitting, which in many studies (e.g. Lee et al., 2012; Matthews et al., 2012) have been identified as significantly increasing the risk of chronic diseases. Thus, exergaming can be recommended as a replacement to traditional video gaming activities that usually take place seated.

Strength and Limitations

Strengths of this systematic review include the systematic review process itself, a methodology based on proven guidelines, and the *a priori* research design. Also, articles were searched from both information systems and healthcare databases for maximal coverage. In addition, the retrieved articles were cross-referenced to find other potentially suitable systematic reviews. All the relevant articles were assessed for quality using the AMSTAR tool, and only articles of good quality were included. This was to ensure that possible false conclusions based on low quality research would be avoided. In addition to answering the research questions, gaps in previous research were also identified.

There are some possible limitations to this research. Even though the search strategy aimed for maximal coverage of suitable studies, it is still possible that not all the relevant articles were found. Due to the nature of this study (systematic review), some of the limitations of the included articles (reported in the Appendix) might also have affected the results of this article. There was also some overlap in the studies included among the systematic reviews, which might have had some effect on the results of this systematic review. Finally, as none of the included articles focused on mobile-based exergaming, the results can only be examined with respect to console-based exergaming.

ACKNOWLEDGMENT

The author would like to acknowledge support by Professor Taija Juutinen Finni of the Department of Biology of Physical Activity, University of Jyvaskyla, in receiving general help in evaluating the articles and creating the research design for the original version of this article in 2014.

REFERENCES

Barnett, A., Cerin, E., & Baranowski, T. (2011). Active video games for youth: A systematic review. *Journal of Physical Activity & Health*, 8(5), 724–737. doi:10.1123/jpah.8.5.724 PMID:21734319

Best, J. R. (2013). Exergaming in youth: Effects on physical and cognitive health. *Zeitschrift fur Psychologie mit Zeitschrift fur Angewandte Psychologie*, 221(2), 72–78. doi:10.1027/2151-2604/a000137 PMID:25097828

Biddiss, E., & Irwin, J. (2010). Active video games to promote physical activity in children and youth: A systematic review. *Archives of Pediatrics & Adolescent Medicine*, 164(7), 664–672. doi:10.1001/archpediatrics.2010.104 PMID:20603468

Bleakley, C. M., Charles, D., Porter-Armstrong, A., McNeill, M. D., McDonough, S. M., & McCormack, B. (2013). Gaming for health: A systematic review of the physical and cognitive effects of interactive computer games in older adults. *Journal of Applied Gerontology*; Advance online publication. doi:10.1177/0733464812470747 PMID:24652863

Bleakley, C. M., Charles, D., Porter-Armstrong, A., McNeill, M. D., McDonough, S. M., & McCormack, B. (2015). Gaming for health: A systematic review of the physical and cognitive effects of interactive computer games in older adults. *Journal of Applied Gerontology*, *34*(3), 166–189. doi:10.1177/0733464812470747 PMID:24652863

Bochner, R. E., Sorensen, K. M., & Belamarich, P. F. (2015). The impact of active video gaming on weight in youth: A meta-analysis. *Clinical Pediatrics*, *54*(7), 620–628. doi:10.1177/0009922814545165 PMID:25085926

Brox, E., Fernandez-Luque, L., & Tøllefsen, T. (2011). Healthy gaming–video game design to promote health. *Applied Clinical Informatics*, *2*(2), 128–142. doi:10.4338/ACI-2010-10-R-0060 PMID:23616865

Chao, Y. Y., Scherer, Y. K., & Montgomery, C. A. (2014). Effects of using Nintendo Wii™ exergames in older adults: A review of the literature. *Journal of Aging and Health*, *27*(3), 379–402. doi:10.1177/0898264314551171 PMID:25245519

Chen, J. L., & Wilkosz, M. E. (2014). Efficacy of technology-based interventions for obesity prevention in adolescents: A systematic review. *Adolescent Health. Medicine and Therapeutics*, *5*, 159–170.

Connolly, T. M., Boyle, E. A., MacArthur, E., Hainey, T., & Boyle, J. M. (2012). A systematic literature review of empirical evidence on computer games and serious games. *Computers & Education*, *59*(2), 661–686. doi:10.1016/j.compedu.2012.03.004

Cushing, C. C., & Steele, R. G. (2010). A meta-analytic review of eHealth interventions for pediatric health promoting and maintaining behaviors. *Journal of Pediatric Psychology*, *35*(9), 937–949. doi:10.1093/jpepsy/jsq023 PMID:20392790

DeSmet, A., Van Ryckeghem, D., Compernolle, S., Baranowski, T., Thompson, D., Crombez, G., & Vandebosch, H. et al. (2014). A meta-analysis of serious digital games for healthy lifestyle promotion. *Preventive Medicine*, *69*, 95–107. doi:10.1016/j.ypmed.2014.08.026 PMID:25172024

do Carmo, J., Goncalves, R., Batalau, R., & Palmeira, A. L. (2013). Active video games and physical activity in overweight children and adolescents. In *Proceedings of the IEEE 2nd International Conference on Serious Games and Applications for Health (SeGAH)* (pp. 1–5). doi:10.1109/SeGAH.2013.6665323

Dutta, N., & Pereira, M. A. (2015). Effects of active video games on energy expenditure in adults: A systematic literature review. *Journal of Physical Activity & Health*, *12*(6), 890–899. doi:10.1123/jpah.2013-0168 PMID:25134074

Entertainment Software Association (ESA). (2014). *2014 Essential facts about the computer and video game industry (Report)*. Washington, DC: Entertainment Software Association.

Fleming, P. S., Koletsi, D., Seehra, J., & Pandis, N. (2014). Systematic reviews published in higher impact clinical journals were of higher quality. *Journal of Clinical Epidemiology, 67*(7), 754–759. doi:10.1016/j.jclinepi.2014.01.002 PMID:24709031

Foley, L., & Maddison, R. (2010). Use of active video games to increase physical activity in children: A (virtual) reality. *Pediatric Exercise Science, 22*(1), 7–20. doi:10.1123/pes.22.1.7 PMID:20332536

Gao, Z., & Chen, S. (2014). Are field-based exergames useful in preventing childhood obesity? a systematic review. *Obesity Reviews, 15*(8), 676–691. doi:10.1111/obr.12164 PMID:24602072

Gao, Z., Chen, S., Pasco, D., & Pope, Z. (2015). A meta-analysis of active video games on health outcomes among children and adolescents. *Obesity Reviews, 16*(9), 783–794. doi:10.1111/obr.12287 PMID:25943852

Guy, S., Ratzki-Leewing, A., & Gwadry-Sridhar, F. (2011). Moving beyond the stigma: Systematic review of video games and their potential to combat obesity. *International Journal of Hypertension, 2011*, 1–13. doi:10.4061/2011/179124 PMID:21629863

Hall, A. K., Chavarria, E., Maneeratana, V., Chaney, B. H., & Bernhardt, J. M. (2012). Health benefits of digital videogames for older adults: A systematic review of the literature. *Games For Health: Research, Development, and Clinical Applications, 1*(6), 402–410. doi:10.1089/g4h.2012.0046 PMID:26192056

Hieftje, K., Edelman, E. J., Camenga, D. R., & Fiellin, L. E. (2013). Electronic media-based health interventions promoting behavior change in youth: A systematic review. *JAMA Pediatrics, 167*(6), 574–580. doi:10.1001/jamapediatrics.2013.1095 PMID:23568703

Höchsmann, C., Schüpbach, M., & Schmidt-Trucksäss, A. (2016). Effects of exergaming on physical activity in overweight individuals. *Sports Medicine (Auckland, N.Z.), 46*(6), 845–860. doi:10.1007/s40279-015-0455-z PMID:26712512

Ickes, M. J., Erwin, H., & Beighle, A. (2013). Systematic review of recess interventions to increase physical activity. *Journal of Physical Activity & Health, 10*(6), 910–926. doi:10.1123/jpah.10.6.910 PMID:23074100

Jaspers, M. W., Smeulers, M., Vermeulen, H., & Peute, L. W. (2011). Effects of clinical decision-support systems on practitioner performance and patient outcomes: A synthesis of high-quality systematic review findings. *Journal of the American Medical Informatics Association, 18*(3), 327–334. doi:10.1136/amiajnl-2011-000094 PMID:21422100

Kari, T. (2014). Can exergaming promote physical fitness and physical activity?: A systematic review of systematic reviews. *International Journal of Gaming and Computer-Mediated Simulations, 6*(4), 59–77. doi:10.4018/ijgcms.2014100105

Kari, T. (2015). Explaining the adoption and habits of playing exergames: the role of physical activity background and digital gaming frequency. In *Proceeding of the Twenty First American Conference on Information Systems 2015*.

Kari, T., & Makkonen, M. (2014). Explaining the usage intentions of exergames. In *Proceedings of the Thirty Fifth International Conference on Information Systems 2014*.

Kari, T., Makkonen, M., Moilanen, P., & Frank, L. (2012). The habits of playing and the reasons for not playing exergames: gender differences in Finland. In *Proceedings of The 25th Bled eConference* (pp. 512–526).

Kari, T., Makkonen, M., Moilanen, P., & Frank, L. (2013). The habits of playing and the reasons for not playing exergames: age differences in Finland. *International Journal on WWW/Internet, 11*, 30–42.

Kohl, H. W. III, Craig, C. L., Lambert, E. V., Inoue, S., Alkandari, J. R., Leetongin, G., & Kahlmeier, S. (2012). The pandemic of physical inactivity: Global action for public health. *Lancet, 380*(9838), 294–305. doi:10.1016/S0140-6736(12)60898-8 PMID:22818941

Lamboglia, C. M. G. F., Silva, V. T. B. L. D., Vasconcelos Filho, J. E. D., Pinheiro, M. H. N. P., Munguba, M. C. D. S., Silva Júnior, F. V. I., & Silva, C. A. B. D. et al. (2013). Exergaming as a strategic tool in the fight against childhood obesity: A systematic review. *Journal of Obesity, 2013*, 1–8. doi:10.1155/2013/438364 PMID:24319594

Larsen, L. H., Schou, L., Lund, H. H., & Langberg, H. (2013). The physical effect of exergames in healthy elderly—a systematic review. *Games For Health: Research, Development, and Clinical Applications, 2*(4), 205–212. doi:10.1089/g4h.2013.0036 PMID:26192224

Laufer, Y., Dar, G., & Kodesh, E. (2014). Does a Wii-based exercise program enhance balance control of independently functioning older adults? a systematic review. *Clinical Interventions in Aging, 9*, 1803–1813. doi:10.2147/CIA.S69673 PMID:25364238

LeBlanc, A. G., Chaput, J. P., McFarlane, A., Colley, R. C., Thivel, D., Biddle, S. J., & Tremblay, M. S. et al. (2013). Active video games and health indicators in children and youth: A systematic review. *PLoS ONE, 8*(6), e65351. doi:10.1371/journal.pone.0065351 PMID:23799008

Lee, I., Shiroma, E. J., Lobelo, F., Puska, P., Blair, S. N., & Katzmarzyk, P. T. (2012). Effect of physical inactivity on major non-communicable diseases worldwide: An analysis of burden of disease and life expectancy. *Lancet, 380*(9838), 219–229. doi:10.1016/S0140-6736(12)61031-9 PMID:22818936

Liberati, A., Altman, D. G., Tetzlaff, J., Mulrow, C., Gøtzsche, P. C., Ioannidis, J. P., & Moher, D. et al. (2009). The PRISMA statement for reporting systematic reviews and meta analyses of studies that evaluate health care interventions: Explanation and elaboration. *Annals of Internal Medicine, 151*(4), W-65–W-94. doi:10.7326/0003-4819-151-4-200908180-00136 PMID:19622512

Lu, A. S., Kharrazi, H., Gharghabi, F., & Thompson, D. (2013). A systematic review of health videogames on childhood obesity prevention and intervention. *Games For Health: Research, Development, and Clinical Applications, 2*(3), 131–141. doi:10.1089/g4h.2013.0025 PMID:24353906

Maddison, R., Simons, M., Straker, L., Witherspoon, L., Palmeira, A., & Thin, A. (2013). Active video games: An opportunity for enhanced learning and positive health effects? *Cognitive Technology, 18*, 6–13.

Maitland, C., Stratton, G., Foster, S., Braham, R., & Rosenberg, M. (2013). A place for play? The influence of the home physical environment on children's physical activity and sedentary behaviour. *The International Journal of Behavioral Nutrition and Physical Activity, 10*. PMID:23958282

Matthews, C. E., Chen, K. Y., Freedson, P. S., Buchowski, M. S., Beech, B. M., Pate, R. R., & Troiano, R. P. (2008). Amount of time spent in sedentary behaviors in the United States, 2003–2004. *American Journal of Epidemiology, 167*(7), 875–881. doi:10.1093/aje/kwm390 PMID:18303006

Matthews, C. E., George, S. M., Moore, S. C., Bowles, H. R., Blair, A., Park, Y., & Schatzkin, A. et al. (2012). Amount of time spent in sedentary behaviors and cause-specific mortality in US adults. *The American Journal of Clinical Nutrition, 95*(2), 437–445. doi:10.3945/ajcn.111.019620 PMID:22218159

Moher, D., Liberati, A., Tetzlaff, J., & Altman, D. G. (2009). Preferred reporting items for systematic reviews and meta-analyses: The PRISMA statement. *Annals of Internal Medicine, 151*(4), 264–269. doi:10.7326/0003-4819-151-4-200908180-00135 PMID:19622511

Molina, K. I., Ricci, N. A., de Moraes, S. A., & Perracini, M. R. (2014). Virtual reality using games for improving physical functioning in older adults: A systematic review. *Journal of Neuroengineering and Rehabilitation, 11*(1), 1–20. doi:10.1186/1743-0003-11-156 PMID:25399408

Mueller, F., Edge, D., Vetere, F., Gibbs, M. R., Agamanolis, S., Bongers, B., & Sheridan, J. G. (2011). Designing sports: a framework for exertion games. In *Proceedings of the SIGCHI Conference on Human Factors in Computing Systems* (pp. 2651–2660). doi:10.1145/1978942.1979330

Newzoo. (2015). *2015 Global games market report, 5/2015* (Report). Amsterdam: Newzoo.

Norris, E., Hamer, M., & Stamatakis, E. (2016). Active video games in schools and effects on physical activity and health: A systematic review. *The Journal of Pediatrics, 172*, 40–46. doi:10.1016/j.jpeds.2016.02.001 PMID:26947570

Osorio, G., Moffat, D. C., & Sykes, J. (2012). Exergaming, exercise, and gaming: Sharing motivations. *Games For Health: Research, Development, and Clinical Applications, 1*(3), 205–210. doi:10.1089/g4h.2011.0025 PMID:26193438

Parrish, A. M., Okely, A. D., Stanley, R. M., & Ridgers, N. D. (2013). The effect of school recess interventions on physical activity. *Sports Medicine (Auckland, N.Z.), 43*(4), 287–299. doi:10.1007/s40279-013-0024-2 PMID:23512170

Peng, W., Crouse, J. C., & Lin, J. H. (2013). Using active video games for physical activity promotion: A systematic review of the current state of research. *Health Education & Behavior, 40*(2), 171–192. doi:10.1177/1090198112444956 PMID:22773597

Peng, W., Lin, J. H., & Crouse, J. (2011). Is playing exergames really exercising? A meta-analysis of energy expenditure in active video games. *Cyberpsychology, Behavior, and Social Networking, 14*(11), 681–688. doi:10.1089/cyber.2010.0578 PMID:21668370

Płaszewski, M., & Bettany-Saltikov, J. (2014). Are current scoliosis school screening recommendations evidence-based and up to date? A best evidence synthesis umbrella review. *European Spine Journal.* doi:10.1007/s00586-014-3307-x PMID:24777669

Primack, B. A., Carroll, M. V., McNamara, M., Klem, M. L., King, B., Rich, M., & Nayak, S. et al. (2012). Role of video games in improving health-related outcomes: A systematic review. *American Journal of Preventive Medicine, 42*(6), 630–638. doi:10.1016/j.amepre.2012.02.023 PMID:22608382

Prior, M., Guerin, M., & Grimmer-Somers, K. (2008). The effectiveness of clinical guideline implementation strategies–a synthesis of systematic review findings. *Journal of Evaluation in Clinical Practice, 14*(5), 888–897. doi:10.1111/j.1365-2753.2008.01014.x PMID:19018923

Rahmani, E., & Boren, S. A. (2012). Videogames and health improvement: A literature review of randomized controlled trials. *Games For Health: Research, Development, and Clinical Applications, 1*(5), 331–341. doi:10.1089/g4h.2012.0031 PMID:26191999

Ruivo, J. A. (2014). Exergames and cardiac rehabilitation: A review. *Journal of Cardiopulmonary Rehabilitation and Prevention, 34*(1), 2–20. doi:10.1097/HCR.0000000000000037 PMID:24370759

Saunders, T. J., Chaput, J. P., & Tremblay, M. S. (2014). Sedentary behaviour as an emerging risk factor for cardiometabolic diseases in children and youth. *Canadian Journal of Diabetes, 38*(1), 53–61. doi:10.1016/j.jcjd.2013.08.266 PMID:24485214

Seo, H. J., & Kim, K. U. (2012). Quality assessment of systematic reviews or meta-analyses of nursing interventions conducted by Korean reviewers. *BMC Medical Research Methodology, 12.* PMID:22928687

Shea, B. J., Grimshaw, J. M., Wells, G. A., Boers, M., Andersson, N., Hamel, C., & Bouter, L. M. et al. (2007). Development of AMSTAR: A measurement tool to assess the methodological quality of systematic reviews. *BMC Medical Research Methodology, 7.* PMID:17302989

Shea, B. J., Hamel, C., Wells, G. A., Bouter, L. M., Kristjansson, E., Grimshaw, J., & Boers, M. et al. (2009). AMSTAR is a reliable and valid measurement tool to assess the methodological quality of systematic reviews. *Journal of Clinical Epidemiology, 62*(10), 1013–1020. doi:10.1016/j.jclinepi.2008.10.009 PMID:19230606

Smith, V., Devane, D., Begley, C. M., & Clarke, M. (2011). Methodology in conducting a systematic review of systematic reviews of healthcare interventions. *BMC Medical Research Methodology, 11.* PMID:21291558

Sween, J., Wallington, S. F., Sheppard, V., Taylor, T., Llanos, A. A., & Adams-Campbell, L. L. (2013). The role of exergaming in improving physical activity: a review. *Journal of Physical Activity & Health.*

Sween, J., Wallington, S. F., Sheppard, V., Taylor, T., Llanos, A. A., & Adams-Campbell, L. L. (2014). The role of exergaming in improving physical activity: A review. *Journal of Physical Activity & Health, 11*(4), 864–870. doi:10.1123/jpah.2011-0425 PMID:25078529

Taylor, L. M., Kerse, N., Frakking, T., & Maddison, R. (2016). Active video games for improving physical performance measures in older people: a meta-analysis. *Journal of Geriatric Physical Therapy.*

Taylor, M. J., McCormick, D., Impson, R., Shawis, T., & Griffin, M. (2011). Activity promoting gaming systems in exercise and rehabilitation. *Journal of Rehabilitation Research and Development, 48*(10), 1171–1186. doi:10.1682/JRRD.2010.09.0171 PMID:22234662

Thorp, A. A., Owen, N., Neuhaus, M., & Dunstan, D. W. (2011). Sedentary behaviors and subsequent health outcomes in adults: A systematic review of longitudinal studies, 1996–2011. *American Journal of Preventive Medicine, 41*(2), 207–215. doi:10.1016/j.amepre.2011.05.004 PMID:21767729

Tremblay, M. S., LeBlanc, A. G., Kho, M. E., Saunders, T. J., Larouche, R., Colley, R. C., & Gorber, S. C. et al. (2011). Systematic review of sedentary behaviour and health indicators in school-aged children and youth. *The International Journal of Behavioral Nutrition and Physical Activity, 8.* PMID:21936895

U.S. Department of Health and Human Services. (2008). *2008 Physical Activity Guidelines for Americans (ODPHP Publication No. U0036).* Washington, DC: ODPHP.

Van Camp, C. M., & Hayes, L. B. (2012). Assessing and increasing physical activity. *Journal of Applied Behavior Analysis, 45,* 871–875. PMID:23322945

Van Diest, M., Lamoth, C. J., Stegenga, J., Verkerke, G. J., & Postema, K. (2013). Exergaming for balance training of elderly: State of the art and future developments. *Journal of Neuroengineering and Rehabilitation, 10.* PMID:24063521

Velazquez, A., Campos-Francisco, W., García-Vázquez, J. P., López-Nava, H., Rodríguez, M. D., Pérez-San Pablo, A. I., . . . Favela, J. (2014). Exergames as tools used on interventions to cope with the effects of ageing: a systematic review. In *Proceedings of the 6th International Work-Conference, IWAAL: Ambient Assisted Living and Daily Activities* (pp. 402–405). doi:10.1007/978-3-319-13105-4_59

Warburton, D., Nicol, C., & Bredin, S. (2006). Health benefits of physical activity: The evidence. *Canadian Medical Association Journal, 174*(6), 801–809. doi:10.1503/cmaj.051351 PMID:16534088

World Health Organization (WHO). (2010). *Global recommendations on physical activity for health (Report).* Geneva: WHO Press.

KEY TERMS AND DEFINITIONS

Active Video Games: Synonym for exergames.

AMSTAR: An 11-item instrument for evaluating the methodological quality of systematic reviews.

Exergames: Digital gaming concept combining exercise and games by requiring physical effort from the player that determines the outcome of the game.

Exergaming: A form of digital gaming requiring aerobic physical effort – exceeding sedentary activity level and including strength-, balance-, or flexibility-related activity – from the player that determines the outcome of the game.

Physical Activity: Bodily movement produced by skeletal muscles that requires energy expenditure.

Physical Fitness: A general state of health and well-being with various different measures.

Systematic Review: A type of literature review that systematically searches and critically analyses multiple research studies or articles.

APPENDIX

Table 4. Reported limitations and funding of the included systematic reviews

Reference	Reported Limitations	Funding
Barnett et al., 2011	• Number and quality of research articles in the area of AVGs. • Out-datedness due to rapidly evolving research area. • Potential publication bias due to studies reporting positive results having a better chance of being published. • Selection bias due to the inability to identify relevant studies not included in the selected search engines. • Bias in the assessment of study quality due to information necessary to evaluate the quality of a study being inadequately reported.	Primarily funded by a grant from the National Institute of Diabetes & Digestive & Kidney Diseases (5 U44 DK66724-01). Partially funded with federal funds from the USDA/ARS under Cooperative Agreement No. 58-6250-6001.
Biddiss & Irwin, 2010	• Quality of research articles reviewed. • Regarding energy expenditure measurements, nonstandardised protocols may have contributed to some of the variations observed among studies. • Quantitative interstudy comparisons of activity patterns were not feasible owing to variations in study methods and reporting. • The most common risks for bias included unconcealed allocation, lack of blinding (where possible), and selectively reported outcomes.	Study was supported by the Natural Sciences and Research Council of Canada, by the Canadian Institutes of Health Research, and by the Bloorview Kids Foundation.
Larsen et al., 2013	• Limited number of studies that met all eligibility criteria. • Included studies varied in terms of type of intervention, type of control, outcome measures, and methodological quality. • A publication bias may have occurred, as well as language bias. • The identified studies are limited to our key word search, which might have been insufficient because the use of terms varies greatly in this new field.	We are grateful for funding from the Department of Public Health, University of Copenhagen.
LeBlanc et al., 2013	• Relatively low quality of studies in this field of research. • The review included studies that were largely based on what could be deemed "first generation" AVGs.	This study was supported by funds from Active Healthy Kids Canada. The organisation had no role in the design and conduct of the study; the collection, management, analysis and interpretation of the data; or the preparation, review and approval of the manuscript.
Lu et al., 2013	• Only English language articles were included. • The selected articles may be subject to publication bias for positive findings.	This project was partially funded by the National Cancer Institute (grant 1R21CA158917-01A1; "The Narrative Impact of Active Video Games on Physical Activity," PI: Amy Shirong Lu, PhD).
Peng et al., 2013	• The AVGs in this review included only those available off-the-shelf and are not designed with the purpose to increase physical activity. • The sample sizes of all the included studies were very small, limiting adequate power of these research studies. • Six of the 13 intervention studies did not provide an adequate design to test for effectiveness of the AVG intervention because of lack of a control group without AVG treatment.	This research was supported by a grant from the Robert Wood Johnson Foundation's Pioneer Portfolio through its national program, Health Games Research.
Bochner et al., 2015	• The meta-analysis is limited by the methodology problems and bias inherent in the RCTs of exergaming interventions to date. • Combining studies of 7- to 8-year-olds with studies of 18- to 19-year-olds may conceal an interaction effect of age on weight outcomes for exergaming interventions. • Instead of using SMD of weight change as outcome measure, the use of BMI z –score change is a better measure.	The author(s) received no financial support for the research, authorship, and/or publication of this article.
Gao et al., 2015	• The authors were not able to categorize children/adolescents into subgroups because some studies did not provide detailed information on age. • The meta-analysis holistically assessed multiple physiological and psychological effects of AVGs (e.g. PA, enjoyment), but some of these included outcome variables might have been defined or measured differently. • Two different ways of obtaining effect size were utilized to capture treatment effects of AVGs and although the method is deemed conventional and has been previously utilized in other similar research, it might have brought upon bias to the meta-analysis. • Summative findings based upon a small number of empirical studies are by no means conclusive. • The review only included published studies for analysis, raising the issue of publication bias.	The authors have no financial disclosures.
Höchsmann et al., 2016	• The high levels of heterogeneity among the studies. • The inconsistent results regarding the degree of increase in objectively measured PA parameters as well as the greatly differing settings across the included studies. • Only one study had a low risk of bias and that 10 of 11 studies were cross-sectional. • None of the included studies recruited patients with T2DM. • Study samples of included articles might bias the results.	This study was conducted with internal support by the Department of Sports, Exercise and Health, University of Basel, Basel, Switzerland. No external sources of funding were used to assist in the preparation of this article.

Table 5. Publication years of the studies

Publication Years of Included Systematic Reviews	
2010	1
2011	1
2012	0
2013	4
2015	2
2016	1
Total	9
Publication Years of Studies Reviewed in Systematic Reviews	
2002	2
2003	0
2004	0
2005	0
2006	10
2007	20
2008	39
2009	32
2010	30
2011	28
2012	30
2013	4
2014	6
Total	201

Chapter 14
Is Artificial Intelligence (AI) Friend or Foe to Patients in Healthcare?
On Virtues of Dynamic Consent – How to Build a Business Case for Digital Health Applications

Veronika Litinski
MaRS Discovery, Canada

ABSTRACT

Failure to appropriately measure Value is one of the reasons for slow reform in health. Value brings together quality and cost, both defined around the patient. With technology we can measure value in the new ways: commercially developed algorithms are capable of mining large, connected data sets to present accurate information for patients and providers. But how do we align these new capabilities with clinical and operational realities, and further with individual privacy? The right amount of information, shared at the right time, can improve practitioners' ability to choose treatments, and patients' motivation to provide consent and follow the treatment. Dynamic Consent, where IT is used to determine just what patients are consenting to share, can address the inherent conflict between the demand from AI for access to data and patients' privacy principles. This chapter describes a pragmatic Commercial Development framework for building digital health tool. It overlays Value Model for healthcare IT investments with Patient Activation Measures and innovation management techniques.

DOI: 10.4018/978-1-5225-1817-4.ch014

ARTIFICIAL INTELLIGENCE (AI): THE PATIENT'S FRIEND OR FOE?

Where can AI improve health services? The short answer is, wherever Big Data lives. Policy makers and healthcare administrators are grappling with the recent emergence of Big Data in healthcare. These can include large linked data (from electronic patient records,) streams of real-time geo-located health data (collected by personal wearable devices, etc.) and open data (from shared datasets.) Together these form Big Data, a realm rich in new research opportunities and avenues for commercial exploitation. (Kostkova, 2015)

AI in Health Systems

It is nearly impossible for doctors to stay abreast of all the new and changing rules governing their fields, on top of the constant innovations taking place therein.

In the paper, Analysis of Questions Asked by Family Doctors Regarding Patient Care, (Ely, J. W. et al. 1999) observed 103 physicians over one workday. Those physicians asked 1,101 clinical questions during the day. The majority of those questions (64%) were never answered. Among questions that did get answered, the physicians spent less than two minutes looking for their answers.

Obviously, providing quick answers to clinical questions will always improve the quality of healthcare. No wonder the Chief Health Officer at IBM Corporation, Rhee Kyi, a physician earlier in his career, recognizes the role IBM Watson will play in healthcare delivery. Watson, and other commercial solutions, promise to provide insights, reveal patterns and relationships across data sets. The allure of Watson lies in its being designed to work with unstructured data, such as genetic data and the free text portions of electronic health records.

The expectation is that research on large, shared medical datasets will provide radically new pathways for improving health systems as well as individual care. Facilitating personalized or "stratified medicine," such open data can shed light on causes of disease, and the effects of treatment.

Some of the most powerful applications can be found in Public Health, where data sets from communities of practice, social networks, and wearable devices can be mined for a wide spectrum of public health monitoring, and launch of persuasive technologies for public health interventions. However, these fascinating opportunities develop against a backdrop of decades of under-investment in public health systems, which lack the resources to tackle the full range of health threats, from potential chemical or biological attacks, to serious chronic disease epidemics, or emerging infectious diseases like Zika. (*Trust For America's Health*, 2016)

The allure of analytics here is obvious. It can help health systems crunch data to improve care quality and reduce costs, especially for organizations that aim to profit under shared savings or financial risk contracts. How can we balance cost, value and liability in a regulated healthcare industry?

Me, My Health Care Circle, and AI

Another area where AI can be hugely helpful is in presenting data and helping patients make sense of it. After all, they are confronted with the same challenge as their doctors: quantities of specialized information that can be life saving, or just the opposite. The patient's informed consent is required in every aspect of care – from their contributing biological samples preparing for complex surgeries, to accepting a given course of treatment. How do we empower patients to make truly informed decisions, while allowing developers access to the streams of data?

Respect for a patient's individual autonomy is an established principle in modern medicine. In the past half century, the concept of autonomy has promoted patients from passive recipients of care to partners in planning their own treatments.

The notion of patient empowerment is reflected by developments in regulation and guidance. Think of phrases such as "patient led care," "patient engagement" and "shared treatment decision-making".

The new strategy of patient involvement in health services is emerging in conjunction with initiatives for deepening inter-professional collaboration, all with the further aim of providing team-based care. Policy-makers envision some non-physician providers' expanding scope of practice going hand-in-hand with this increased focus on patient-centered care. Can AI help deepen the trust between patients and the professionals in their care circle?

Research shows that high-performing teams are not built piecemeal. They achieve superior levels of cooperation because their members trust one another. Trust and a strong sense of group identity build confidence in their effectiveness as a team. In other words, such teams possess high levels of group EI (emotional intelligence).

The right amount of information, shared at the right time, can promote significant improvement in patients' ability to choose the right treatments.

In a randomized controlled trial at two hospitals in Boston researchers studied the impact of a video-based decisions support tool for patients in the hospital. Decisions about cardiopulmonary resuscitation (CPR) and intubation are core parts of advance care planning, particularly for seriously ill, hospitalized patients. However, these discussions are often avoided. Seriously ill patients who viewed a video about CPR and intubation were less likely to want these treatments. Better informed about their options, they gave orders to forgo CPR/ intubation, and discussed their preferences with providers. This study brings into question what represents Informed Consent in the emerging world of AI and Big data? (El-Jawahri, et al., 2015)

Anonymizing data is a recognized pre-condition for its collection. It allows access to health data without compromising the patient's right to privacy or security. Sayo, founder of Self-Care Catalysts, makes a compelling case for codifying trust between the givers and the gatherers of data: patients who give their health data should have greater access to it themselves. They should be able to track it, and see how their data is being used. There should also be an available, clearly delineated process of opting out of data sharing. (*Nuffield Council on Bioethics,* 2015)

Researchers in the United Kingdom have tested the concept of Dynamic Consent. (Spencer, K. et al., 2016). Here, information technology is used to determine just what patients are consenting to share. A succession of digital interface screens is presented to the patient. Information and choices about data gathering, and its potential uses, are delineated. Patients are thus enabled to tailor consent according to their own preferences.

However, this concept is bound to come into conflict with the demand from AI for access to large pools of patient data. This is useful in training AI's predictive function, which is not always related to a specific patient's care. These secondary uses of identifiable patients' data, (e.g. to develop commercial products,) represent unchartered waters for public payers, patient advocates and commercial vendors. Google's company, DeepMind, launched several projects with large health systems that bring out important questions about the commercial exploitation of individuals' data and publicly funded health systems.

These systems are fertile ground for "schooling" AI programs owned by powerful global corporations. (techcrunch.com, 2016)

There is great potential to be realized by combining data with analytics, and technology with expertise. Many ills can be more efficiently cured, once value is understood and paid for. However, a patient centric, value-defining framework – one capable of informing data-sharing in the new healthcare sphere – does not yet exist.

The Office of the National Coordinator for Health Information Technology, United States Government Health and Human Services (ONC) has identified patient-generated health data (PGHD) as an important issue for advancing patient engagement. It has initiated a series of activities to gain more information about PGHD's value, and the various approaches to its implementation. The PGHD policy framework project is integral to Stage 3 of the Meaningful Use Rule, and the U.S. administration's Precision Medicine Initiative. (HealthIT.gov, 2016)

Institutional View: Focus Areas and Investment

While value dimensions are known, (Institute for Healthcare Improvement, 2016) decision-makers' perspectives still vary widely. And the ways organizations are structured to gather data and make decisions are equally diverse.

The problem of establishing connections between processes of care and their outcomes is not trivial either. However, a number of frameworks have been evaluated (Dwamena et al, 2012; Ryan et al, 2012; Scott, et al, 2011; Bircher, 2016). Furthermore, there is the widely acknowledged need for meaningful measures: feasible, affordable, and embedded in the care delivery system (Beck, 2013).

Digital tools create opportunities to advance the quality of measurements, integrate them with electronic medical records, and allow healthcare practitioners to focus attention where it is needed most.

In practice, the issue of measurement arises at the point of introducing a process redesign. Each new idea within such redesigns has its own story of relative risks and advantages.

Finally, most innovative projects in health care will bring together a diverse set of perspectives, expertise and expectations. The diversity of language and approaches to framing problems make development and evaluation of new products complex. This in turn slows down development and adoption by users.

Can we develop a business case for engaging, game-like applications in Health? We shall describe processes, parameters and methodologies for doing just that.

APPROACH

The Lean Start-up Methodology (Ries, 2011) is a widely used framework for developing new software products. Thinking about process redesign as "validated learning" prepares foundations for Growth Mindset among all participants, from builders to the business managers involved in any given project.

Through decades of research on achievement and success, Stanford University psychologist, Carol Dweck (Dweck C, 2007) discovered what she has termed, "growth mindset". It is an approach to problem-solving that stimulates the resilience essential to getting things done. It also plays an especially important role in long development and implementation projects, which are typical for healthcare. Most take 18-24 months to move from Pilot to Project, to System-wide deployment.

Creating and launching digital tools for health are no simple tasks. Perhaps only one thing is certain: your team will go through multiple iterations of the Build-Learn-Measure cycle on its path to developing a relevant value proposition for users, and demonstrating value to business managers. Resilience is key. In short, your team will reach new heights if all members learn to embrace the occasional tumble.

Who Is at the Table?

To succeed while introducing innovation in a multi-stakeholder environment, it is important to map out priorities for each stakeholder, and make sure that all relevant points of view are considered.

Developers of innovative solutions face the significant challenge of carving a path that both defines and measures success. Typically, the path will address at least these 4 perspectives:

1. Describing an IT development project, it is usual to focus on the tactical elements of delivery: meeting specifications, working within time and budget constraints, and developing the robust architecture necessary to meeting expected levels of quality and scalability.
2. Talking about successful management, the focus is on strategic achievements: meeting an organization's business goals, contributing to competitive advantage, generating financial results, and allocating resources wisely.
3. Discussing quality in healthcare, we must involve measures specific to certain care settings: for example, in rehabilitation, the FIM® instrument helps care providers assess patients' physical and cognitive status.
4. Patients confronting a new interface within the care system will seek simplicity and support on their journey towards self-management and improved health.

Payer's Perspective: Value Dials to Understand Benefits

Healthcare payers – whether these are private insurers, sickness funds or, as is the case in many parts of the world, governments – have the responsibility to provide health care to a pre-defined population within a fixed spending envelope. In this environment some form of priority setting must occur (Mitton & Donaldson, 2004). In the recent past, it was not uncommon to allocate resources in health organizations on the basis of historical or political patterns. Although a lot of work is underway in outcomes research (Pincus, 2016), connections between processes of care and outcomes remain imperfectly understood.

Such connections represent information important in the determining of values obtained from health care investments of any kind. Some of information technology's brightest thinkers have long advocated use of the Value Model when discussing health IT investments. It is an industry-tested approach to discussing and measuring the benefits of such investments, and it focuses upon quantifiable benefits that produce financial impact. The Value Model asks two simple questions:

- Where are we going?
- How will we know we've arrived?

Developed by Intel, the model expresses the "where to" question as a value dial, a starting point for specifying what you want to achieve. Intel's 'value dials' are broad categories of benefits through which an IT investment may deliver strategic value.

The value dials mirror quality indicators defined by the healthcare system, such as patient safety and access, cost optimization, and staff satisfaction. We see some of the significant benefits from applying a value dials framework when we discuss which performance indicators are most relevant to specific HIT-enabled projects, to patient priorities, to organizational goals, and/or to the culture as a whole.

Once value dials are established, the next step is to associate each value dial with a set of observable, quantifiable metrics ('Key Performance Indicators' in Intel's parlance). Each KPI is usually derived from an underlying calculation. The calculation is derived from metrics already collected by a healthcare institution.

With the advent of digital tools put in the hands of patients, there is now an opportunity to add metrics that truly reflect their experiences throughout the care process. Thus, digital tools make it possible for patients to become efficient 'reporters' to the healthcare provider. This in turn supports clinical decision-making and leads to improved outcomes.

Measuring the impact of such patient engagement in health care outcomes is not yet well understood. It may be that solutions will be found at the intersection of system-generated measures and psychometric methods for data collection and analysis. Psychometrics offers quantitative models for psychological phenomena, such as patient engagement. (Dubbels, 2016).

Thus, psychometrics can contribute key elements for ROI analyses of digital health interventions. All this helps diminish the risk and uncertainty associated with the costs of development. In this way, serious games may serve as practice innovations, helping to make care more efficient, effective, and satisfying to patients and providers.

What Represents "Engagement" in the Health Context?

As shown in the 2010 editorial (Nash D, 2010) there is a growing body of evidence demonstrates that patients who are more actively involved in their health care experience better health outcomes and incur lower costs.

'The insider perspective of the illness experience' (Thorne and Paterson, 2000) is gaining more central consideration within service redesign debates. While there are examples of tools improving communications at the bedside, such as the Interactive Patient Whiteboard™, there are many fewer tools suited to community and home care settings.

The efforts of Judith Hibbard and her colleagues (Hibbard, 2004; Hibbard 2013) have helped to create the Patient Activation Measure (PAM), a tool that quantifies an individual's level of activation, or engagement, in their care.

Patients' scores are assigned to one of four stages of activation:

Stage 1: The patient does not yet understand that an active role is important.
Stage 2: The patient lacks the knowledge and/or confidence to take action.
Stage 3: The patient is beginning to take action.
Stage 4: The patient is maintaining behaviors (e.g. 30 minutes of aerobic exercise daily) over time.

High PAM scores correlate positively with self-management behaviors, the use of self-directed services, and high rates of adherence to medication regimens.

"Patient Activation" refers to a patient's knowledge, skills, ability, and willingness to manage his or her own health and care. "Patient engagement" is a broader concept that combines patient activation with interventions designed to increase activation and promote positive patient behavior.

By combining PAM with an understanding of the components of motivation the developers of patient engagement tools can begin designing better interventions.

Case Study

In the case of the Home Assessment Tool (HAT) developed at Cogniciti, (www.cogniciti.com) the team started with very simple, pragmatic questions: How would our target users find HAT amid the clutter of web applications? What words would they use for searches? What would make them try the assessment and trust the results? In order to develop meaningful health interventions that could drive behavior change we needed to understand consumers' day-to-day experiences, ie. the full complexity of their decisions regarding aging-related cognitive change.

The Patient Journey is a practical tool for garnering these insights. Patient decision conflicts arise when values, beliefs, and knowledge associated with their "normal" selves conflict with their experience of the new health environment faced in illness.

Uncertainties associated with choosing a healthcare intervention represent barriers. Often, a treatment is rejected based on fears, not of side effects, but of associated losses of physical freedom, connectedness to family and friends, or a general decline in quality of life. Understanding the conflicts underlying their decisions is crucial to influencing patients to adopt or adhere to an intervention.

Commercial Development Framework

Successful innovative projects in digital health typically go through the milestones defined by the "3 Ps":

1. Identify and understand Problems that the customers, (patients and healthcare providers) actually have and care about.
2. Construct a Path to success for customers to investigate, compare, test and purchase. This includes building a demo or a prototype technology, developing a revenue model, and gathering early indications of the marketing equation (i.e. cost of customer acquisition and customer lifetime value).
3. Develop Proof that the healthcare outcomes and value are real.

Once an application has reached the 3rd milestone it represents the complete package of information required for scaling up across the healthcare landscape. The opposite is also true: without such a package it is very difficult to secure the financial and human resources to implement an innovative solution at a meaningful scale.

Process Map

The process map serves three purposes:

First, it is a shared "sand box" where each stakeholder – users, buyers, and developers – can see how their individual perspectives and objectives fit together. Every time a new idea for a feature comes up the team can decide whether it aligns with the overall plan.

Second, it identifies building blocks for a project plan.

Third, it establishes the foundation for an investment pitch. Whether you are pitching to an internal audience or outside investment, it is important to create a narrative that addresses emotional, rational, and financial considerations. The Process Map (Table 1) contains key points that make explicit how the innovative application will deliver on each level.

Table 1. Process map

Target Audience
• Understand user's motivations • Patient Journey • Clinical flow • Business drivers
Define What You Want to Do for the Target Audience
• Audience pain points • Business drivers, e.g. enhancement/brand loyalty; alignment with audience expectations, alignment with the current business model, value dials defined in the strategic plan • Alignment with the business objectives of a sponsor/buyer
Desired Functionality
Where and how the application will be used
Technology Resources
• Scalability across platforms, screens, privacy and security requirements, integration and inter-operability • Clinical validation: meaningful improvement vs. treatment as usual • Workflow integration
Speed to Market
Define metrics early to make decisions through launch and ongoing support; e.g. Efficacy vs. Uptake; utility across the care pathway.

Table 2. Sample budget

	Activities	Range
Milestone 1: Problem	• Interviews with clinical users • Primary research with patients • Patient journey mapping • Mock-ups and models	$30K-$100K
	• Market segmentation • Test business model with a short list of prospective partners • Establish path to pilots.	$30K-$50K
Milestone 2: Path	Stand alone application/treatment/intervention, validated with patients in a controlled setting	$100K-$300K
	Direct market research with consumers to develop messaging and pricing, and to understand perceived trust-worthiness of various channels (e.g. pharmacies, insurance, social media, primary care)	$50K-$100K
	Complete solution designed to integrate with clinical systems and ensure compliance with data security and privacy regulations	$100K-$300K
	Front end UX and dashboards, with inputs from users, buyers and business partners	$100K-$200K
Milestone 3: Proof	• Design measures to assess business and clinical outcomes • Structure and run a pilot implementation • Collaborate with independent clinical users to collect data.	$100K-$500K

This case study demonstrates utilization of the Commercial Development Framework described above for development of an online memory self-assessment for older adults by Cogniciti (www.cogniciti.com). The assessment was developed in collaboration with clinicians and researchers from Baycrest Hospital for Geriatric Care.

The tool is based on existing in-hospital tests that the research team rated as most sensitive for age-related brain health issues, including memory loss, attention loss, and decline in executive function. The self-assessment can be completed anonymously and in the privacy of home settings, and without the assistance of a health care professional All of which helps to lessen bias and provide a better picture of cognitive and mood health. Cogniciti's customers can determine how their cognitive function compares to population norms, and they are offered coping tools to support overall wellness and brain health.

Identifying brain health issues earlier supports earlier intervention, which may improve both quality of life and brain health outcomes. Anonymized and aggregated data are available to companies developing treatments for Mild Cognitive Impairment and Alzheimer.

Cogniciti's Assessment Tool generates a clinically relevant report based on population norms. The assessment report addresses an important communication gap in brain health monitoring.

- For those with health issues beyond what is expected in normal aging, combining a timely visit to the doctor's office with a means to clearly explain specific areas of difficulty helps doctors decide whether or not further investigation is warranted.
- For members of the inter-professional healthcare team the assessment report is a tool to triage patients in an expedient manner and gather all relevant information (meds, lifestyle, history, etc.) into a convenient format.
- For R&D groups developing interventions for mild cognitive impairment, these assessment data represent a rich resource for better targeting treatments.

CONCLUSION

Ways to reduce cost, improve quality, and improve customer engagement are top of mind for healthcare leaders. The health care delivery system that we are so familiar with was built in the 60's for a model focused upon hospitals and providers. As we transition care to lower cost centres, and put more focus on the wellness of individuals, we are in effect shifting our attention (and corresponding investments) away from institutional care, upstream towards prevention and better quality of life for consumers.

We can now build economical and powerful apps that deliver succinct, task oriented user experiences, thereby supporting patient-centred and collaborative care. By shifting some of the clinical responsibilities to lower cost settings, and powering clinical decisions with AI-mediated analytics, healthcare administrators aim to solve acute operational, economic and clinical problems.

However, to get the full economic potential and quality benefit from this Shift, healthcare is also going through a business re-design - realigning roles and accountabilities for providers, and developing entirely new ways of engaging empowered and informed consumers. The value chain of a $10 trillion global healthcare industry is changing, causing disruptions in established business models and opening myriad opportunities for innovation.

In his 2010, *Value In Health Care* framework, Michael E. Porter (2010) explains that Value brings together quality and cost, both defined around the patient. In his view, our system's failures to measure this Value – and to adopt it as the central goal in health care – have hobbled true innovation, allowing instead pseudo-innovations without meaningful value benefits. It has also resulted in ill-advised strategies for cost containment, including the micromanagement of physician practices, which imposes significant costs of its own. Failure to appropriately measure Value is one of the principal reasons that reform in health care has proven so problematic, as compared with reforms in other fields.

With advances in technology, we are now able to measure value in ways unachievable in the past. This journey has seen the introduction of an entirely new set of players, digital players. Commercially developed algorithms are capable of mining large, connected data sets and applications to present accurate information for patients and providers when they need it.

But how do we align these new digital capabilities with clinical and operational priorities, and further with individual privacy? Value exchanges in traditional consumer markets are not always altogether private. A lot more may be at stake for individuals choosing among surgeries vs. those choosing among brands of computer.

While technology tools – pervasive cloud technologies, mobility and analytics – have become readily, commercially available, an ethical value framework for their uses is as yet ill defined at best.

Healthcare systems around the world are reaching out for solutions. The trick is to re-engineer these health care systems to improve population health and provide quality care, all while confronted with persistent structural and cost pressures.

We need to empower quality and regulatory agencies to develop guidelines for data sharing that balance commercial innovation, the economics of a publicly funded healthcare sector, and individuals' ownership of their health data.

ACKNOWLEDGMENT

Lee Gotham: Editor, Corporate Communications, Konona Health

REFERENCES

Beck, S. L., Weiss, M. E., Ryan-Wenger, N., Donaldson, N. E., Aydin, C., Towsley, G. L., & Gardner, W. (2013, Apr). *Measuring nurses' impact on health care quality: Progress, challenges, and future directions.* Retrieved from http://www.ncbi.nlm.nih.gov/pubmed/23502913

Bircher, J., & Hahn, E. G. (2016, Feb 12) *Understanding the nature of health: New perspectives for medicine and public health. Improved wellbeing at lower costs.* Retrieved from http://www.ncbi.nlm.nih.gov/pmc/articles/PMC4837984/

Consumer e-Health: Patient-Generated Health Data. (n.d.). Retrieved from https://www.healthit.gov/policy-researchers-implementers/patient-generated-health-data

Dubbels, B. (2016). *The Vegas Effect: Serious Games Can Ensure Serious Learning.* Retrieved from https://www.academia.edu/9816169/The_Vegas_Effect_Serious_Games_Can_Ensure_Serious_Learning

Dwamena, F., Holmes-Rovner, M., Gaulden, C. M., Jorgenson, S., Sadigh, G., Sikorskii, A., & Olomu, A. et al. (2012, December12). Interventions for providers to promote a patient-centred approach in clinical consultations. *Cochrane Database of Systematic Reviews.* Retrieved from http://www.ncbi.nlm.nih. gov/pubmed/23235595 PMID:23235595

Dweck, C. (2007). *Mindset: The New Psychology of Success.* New York: Ballantine Books.

El-Jawahri, A., Mitchell, S. L., Paasche-Orlow, M. K., Temel, J. S., Jackson, V. A., Rutledge, R. R., & Gillick, M. R. et al. (2015, August). A Randomized Controlled Trial of a CPR and Intubation Video Decision Support Tool for Hospitalized Patients. *Journal of General Internal Medicine.*

Ely, J. W., Osheroff, J. A., Ebell, M. H., Bergus, G. R., Levy, B. T., Chambliss, M. L., & Evans, E. R. (1999, August7). Analysis of questions asked by family doctors regarding patient care. *BMJ (Clinical Research Ed.).*

Hibbard, J. H. (2013). *Patient Engagement, Health Policy Briefs.* Retrieved from http://www.healthaffairs.org/healthpolicybriefs/brief.php?brief_id=86

Hibbard, J. H., Stockard, J., Mahoney, E. R., & Tusler, M. (2004, August). Development of the Patient Activation Measure (PAM): Conceptualizing and Measuring Activation in Patients and Consumers. *Health Services Research.*

Institute for Healthcare Improvement. (2016). Retrieved from http://www.ihi.org/Engage/Initiatives/TripleAim/Pages/MeasuresResults.aspx

Investing in America's Health: A State-by-State Look at Public Health Funding and Key Health Facts. (2016, Apr). Trust for America's Health. Retrieved from http://healthyamericans.org/report/126/

Kostkova, P. (2015, May 5). *Frontiers in Public Health.* ubh.2015.0013410.3389/fp

Lomas, N. (2016, May 18). *Reporting for techcrunch.com, UK's MHRA (medicines and healthcare devices regulator) spokesperson in talks with Google/DeepMind over its Streams app.* Retrieved from https://techcrunch.com/2016/05/18/uk-healthcare-products-regulator-in-talks-with-googledeepmind-over-its-streams-app/

Mitton, C., & Donaldson, C. (2004). *Health care priority setting: Principles, Practice and Challenges, Cost Effectiveness and Resource Allocation* Retrieved from http://www.ncbi.nlm.nih.gov/pmc/articles/PMC411060/

Nash, D. (2010). *P & T: a Peer-reviewed Journal for Formulary Management.* Retrieved from http://europepmc.org/abstract/PMC/PMC2873722

Pincus, H. A., Hudson Scholle, S., Spaeth-Rublee, B., Hepner, K. A., & Brown, J. (2016, June 24). *Quality Measures For Mental Health And Substance Use: Gaps, Opportunities, And Challenges.* Retrieved from http://content.healthaffairs.org/content/35/6/1000.abstract?=right

Porter, M. E. (2010). What Is Value in Health Care? *The New England Journal of Medicine, 363*(26), 2477–2481. doi:10.1056/NEJMp1011024 PMID:21142528

Ries, E. (2011The Lean Startup. *Crown Publishing Group.*

Ryan, A. M., & Doran, T. (2012, Mar). *The effect of improving processes of care on patient outcomes: evidence from the United Kingdom's quality and outcomes framework.* Med Care. Retrieved from http://www.ncbi.nlm.nih.gov/pubmed/22329994

Scott, A., Sivey, P., Ait Ouakrim, D., Willenberg, L., Naccarella, L., Furler, J., & Young, D. (2011, September7). The effect of financial incentives on the quality of health care provided by primary care physicians. *Cochrane Database of Systematic Reviews.* doi:10.1002/14651858.CD008451.pub2 PMID:21901722

Spencer, K., Sanders, C., Whitley, E. A., Lund, D., Kaye, J., & Dixon, W. G. (2016). Patient Perspectives on Sharing Anonymized Personal Health Data Using a Digital System for Dynamic Consent and Research Feedback: A Qualitative Study. *Journal of Medical Internet Research, 18*(4), e66. doi:10.2196/jmir.5011 PMID:27083521

The Collection, Linking and Use of Data in Biomedical Research and Health Care: Ethical Issues. (2015). Nuffield Council on Bioethics. Retrieved from http://nuffieldbioethics.org/project/biological-health-data/

Thorne, S.E., & Paterson, B.L. (2000). Two decades of insider research: What we know and don't know about chronic illness experience. Annual Review of Nursing Research.

Compilation of References

Abernathy, T., & Rouse, R. (2014). *Death to the Three Act Structure! Toward a Unique Structure for Game Narratives.* Retrieved July 5, 2016, from http://www.gdcvault.com/play/1020050/Death-to-the-Three-Act

Adams, R. (2009). *Watership down: A novel.* Simon and Schuster. Retrieved from https://books.google.com/books?hl=en&lr=&id=ittzoegmRpAC&oi=fnd&pg=PA3&dq=watership+down&ots=RmUTuRNLZj&sig=LOGjx4-9kPRPKfDElmk-56ZNbeg

Aggarwal, R., Ward, J., Balasundaram, I., Sains, R., Athanasiou, T., & Darzi, A. (2007). Proving the Effectiveness of Virtual Reality Simulation for Training in Laparoscopic Surgery. *Annals of Surgery, 246*(5), 771–779. doi:10.1097/SLA.0b013e3180f61b09 PMID:17968168

Ahlquist, J. (2007). *Game Development Essentials: Game Artificial Intelligence.* New York: Thomson.

Al, C. C. (2009). Relationships Between Gaming Attributes and Learning Outcomes. *Simulation & Gaming, 40*(2), 217–266.

Alexander, A. L., Brunye, T., & Sidman, J. (2005). From gaming to training: A review of studies on fidelity, immersion, presence and buy-in and their effects on transfer in pc-based simulations and games. *DARWARS Conference Proceedings.* Accessed at http://www.aptima.com/publications/2005_Alexander_Brunye_Sidman_Weil.pdf

Al, H. S. (2010). Prevention of Central Venous Catheter Bloodstream Infections. *Journal of Intensive Care Medicine, 25*(3), 131–138. doi:10.1177/0885066609358952 PMID:20089527

Allard, F., & Starkes, J. L. (1991). Motor-skill experts in sports, dance, and other domains. In *Toward a general theory of expertise: Prospects and limits*, (pp. 126-152). Academic Press.

Alonzo, M., & Aiken, M. (2004). Flaming in electronic communication. *Decision Support Systems, 36*(3), 205–213. doi:10.1016/S0167-9236(02)00190-2

Althabe, F., & Belizán, J. (2006). Caesarean section: The paradox. *Lancet, 368*(9546), 1472–1473. doi:10.1016/S0140-6736(06)69616-5 PMID:17071266

Ames, C. (1992). Classrooms: Goals, structures, and student motivation. *Journal of Educational Psychology, 84*(3), 261–271. doi:10.1037/0022-0663.84.3.261

Ames, C. A. (1990). Motivation: What teachers need to know. *Teachers College Record, 90*(3), 409–421.

Andreatta, P., Chen, Y., & Marsh, M. C. K. (2010). *Simulation based training improves applied clinical placement of ultrasound-guided PICCs.* Supp Care Cancer.

Anesthesiology, A. S. of. (2010). *Central Venous Access Guidelines Draft.* Retrieved from www.asahq.org/clinical/CentralVenousAccessGuidelinesDraft06142010.pdf

Angehrn, A. A. (2006). L2C: Designing simulation-based learning experiences for collaboration competencies development. Association for Learning Technology, 31.

App Store [computer software]. Cupertino, CA: Apple, Inc.

Applied Research Associates. (2016). *BioGears Physiology Engine*. Retrieved on June 26th, 2016 at www.biogearsengine.com

Arnett, J. J. (2010). *Adolescence and emerging adulthood: A cultural approach* (4th ed.). Upper Saddle River, NJ: Pearson-Prentice Hall.

Baddeley, A. (1992). Working memory. *Science*, *255*(5044), 556–559. doi:10.1126/science.1736359 PMID:1736359

Bailey, R., Wise, K., & Bolls, P. (2009). How avatar customizability affects childrens arousal and subjective presence during junk food-sponsored online video games. *Cyberpsychology & Behavior*, *12*(3), 277–283. doi:10.1089/cpb.2008.0292 PMID:19445632

Ball, K., Berch, D. B., Helmers, K. F., Jobe, J. B., Leveck, M. D., Marsiske, M., & Willis, S. L et al.. (2002). Effects of cognitive training interventions with older adults: A randomized controlled trial. *Journal of the American Medical Association*, *288*(18), 2271–2281. doi:10.1001/jama.288.18.2271 PMID:12425704

Baltes, B. B., Dickson, M. W., Sherman, M. P., Bauer, C. C., & LaGanke, J. S. (2002). Comptuer-mediated communication and group decision making: A meta-analysis. *Organizational Behavior and Human Decision Processes*, *87*(1), 156–179. doi:10.1006/obhd.2001.2961

Bandura, A. (1986). *Social foundations of thought and action: A social cognitive theory*. Englewood Cliffs, NJ: Prentice-Hall.

Bandura, A. (1997). *Self-efficacy: The exercise of control*. New York: W.H. Freeman.

Baniqued, P. L., Lee, H., Voss, M. W., Basak, C., Cosman, J. D., DeSouza, S., & Kramer, A. F. et al. (2013). Selling points: What cognitive abilities are tapped by casual video games? *Acta Psychologica*, *142*(1), 74–86. doi:10.1016/j.actpsy.2012.11.009 PMID:23246789

Barab, S. A., Pettyjohn, P., Gresalfi, M., Volk, C., & Solomou, M. (2012). Game-based curriculum and transformational play: Designing to meaningfully positioning person, content, and context. *Computers & Education*, *58*(1), 518–533. doi:10.1016/j.compedu.2011.08.001

Barab, S., Thomas, M., Dodge, T., Carteaux, R., & Tuzun, H. (2005). Making learning fun: Quest Atlantis, a game without guns. *Educational Technology Research and Development*, *53*(1), 86–107. doi:10.1007/BF02504859

Baranowski, T., Buday, F., Thompson, D. I., & Baranowski, J. (2008). Playing for real: Video games and stories for health-related behavior change. *American Journal of Preventive Medicine*, *34*(1), 74–82. doi:10.1016/j.amepre.2007.09.027 PMID:18083454

Bargh, J. A., & Chartrand, T. L. (1999). The unbearable automaticity of being. *The American Psychologist*, *54*(7), 462–479. doi:10.1037/0003-066X.54.7.462

Bargh, J. A., Chen, M., & Burrows, L. (1996). Automaticity of social behavior: Direct effects of trait construct and stereotype activation on action. *Journal of Personality and Social Psychology*, *71*(2), 230–244. doi:10.1037/0022-3514.71.2.230 PMID:8765481

Barnett, A., Cerin, E., & Baranowski, T. (2011). Active video games for youth: A systematic review. *Journal of Physical Activity & Health*, *8*(5), 724–737. doi:10.1123/jpah.8.5.724 PMID:21734319

Barsuk, J. H., McGahie, W. C., Cohen, E. R., & Balachandran, J. S. (2009). Use of simulation based mastery learning to improve the quality of central venous catheter placement in a medical intensive care unit. *Journal of Hospital Medicine, 7*(7), 397–403. doi:10.1002/jhm.468 PMID:19753568

Baumgart, M., Snyder, H. M., Carrillo, M. C., Fazio, S., Kim, H., & Johns, H. (2015). Summary of the evidence on modifiable risk factors for cognitive decline and dementia: A population –based perspective. *Alzheimers & Dementia, 11*(6), 718–726. doi:10.1016/j.jalz.2015.05.016 PMID:26045020

Beck, S. L., Weiss, M. E., Ryan-Wenger, N., Donaldson, N. E., Aydin, C., Towsley, G. L., & Gardner, W. (2013, Apr). *Measuring nurses' impact on health care quality: Progress, challenges, and future directions.* Retrieved from http://www.ncbi.nlm.nih.gov/pubmed/23502913

Behm-Morawitz, E., & Mastro, D. (2009). The Effects of the Sexualization of Female Video Game Characters on Gender Stereotyping and Female Self-Concept. *Sex Roles, 61*(11), 808–823. doi:10.1007/s11199-009-9683-8

Belchior, P., Marsiske, M., Sisco, S., Yam, A., Bavelier, D., Ball, K., & Mann, W. C. (2013). Video game training to improve selective visual attention in older adults. *Computers in Human Behavior, 29*(4), 1318–1324. doi:10.1016/j.chb.2013.01.034 PMID:24003265

Belchior, P., Marsiske, M., Sisco, S., Yam, A., & Mann, W. (2012). Older adults engagement with a video game training program. *Activities, Adaptation and Aging, 36*(4), 269–279. doi:10.1080/01924788.2012.702307 PMID:23504652

Belizán, J., Althabe, F., & Carrerata, M. (2007). Health consequences of the increasing caesarean section rates. *Epidemiology (Cambridge, Mass.), 18*(4), 485–486. doi:10.1097/EDE.0b013e318068646a PMID:17568221

Benford, S., Schnadelbach, H., Koleva, B., Anastasi, R., Greenhalgh, C., Rodden, T., … Steed, A. (2005). Expected, sensed, and desired: A framework for designing sensing-based interaction. *ACM Transactions on Computer-Human Interaction, 12*(1), 3-30. doi: 1073-0616/05/0300-003

Bers, M. (2001). Identity construction environments: Developing personal and moral values through the design of a virtual city. *Journal of the Learning Sciences, 10*(4), 365–415. doi:10.1207/S15327809JLS1004new_1

Bessiere, K., Seay, A. F., & Kiesler, S. (2007). The ideal elf: Identity exploration in World of Warcraft. *Cyberpsychology & Behavior, 10*(4), 530–537. doi:10.1089/cpb.2007.9994 PMID:17711361

Best, J. R. (2013). Exergaming in youth: Effects on physical and cognitive health. *Zeitschrift fur Psychologie mit Zeitschrift fur Angewandte Psychologie, 221*(2), 72–78. doi:10.1027/2151-2604/a000137 PMID:25097828

Bianchi-Berthouze, N., Kim, W. W., & Patel, D. (2007). Does body movement engage you more in digital game play? and why? In *Proceedings of the 2nd international conference on Affective Computing and Intelligent Interaction, ACII '07.* Berlin: Springer-Verlag. doi:10.1007/978-3-540-74889-2_10

Biddiss, E., & Irwin, J. (2010). Active video games to promote physical activity in children and youth: A systematic review. *Archives of Pediatrics & Adolescent Medicine, 164*(7), 664–672. doi:10.1001/archpediatrics.2010.104 PMID:20603468

Bircher, J., & Hahn, E. G. (2016, Feb 12) *Understanding the nature of health: New perspectives for medicine and public health. Improved wellbeing at lower costs.* Retrieved from http://www.ncbi.nlm.nih.gov/pmc/articles/PMC4837984/

Birk, M. V., Atkins, C., Bowey, J. T., & Mandryk, R. L. (2016). *Fostering intrinsic motivation through avatar identification in digital games.* Paper presented at CHI 2016, San Jose, CA. http://doi.org/ doi:10.1145/2858036.2858062

Bleakley, C. M., Charles, D., Porter-Armstrong, A., McNeill, M. D., McDonough, S. M., & McCormack, B. (2013). Gaming for health: A systematic review of the physical and cognitive effects of interactive computer games in older adults. *Journal of Applied Gerontology*; Advance online publication. doi:10.1177/0733464812470747 PMID:24652863

Blum, M. G., Powers, T. W., & Sundaresan, S. (2004). Bronchoscopy simlulator effectively prepares junior residents to competently perform basic clinical bronchoscopy. *The Annals of Thoracic Surgery, 78*(1), 287–291. doi:10.1016/j.athoracsur.2003.11.058 PMID:15223446

Bochner, R. E., Sorensen, K. M., & Belamarich, P. F. (2015). The impact of active video gaming on weight in youth: A meta-analysis. *Clinical Pediatrics, 54*(7), 620–628. doi:10.1177/0009922814545165 PMID:25085926

Bogost, I. (2007). *Persuasive games: The expressive power of video games.* Cambridge, MA: MIT Press.

Bozoki, A., Radovanovic, M., Winn, B., Heeter, C., & Anthony, J. C. (2013). Effects of a computer-based cognitive exercise program on age-related cognitive decline. *Archives of Gerontology and Geriatrics, 57*(1), 1–7. doi:10.1016/j.archger.2013.02.009 PMID:23542053

Braitman, K. A., & McCartt, A. T. (2008). Characteristics of older drivers who self-limit their driving. *Annals of Advances in Automotive Medicine, 52*, 254–254. PMID:19026241

Britt,, R.C., & Reed,, S.F. (2007). Central line simulation: A new training algorithm. *The American Surgeon, 73*(7), 682–683. PMID:17674940

Brown, C. L., Gibbons, L. E., Kennison, R. F., Robitalle, A., Lindwall, M., Mitchell, M. B., & Mungas, D. et al. (2012). Social Activity and Cognitive Functioning Over Time. *Journal of Aging Research, 2012*, 287438. doi:10.1155/2012/287438 PMID:22991665

Brox, E., Fernandez-Luque, L., & Tøllefsen, T. (2011). Healthy gaming–video game design to promote health. *Applied Clinical Informatics, 2*(2), 128–142. doi:10.4338/ACI-2010-10-R-0060 PMID:23616865

Buonomano, D. V., & Merzenich, M. M. (1998). Cortical plasticity: From synapses to maps. *Annual Review of Neuroscience, 21*(1), 149–186. doi:10.1146/annurev.neuro.21.1.149 PMID:9530495

Business Wire. (2016, June 21). *In-Game Purchases and Construction Toys Drive Global Growth for Toys and Games in 2015.* Retrieved August 15, 2016, from http://www.businesswire.com/news/home/20160621005113/en/In-Game-Purchases-Construction-Toys-Drive-Global-Growth

C Programming Tutorial. (n.d.). Retrieved from http://www.cprogramming.com/tutorial.html

Cannon, W. B. (1987). The James-Lange theory of emotions: A critical examination and an alternative theory. *The American Journal of Psychology, 100*(3/4), 567–586. doi:10.2307/1422695 PMID:3322057

Cassavaugh, N. D., & Kramer, A. F. (2009). Transfer of computer-based training to simulated driving in older adults. *Applied Ergonomics, 40*(5), 943–952. doi:10.1016/j.apergo.2009.02.001 PMID:19268912

Centers for Disease Control Data and Statistics. (2011). *New data on older drivers.* Retrieved from http://www.cdc.gov/Features/dsOlderDrivers/

Champagne, D. L., Bagot, R. C., van Hasselt, F., Ramakers, G., Meaney, M. J., de Kloet, E. R., & Krugers, H. (2008). Maternal care and hippocampal plasticity: Evidence for experience-dependent structural plasticity, altered synaptic functioning, and differential responsiveness to glucocorticoids and stress. *The Journal of Neuroscience, 28*(23), 6037–6045. doi:10.1523/JNEUROSCI.0526-08.2008 PMID:18524909

Chandler, D., & Griffiths, M. (2004). Who is the fairest of them all? Gendered readings of Big Brother 2 (UK). In E. Mathijs & J. Jones (Eds.), *Big Brother International: Format, Critics and Publics* (pp. 40–61). London, UK: Wallflower Press.

Chan, K., & Paterson-Brown, S. (2002). How do fathers feel after accompanying their partners in labour and delivery? *Journal of Obstetrics & Gynaecology, 22*(1), 11–15. doi:10.1080/01443610120101628 PMID:12521719

Chao, Y. Y., Scherer, Y. K., & Montgomery, C. A. (2014). Effects of using Nintendo Wii™ exergames in older adults: A review of the literature. *Journal of Aging and Health*, *27*(3), 379–402. doi:10.1177/0898264314551171 PMID:25245519

Charmaz, K. (2006). *Constructing Grounded Theory: A Practical Guide through Qualitative Analysis*. Thousand Oaks, NJ: Sage Publications.

Chen, J. L., & Wilkosz, M. E. (2014). Efficacy of technology-based interventions for obesity prevention in adolescents: A systematic review. *Adolescent Health. Medicine and Therapeutics*, *5*, 159–170.

Cheung, I., & McCartt, A. T. (2010). *Declines in fatal crashes of older drivers: Changes in crash risk & survivability.* Arlington, VA: Insurance Institute for Highway Safety.

Child of Eden [Computer software]. Montreuil-sous-Bois, France: Ubisoft.

Childress, M. D., & Braswell, R. (2006). Using massively multiplayer online role-playing games for online learning. *Distance Education*, *27*(2), 187–196. doi:10.1080/01587910600789522

Christy, K. R., & Fox, J. (2016). Transportability and presence as predictors of avatar identification within narrative video games. *Cyberpsychology, Behavior, and Social Networking*, *19*(4), 283–287. doi:10.1089/cyber.2015.0474 PMID:26919032

Civilization [computer software]. Alameda, CA: MicroProse.

Clark, R. C., & Mayer, R. E. (2008). e-learning and the science of instruction: Proven guidelines for consumers and designers of multimedia learning. San Francisco: Pfeiffer.

Clarke, J., Dede, C., Ketelhut, D. J., & Nelson, B. (2006). A design-based research strategy to promote scalability for educational innovations. *Educational Technology*, *46*(3), 27–36.

Cohen, J. (1988). *Statistical power analysis for the behavioral sciences* (2nd ed.). Hillsdale, NJ: Lawrence Erlbaum Associates, Publishers.

Cohen, J. (1999). Favorite characters of teenage viewers of Israeli serials. *Journal of Broadcasting & Electronic Media*, *43*(3), 327–345. doi:10.1080/08838159909364495

Cohen, J. (2001). Defining identification: A theoretical look at the identification of audiences with media characters. *Mass Communication & Society*, *4*(3), 245–264. doi:10.1207/S15327825MCS0403_01

Colcombe, S. J., & Kramer, A. F. (2003). Fitness effects on the cognitive function of older adults: A meta-analytic study. *Psychological Science*, *14*(2), 125–130. doi:10.1111/1467-9280.t01-1-01430 PMID:12661673

Connolly, T. M., Boyle, E. A., MacArthur, E., Hainey, T., & Boyle, J. M. (2012). A systematic literature review of empirical evidence on computer games and serious games. *Computers & Education*, *59*(2), 661–686. doi:10.1016/j.compedu.2012.03.004

Consumer e-Health: Patient-Generated Health Data. (n.d.). Retrieved from https://www.healthit.gov/policy-researchers-implementers/patient-generated-health-data

Cooper, J., & Taqueti, V. (2008). A brief history of the development of mannequin simulators for clinical education and training. *Postgraduate Medical Journal*, *84*(997), 563–570. doi:10.1136/qshc.2004.009886 PMID:19103813

Cormier, D. (2009). MUVE eventedness: An experience like any other. *British Journal of Educational Technology*, *40*(3), 543–546. doi:10.1111/j.1467-8535.2009.00956.x

Craik, F. I. M., & Bialystok, E. (2006). Planning and task management in older adults: Cooking breakfast. *Memory & Cognition*, *34*(6), 1236–1249. doi:10.3758/BF03193268 PMID:17225505

Creswell, J. W. (2005). *Educational Research: planning, conducting, and evaluating quantitative and qualitative research* (2nd ed.). Merrill.

Csikszentmihalyi, M. (2014). Play and Intrinsic Rewards. In Flow and the Foundations of Positive Psychology (pp. 135–153). Springer. Retrieved from http://link.springer.com/chapter/10.1007/978-94-017-9088-8_10

Csikszentmihalyi, M., & Bennett, S. (1971). An exploratory model of play. *American Anthropologist, 73*(1), 45–58. doi:10.1525/aa.1971.73.1.02a00040

Cushing, C. C., & Steele, R. G. (2010). A meta-analytic review of eHealth interventions for pediatric health promoting and maintaining behaviors. *Journal of Pediatric Psychology, 35*(9), 937–949. doi:10.1093/jpepsy/jsq023 PMID:20392790

Dahlin, E., Stigsdotter-Neely, A., Larsson, A., Backman, L., & Nyberg, L. (2008). Transfer of learning after updating mediated by the striatum. *Science, 320*(5882), 1510–1512. doi:10.1126/science.1155466 PMID:18556560

Dance Central [Computer software]. Redmond, WA: Microsoft.

Dance Central 2 [Computer software]. Redmond, WA: Microsoft.

Dance Central 3 [Computer software]. Redmond, WA: Microsoft.

Daviglus, M. L., Bell, C. C., Berrettini, W., Bowen, P. E., Connolly, E. S., & Cox, N. J. (2010, April 26–28). ... Trevisan, M. (2010). *National Institutes of Health State-of-the-Science Conference Statement: Preventing Alzheimer's Disease and Cognitive Decline. NIH Consensus and State-of-the-Science Statements, 27*(4), 1–30. doi:10.7326/0003-4819-153-3-201008030-00260 PMID:20445638

Davis, A., Murphy, J., Owens, D., Khazanchi, D., & Zigurs, I. (2009). Avatars, people, and virtual worlds: Foundations for research in metaverses. *Journal of the Association for Information Systems, 10*(2), 90–117.

Davis-Floyd, R. E. (2004). *Birth as an american rite of passage: With a new preface.* University of California Press. doi:10.1525/california/9780520229327.001.0001

Davis, M. H. (1983). Measuring individual differences in empathy: Evidence for a multidimensional approach. *Journal of Personality and Social Psychology, 44*(1), 113–126. doi:10.1037/0022-3514.44.1.113

Dead Rising 3 [Computer software]. Redmond, WA: Microsoft.

Deci, E. L. (1971). Effects of externally mediated rewards on intrinsic motivation. *Journal of Personality and Social Psychology, 18*(1), 105–115. doi:10.1037/h0030644

Deci, E. L., & Ryan, R. M. (1985). *Intrinsic motivation and self-determination in human behavior.* New York, NY: Plenum Press. doi:10.1007/978-1-4899-2271-7

Declercq, E., Sakala, C., Corry, M., & Applebaum, S. (2007). Listening to mothers II: Report of the second national US survey of womens childbearing experiences. *Journal of Perinatal Education, 16*(4), 9–14. doi:10.1624/105812407X244769 PMID:18769512

Delwiche, A. (2006). Massively multiplayer online games (MMOs) in the new media classroom. *Journal of Educational Technology & Society, 9,* 160–172.

DeNeve, K. M., & Heppner, M. J. (1997). Role play simulations: The assessment of an active learning technique and comparisons with traditional lectures. *Innovative Higher Education, 21*(3), 231–246. doi:10.1007/BF01243718

DeSmet, A., Van Ryckeghem, D., Compernolle, S., Baranowski, T., Thompson, D., Crombez, G., & Vandebosch, H. et al. (2014). A meta-analysis of serious digital games for healthy lifestyle promotion. *Preventive Medicine, 69,* 95–107. doi:10.1016/j.ypmed.2014.08.026 PMID:25172024

Dickey, M. D. (2005). Three-dimensional virtual worlds and distance learning: Two case studies of Active Worlds as a medium for distance education. *British Journal of Educational Technology, 36*(3), 439–451. doi:10.1111/j.1467-8535.2005.00477.x

Dickey, M. D. (2007). Game design and learning: A conjectual analysis of how massively mutliple online role-playing games (MMORPGs) foster intrinsic motivation. *Educational Technology Research and Development, 55*(3), 253–273. doi:10.1007/s11423-006-9004-7

Diehl, M., Willis, S., & Schaie, K. W. (1995). Everyday problem solving in older adults: Observational assessment and cognitive correlates. *Psychology and Aging, 10*(3), 478–491. doi:10.1037/0882-7974.10.3.478 PMID:8527068

do Carmo, J., Goncalves, R., Batalau, R., & Palmeira, A. L. (2013). Active video games and physical activity in overweight children and adolescents. In *Proceedings of the IEEE 2nd International Conference on Serious Games and Applications for Health (SeGAH)* (pp. 1–5). doi:10.1109/SeGAH.2013.6665323

Doidge, N. (2007). *The Brain That Changes Itself: Stories of personal triumph from the frontiers of brain science.* New York, NY: Penguin Group.

Dolgov, I., Graves, W. J., Nearents, M. R., Schwark, J. D., & Brooks Volkman, C. (2014). Effects of cooperative gaming and avatar customization on subsequent spontaneous helping behavior. *Computers in Human Behavior, 33,* 49–55. doi:10.1016/j.chb.2013.12.028

Dong, Y., Suri, H. S., Cook, D. A., Kashani, K. B., Mullon, J. J., Enders, F. T., & Ziv, A. D. W. et al. (2010). Simulation-based objective assessment discerns clinical proficiency in central line placement: A construct validation. *Chest, 137*(5), 1050–1056. doi:10.1378/chest.09-1451 PMID:20061397

Donoghue, A. J., Durbin, D. R., Nadel, F. M., Stryjewski, G. R., Kost, S. I., & Nadkarny, V. (2008). Perception of Realism During Mock Resuscitations by Pediatric Housestaff: The Impact of simulated Physical Features. *J Soc Simulation in Healthcare, 3*(3), 113–137.

Dove, T. (2002). The Space between: Telepresence, re-animation and the re-casting of the invisible. In M. Reiser & A. Zapp (Eds.), *New screen media: cinema/art/narrative.* London: British Film Institute.

Downs, E., & Smith, S. (2010). Keeping abreast of hypersexuality: A video game character content analysis. *Sex Roles,* 1–13.

Draganski, B., & May, A. (2008). Training-induced structural changes in the adult human brain. *Behavioural Brain Research, 192*(1), 137–142. doi:10.1016/j.bbr.2008.02.015 PMID:18378330

Dubbels, B. (2008). Video games, reading, and transmedial comprehension. In Handbook of research on effective electronic gaming in Education (pp. 251–276). Academic Press.

Dubbels, B. (2016). *The Vegas Effect: Serious Games Can Ensure Serious Learning.* Retrieved from https://www.academia.edu/9816169/The_Vegas_Effect_Serious_Games_Can_Ensure_Serious_Learning

Dubbels, B. (2013). Gamification, Serious Games, Ludic Simulation, and other Contentious Categories. *International Journal of Gaming and Computer-Mediated Simulations, 5*(2), 1–19. doi:10.4018/jgcms.2013040101

Ducheneaut, N., Wen, M. D., Yee, N., & Wadley, G. (2009). Body and mind: A study of avatar personalization in three virtual worlds.*ACM Conference on Human Factors in Computing Systems*. doi:10.1145/1518701.1518877

Ducheneaut, N., Yee, N., Nickell, E., & Moore, R. J. (2006). Alone together?: Exploring the social dynamics of massively multiplayer online games.*Proceedings of the SIGCHI Conference on Human Factors in Computing CHI '06* (pp. 407-416). ACM. doi:10.1145/1124772.1124834

Dutta, N., & Pereira, M. A. (2015). Effects of active video games on energy expenditure in adults: A systematic literature review. *Journal of Physical Activity & Health*, *12*(6), 890–899. doi:10.1123/jpah.2013-0168 PMID:25134074

Dwamena, F., Holmes-Rovner, M., Gaulden, C. M., Jorgenson, S., Sadigh, G., Sikorskii, A., & Olomu, A. et al. (2012, December12). Interventions for providers to promote a patient-centred approach in clinical consultations. *Cochrane Database of Systematic Reviews*. Retrieved from http://www.ncbi.nlm.nih.gov/pubmed/23235595 PMID:23235595

Dweck, C. (2007). *Mindset: The New Psychology of Success*. New York: Ballantine Books.

Edwards, J. D., Delahunt, P. B., & Mahncke, H. W. (2009). Cognitive speed of processing training delays driving cessation. *The Journals of Gerontology. Series A, Biological Sciences and Medical Sciences*, *64*(12), 1262–1267. doi:10.1093/gerona/glp131 PMID:19726665

Elder Scrolls, V. *Skyrim* [Computer software]. Rockville, MD: Bethesda Softworks.

El-Jawahri, A., Mitchell, S. L., Paasche-Orlow, M. K., Temel, J. S., Jackson, V. A., Rutledge, R. R., & Gillick, M. R. et al. (2015, August). A Randomized Controlled Trial of a CPR and Intubation Video Decision Support Tool for Hospitalized Patients. *Journal of General Internal Medicine*.

El-Shinnawy, M., & Vinze, A. S. (1997). Technology, culture, and persuasiveness: A study of choiceshifts in group settings. *International Journal of Human-Computer Studies*, *47*(3), 473–496. doi:10.1006/ijhc.1997.0138

Elson, V. L. (1997). *Childbirth in American movies and television: Patterns of portrayal and audience impact* (Unpublished doctoral dissertation). University of Massachusetts at Amherst.

Ely, J. W., Osheroff, J. A., Ebell, M. H., Bergus, G. R., Levy, B. T., Chambliss, M. L., & Evans, E. R. (1999, August7). Analysis of questions asked by family doctors regarding patient care. *BMJ (Clinical Research Ed.)*.

England, P., & Horowitz, R. (1998). *Birthing From Within: An Extra-Ordinary Guide to Childbirth Preparation*. Albuquerque, NM: Partera Press.

Entertainment Software Association (ESA). (2014). *2014 Essential facts about the computer and video game industry (Report)*. Washington, DC: Entertainment Software Association.

Erikson, E. (1968). *Identity youth and crisis*. New York: Norton.

Etnier, J. L., Salazar, W., Landers, D. M., Petruzzello, S. J., Han, M., & Nowell, P. (1997). The influence of physical fitness and exercise upon cognitive functioning: A meta-analysis. *Journal of Sport & Exercise Psychology*, *19*(3), 249–277. doi:10.1123/jsep.19.3.249

European Commission. (2014, July). *In-app purchases: Joint action by the European Commission and Member States is leading to better protection for consumers in online games*. Retrieved August 15, 2016, from http://europa.eu/rapid/press-release_IP-14-847_en.htm

Fabian, H., Rådestad, I., & Waldenström, U. (2005). Childbirth and parenthood education classes in Sweden. Womens opinion and possible outcomes. *Acta Obstetricia et Gynecologica Scandinavica*, *84*(5), 436–443. doi:10.1111/j.0001-6349.2005.00732.x PMID:15842207

Fable the Journey [Computer software]. Redmond, WA: Microsoft.

Fares, L.G., II, & Block, P.H. (1986). House staff results with subclavian cannulation. *Am Surg, 52*(2), 108–111.

Fatherhood Institute. (2007). Fathers at the birth and after: Impact on mothers. In *Fatherhood Institute Research Summary: Fathers Attending Births*. Author.

Feng, J., Spence, I., & Pratt, J. (2007). Playing an action video game reduces gender differences in spatial cognition. *Psychological Science, 18*(10), 850–855. doi:10.1111/j.1467-9280.2007.01990.x PMID:17894600

Fischer, P., Kastenmüller, A., & Greitemeyer, T. (2010). Media violence and the self: The impact of personalized gaming characters in aggressive video games in aggressive behavior. *Journal of Experimental Social Psychology, 46*(1), 192–195. doi:10.1016/j.jesp.2009.06.010

Fisher, A. G. (2006). Assessment of Motor and Process Skills: Vol. 1. *Development, standardization, and administration manual* (6th ed.). Fort Collins, CO: Three Star Press.

Flanagan, M. (1999). Mobile identities, digital stars, and post-cinematic selves. *Wide Angle., 21*(1), 77–93. doi:10.1353/wan.1999.0002

Fleming, P. S., Koletsi, D., Seehra, J., & Pandis, N. (2014). Systematic reviews published in higher impact clinical journals were of higher quality. *Journal of Clinical Epidemiology, 67*(7), 754–759. doi:10.1016/j.jclinepi.2014.01.002 PMID:24709031

Fletcher, G., Flin, R., McGeorge, P., Glavin, R., & Maran, N. P. R. (2003). Non-technical skills (ANTS): Evaluation of a behavioural marker system. *British Journal of Anaesthesia, 90*(5), 580–588.

Flight Sim X [computer software]. Redmond, WA: Microsoft Corporation.

Foley, L., & Maddison, R. (2010). Use of active video games to increase physical activity in children: A (virtual) reality. *Pediatric Exercise Science, 22*(1), 7–20. doi:10.1123/pes.22.1.7 PMID:20332536

Fox, J., & Bailenson, J. N. (2009). Virtual self-modeling: The effects of vicarious reinforcement and identification on exercise behaviors. *Media Psychology, 12*(1), 1–25. doi:10.1080/15213260802669474

Fricker, S. J., Kuperwaser, M. C., & Stromberg, A. E. (1981). Use of a video-game/stripe presentation for amblyopia therapy. *Journal of Pediatric Ophthalmology and Strabismus, 18*(2), 11–16.

Fried, G. M., Feldman, L. S., Vassiliou, M. C., Fraser, S. A., Stanbridge, D., Ghitulescu, G., & Andrew, C. G. (2004). Proving the value of simulation in laparoscopic surgery. *Annals of Surgery, 240*(3), 518–525. doi:10.1097/01.sla.0000136941.46529.56 PMID:15319723

Fron, J., Fullerton, T., Ford Morie, J., & Pearce, C. (2007). *Playing dress-up: Costumes, role-play and imagination.* Philosophy of Computer Games Conference, Reggio Emilia, Italy.

Fuchs, M. (2012). Ludic interfaces. Driver and product of gamification. *GAME*. Retrieved July 12, 2012, from http://www.gamejournal.it/ludic-interfaces-driver-and-product-of-gamification/

Fuchs, M., & Strouhal, E. (2008). *Games. Kunst und Politik der Spiele*. Wien, Austria: Sonderzahl Verlag.

Ganesh, S., van Schie, H. T., de Lange, F. P., Thompson, E., & Wigboldus, D. H. (2011). How the human brain goes virtual: Distinct cortical regions of the person-processing network are involved in self-identification with virtual agents. *Cereb Cortex., 22*(7), 1577–1585. doi:10.1093/cercor/bhr227 PMID:21917741

Gao, Z., & Chen, S. (2014). Are field-based exergames useful in preventing childhood obesity? a systematic review. *Obesity Reviews*, *15*(8), 676–691. doi:10.1111/obr.12164 PMID:24602072

Gao, Z., Chen, S., Pasco, D., & Pope, Z. (2015). A meta-analysis of active video games on health outcomes among children and adolescents. *Obesity Reviews*, *16*(9), 783–794. doi:10.1111/obr.12287 PMID:25943852

Garris, R., Ahlers, R., & Driskell, J. E. (2002). Games, motivation, and learning: A research and practice model. *Simulation & Gaming*, *33*(4), 441–467. doi:10.1177/1046878102238607

Garry's Mod [computer software]. Walsall, UK: Facepunch Studios LTD.

Gaskin, I. (2003). *Ina May's Guide to Childbirth*. Bantam Books.

Gee, J. P. (2003). What video games have to teach us about learning and literacy. *Computers in Entertainment*, *1*(1), 20–20. doi:10.1145/950566.950595

Gee, J. P. (2004). Learning by design: Games as learning machines. *Interactive Educational Multimedia*, *8*, 15–23.

Giant Bomb. (2011, July). *So much grind... - Red Dead Redemption - Giant Bomb*. Retrieved August 11, 2016, from http://www.giantbomb.com/red-dead-redemption/3030-25249/forums/so-much-grind-505106/

Giddings, S. (2007). I'm the one who makes the Lego Racers go: Virtual and actual space in videogame play. In S. Weber & S. Dixon (Eds.), *Growing Up Online: Young People and Digital Technologies* (pp. 35–48). New York: Palgrave Macmillan. doi:10.1057/9780230607019_3

Giddings, S., & Kennedy, H. (2008). Little jesuses and fuck-off robots: On aesthetics, cybernetics, and not being very good at Lego Star Wars. In M. Swalwell & J. Wilson (Eds.), *The Pleasures of Computer Gaming: Essays on Cultural History, Theory and Aesthetics* (pp. 13–32). Jefferson, NC: McFarland.

Githens, P., Glass, C., Sloan, F., & Entman, S. (1993). Maternal recall and medical records: An examination of events during pregnancy, childbirth, and early infancy. *Birth (Berkeley, Calif.)*, *20*(3), 136–141. doi:10.1111/j.1523-536X.1993. tb00438.x PMID:8240621

Goer, H. (1999). *The Thinking Woman's Guide to a Better Birth*. Perigee.

Goodman, P., Mackey, M., & Tavakoli, A. (2004). Factors related to childbirth satisfaction. *Journal of Advanced Nursing*, *46*(2), 212–219. doi:10.1111/j.1365-2648.2003.02981.x PMID:15056335

GoSupermodel [PC Game]. Copenhagen, Denmark: watAgame.

Gould, M. M. D. (2003). Preventing Complications of Central Venous Catheterization. *The New England Journal of Medicine*, *348*(12), 1123–1131. doi:10.1056/NEJMra011883 PMID:12646670

Grand Theft Auto IV [computer software]. New York: Rockstar Games.

Grant, T., McNeil, M. A., & Luo, X. (2010). Absolute and Relative Value of Patient Simulator Features as Perceived by Medical Undergraduates. *J Soc Simulation in Healthcare*, *5*(4), 213–218.

Green, C. S., Pouget, A., & Bavelier, D. (2010). Improved probabilistic inference as a general learning mechanism with action video games. *Current Biology*, *20*(17), 1573–1579. doi:.cub.2010.07.04010.1016/j

Green, C. S., & Bavelier, D. (2003). Action video game modifies visual attention. *Nature*, *423*(6939), 534–537. doi:10.1038/nature01647 PMID:12774121

Gustafsson, A., Bång, M., & Svahn, M. (2009). Power explorer: A casual game style for encouraging long term behavior change among teenagers. In *Proceedings of the International Conference on Advances in Computer Entertainment Technology* (pp. 182-189. New York: ACM. doi:10.1145/1690388.1690419

Guy, S., Ratzki-Leewing, A., & Gwadry-Sridhar, F. (2011). Moving beyond the stigma: Systematic review of video games and their potential to combat obesity. *International Journal of Hypertension, 2011,* 1–13. doi:10.4061/2011/179124 PMID:21629863

Hall, A. K., Chavarria, E., Maneeratana, V., Chaney, B. H., & Bernhardt, J. M. (2012). Health benefits of digital videogames for older adults: A systematic review of the literature. *Games For Health: Research, Development, and Clinical Applications, 1*(6), 402–410. doi:10.1089/g4h.2012.0046 PMID:26192056

Hallgren, A., Kilhgren, M., Forslin, L., & Norberg, A. (1999). Swedish fathers involvement in and experiences of childbirth preparation and childbirth. *Midwifery, 15*(1), 6–15. doi:10.1016/S0266-6138(99)90032-3 PMID:10373868

Halo: Combat Evolved [Computer software]. Redmond, WA: Microsoft.

Halo: Combat Evolved Anniversary Edition [Computer software]. Redmond, WA: Microsoft.

Hamilton, J. G. (2009). Identifying with an Avatar: A multidisciplinary perspective. *Proceedings of Cumulus Conference '09.*

Handfield, B., Turnbull, S., & Bell, R. J. (2006). What do obstetricians think about media influences on their patients? *Australian and New Zealand Journal of Obstetrics and Gynaecology, 46*(5), 379–383. doi:10.1111/j.1479-828X.2006.00621.x PMID:16953850

Hargrove, M. B., Nelson, D. L., & Cooper, C. L. (2013). Generating eustress by challenging employees. *Organizational Dynamics, 42*(1), 61–69. doi:10.1016/j.orgdyn.2012.12.008

Hefner, D., Klimmt, C., & Vorderer, P. (2007). Identification with the player character as determinant of video game enjoyment. In L. Ma, M. Rauterberg, & R. Nakatsu (Eds.), *Entertainment computing–International Conference of Entertainment Computing* (pp. 39–48). Berlin: Springer. doi:10.1007/978-3-540-74873-1_6

Herold, D. K. (2012). Second life and academia: Reframing the debate between supporters and critics. *Journal of Virtual Worlds Research.* Retrieved from http://journals.tdl.org/jvwr/index.php/jvwr/article/view/6156/5976

Hertzog, C., Kramer, A. F., Wilson, R. S., & Lindenberger, U. (2009). Enrichment effects on adult cognitive development: Can the functional capacity of older adults be preserved or enhanced? *Psychological Science in the Public Interest, 9,* 1–65. PMID:26162004

Hibbard, J. H. (2013). *Patient Engagement, Health Policy Briefs.* Retrieved from http://www.healthaffairs.org/healthpolicybriefs/brief.php?brief_id=86

Hibbard, J. H., Stockard, J., Mahoney, E. R., & Tusler, M. (2004, August). Development of the Patient Activation Measure (PAM): Conceptualizing and Measuring Activation in Patients and Consumers. *Health Services Research.*

Hieftje, K., Edelman, E. J., Camenga, D. R., & Fiellin, L. E. (2013). Electronic media-based health interventions promoting behavior change in youth: A systematic review. *JAMA Pediatrics, 167*(6), 574–580. doi:10.1001/jamapediatrics.2013.1095 PMID:23568703

Higgins, E. T. (1987). Self-Discrepancy: A Theory Relating Self and Affect. *Psychological Review, 94*(3), 319–341. doi:10.1037/0033-295X.94.3.319 PMID:3615707

Higgins, E. T. (1996). Knowledge activation: Accessibility, applicability, and salience. In E. T. Higgins & A. W. Kruglanski (Eds.), *Social psychology: Handbook of basic principles.* New York: Guilford Press.

Hindin, S., & Zelinski, E. M. (2012). Extended practice and aerobic exercise interventions benefit untrained cognitive outcomes in older adults: A meta-analysis. *Journal of the American Geriatrics Society*, *60*(1), 136–141. doi:10.1111/j.1532-5415.2011.03761.x PMID:22150209

Hindrichs, U., & Carpendale, S. (2011). Gestures in the Wild: Studying Multi-Touch Gesture Sequences on Interactive Tabletop Exhibits. In *Proceedings of the SIGCHI Conference on Human Factors in Computing Systems, CHI '11*, (pp. 3023-3032). New York: ACM.

Hitchens, M., Drachen, A., & Richards, D. (2012). An investigation of player to player character identification via personal pronouns.*Proceedings of The 8th Australasian Conference on Interactive Entertainment: Playing the System.* doi:10.1145/2336727.2336738

Höchsmann, C., Schüpbach, M., & Schmidt-Trucksäss, A. (2016). Effects of exergaming on physical activity in over-weight individuals. *Sports Medicine (Auckland, N.Z.)*, *46*(6), 845–860. doi:10.1007/s40279-015-0455-z PMID:26712512

Hodent, C. (2015, March 31). *Gamer's Brain: Neuroscience, UX & Design.* Retrieved from http://celiahodent.com/the-gamers-brain/

Hoffner, C., & Buchanan, M. (2005). Young adults wishful identification with television characters: The role of perceived similarity and character attributes. *Media Psychology*, *7*(4), 325–351. doi:10.1207/S1532785XMEP0704_2

Hoffner, C., & Cantor, J. (1991). Perceiving and responding to mass media characters. In J. Bryant & D. Zillmann (Eds.), *Responding to the screen: Reception and reaction processes* (pp. 63–101). Hillsdale, NJ: Lawrence Erlbaum Associates, Inc.

Hollingdale, J., & Greitemeyer, T. (2013). The changing face of aggression: The effect of personalized avatars in a violent video game on levels of aggressive behavior. *Journal of Applied Social Psychology*, *43*(9), 1862–1868. doi:10.1111/jasp.12148

Holloway, A. (2010). *System design and evaluation of The Prepared Partner: a labor and childbirth game* (Unpublished master's thesis). University of California, Santa Cruz, CA.

Holloway, A., & Kurniawan, S. (2010). System design evolution of The Prepared Partner: How a labor and childbirth game came to term. In Meaningful play. Academic Press.

Holloway, A., & Kurniawan, S. (2011). The Prepared Partner: Can a video game teach labor and childbirth support techniques? In Information quality in ehealth. Graz, Austria: Academic Press.

Holloway, A., Rubin, Z., & Kurniawan, S. (2012). What video games have to teach us about childbirth and childbirth support. In *Proceedings of the first workshop on design patterns in games* (p. 4). doi:10.1145/2427116.2427120

Holzinger, A. (2005). Usability engineering methods for software developers. *Communications of the ACM*, *48*(1), 71–74. doi:10.1145/1039539.1039541

Hopson, J. (2001, April). *Behavioral Game Design* [Gamasutra]. Retrieved from http://www.gamasutra.com/view/feature/131494/behavioral_game_design.php

Hubel, D. H. (1988). Deprivation and development. In *Eye, Brain and Vision* (pp. 191–217). New York: Scientific American Library.

Hubel, D. H., & Wiesel, T. N. (1970). The period of susceptibility to the physiological effects of unilateral eye closure in kittens. *The Journal of Physiology*, *206*(2), 419–436. doi:10.1113/jphysiol.1970.sp009022 PMID:5498493

Ickes, M. J., Erwin, H., & Beighle, A. (2013). Systematic review of recess interventions to increase physical activity. *Journal of Physical Activity & Health*, *10*(6), 910–926. doi:10.1123/jpah.10.6.910 PMID:23074100

Institute for Healthcare Improvement. (2016). Retrieved from http://www.ihi.org/Engage/Initiatives/TripleAim/Pages/MeasuresResults.aspx

Investing in America's Health: A State-by-State Look at Public Health Funding and Key Health Facts. (2016, Apr). Trust for America's Health. Retrieved from http://healthyamericans.org/report/126/

IOM (Institute of Medicine). 2015. *Cognitive aging: Progress in understanding and opportunities for action.* Washington, DC: The National Academies Press. Retrieved from http://search.proquest.com/docview/1712600597?accountid=14749

Ivan, T. (2009). NPD: 26 Percent Of Kids Own A Game Console. *EDGE.* Retrieved from http://www.edge-online.com/news/npd-26-percent-kids-own-game-console

Jacoby, L. L., & Kelley, C. M. (1987). Unconscious influences of memory for a prior event. *Personality and Social Psychology Bulletin, 13*(3), 314–336. doi:10.1177/0146167287133003

James, B. D., Wilson, R. S., Barnes, L. L., & Bennett, D. A. (2011). Late-life social activity and cognitive decline in old age. *Journal of the International Neuropsychological Society, 17*(06), 998–1005. doi:10.1017/S1355617711000531 PMID:22040898

Jansz, J. (2005). The emotional appeal of violent video games for adolescent males. *Communication Theory, 15*(3), 219–241. doi:10.1111/j.1468-2885.2005.tb00334.x

Jaspers, M. W., Smeulers, M., Vermeulen, H., & Peute, L. W. (2011). Effects of clinical decision-support systems on practitioner performance and patient outcomes: A synthesis of high-quality systematic review findings. *Journal of the American Medical Informatics Association, 18*(3), 327–334. doi:10.1136/amiajnl-2011-000094 PMID:21422100

Java Made Easy. (n.d.). Retrieved from http://www.java-made-easy.com/

Jenkins, W. M., Merzenich, M. M., Ochs, M. T., Allard, T., & Guic-robles, E. (1990). Functional reorganization of primary somatosensory cortex in adult owl monkeys after controlled tactile stimulation. *Journal of Neurophysiology, 63*, 82–104. PMID:2299388

Jessup, L. M., Connolly, T., & Galegher, J. (1990). The effects of anonymity on GDSS group process with an idea-generating task. *Management Information Systems Quarterly, 14*(3), 313–321. doi:10.2307/248893

Jick, T. D. (1979). Mixing qualitative and quantitative methods: Triangulation in action. *Administrative Science Quarterly, 24*(4), 602–611. doi:10.2307/2392366

Jobe, J. B., Smith, D. M., Ball, K., Tennstedt, S. L., Marsiske, M., Willis, S. L., & Kleinman, K. et al. (2001). ACTIVE: A cognitive intervention trial to promote independence in older adults. *Controlled Clinical Trials, 22*(4), 453–479. doi:10.1016/S0197-2456(01)00139-8 PMID:11514044

John, B., & Talbot, T. B. (2013). *Virtual Child Witness.* International Pediatric Simulation Society Proceedings.

John, J. T., & Samuel, R. (2000). Herd immunity and herd effect: New insights and definitions. *European Journal of Epidemiology, 16*(7), 601–606. doi:10.1023/A:1007626510002 PMID:11078115

Jong, B.-S., Lai, C.-H., Hsia, Y.-T., & Lin, T.-W. (2013). Effects of anonymity in group discussion on peer interaction and learning achievement. *IEEE Transactions on Education, 56*(3), 292–299. doi:10.1109/TE.2012.2217379

Kafai, Y. B., Fields, D. A., & Cook, M. S. (2010). Your second selves: Player-designed avatars. *Games and Culture, 5*(1), 23–42. doi:10.1177/1555412009351260

Kari, T., Makkonen, M., Moilanen, P., & Frank, L. (2013). The habits of playing and the reasons for not playing exer-games: age differences in Finland. *International Journal on WWW/Internet, 11*, 30–42.

Kari, T. (2014). Can exergaming promote physical fitness and physical activity?: A systematic review of systematic reviews. *International Journal of Gaming and Computer-Mediated Simulations*, *6*(4), 59–77. doi:10.4018/ijgcms.2014100105

Kari, T. (2015). Explaining the adoption and habits of playing exergames: the role of physical activity background and digital gaming frequency. In *Proceeding of the Twenty First American Conference on Information Systems 2015.*

Kari, T., & Makkonen, M. (2014). Explaining the usage intentions of exergames. In *Proceedings of the Thirty Fifth International Conference on Information Systems 2014.*

Kari, T., Makkonen, M., Moilanen, P., & Frank, L. (2012). The habits of playing and the reasons for not playing exergames: gender differences in Finland. In *Proceedings of The 25th Bled eConference* (pp. 512–526).

Kato, P. M., Cole, S. W., Bradlyn, A. S., & Pollock, B. H. (2008). A video game improves behavioral outcomes in. adolescents and young adults with cancer: A randomized trial. *Pediatrics*, *122*(2), 305–317. doi:10.1542/peds.2007-3134 PMID:18676516

Kaufman, G., & Flanagan, M. (2016a). High-low split: Divergent cognitive construal levels triggered by digital and non-digital platforms. In *Proceedings of the 2016 CHI Conference on Human Factors in Computing Systems* (pp. 2773-2777). ACM. doi:10.1145/2858036.2858550

Kaufman, G., & Flanagan, M. (2016b). Playing the system: Comparing the efficacy and impact of digital and non-digital versions of a collaborative strategy game. In *Proceedings of the 2016 DiGRA/FDG Conference.*

Kazdin, A. E., & Bootzin, R. R. (1972). The token economy: An evaluative review. *Journal of Applied Behavior Analysis*, *5*(3), 343–372. doi:10.1901/jaba.1972.5-343 PMID:16795358

Kennison, R. F., Petway, K. T II, & Zelinski, E. M. (under review). *Cognitive reserve and cohort effects interact in psychometric measures of the Long Beach Longitudinal Study.*

Kenny, P. G., Parsons, T. D., & Rizzo, A. A. (2009). Human Computer Interaction in Virtual Standardized Patient Systems. In Human-Computer Interaction, Part IV, HCII, (LNCS), (vol. 5613, pp. 514-523). Berlin: Springer.

Ketelhut, D. J. (2007). The impact of student self-efficacy on scientific inquiry skills: An exploratory investigation in River City, a multi-user virtual environment. *Journal of Science Education and Technology*, *16*(1), 99–111. doi:10.1007/s10956-006-9038-y

Ketelhut, D. J., Dede, C., Clarke, J., Nelson, B., & Bowman, C. (2007). Studying situated learning in a multi-user virtual environment. In R. E. Mayer (Ed.), *Assessment of problem solving using simulations* (pp. 37–58). Mahwah, NJ: Lawrence Erlbaum Associates.

Ketelhut, D. J., & Nelson, B. C. (2010). Designing for real-world scientific inquiry in virtual environments. *Educational Research*, *52*(2), 151–167. doi:10.1080/00131881.2010.482741

Kiernan, K., & Smith, K. (2003). Unmarried parenthood: new insights from the millennium cohort study. *Population Trends - London*, 26–33.

Kim, I. (2009). *A Study on the Factors and the Principles of the Fantasy in the Educational Context* (Doctoral Dissertation). Seoul National University.

Kim, J. (2014, March). *The Compulsion Loop Explained* [Gamasutra]. Retrieved from http://www.gamasutra.com/blogs/JosephKim/20140323/213728/The_Compulsion_Loop_Explained.php

Kim, S. H., Lee, J., & Thomas, M. K. (2012). Between purpose and method: A review of educational research on 3D virtual worlds. *Journal of Virtual Worlds Research*. Retrieved from http://jvwr-ojs-utexas.tdl.org/jvwr/index.php/jvwr/article/view/2151/5973

Kim, T. (2008, November 6). In-Depth: Eye To Eye – The History of EyeToy. *Gamasutra*. Retrieved from http://www.gamasutra.com/php-bin/news_index.php?story=20975

Kim, C., Lee, S., & Kang, M. (2012). I became and attractive person in the virtual world: Users identification with virtual communities and avatars. *Computers in Human Behavior*, *28*(1), 1663–1669. doi:10.1016/j.chb.2012.04.004

Kimmons, R., Liu, M., Kang, J., & Santana, L. (2012). Attitude, Achievement, and Gender in a Middle School Science-based Ludic Simulation for Learning. *Journal of Educational Technology Systems*, *40*(4), 341–370. doi:10.2190/ET.40.4.b

Kinect Adventures [Computer software]. Redmond, WA: Microsoft.

Kinect Disneyland Adventures [Computer software]. Redmond, WA: Microsoft.

Kinect Joyride [Computer software]. Redmond, WA: Microsoft.

Kinect Party [Computer software]. Redmond, WA: Microsoft.

Kinect Rush: , *A Disney Pixar Adventure* [Computer software]. Redmond, WA: Microsoft.

Kinect Sports [Computer software]. Redmond, WA: Microsoft.

Kinect Sports Season 2 [Computer software]. Redmond, WA: Microsoft.

King, E. B., Madera, J. M., Hebl, M. K., Knight, J. L., & Mendoza, S. A. (2004). Career self-management: Its nature, causes and consequences. *Journal of Vocational Behavior*, *65*(1), 112–133. doi:10.1016/S0001-8791(03)00052-6

Klaus, M., Kennell, J., & Klaus, P. (1993). *Mothering the Mother: How a Doula Can Help You Have a Shorter*. Perseus Books.

Klaus, M., Kennell, J., & Klaus, P. (2002). *The Doula Book*. Da Capo Press.

Klimmt, C., Hefner, D., & Vorderer, P. (2009). The video game experience as true identification: A theory of enjoyable alterations of players self-perception. *Communication Theory*, *19*(4), 351–373. doi:10.1111/j.1468-2885.2009.01347.x

Klimmt, C., Hefner, D., Vorderer, P., Roth, C., & Blake, C. (2010). Identification with video game characters as automatic shift of self-perceptions. *Media Psychology*, *13*(4), 323–338. doi:10.1080/15213269.2010.524911

Knight J.F., Carlet S., Tregunna B., Jarvis S., Smithies R., de Freitas S., Dunwell I., & Mackway-Jones K. (2010). *Serious gaming technology in major incident triage training: A pragmatic controlled trial*. Academic Press.

Koehne, B., Bietz, M. J., & Redmiles, D. (2013). *Identity Design in Virtual Worlds*. Paper presented at the 4th International Symposium, IS-EUD 2013, Copenhagen, Denmark.

Kohl, H. W. III, Craig, C. L., Lambert, E. V., Inoue, S., Alkandari, J. R., Leetongin, G., & Kahlmeier, S. (2012). The pandemic of physical inactivity: Global action for public health. *Lancet*, *380*(9838), 294–305. doi:10.1016/S0140-6736(12)60898-8 PMID:22818941

Kolb, A., & Kolb, D. (2009). The learning way: Meta-cognitive aspects of experiential learning. *Simulation & Gaming*, *40*(3), 297–327. doi:10.1177/1046878108325713

Kostkova, P. (2015, May 5). *Frontiers in Public Health*. ubh.2015.0013410.3389/fp

Kumar, J., & Herger, M. (2016). *Gamification at Work: Designing Engaging Business Software*. Interaction Design Foundation. Retrieved from https://www.interaction-design.org/literature/book/gamification-at-work-designing-engaging-business-software

Lamboglia, C. M. G. F., Silva, V. T. B. L. D., Vasconcelos Filho, J. E. D., Pinheiro, M. H. N. P., Munguba, M. C. D. S., Silva Júnior, F. V. I., & Silva, C. A. B. D. et al. (2013). Exergaming as a strategic tool in the fight against childhood obesity: A systematic review. *Journal of Obesity, 2013*, 1–8. doi:10.1155/2013/438364 PMID:24319594

Landers, R. N., & Callan, R. C. (2012). Training evaluation in virtual worlds: Development of a model. *Journal of Virtual Worlds Research*. Retrieved from http://journals.tdl.org/jvwr/index.php/jvwr/article/view/6335/6300

Lane, J., & Lane, A. (2001). Self-efficacy and academic performance. *Social Behavior and Personality, 29*(7), 687–694. doi:10.2224/sbp.2001.29.7.687

Larsen, L. H., Schou, L., Lund, II. II., & Langberg, H. (2013). The physical effect of exergames in healthy elderly—a systematic review. *Games For Health: Research, Development, and Clinical Applications, 2*(4), 205–212. doi:10.1089/g4h.2013.0036 PMID:26192224

Latham, G. P., & Locke, E. A. (1979). Goal setting: A motivational technique that works. *Organizational Dynamics, 8*(2), 6880. doi:10.1016/0090-2616(79)90032-9

Laufer, Y., Dar, G., & Kodesh, E. (2014). Does a Wii-based exercise program enhance balance control of independently functioning older adults? a systematic review. *Clinical Interventions in Aging, 9*, 1803–1813. doi:10.2147/CIA.S69673 PMID:25364238

Leathrum, J. F., Mielke, R. R., Audette, R., McKenzie, F., Armstrong, R. K., Miller, G. T., . . . Scerbo, M. W. (2015). An Architecture to Support Integrated Manikin-Based Simulations. *Society for Modeling & Simulation International Conference Proceedings*. SCSC.

Leavitt, J. W. (2009). *How did men end up in the delivery room?* George Mason University's History News Network. Retrieved May 13, 2013, from http://www.hnn.us/articles/116291.html

LeBlanc, A. G., Chaput, J. P., McFarlane, A., Colley, R. C., Thivel, D., Biddle, S. J., & Tremblay, M. S. et al. (2013). Active video games and health indicators in children and youth: A systematic review. *PLoS ONE, 8*(6), e65351. doi:10.1371/journal.pone.0065351 PMID:23799008

Lee, I., Shiroma, E. J., Lobelo, F., Puska, P., Blair, S. N., & Katzmarzyk, P. T. (2012). Effect of physical inactivity on major non-communicable diseases worldwide: An analysis of burden of disease and life expectancy. *Lancet, 380*(9838), 219–229. doi:10.1016/S0140-6736(12)61031-9 PMID:22818936

Lee, K. M. (2004). Presence, explicated. *Communication Theory, 14*(1), 27–50. doi:10.1111/j.1468-2885.2004.tb00302.x

Lepper, M. R., & Greene, D. (1975). Turning play into work: Effects of adult surveillance and extrinsic rewards on childrens intrinsic motivation. *Journal of Personality and Social Psychology, 31*(3), 479–486. doi:10.1037/h0076484

Lepper, M. R., Iyengar, S. S., & Corpus, J. H. (2005). Intrinsic and extrinsic motivational orientations in the classroom: Age differences and academic correlates. *Journal of Educational Psychology, 97*(2), 184–196. doi:10.1037/0022-0663.97.2.184

Liberati, A., Altman, D. G., Tetzlaff, J., Mulrow, C., Gøtzsche, P. C., Ioannidis, J. P., & Moher, D. et al. (2009). The PRISMA statement for reporting systematic reviews and meta analyses of studies that evaluate health care interventions: Explanation and elaboration. *Annals of Internal Medicine, 151*(4), W-65–W-94. doi:10.7326/0003-4819-151-4-200908180-00136 PMID:19622512

Lim, S. (2006). *The effect of avatar choice and visual POV on game play experience* (Unpublished doctoral dissertation). Stanford University, Stanford, CA.

Lim, S., & Reeves, B. (2009). Being in the game: Effects of avatar choice and point of view on psychophysiological responses during play. *Media Psychology*, *12*(4), 348–370. doi:10.1080/15213260903287242

Lincoln, Y. S., & Guba, E. D. (1985). *Naturalistic Inquiry*. Thousand Oaks, CA: Sage Publications, Inc.

Lindley. (2003). *Game taxonomies: A high level framework for game analysis and design*. Retrieved June 18, 2012, from http://www.gamasutra.com/view/feature/2796/game_taxonomies_a_high_level_.php

Lindley, S. E., Le Couteur, J., & Berthouze, N. L. (2008). Stirring up experience through movement in game play: effects on engagement and social behaviour. In *Proceedings of the SIGCHI Conference on Human Factors in Computing Systems, CHI '08*, (pp. 511–514). New York: ACM. doi:10.1145/1357054.1357136

Lindwall, M., Cimino, C. R., Gibbons, L. E., Mitchell, M. B., Benitez, A., Brown, C. L., & Piccinin, A. M. et al. (2012). Dynamic associations of change in physical activity and change in cognitive function: Coordinated and integrated analyses of four longitudinal studies. *Journal of Aging Research*, *2012*, 493598. doi:10.1155/2012/493598 PMID:23029615

Linser, R., Ree-Lindstad, N., & Vold, T. (2007). *Black Blizzard: Designing role-play simulations for education*. Retrieved from http://www.eric.ed.gov/ERICWebPortal/contentdelivery/servlet/ERICServlet?accno=ED500156

Li, R. W., Ngo, C., Nguyen, J., & Levi, D. M. (2011, August). Video-game play induces plasticity in the visual system of adults with amblyopia. *PLoS Biology*, *9*(8). doi:10.1371/journal.pbio.1001135 PMID:21912514

Li, R., Polat, U., Makous, W., & Bavelier, D. (2009, May). Enhancing the contrast sensitivity function through action video game training. *Nature Neuroscience*, *12*(5), 549–551. doi:10.1038/nn.2296 PMID:19330003

Liu, C. (2009). Second life learning community: A peer-based approach to involving more faculty members in Second Life.*Proceedings of the Second Life Education Workshop at the Second Life Community Convention*, (pp. 6-10).

Liu, M., Horton, L., Lee, J., Kang, J., Rosenblum, J., O'Hair, M., & Lu, C. W. (2014). *Creating a Multimedia Enhanced Problem-Based Learning Environment for Middle School Science: Voices from the Developers. Interdisciplinary Journal of Problem-Based Learning, 8(1)*. doi:10.7771/1541-5015.1422

Liu, M., Horton, L., Olmanson, J., & Toprac, P. (2011). A study of learning and motivation in a new media enriched environment for middle school science. *Educational Technology Research and Development*, *59*(2), 249–265. doi:10.1007/s11423-011-9192-7

Lomas, N. (2016, May 18). *Reporting for techcrunch.com, UK's MHRA (medicines and healthcare devices regulator) spokesperson in talks with Google/DeepMind over its Streams app*. Retrieved from https://techcrunch.com/2016/05/18/uk-healthcare-products-regulator-in-talks-with-googledeepmind-over-its-streams-app/

Looy, J. V. (2015). Online games, characters, avatars, and identity. *The International Encyclopedia of Digital Communication and Society*. Retrieved from http://onlinelibrary.wiley.com/doi/10.1002/9781118767771.wbiedcs106/full

Looy, J. V., Courtois, C., & Vocht, M. D. (2010). *Player identification in online games: Validation of a scale for measuring identification in mmorpgs*. Paper presented at the 3rd International Conference on Fun and Games, Leuven, Belgium.

Looy, J. V., Courtois, C., Vocht, M. D., & De Marez, L. (2012). Player identification in online games: Validation of a scale for measuring identification in MMOGs. *Media Psychology*, *15*(2), 197–221. doi:10.1080/15213269.2012.674917

Lord of the Rings Online [PC Game]. Warner Bros. Entertainment Inc.

Lövdén, M., Bodammer, N. C., Kühn, S., Kaufmann, J., Schütze, H., Tempelmann, C., & Lindenberger, U. et al. (2010). Experience-dependent plasticity of white-matter microstructure extends into old age. *Neuropsychologia, 48*(13), 3878–3883. doi:10.1016/j.neuropsychologia.2010.08.026 PMID:20816877

Lozano, S. C., Hard, B. M., & Tversky, B. (2007). Putting action in perspective. *Cognition, 103*(3), 480–490. doi:10.1016/j.cognition.2006.04.010 PMID:16765339

Lu, A. S., Kharrazi, H., Gharghabi, F., & Thompson, D. (2013). A systematic review of health videogames on childhood obesity prevention and intervention. *Games For Health: Research, Development, and Clinical Applications, 2*(3), 131–141. doi:10.1089/g4h.2013.0025 PMID:24353906

Lumley, J., & Brown, S. (1993). Attenders and nonattenders at childbirth education classes in Australia: How do they and their births differ? *Birth (Berkeley, Calif.), 20*(3), 123–130. doi:10.1111/j.1523-536X.1993.tb00435.x PMID:8240618

Lupien, S. J., Maheu, F., Tu, M., Fiocco, A., & Schramek, T. E. (2007). The effects of stress and stress hormones on human cognition: Implications for the field of brain and cognition. *Brain and Cognition, 65*(3), 209–237. doi:10.1016/j.bandc.2007.02.007 PMID:17466428

Maccoby, E. E., & Wilson, W. C. (1957). Identification and observational learning from films. *Journal of Abnormal and Social Psychology, 55*(1), 76–87. doi:10.1037/h0043015 PMID:13462664

Maddison, R., Simons, M., Straker, L., Witherspoon, L., Palmeira, A., & Thin, A. (2013). Active video games: An opportunity for enhanced learning and positive health effects? *Cognitive Technology, 18*, 6–13.

Mahmassani, H. S., Chen, R. B., Huang, Y., Williams, D., & Contractor, N. (2010). Time to play? Activity engagement in multiplayer online role-playing games. *Transportation Research Record, 2157*(2), 129–137. doi:10.3141/2157-16

Mahncke, H. W., Bronstone, A., & Merzenich, M. M. (2006). Brain plasticity and functional losses in the aged: Scientific bases for a novel intervention. *Reprogramming the Brain, 157*, 81–109. doi:10.1016/S0079-6123(06)57006-2 PMID:17046669

Maitland, C., Stratton, G., Foster, S., Braham, R., & Rosenberg, M. (2013). A place for play? The influence of the home physical environment on children's physical activity and sedentary behaviour. *The International Journal of Behavioral Nutrition and Physical Activity, 10*. PMID:23958282

Mandler, J. M. (1984). *Stories, scripts, and scenes: Aspects of schema theory.* Hillsdale, NJ: Lawrence Erlbaum Associates.

Mania, K., Wooldridge, D., Coxon, M., & Robinson, A. (2006). The effects of visual and interaction fidelity on spatial cognition in immersive virtual environments. *IEEE Transactions on Visualization and Computer Graphics, 12*(3), 396–404. doi:10.1109/TVCG.2006.55 PMID:16640253

Mantovani, F., & Castelnuovo, G. (2003). Sense of presence in virtual training: enhancing skills acquisition and transfer of knowledge through learning experience in virtual environments. In G. Riva, F. Davide, & W. A. IJsselsteijn (Eds.), *Being there: Concepts, effects and measurement of user presence in synthetic environments* (pp. 167–181). Amsterdam, The Netherlands: Ios Press.

Mark, D. (2009). *Behavioral Mathematics for Game AI.* Boston: Charles River Media.

Markus, H., & Nurius, P. (1986). Possible selves. *The American Psychologist, 41*(9), 954–969. doi:10.1037/0003-066X.41.9.954

Mass Effect 3 [Computer software]. Redwood City, CA: Electronic Arts.

Matthews, C. E., Chen, K. Y., Freedson, P. S., Buchowski, M. S., Beech, B. M., Pate, R. R., & Troiano, R. P. (2008). Amount of time spent in sedentary behaviors in the United States, 2003–2004. *American Journal of Epidemiology, 167*(7), 875–881. doi:10.1093/aje/kwm390 PMID:18303006

Matthews, C. E., George, S. M., Moore, S. C., Bowles, H. R., Blair, A., Park, Y., & Schatzkin, A. et al. (2012). Amount of time spent in sedentary behaviors and cause-specific mortality in US adults. *The American Journal of Clinical Nutrition, 95*(2), 437–445. doi:10.3945/ajcn.111.019620 PMID:22218159

McArdle, J. J., & Prindle, J. J. (2008). A latent change score analysis of a randomized clinical trial in reasoning training. *Psychology and Aging, 23*(4), 702–719. doi:10.1037/a0014349 PMID:19140642

McAuley, E., Morris, K. S., Motl, R. W., Hu, L., Konopak, J. F., & Elavsky, S. (2007). Long-term follow-up of physical activity behavior in older adults. *Health Psychology, 25*(3), 375–380. doi:10.1037/0278-6133.26.3.375 PMID:17500625

McDaniel, M. A., Binder, E. F., Bugg, J. M., Waldum, E. R., Dufault, C., Meyer, A., & Kudelka, C. et al. (2014). Effects of cognitive training with and without aerobic exercise on cognitively demanding everyday activities. *Psychology and Aging, 29*(3), 717–730. doi:10.1037/a0037363 PMID:25244489

McDonald, D., & Kim, H. (2001). When I die, I feel small: Electronic game characters and the social self. *Journal of Broadcasting & Electronic Media, 45*(2), 241–258. doi:10.1207/s15506878jobem4502_3

McGinnis, D., & Zelinski, E. M. (2000). Understanding unfamiliar words: The influence of processing resources, vocabulary knowledge, and age. *Psychology and Aging, 15*(2), 335–350. doi:10.1037/0882-7974.15.2.335 PMID:10879587

McGonigal, J. (2011). *Reality is broken: Why games make us better and how they can change the world*. Penguin Press HC.

Medlock, M. C., Wixon, D., McGee, M., & Welsh, D. (2005). The rapid iterative test and evaluation method: Better products in less time. In *Costjustifying Usability: An Update for the Internet Age*, (pp. 489–517). Academic Press.

Medlock, M. C., Wixon, D., Terrano, M., Romero, R., & Fulton, B. (2002). *Using the RITE method to improve products: A definition and a case study*. Usability Professionals Association. Retrieved from http://www.computingscience.nl/docs/vakken/musy/RITE.pdf

Melby-Lervag, M., & Hulme, C. (2013). Is working memory training effective? A meta-analytic review. *Developmental Psychology, 49*(2), 270–291. doi:10.1037/a0028228 PMID:22612437

Merrer, J., De Jonghe, B., & Golliot, F. (2001). French Catheter Study Group in Intensive Care. Complications of femoral and subclavian venous catheterization in critically ill patients: A randomized control trial. *Journal of the American Medical Association, 286*(6), 700–707. doi:10.1001/jama.286.6.700 PMID:11495620

Meyer, C., & Schwager, A. (2007a). Customer Experience. *Harvard Business Review*, 1–11. PMID:17345685

Meyer, C., & Schwager, A. (2007b). Understanding customer experience. *Harvard Business Review, 85*(2), 116. PMID:17345685

Meyer, D. E., & Schvaneveldt, R. W. (1971). Facilitation in recognizing pairs of words: Evidence of a dependence between retrieval operations. *Journal of Experimental Psychology, 90*(2), 227–234. doi:10.1037/h0031564 PMID:5134329

Mitchell, M. B., Cimino, C. R., Benitez, A., Brown, C. L., Gibbons, L. E., Kennison, R. F., & Piccinin, A. M. et al. (2012). Cognitively stimulating activities: Effects on cognition across four studies with up to 21 years of longitudinal data. *Journal of Aging Research, 2012*, 461592. doi:10.1155/2012/461592 PMID:23024862

Mitgutsch, K., & Alvarado, N. (2012). Purposeful by design?: a serious game design assessment framework. In *Proceedings of the International Conference on the Foundations of Digital Games* (pp. 121–128). ACM. doi:10.1145/2282338.2282364

Mitton, C., & Donaldson, C. (2004). *Health care priority setting: Principles, Practice and Challenges, Cost Effectiveness and Resource Allocation* Retrieved from http://www.ncbi.nlm.nih.gov/pmc/articles/PMC411060/

Moher, D., Liberati, A., Tetzlaff, J., & Altman, D. G. (2009). Preferred reporting items for systematic reviews and meta-analyses: The PRISMA statement. *Annals of Internal Medicine, 151*(4), 264–269. doi:10.7326/0003-4819-151-4-200908180-00135 PMID:19622511

Molina, K. I., Ricci, N. A., de Moraes, S. A., & Perracini, M. R. (2014). Virtual reality using games for improving physical functioning in older adults: A systematic review. *Journal of Neuroengineering and Rehabilitation, 11*(1), 1–20. doi:10.1186/1743-0003-11-156 PMID:25399408

Montoya, M. M., Massey, A. P., & Lockwood, N. S. (2011). 3D collaborative virtual environments: Exploring the link between collaborative behaviors and team performance. *Decision Sciences, 42*(2), 451–476. doi:10.1111/j.1540-5915.2011.00318.x

Moore, D. J., Palmer, B. W., Patterson, T. L., & Jesre, D. V. (2007). A review of performance-based measures of functional living skills. *Journal of Psychiatric Research, 41*(1-2), 97–117. doi:10.1016/j.jpsychires.2005.10.008 PMID:16360706

Morgan, B., Bulpitt, C., Clifton, P., & Lewis, P. (1982). Analgesia and satisfaction in childbirth (the Queen Charlottes 1000 mother survey). *Lancet, 320*(8302), 808–810. doi:10.1016/S0140-6736(82)92691-5 PMID:6126674

Morgan, P. J., & Cleave-Hogg, D. (2002). A worldwide survey of the use of simulation in anesthesia. *Canadian Journal of Anaesthesia, 49*(7), 659–662. doi:10.1007/BF03017441 PMID:12193481

Morris, T., & McInerney, K. (2010). Media representations of pregnancy and childbirth: An analysis of reality television programs in the United States. *Birth (Berkeley, Calif.), 37*(2), 134–140. doi:10.1111/j.1523-536X.2010.00393.x PMID:20557536

Mueller, F., Edge, D., Vetere, F., Gibbs, M. R., Agamanolis, S., Bongers, B., & Sheridan, J. G. (2011). Designing sports: a framework for exertion games. In *Proceedings of the SIGCHI Conference on Human Factors in Computing Systems* (pp. 2651–2660). doi:10.1145/1978942.1979330

Mueller, F., & Isbister, K. (in press). Movement Based Game Guidelines. In *Proceedings of the SIGCHI Conference on Human Factors in Computing Systems, CHI '14*. New York: ACM.

Murphy, S. D. (2004). Live in your world, play in ours: The spaces of video game identity. *Journal of Visual Culture, 3*(2), 223–238. doi:10.1177/1470412904044801

Nash, D. (2010). *P & T: a Peer-reviewed Journal for Formulary Management*. Retrieved from http://europepmc.org/abstract/PMC/PMC2873722

Nelson, B. (2007). Exploring the use of individualized, reflective guidance in an educational multi-user virtual environment. *Journal of Science Education and Technology, 16*(1), 83–97. doi:10.1007/s10956-006-9039-x

Nelson, B., Ketelhut, D. J., Clarke, J., Bowman, C., & Dede, C. (2005). Design-based research strategies for developing a scientific inquiry curriculum in a multi-user virtual environment. *Educational Technology, 45*(1), 21–27.

Newman, J. (2002). The myth of the ergodic videogame. *The International Journal of Computer Game Research., 2*(1), 1–8.

Newzoo. (2015). *2015 Global games market report, 5/2015* (Report). Amsterdam: Newzoo.

Nichols, M. (1995). Adjustment to new parenthood: Attenders versus nonattenders at prenatal education classes. *Birth (Berkeley, Calif.), 22*(1), 21–26. doi:10.1111/j.1523-536X.1995.tb00549.x PMID:7741947

Nintendo. (2009). *Nintendo Annual Report 2009*. Retrieved from http://www.nintendo.co.jp/ir/pdf/2009/annual0903e.pdf

Norman, D. (2010). Natural User Interfaces are Not Natural. *Interaction, 17*(3), 6–10. doi:10.1145/1744161.1744163

Norman, D. (2013). *The Design of Everyday things, Revised and Expanded Edition*. New York: Basic Books.

Norris, E., Hamer, M., & Stamatakis, E. (2016). Active video games in schools and effects on physical activity and health: A systematic review. *The Journal of Pediatrics, 172*, 40–46. doi:10.1016/j.jpeds.2016.02.001 PMID:26947570

OBrien, H. L., & Toms, E. G. (2010). The development and evaluation of a survey to measure user engagement. *Journal of the American Society for Information Science and Technology, 61*(1), 50–69. doi:10.1002/asi.21229

Odent, M. (1999). Is the participation of the father at birth dangerous? *Midwifery Today*, (51), 23.

Okita, S. Y., Turkay, S., Kim, M., & Murai, Y. (2013). When observation beats doing: Learning by teaching with virtual peers and the effects of technological design choices on learning. *Computers & Education, 63*, 176–196. doi:10.1016/j.compedu.2012.12.005

Ortoleva, P. (2012). Homo ludicus. The ubiquity of play and its roles in present society. *GAME*. Retrieved from http://www.gamejournal.it/homo-ludicus-the-ubiquity-and-roles-of-play-in-present-society/

Osborne, J., Simon, S., & Collins, S. (2003). Attitudes towards science: A review of the literature and its implication. *International Journal of Science Education, 25*(9), 1049–1079. doi:10.1080/0950069032000032199

Osin, E., Malyutina, A., & Kosheleva, N. V. (2015). Self-Transcendence Facilitates Meaning-Making and Flow Experience: Evidence from a Pilot Experimental Study (SSRN Scholarly Paper No. ID 2576658). Rochester, NY: Social Science Research Network. Retrieved from http://papers.ssrn.com/abstract=2576658

Osin, E. N., Malyutina, A. A., & Kosheleva, N. V. (2016). self-transcendence facilitates meaning-making and flow: Evidence from a pilot experimental study. *International Journal of Psychology, 5*. Retrieved from http://psychologyinrussia.com/volumes/pdf/2016_2/psychology_2016_2_7.pdf

Osorio, G., Moffat, D. C., & Sykes, J. (2012). Exergaming, exercise, and gaming: Sharing motivations. *Games For Health: Research, Development, and Clinical Applications, 1*(3), 205–210. doi:10.1089/g4h.2011.0025 PMID:26193438

Overmier, J. B. (2002). On learned helplessness. *Integrative Physiological and Behavioral Science, 37*(1), 4–8. doi:10.1007/BF02688801 PMID:12069364

Owsley, C., Sloane, M., McGwin, G. Jr, & Ball, K. (2002). Timed instrumental activities of daily living tasks: Relationship to cognitive function and everyday performance assessments in older adults. *Gerontology, 48*(4), 254–265. doi:10.1159/000058360 PMID:12053117

Pagulayan, R., Keeker, K., Fuller, T., Wixon, D., & Romero, R. (2007). User-centered Design in Games. In A. Sears & J. Jacko (Eds.), *The Human-Computer Interaction Handbook: Fundamentals, Evolving Technologies, and Emerging Applications* (pp. 742–758). Hillsdale, NJ: Earlbaum. doi:10.1201/9781410615862.ch37

Paradise, A. (2008). *2008 state of the industry in leading enterprises: ASTD's annual review of trends in workplace learning and performance*. Alexandria, VA: American Society for Training & Development.

Park, B.-W., & Lee, K. C. (2011). Exploring the value of purchasing online game items. *Computers in Human Behavior, 27*(6), 2178–2185. doi:10.1016/j.chb.2011.06.013

Park, D. C., Gutchess, A. H., Meade, M. L., & Stine-Morrow, E. A. L. (2007). Improving cognitive function in older adults: Nontraditional approaches. *Journals of Gerontology, Series B, 62B*(Special Issue 1SI1), 45–52. doi:10.1093/geronb/62.special_issue_1.45 PMID:17565164

Parrish, A. M., Okely, A. D., Stanley, R. M., & Ridgers, N. D. (2013). The effect of school recess interventions on physical activity. *Sports Medicine (Auckland, N.Z.), 43*(4), 287–299. doi:10.1007/s40279-013-0024-2 PMID:23512170

Peng, W., Crouse, J. C., & Lin, J. H. (2013). Using active video games for physical activity promotion: A systematic review of the current state of research. *Health Education & Behavior, 40*(2), 171–192. doi:10.1177/1090198112444956 PMID:22773597

Peng, W., Lin, J. H., & Crouse, J. (2011). Is playing exergames really exercising? A meta-analysis of energy expenditure in active video games. *Cyberpsychology, Behavior, and Social Networking, 14*(11), 681–688. doi:10.1089/cyber.2010.0578 PMID:21668370

Pereira, A. C., Huddleston, D. E., Brickman, A. M., Sosunov, A. A., Hen, R., McKhann, G. M., …Small, S. A. (2007). An in vivo correlate of exercise-induced neurogenesis in the adult dentate gyrus. *Proceedings of the National Academy of Sciences, 104,* 5638-5643. doi:10.1073/pnas.0611721104

Piaget, J. (1951). *Play, dreams, and imitation in childhood.* New York: W. W. Norton & Company.

Pieramico, V., Esposito, R., Sensi, F., Cilli, F., Mantini, D., Mattei, P. A., & Sensi, S. L. et al. (2012). Combination training in aging individuals modifies functional connectivity and cognition, and is potentially affected by dopamine-related genes. *PLoS ONE, 7*(8), e43901. doi:10.1371/journal.pone.0043901 PMID:22937122

Pincus, H. A., Hudson Scholle, S., Spaeth-Rublee, B., Hepner, K. A., & Brown, J. (2016, June 24). *Quality Measures For Mental Health And Substance Use: Gaps, Opportunities, And Challenges.* Retrieved from http://content.healthaffairs.org/content/35/6/1000.abstract?=right

Pine, B. J., & Gilmore, J. H. (1998). Welcome to the experience economy. *Harvard Business Review, 76,* 97–105. PMID:10181589

Pingault, , Tremblay, R. E., Vitaro, F., Carbonneau, R., Genolini, C., Falissard, B., & Côté, S. M. (2011). Childhood Trajectories of Inattention and Hyperactivity and Prediction of Educational Attainment in Early Adulthood: A 16-Year Longitudinal Population-Based Study. *The American Journal of Psychiatry, 168*(11), 1164–1170. doi:10.1176/appi.ajp.2011.10121732 PMID:21799065

Płaszewski, M., & Bettany-Saltikov, J. (2014). Are current scoliosis school screening recommendations evidence-based and up to date? A best evidence synthesis umbrella review. *European Spine Journal.* doi:10.1007/s00586-014-3307-x PMID:24777669

Polley, D. B., Steinberg, E. E., & Merzenich, M. M. (2006). Perceptual learning directs auditory cortical map reorganization through top-down influences. *The Journal of Neuroscience, 26*(18), 4970–4982. doi:10.1523/JNEUROSCI.3771-05.2006 PMID:16672673

Porter, M. E. (2010). What Is Value in Health Care? *The New England Journal of Medicine, 363*(26), 2477–2481. doi:10.1056/NEJMp1011024 PMID:21142528

Primack, B. A., Carroll, M. V., & McNamara, M. (2012, June). Role of video games in improv- ing health-related outcomes: A systematic review. *American Journal of Preventive Medicine, 42*(6), 630–638. doi:10.1016/j.amepre.2012.02.023 PMID:22608382

Prior, M., Guerin, M., & Grimmer-Somers, K. (2008). The effectiveness of clinical guideline implementation strategies–a synthesis of systematic review findings. *Journal of Evaluation in Clinical Practice*, *14*(5), 888–897. doi:10.1111/j.1365-2753.2008.01014.x PMID:19018923

Przybylski, A. K., Rigby, C. S., & Ryan, R. M. (2010). A motivational model of video game engagement. *Review of General Psychology*, *14*(2), 154–166. doi:10.1037/a0019440

Puss in Boots [Computer software]. Agoura Hills, CA: THQ.

Raad,, I., Darouiche,, R., & Dupuis,, J. (1997). Central venous catheters coated with minocycline and rifmapin for the prevention of catheter-related colonization and bloodstream infections. A randomized, double blind trial. *Annals of Internal Medicine*, *127*(4), 267–274. doi:10.7326/0003-4819-127-4-199708150-00002 PMID:9265425

Raessens, J. (2006). Playful identities, or the ludification of culture. *Games and Culture*, *1*(1), 52–57. doi:10.1177/1555412005281779

Rahmani, E., & Boren, S. A. (2012). Videogames and health improvement: A literature review of randomized controlled trials. *Games For Health: Research, Development, and Clinical Applications*, *1*(5), 331–341. doi:10.1089/g4h.2012.0031 PMID:26191999

Ratan, R., Rikard, R., Wanek, C., McKinley, M., Johnson, L., & Sah, Y. J. (2016). *Introducing Avatarification: An Experimental Examination of How Avatars Influence Student Motivation* (pp. 51–59). IEEE; doi:10.1109/HICSS.2016.15

Rebok, G. W., Ball, K., Guey, L. T., Jones, R. N., Kim, H.-Y., King, J. W., & Willis, S. L. et al. (2014). Ten-year effects of the Advanced Cognitive Training for Independent and Vital Elderly cognitive training trial on cognition and everyday functioning in older adults. *Journal of the American Geriatrics Association*, *62*(1), 16–24. doi:10.1111/jgs.12607 PMID:24417410

Reeves, S., Benford, S., & O'Malley, C. (2005). Designing the Spectator Experience. In *Proceedings of CHI 2005*.

Reijmersdal, E. A. V., Jansz, J., Peters, O., & van Noort, G. (2013). Why girls go pink: Game character identification and game-players motivations. *Computers in Human Behavior*, *29*(6), 2640–2649. doi:10.1016/j.chb.2013.06.046

Reinig, B. A., & Mejias, R. J. (2004). The effects of national culture and anonymity on flaming and criticalness in GSS-supported discussions. *Small Group Research*, *35*(6), 698–723. doi:10.1177/1046496404266773

Ren, L., Qiu, H., Wang, P., & Lin, P. M. C. (2016). Exploring customer experience with budget hotels: Dimensionality and satisfaction. *International Journal of Hospitality Management*, *52*, 13–23. doi:10.1016/j.ijhm.2015.09.009

Rideout, V. J., Foehr, U. G., & Roberts, D. F. (2010). *Generation M2: Media in the lives of 8- to 18-year-olds.* Kaiser Family Foundation. Retrieved from http://www.kff.org/ entmedia/upload/8010.pdf

Rieber, L. P. (1996). Seriously considering play: Designing interactive learning environments based on the blending of microworlds, simulations, and games. *Educational Technology Research and Development*, *44*(2), 43–58. doi:10.1007/BF02300540

Riedl, M. O., & Young, R. M. (2006). From Linear Story Generation to Branching Story Graphs. *IEEE Computer Graphics and Applications*, *26*(3), 23–31. doi:10.1109/MCG.2006.56 PMID:16711214

Ries, E. (2011The Lean Startup. *Crown Publishing Group*.

Roberts, N. (1976). *Simulation gaming: A critical review.* Retrieved July 12, 2012, from http://www.eric.ed.gov/ERIC-WebPortal/contentdelivery/servlet/ERICServlet?accno=ED137165

Roberts, J. S., McLaughlin, S. J., & Connell, C. M. (2014). Public beliefs and knowledge about risk and protective factors for Alzheimers disease. *Alzheimers & Dementia, 10*(5Supplement), S381–S389. doi:10.1016/j.jalz.2013.07.001 PMID:24630852

Robertson, D. A., & Kenny, R. A. (2015). Negative perceptions of aging modify the association between frailty and cognitive function in older adults. *Personality and Individual Differences.* doi:10.1016/j.paid.2015.12.010

Rose, N. S., Luo, L., Bialystock, E., Hering, A., Lau, K., & Craik, F. I. M. (2015). Cognitive processes in the Breakfast Task: Planning and monitoring. *Canadian Journal of Experimental Psychology, 69*(3), 252–263. doi:10.1037/cep0000054 PMID:25938251

Rosen, B. T., Uddin, P. Q., Harrington, A. R., Ault, B. W., & Ault, M. J. (2009). Does personalized vascular access training on a nonhuman tissue model allow for learning and retention of central line placement skills? Phase II of the procedural patient safety initiative (PPSI-II). *Journal of Hospital Medicine, 4*(7), 423–429. doi:10.1002/jhm.571 PMID:19753570

Ruivo, J. A. (2014). Exergames and cardiac rehabilitation: A review. *Journal of Cardiopulmonary Rehabilitation and Prevention, 34*(1), 2–20. doi:10.1097/HCR.0000000000000037 PMID:24370759

Rumelhart, D. E. (1980). Schemata: the building blocks of cognition. In R. J. Spiro et al. (Eds.), *Theoretical Issues in Reading Comprehension*. Hillsdale, NJ: Lawrence Erlbaum.

Ryan, A. M., & Doran, T. (2012, Mar). *The effect of improving processes of care on patient outcomes: evidence from the United Kingdom's quality and outcomes framework*. Med Care. Retrieved from http://www.ncbi.nlm.nih.gov/pubmed/22329994

Ryan, R. M., Rigby, C. S., & Przybylski, A. (2006). The motivational pull of video games: A self-determination theory approach. *Motivation and Emotion, 30*(4), 344–360. doi:10.1007/s11031-006-9051-8

Sackett, A. M., Meyvis, T., Nelson, L. D., Converse, B. A., & Sackett, A. L. (2010). Youre having fun when time flies the hedonic consequences of subjective time progression. *Psychological Science, 21*(1), 111–117. doi:10.1177/0956797609354832 PMID:20424031

Salmon, G. (2009). The future for (second) life and learning. *British Journal of Educational Technology, 40*(3), 526–538. doi:10.1111/j.1467-8535.2009.00967.x

Salthouse, T. A. (2004). What and when of cognitive aging. *Current Directions in Psychological Science, 13*(4), 140–144. doi:10.1111/j.0963-7214.2004.00293.x

Saunders, T. J., Chaput, J. P., & Tremblay, M. S. (2014). Sedentary behaviour as an emerging risk factor for cardiometabolic diseases in children and youth. *Canadian Journal of Diabetes, 38*(1), 53–61. doi:10.1016/j.jcjd.2013.08.266 PMID:24485214

Schaie, K. W. (2005). *Developmental influences on adult intelligence*. Oxford, UK: Oxford University Press. doi:10.1093/acprof:oso/9780195156737.001.0001

Schlaug, G. (2001). The brain of musicians: Structural and functional adaptation. *Annals of the New York Academy of Sciences*, 281–289. PMID:11458836

Schmierbach, M., Limperos, A. M., & Woolley, J. K. (2012). Feeling the Need for (Personalized) Speed: How Natural Controls and Customization Contribute to Enjoyment of a Racing Game Through Enhanced Immersion. *Cyberpsychology, Behavior, and Social Networking, 15*(7), 364–369. doi:10.1089/cyber.2012.0025 PMID:22687145

Schneider, B. A., & Pichora-Fuller, M. K. (2000). Implications of perceptual deterioration for cognitive aging research. In F. I. M. Craik & T. A. Salthouse (Eds.), *The handbook of aging and cognition* (pp. 155–219). Mahwah, NJ: Erlbaum.

Schneider, E. F., Lang, A., Shin, M., & Bradley, S. D. (2004). Death with a story: How story impacts emotional, motivational, and physiological responses to first-person shooter video games. *Human Communication Research, 30*(3), 361–375.

Schouten, J. W., McAlexander, J. H., & Koenig, H. F. (2007). Transcendent customer experience and brand community. *Journal of the Academy of Marketing Science, 35*(3), 357–368. doi:10.1007/s11747-007-0034-4

Schultheiss, D. (2007). Long-term motivations to play MMOGs: A longitudinal study on motivations, experience and behavior. In A. Baba (Ed.), *DiGRA 2007-Situated Play (Proceedings of Digital Games Research Association International Conference 2007)* (pp. 344–348).

Schunk, D. H. (1995). Self-efficacy and education and instruction. In J. E. Maddux (Ed.), *Theory, research, and application* (pp. 281–303). New York: Plenum Press.

Schwind, V., Wolf, K., Henze, N., & Korn, O. (2015). *Determining the characteristics of preferred virtual faces using an avatar generator.* Paper presented at ChiPlay 2015. doi:10.1145/2793107.2793116

Scott, A., Sivey, P., Ait Ouakrim, D., Willenberg, L., Naccarella, L., Furler, J., & Young, D. (2011, September7). The effect of financial incentives on the quality of health care provided by primary care physicians. *Cochrane Database of Systematic Reviews.* doi:10.1002/14651858.CD008451.pub2 PMID:21901722

Seo, H. J., & Kim, K. U. (2012). Quality assessment of systematic reviews or meta-analyses of nursing interventions conducted by Korean reviewers. *BMC Medical Research Methodology*, 12. PMID:22928687

Sharma, J., Angelucci, A., & Sur, M. (2000). Induction of visual orientation modules in aud cortex. *Nature, 404*(6780), 841–847. doi:10.1038/35009043 PMID:10786784

Shaw, A. (2011). "He could be a bunny rabbit for all I care": Exploring identification in digital games. *Proceedings of DiGRA 2011: Think Design Play: The fifth international conference of the Digital Research Association* (DIGRA).

Shea, B. J., Grimshaw, J. M., Wells, G. A., Boers, M., Andersson, N., Hamel, C., & Bouter, L. M. et al. (2007). Development of AMSTAR: A measurement tool to assess the methodological quality of systematic reviews. *BMC Medical Research Methodology*, 7. PMID:17302989

Shea, B. J., Hamel, C., Wells, G. A., Bouter, L. M., Kristjansson, E., Grimshaw, J., & Boers, M. et al. (2009). AMSTAR is a reliable and valid measurement tool to assess the methodological quality of systematic reviews. *Journal of Clinical Epidemiology, 62*(10), 1013–1020. doi:10.1016/j.jclinepi.2008.10.009 PMID:19230606

Sia, C.-L., Tan, B. C. Y., & Wei, K.-K. (2002). Group polarization and computer-mediated communication: Effects of communication cues, social presence, and anonymity. *Information Systems Research, 13*(1), 70–90. doi:10.1287/isre.13.1.70.92

Simkin, P. (2008). The Birth Partner: A Complete Guide To Childbirth For Dads, Doulas, and All Other Labor Companions (3rd ed.). Harvard Common Press.

Simkin, P. (2011, February 28). Part 2: Pain, suffering, and trauma in labor and subsequent post-traumatic stress disorder: Practical suggestions to prevent PTSD after childbirth. *Science & Sensibility.*

Simkin, P. (1992). Just Another Day in a Womans Life? Part II: Nature and Consistency of Womens Long-Term Memories of Their First Birth Experiences. *Birth (Berkeley, Calif.), 19*(2), 64–81. doi:10.1111/j.1523-536X.1992.tb00382.x PMID:1388434

Simkin, P., & Bolding, A. (2004). Update on nonpharmacologic approaches to relieve labor pain and prevent suffering. *Journal of Midwifery & Womens Health, 49*(6), 489–504. doi:10.1016/S1526-9523(04)00355-1 PMID:15544978

Singer, D. G., Golinkoff, R. M., & Hirsh-Pasek, K. (2006). *Play = learning: How play motivates and enhances children's cognitive and social-emotional growth* (1st ed.). Oxford University Press. doi:10.1093/acprof:oso/9780195304381.001.0001

Skinner, E. A., & Belmont, M. J. (1993). Motivation in the classroom: Reciprocal effects of teacher behavior and student engagement across the school year. *Journal of Educational Psychology, 85*(4), 571–581. doi:10.1037/0022-0663.85.4.571

Smith, A. (2010). *Mobile Access 2010*. Pew Research Center. Available at http://pewinternet.org/Reports/2010/Mobile-Access-2010/Summary-of-Findings.aspx

Smith, G. E., Housen, P., Yaffe, K., Ruff, R., Kennison, R. F., Mahncke, H. W., & Zelinski, E. M. (2009). A cognitive training program based on principles of brain plasticity: Results from the Improvement in Memory with Plasticity-based Adaptive Cognitive Training (IMPACT) study. *Journal of the American Geriatrics Society, 57*(4), 594–603. doi:10.1111/j.1532-5415.2008.02167.x PMID:19220558

Smith, V., Devane, D., Begley, C. M., & Clarke, M. (2011). Methodology in conducting a systematic review of systematic reviews of healthcare interventions. *BMC Medical Research Methodology, 11*. PMID:21291558

Somers-Smith, M. (1999). A place for the partner? Expectations and experiences of support during childbirth. *Midwifery, 15*(2), 101–108. doi:10.1016/S0266-6138(99)90006-2 PMID:10703413

Soutter, A. R. B., & Hitchens, M. (2016). The relationship between character identification and flow state within video games. *Computers in Human Behavior, 55*(B), 1030–1038. http://doi.org/<ALIGNMENT.qj></ALIGNMENT>10.1016/j.chb.2015.11.012

Spencer, K., Sanders, C., Whitley, E. A., Lund, D., Kaye, J., & Dixon, W. G. (2016). Patient Perspectives on Sharing Anonymized Personal Health Data Using a Digital System for Dynamic Consent and Research Feedback: A Qualitative Study. *Journal of Medical Internet Research, 18*(4), e66. doi:10.2196/jmir.5011 PMID:27083521

Squire, K. (2003). Video games in education. *International Journal of Intelligent Games & Simulation, 2*(1), 49–62.

Star Wars: *The Old Republic* [PC Game]. Bioware.

Steam [computer software]. Bellvue, WA: Valve Corporation. Retrieved from http://store.steampowered.com

Steen, M., Downe, S., Bamford, N., & Edozien, L. (2011). Not-patient and and not-visitor: A metasynthesis of fathers' encounters with pregnancy, birth and maternity care. *Midwifery*. PMID:21820778

Stefanidis, D., Korndorffer, J. Jr, Sierra, R., Touchard, C., Dunne, J. B., & Scott, D. J. (2005). Skill retention following proficiency-based laparoscopic simulator training. *Surgery, 138*(2), 165–170. doi:10.1016/j.surg.2005.06.002 PMID:16153423

Steinkuehler, C. A., & Williams, D. (2006). Where everybody knows your (screen) name: Online games as third places.. *Journal of Computer-Mediated Communication, 11*(4), 885–909. doi:10.1111/j.1083-6101.2006.00300.x

Sterman, J. (2002). All models are wrong: Reflections on becoming a systems scientist. *System Dynamics Review, 18*(4), 501–531. doi:10.1002/sdr.261

Stern, Y. (2006). Cognitive reserve and Alzheimer disease. *Alzheimer Disease and Associated Disorders, 20*(Supplement 2), S69–S74. doi:10.1097/00002093-200607001-00010 PMID:16917199

Stern, Y. (2009). Cognitive reserve. *Neuropsychologia, 47*(10), 2015–2028. doi:10.1016/j.neuropsychologia.2009.03.004 PMID:19467352

Strauss, A., & Corbin, J. (1990). *Basics of qualitative research: Grounded theory procedures and techniques*. Thousand Oaks, CA: Sage Publications.

Sween, J., Wallington, S. F., Sheppard, V., Taylor, T., Llanos, A. A., & Adams-Campbell, L. L. (2013). The role of exergaming in improving physical activity: a review. *Journal of Physical Activity & Health*.

Sween, J., Wallington, S. F., Sheppard, V., Taylor, T., Llanos, A. A., & Adams-Campbell, L. L. (2014). The role of exergaming in improving physical activity: A review. *Journal of Physical Activity & Health*, *11*(4), 864–870. doi:10.1123/jpah.2011-0425 PMID:25078529

Sznajder, J. I., Zveibil, F. R., Bitterman, H., & Weiner, P. B. S. (1986). Central vein catheterization. Failure and complication rates by three percutaneous approaches. *Archives of Internal Medicine*, *146*(2), 259–261. doi:10.1001/archinte.1986.00360140065007 PMID:3947185

Takatalo, J., Nyman, G., & Laakosonen, L. (2008). Components of human experience in virtual environments. *Computers in Human Behavior*, *24*(1), 1–15. doi:10.1016/j.chb.2006.11.003

Talbot, T. B. (2008). *SIMapse Nerve Agent Laboratory 2.0 and Nerve Academy CD-ROM*. Referenced at https://ccc.apgea.army.mil/products/info/products.htm

Talbot, T. B. (2012). *Exanguitron 150 Health-Score based trauma simulator demonstration*. Accessed at http://www.doctortalbot.com/healthscore

Talbot, T. B., Rizzo, A., Christofferson, K., & Kalish, N. (2016). *USC Standard Patient virtual standardized patient*. Accessed on June 26th, 2016 at http://www.standardpatient.org

Talbot, T. B., Sagae, K., John, B., & Rizzo, A. A. (2012a). Designing useful virtual standardized patient encounters. *Interservice/Industry Training,Simulation and Education Conference Proceedings*.

Talbot, T. B. (2013). Balancing Physiology, Anatomy & Immersion: How Much Biological Fidelity is Necessary in a Medical Simulation? *Journal of Military Medicine.*, *178*(10S), 26–33. PMID:24084303

Talbot, T. B. (2013). Playing with Biology: Making medical games that appear lifelike.[July-September.]. *International Journal of Gaming and Computer-Mediated Simulations*, *5*(3), 83–96. doi:10.4018/jgcms.2013070106

Talbot, T. B. (2016). *Natural Language Understanding Performance & Use Considerations in Virtual Medical Encounters*. Medicine Meets Virtual Reality Proceedings.

Talbot, T. B., Sagae, K., John, B., & Rizzo, A. A. (2012b). Sorting out the Virtual Patient: How to exploit artificial intelligence, game technology and sound educational practices to create engaging role-playing simulations. *International Journal of Gaming and Computer-Mediated Simulations*, *4*(4).

Taylor, L. M., Kerse, N., Frakking, T., & Maddison, R. (2016). Active video games for improving physical performance measures in older people: a meta-analysis. *Journal of Geriatric Physical Therapy*.

Taylor, N., Kampe, C., & Bell, K. (2015). Me and Lee: Identification and the play of attraction in The Walking Dead. *Game Studies, 15*(1). Retrieved from http://gamestudies.org/1501/articles/taylor

Taylor, M. J., McCormick, D., Impson, R., Shawis, T., & Griffin, M. (2011). Activity promoting gaming systems in exercise and rehabilitation. *Journal of Rehabilitation Research and Development*, *48*(10), 1171–1186. doi:10.1682/JRRD.2010.09.0171 PMID:22234662

Taylor, T. L. (2002). Living digitally: Embodiment in virtual worlds. In R. Schroeder (Ed.), *The Social Life of Avatars: Presence and Interaction in Shared Virtual Environments*. London: Springer-Verlag. doi:10.1007/978-1-4471-0277-9_3

Teng, C.-I. (2010). Customization, immersion satisfaction, and online gamer loyalty. *Computers in Human Behavior*, *26*(6), 1547–1554. doi:10.1016/j.chb.2010.05.029

The Collection, Linking and Use of Data in Biomedical Research and Health Care: Ethical Issues. (2015). Nuffield Council on Bioethics. Retrieved from http://nuffieldbioethics.org/project/biological-health-data/

Thomas, A. (2007). Blurring and breaking through the boundaries of narrative, literacy, and identity in adolescent fan fiction. *A New Literacies Sampler, 29*, 137.

Thomson, C. (2007, August 21). *Halo 3: How Microsoft Labs Invented a New Science of Play.* Retrieved July 7, 2016, from http://archive.wired.com/gaming/virtualworlds/magazine/15-09/ff_halo?currentPage=all

Thorne, S.E., & Paterson, B.L. (2000). Two decades of insider research: What we know and don't know about chronic illness experience. Annual Review of Nursing Research.

Thorp, A. A., Owen, N., Neuhaus, M., & Dunstan, D. W. (2011). Sedentary behaviors and subsequent health outcomes in adults: A systematic review of longitudinal studies, 1996–2011. *American Journal of Preventive Medicine, 41*(2), 207–215. doi:10.1016/j.amepre.2011.05.004 PMID:21767729

Toff, N. (2010). Human Factors in Anaesthesia: Lessons From Aviation. *BJA, 105*(1), 21–25. doi:10.1093/bja/aeq127 PMID:20507856

Tomeo, C., Rich-Edwards, J., Michels, K., Berkey, C., Hunter, D., Frazier, A., & Buka, S. L. et al. (1999). Reproducibility and validity of maternal recall of pregnancy-related events. *Epidemiology (Cambridge, Mass.), 10*(6), 774–777. doi:10.1097/00001648-199911000-00022 PMID:10535796

Toril, P., Reales, J. M., & Ballesteros, S. (2014). Video game training enhances cognition of older adults: A meta-analytic study. *Psychology and Aging, 29*(3), 706–716. doi:10.1037/a0037507 PMID:25244488

Tortell, R., & Morie, F. J. (2006). Videogame play and the effectiveness of virtual environments for training. *Proceedings of the Interservice/Industry Training, Simulation, and Education Conference.*

Tremblay, M. S., LeBlanc, A. G., Kho, M. E., Saunders, T. J., Larouche, R., Colley, R. C., & Gorber, S. C. et al. (2011). Systematic review of sedentary behaviour and health indicators in school-aged children and youth. *The International Journal of Behavioral Nutrition and Physical Activity, 8.* PMID:21936895

Trepte, S., & Reinecke, L. (2010). Avatar creation and video game enjoyment: Effects of life-satisfaction, game competitiveness, and identification with the avatar. *Journal of Media Psychology: Theories, Methods, and Applications, 22*(4), 171–184. doi:10.1027/1864-1105/a000022

Trope, Y., & Liberman, N. (2010). Construal-level theory of psychological distance. *Psychological Review, 117*(2), 440–463. doi:10.1037/a0018963 PMID:20438233

Turkay, S. (2012). User experiences with avatar customization in Second Life and Lord of the Rings Online. *Proceedings of Teachers College Educational Technology Conference.*

Turkay, S., & Adinolf, S. (2010). Free to be me: A survey study on customization with World of Warcraft and City of Heroes/Villains players. *Procedia: Social and Behavioral Sciences, 2*(2), 1840–1845. doi:10.1016/j.sbspro.2010.03.995

Turkle, S. (1994). Constructions and reconstructions of self in virtual reality. Playing in MUDs. *Mind, Culture, and Activity, 1*(3), 158–167. doi:10.1080/10749039409524667

Turkle, S. (1995). *Life on the screen: Identity in the age of Internet.* New York: Simon & Schuster.

Turner, D. C., Robbins, T. W., Clark, L., Aron, A. R., Dowson, J., & Sahakian, B. J. (2003). Cognitive enhancing effects of modafinil in healthy volunteers. *Psychopharmacology, 165*, 260–269. PMID:12417966

Tynan, C., McKechnie, S., & Hartley, S. (2014). Interpreting value in the customer service experience using customer-dominant logic. *Journal of Marketing Management, 30*(9–10), 1058–1081. doi:10.1080/0267257X.2014.934269

U.S. Department of Health and Human Services, National Institutes of Health, NIH Consensus Development Program. (2010). *Preventing Alzheimer's disease and cognitive decline.* Retrieved from http://consensus.nih.gov/2010/docs/alz/ALZ_Final_Statement.pdf

U.S. Department of Health and Human Services. (2008). *2008 Physical Activity Guidelines for Americans (ODPHP Publication No. U0036).* Washington, DC: ODPHP.

Van Camp, C. M., & Hayes, L. B. (2012). Assessing and increasing physical activity. *Journal of Applied Behavior Analysis, 45,* 871–875. PMID:23322945

van der Land, S., Schouten, A. P., van den Hooff, B., & Feldberg, F. (2011). Modelling the metaverse: A theoretical model of effective team collaboration in 3D virtual environments. *Journal of Virtual Worlds Research, 4.* Retrieved from http://journals.tdl.org/jvwr/index.php/jvwr/article/view/6126

van Deusen-Scholl, N., Frei, C., & Dixon, E. (2005). Coconstructing learning: The dynamic nature of foreign language pedagogy in a CMC environment. *CALICO Journal, 22,* 657–678.

Van Diest, M., Lamoth, C. J., Stegenga, J., Verkerke, G. J., & Postema, K. (2013). Exergaming for balance training of elderly: State of the art and future developments. *Journal of Neuroengineering and Rehabilitation, 10.* PMID:24063521

Van Zandt, S., Edwards, L., & Jordan, E. (2005). Lower epidural anesthesia use associated with labor support by student nurse doulas: Implications for intrapartal nursing practice. *Complementary Therapies in Clinical Practice, 11*(3), 153–160. doi:10.1016/j.ctcp.2005.02.003 PMID:16005832

Vasalou, A., & Joinson, A. (2009). Me, myself and I: The role of interactional context on self-presentation through avatars. *Computers in Human Behavior, 25*(2), 510–520. doi:10.1016/j.chb.2008.11.007

Velazquez, A., Campos-Francisco, W., García-Vázquez, J. P., López-Nava, H., Rodríguez, M. D., Pérez-San Pablo, A. I., . . . Favela, J. (2014). Exergames as tools used on interventions to cope with the effects of ageing: a systematic review. In *Proceedings of the 6th International Work-Conference, IWAAL: Ambient Assisted Living and Daily Activities* (pp. 402–405). doi:10.1007/978-3-319-13105-4_59

Verhaeghen, P., & Salthouse, T. A. (1997). Meta-analyses of age-cognition relations in adulthood: Estimates of linear and nonlinear age effects and structural models. *Psychological Bulletin, 122*(3), 231–249. doi:10.1037/0033-2909.122.3.231 PMID:9354147

Villani, D., Gatti, E., Triberti, S., Confalonieri, E., & Riva, G. (2016). Exploration of virtual body-representation in adolescence: The role of age and sex in avatar customization. *SpringerPlus, 5*(1), 740. doi:10.1186/s40064-016-2520-y PMID:27376008

von der Emde, S., Schneider, J., & Kotter, M. (2001). Technically speaking: Transforming language learning through virtual learning environments (MOOs). *Modern Language Journal, 85*(2), 210–225. doi:10.1111/0026-7902.00105

von Feilitzen, C., & Linne, O. (1975). The effects of television on children and adolescents identifying with television characters. *Journal of Communication, 4*(4), 31–55.

Vygotskiĭ, L. S. (1978). *Mind in society: The development of higher psychological processes.* Harvard Univ Pr. Retrieved from http://books.google.com/books?hl=en&lr=&id=RxjjUefze_oC&oi=fnd&pg=PA1&dq=mind+in+sociaety&ots=ogzWQZu1dv&sig=Gc_Qkp0dB85be_VBFRaTmuQnsgU

Vygotsky, L. S. (1978). *Mind and Society: The Development of Higher Mental Processes.* Cambridge, MA: Harvard University Press.

Waddell, T. F., Sundar, S. S., & Auriemma, J. (2015). Can customizing an avatar motivate exercise intentions and health behaviors among those with low health ideals? *Cyberpsychology, Behavior, and Social Networking, 18*(11), 687–690. doi:10.1089/cyber.2014.0356 PMID:26406804

Waggoner, Z. (2009). *My avatar, my self: identity in video role-playing games.* Jefferson, NC: McFarland.

Wang, F., & Burton, J. K. (2013). Second Life in education: A review of publications from its launch to 2011. *British Journal of Educational Technology, 44*(3), 357–371. doi:10.1111/j.1467-8535.2012.01334.x

Wang, F., & Lockee, B. B. (2010). Virtual worlds in distance education: A content analysis study. *The Quarterly Review of Distance Education, 11,* 183–186.

Warburton, D., Nicol, C., & Bredin, S. (2006). Health benefits of physical activity: The evidence. *Canadian Medical Association Journal, 174*(6), 801–809. doi:10.1503/cmaj.051351 PMID:16534088

Ward, L., Merriwether, A., & Caruthers, A. (2006). Breasts are for men: Media, masculinity ideologies, and men's beliefs about women's bodies. *Sex Roles, 55*(9), 703–714.

Watts, M. (2016). *Avatar self-identification, self-esteem, and perceived social capital in the real world: A study of World of Warcraft players and their avatars.* Graduate Thesis and Dissertations. Retrieved from http://scholarcommons.usf.edu/etd/6155

Wayne, D. B., Didwania, A., Feinglass, J., Fudala, M. J., Barsuk, J. H., & McGaghie, W. C. (2008). Simulation-based education improves quality of care during cardiac arrest team responses at an academic teaching hospital: A case-control study. *Chest, 133*(1), 56–61. doi:10.1378/chest.07-0131 PMID:17573509

Weaver, I. C. G., Cervoni, N., Champagne, F. A., DAlessio, A. C., Sharma, S., Seckl, J. R., & Meaney, M. J. et al. (2004). Epigenetic programming by maternal behavior. *Nature Neuroscience, 7*(8), 847–854. doi:10.1038/nn1276 PMID:15220929

Weaver, K. E., & Stevens, A. A. (2007). Attention and sensory interactions within the occipital cortex in the early blind: An fMRI study. *Journal of Cognitive Neuroscience, 19*(2), 315–330. doi:10.1162/jocn.2007.19.2.315 PMID:17280519

Weinreich, P., & Saunderson, W. (Eds.). (2003). *Analyzing identity: Cross-cultural, societal and clinical contexts.* London: Routledge.

Wexler, B. E. (2006). *Brain and Culture: Neurobiology, ideology and Social Change.* Cambridge, MA: MIT Press.

Wexler, B. E., Anderson, M., Fulbright, R. K., & Gore, J. C. (2000). Improved verbal working memory performance and normalization of task-related frontal lobe activation in schizophrenia following cognitive exercises. *The American Journal of Psychology, 157,* 1094–1097. PMID:11007730

Wexler, B. E., & Bell, M. D. (2005). Cog Remedi and Voc Rehabilitation for Schizophrenia. *Schizophrenia Bulletin,* 931–941. doi:10.1093/schbul/sbi038 PMID:16079390

Wexler, B. E., Hawkins, K. A., Rounsaville, B., Anderson, M., Sernyak, M. J., & Green, M. F. (1997). Normal neurocognitive performance after extended practice in patients with schizophrenia. *Schizophrenia Research, 26*(2-3), 173–180. doi:10.1016/S0920-9964(97)00053-4 PMID:9323348

What, R. (2015, November 10). *The boring apocalyptic grind of Fallout 4 reviews.* Retrieved from https://robertwhat.com/2015/11/10/the-boring-apocalyptic-grind-of-fallout-4-reviews/

Whyville [PC Game]. Numedeon.

Williams, K. D. (2011). The effects of homophily, identification, and violent video games on players. *Mass Communication & Society, 14*(1), 3–24. doi:10.1080/15205430903359701

Wixon, D., & Pagulayan, R. (2008). Halo 3: The theory and practice of a research-design partnership. *Interactions, 15*(1), 52–55.

World Health Organization (WHO). (2010). *Global recommendations on physical activity for health (Report).* Geneva: WHO Press.

World of Warcraft [PC Game]. Blizzard entertainment Inc.

Worth, N. (2015). *Players and avatars: The connections between player personality, avatar personality, and behavior in video games.* Retrieved from https://dr.library.brocku.ca/handle/10464/6985

Wykes, T., Huddy, V., Cellard, C., McGurk, S. R., & Czobor, P. (2011). A meta-analysis of cognitive remediation for schizophrenia: Methodology and effect sizes. *The American Journal of Psychiatry, 168*(5), 472–485. doi:10.1176/appi.ajp.2010.10060855 PMID:21406461

Yap, J. (2011). Virtual world labyrinth: An interactive maze that teaches computing.*Proceedings of the Defense Science Research Conference and Expo (DSR).* doi:10.1109/DSR.2011.6026883

Yerkes, R. M., & Dodson, J. D. (1908). The relation of strength of stimulus to rapidity of habit-formation. *The Journal of Comparative Neurology and Psychology, 18*(5), 459–482. doi:10.1002/cne.920180503

Yoon, G., & Vargas, P. T. (2014). Know thy avatar: The unintended effect of virtual-self representation on behavior. *Psychological Science, 25*(4), 1043–1045. doi:10.1177/0956797613519271 PMID:24501111

Zahodne, L. B., Manly, J. J., MacKay-Brandt, A., & Stern, Y. (2013). Cognitive declines precede and predict functional declines in aging and Alzheimers disease. *PLoS ONE, 8*(9), e73645. doi:10.1371/journal.pone.0073645 PMID:24023894

Zech, L., Vye, N. J., Bransford, J.D., Swink, J., Mayfield-Stewart, C., & Goldman, S.R., & Cognition and Technology Group at Vanderbilt. (1994). Bringing geometry into the classroom with videodisc technology. *Mathematics Teaching in the Middle School Journal, 1*(3), 228–233.

Zelinski, E. M. (2009). Far transfer in cognitive training of older adults. *Restorative Neurology and Neuroscience, 27,* 455–471. PMID:19847070

Zelinski, E. M. (in press). Does cognitive training reduce risk for dementia? In G. E. Smith & S. Farias (Eds.), *Handbook of Dementia.* Washington, DC: American Psychological Association.

Zelinski, E. M., Dalton, S. E., & Smith, G. E. (2011). Consumer-based brain fitness programs. In A. Larue & P. Hartman-Stein (Eds.), *Enhancing Cognitive Fitness in Adults: A Guide to the Use and Development of Community Programs* (pp. 45–66). New York: Springer. doi:10.1007/978-1-4419-0636-6_3

Zelinski, E. M., & Gilewski, M. J. (2003). Effects of demographic and health variables on Rasch scaled cognitive sores. *Journal of Aging and Health, 15*(3), 435–464. doi:10.1177/0898264303253499 PMID:12914012

Zelinski, E. M., & Gilewski, M. J. (2004). A 10-Item Rasch Modeled Memory Self Efficacy Scale. *Aging & Mental Health, 8*(4), 293–306. doi:10.1080/13607860410001709665 PMID:15370046

Zelinski, E. M., & Kennison, R. F. (2007). Not your parents test scores: Cohort reduces psychometric aging effects. *Psychology and Aging, 22*(3), 546–557. doi:10.1037/0882-7974.22.3.546 PMID:17874953

Zelinski, E. M., & Lewis, K. L. (2003). Adult age differences in multiple cognitive functions: Differentiation, dedifferentiation or process-specific change?*Psychology and Aging, 18*(4), 727–745. doi:10.1037/0882-7974.18.4.727 PMID:14692860

Zelinski, E. M., & Reyes, R. (2009). Cognitive benefits of computer games for older adults. *Gerontechnology (Valkenswaard)*, *8*(4), 220–235. doi:10.4017/gt.2009.08.04.004.00 PMID:25126043

Zelinski, E. M., Spina, L. M., Yaffe, K., Ruff, R., Kennison, R. F., Mahncke, H. W., & Smith, G. E. (2011). Improvement in Memory with Plasticity-based Adaptive Cognitive Training (IMPACT): Results of the 3-Month Follow-up. *Journal of the American Geriatrics Society*, *59*(2), 258–265. doi:10.1111/j.1532-5415.2010.03277.x PMID:21314646

Zhong, Z., & Yao, M. (2012). Gaming motivations, avatar-self-identification and symptoms of online game addiction. *Asian Journal of Communication*, *23*(5), 555–573. doi:10.1080/01292986.2012.748814

Zimmerman, E. (2007). Gaming literacy: Game design as a model for literacy in the 21st century. *Harvard Interactive Media Review*, *1*, 30–35.

Zoo Tycoon [Computer software]. Redmond, WA: Microsoft.

About the Contributors

Brock Dubbels specializes in user experience, user research, and assessment. He helped create the GScale Game Development and Testing Laboratory at McMaster University, and is currently in the Department of Psychology Neuroscience & Behaviour. He has worked as a Fulbright Scholar at the Norwegian Institute of Science and Technology; at Xerox PARC and Oracle, and as a research associate at the Center for Cognitive Science at the University of Minnesota. His specialties include user research, user experience, and software project management. He teaches course work on user experience research. games and cognition, and how learning research can improve game design for return on investment (ROI). He is the founder and principal learning architect at www.vgalt.com for design, production, usability assessment and evaluation of learning systems and games.He is also the founder of the HammerTown-CoderDojo.org, an organization providing free programming instruction to children, and is the Editor in Chief of the International Journal of Games and Computer Mediated Simulations. He currently on the UXPA-MN board and facilitates the UXPA Mentorship program.

* * *

Rachel Callan is a doctoral student at Old Dominion University in Richard Landers' lab and an internal researcher at an insurance company. Her research interests focus on the use of technology in employee selection and training contexts, including how individual differences like experience and personality may have direct and indirect on outcomes. More recently she has turned her attention to the use of gamification in work settings and the use of social networking data in selection. She is equally interested in how these technologies can improve human resource management process and potential pitfalls of utilizing these technologies in the workplace.

Kristie Fisher was a design researcher at Microsoft Game Studios from 2011 – 2015. She now works as a user experience researcher at Google.

Andrew Goldberg is an Assistant Professor at the Icahn School of Medicine School of Medicine at Mount Sinai. He is an integral instructor and educator for the Mount Sinai HELPS center. His research interests include human simulation and the utility of failure, serious gaming, as well as disaster preparedness training.

Alexandra Holloway, as an interaction designer, imagines how we will control space robots in the future, at NASA's Jet Propulsion Laboratory in Pasadena, CA. Dr. Holloway leads user-centered investigations into current and future practices and interactions, specifically in high-stakes areas where humans and automation meet. Dr. Holloway's deeply ethnographic approach results in intimate understanding of human-computer interaction issues in these real-time systems. Previously, Dr. Holloway designed, developed, and tested a suite of learning games about labor support and breastfeeding, including Digital Birth, an iPhone game to be used in collaboration with the University of California San Francisco Medical Center.

Jina Kang is a Ph.D. candidate in the Learning Technologies Program at the University of Texas at Austin. She has been working as a teaching assistant for the classes related to design strategies and interactive multimedia production. Her research interests are in learning analytics, in which she is currently focusing on visualizing students' learning behavior in serious games and providing just-in- time feedback to help teachers track and understand the learning paths.

Tuomas Kari is currently a project researcher / Ph.D. candidate (Information Systems Science) at the University of Jyväskylä, Finland. His dissertation is about the usage of exergames. His research interest is the use of technology in everyday life, especially in the context of health and wellness. His topics of research include exergames, exergaming, sports-, health-, and wellness technology, information systems usage, user behaviour, adoption and diffusion, and gamification. He has published, for example, in International Conference on Information Systems (ICIS) and International Journal of Gaming and Computer-Mediated Simulations (IJGCMS).

Daniel Katz is an Assistant Professor at the Icahn School of Medicine at Mount Sinai. He is also the director of the serious gaming division of the Mount Sinai HELPS Center. His research interests include simulation and gaming as well as obstetric anesthesiology.

Geoff Kaufman is an Assistant Professor in the Human-Computer Interaction Institute at Carnegie Mellon University. His research focuses on studying the psychological/social impact of fictional narratives, games, and computer-mediated interactions; uncovering and empirically verifying user-specific, design-specific, and situational variables that increase that impact; and extrapolating techniques and best practices for the creation of stories, games, and playful technologies as "interventions" for social change.

Khizer Khaderi is a renowned Neuro-Ophthalmologist and Founder/CEO of Vizzario Inc. Dr. Khaderi's expertise focuses on the measurement of visual function, including elements of visual psychophysics, retinal ganglion expression and biometric measurements of oculomotor and pupillary function. He has developed novel technologies in these areas, and has several patents for his inventions. These patents focus on visual processing profiles and monitoring brain injury through wearable technologies. Dr. Khaderi has worked with many of the BMI/BCI related technologies in developing his patents, including EEG (Emotiv, Neurosky, Melon, NeuroFocus), pupillometry and eye tracking (SMI, Tobii, Arrington, EyeTribe, EyeLink). He is the former Director of Neuro-Ophthalmology at UC Davis Medical Center, where he founded the Sports Vision Lab. Dr. Khaderi is currently an adjunct associate professor of Ophthalmology at the University of Utah Moran Eye Center. Dr. Khaderi is a leader in both health and vision technologies, including his position as Associate Director for Health Technology Innovation at CITRIS Health, where he is involved in strategic industry partnerships around health tech. He also consults and serves on boards of vision insurance (VSP), augmented reality (Magic Leap, Daqri) and wearable (Medella Health, Ceeable) companies. In addition, he was selected as one of Sacramento's 40 under 40 and by the the UC-system wide CITRIS group to write a proposal for President Obama's Council of Advisors on Science and Technology regarding vision technology and the aging population.

Royce Kimmons is an Assistant Professor of Instructional Psychology and Technology at Brigham Young University where he studies technology integration in K-12/higher education, emergent technologies, open education, and social networks. More information about Dr. Kimmons and his work may be found on his website at http://roycekimmons.com.

Charles K. Kinzer is Emeritus Professor of Education and Technology at Teachers College (TC) Columbia University, and former Director of the TC Game Research Lab, and principal investigator, at the Teachers College site, of the Games for Learning Institute. His work has been published widely and presented at the Serious Games Summit, Games Learning and Society, Meaningful Play, Games for Change, the American Educational Research Association, GDC, LRA, and other professional and corporate meetings, and has been funded by the USDOE/IES, NSF, the Robert Wood Johnson Foundation, Microsoft Games, and others. He continues to teach courses and work extensively with technology in schools and other settings, in areas from software development and simulations, to virtual environments and games, to reconceptualize educational opportunities for teaching and learning through technology and design across literacy and STEM content areas.

Richard N. Landers is an Associate Professor of Industrial/Organizational Psychology at Old Dominion University in Norfolk, VA, USA. His research program concerns the use of innovative technologies in assessment, employee selection, adult learning, and research methods, with his work appearing in Journal of Applied Psychology, Industrial and Organizational Psychology Perspectives, Computers in Human Behavior, Simulation & Gaming, Social Science Computer Review, and Psychological Methods, among others. Recent topics have included big data, game-based learning, game-based assessment, gamification, unproctored Internet-based testing, mobile devices, virtual reality, and online social media. His research and writing has been featured in Forbes, Business Insider, Science News, Popular Science, Maclean's, and the Chronicle of Higher Education, among others. He currently serves as Associate Editor of Computers in Human Behavior, Simulation & Gaming, and the International Journal of Gaming and Computer-Mediated Simulations, and he is also part of the steering committee of the Coalition for Technology in Behavioral Science. He was Old Dominion University's 2014 and 2015 nominee for the State Council for Higher Education in Virginia Rising Star Outstanding Faculty Award. He is also author of a statistics textbook, A Step-by-Step Introduction to Statistics for Business, and editor of Social Media in Employee Selection.

Jaejin Lee is Research Professor in Center for Teaching and Learning at the University of Seoul, South Korea. His research interests focus on educational uses of new media and 3D educational game in public education. His R&D experience includes designing 3D learning objects and environments and examining the effectiveness of immersive, rich media environments for science learning and engagement. Recently, he is interested in the use of Game Based Learning (GBL) in public classrooms and integration of gamification elements in diverse teaching and learning environments such as flipped instruction and blended learning. He is also interested in developing new data analysis techniques using data mining and data visualization for the examination of learning patterns in GBL and other online learnings.

Jerry Lin was a graduate student at USC where he explored synthesizing emotion in cognitive systems as part of the USC Games program. He is now a machine learning and big data engineer at LinkedIn Corp.

Veronika Litinski is a company builder, health technology innovator and a financier. Her track record for new venture creation, managing change and identifying growth opportunities distinguishes her among those working hard to realize a health transformation agenda. At present, Veronika is establishing Konona Health, a management company and digital health accelerator. Recently, she joined its first graduate, a Personalized Medicine company (www.pillcheck.ca). She led the launch of Cogniciti, a for-profit arm of Baycrest Hospital, the world's leading centre for the study of memory and aging. Cogniciti's mission is to help the millions of adults with memory concerns get earlier assessment, diagnosis and treatment. Before taking on a leadership role with Cogniciti, Veronika led the Health Care and Life Sciences practice at MaRS Discovery District in Toronto. Prior to joining MaRS, Veronika worked in Venture Finance with GATX Capital in San Francisco, where she managed international Venture Partnerships. Veronika began her career in cancer research at Lawrence Berkeley National Laboratory.

Min Liu, Ed.D., is Professor of Learning Technologies at the University of Texas at Austin. She is the Program Coordinator & Graduate Advisor. Her teaching and research interests center on educational uses of new media and other emerging technologies and their impact on teaching and learning for learners at all age levels. She has published over 65 research articles in leading peer-reviewed educational technology journals (e.g., Educational Technology Research and Development (EDR&D), Computers in Human Behavior (CHB), Journal of Research on Technology in Education (JRTE), Journal of Educational Computing Research (JECR), Interdisciplinary Journal of Problem-Based Learning, (IJPBL), The American Journal of Distance Education, (AJDE), Journal of Educational Technology & Society, Journal of Interactive Learning Research, The International Journal of Gaming and Computer-Mediated Simulations), ten peer-reviewed book chapters, 48 peer-reviewed conference proceeding papers, and presents regularly at national and international conferences. She has also served on numerous editorial boards for peer-reviewed research journals, including: Educational Technology Research and Development, Interdisciplinary Journal of Problem-based Learning, Computers in Human Behavior, Journal of Research on Technology in Education, Journal of Educational Computing Research, Journal of Computing in Childhood Education. Her current R&D projects include studying the design and effectiveness of immersive, rich media environments on learning and motivation; learning analytics and data visualizations; understanding MOOCs as an emerging online learning tool; examining the affordances and constraints of using mobile technologies in teaching and learning; and use of Web 2.0 tools to facilitate instruction.

Timothy Nichols is a research manager in the Windows & Devices Group at Microsoft.

Roma Patel is an Assistant Professor of Clinical Ophthalmology; Section Chief of Ophthalmology, Sacramento Veterans Affairs Hospital.

Thomas B. Talbot, MD, is the principal medical expert at the USC Institute for Creative Technologies and Associate Research Professor of Medical Education at USC Keck School of Medicine. He has a medical degree and M.S. in Molecular Biology from Wayne State University and a B.S. in Spanish Literature from Hillsdale College. Dr. Talbot researches medical simulation technologies including medical virtual reality, virtual standardized patients, medical games, and enabling technologies. A pediatrician and war veteran, he created a major medical simulation and gaming initiative for the US Defense Department. Major efforts he initiated there include the Combat Casualty Training Consortia, Public Physiology Research Engine (BioGears) and the Advanced Modular Manikin. Current work includes advancement of virtual standardized patients, virtual reality gestural interfaces and emotionally intelligent conversational computers.

Selen Turkay holds a doctorate in Instructional Technology and Media from Teachers College Columbia University. Currently, she is a postdoc research fellow at the Vice Provost for Advances in Learning Research Group, Harvard University. Her general research interests include design of personalized, interactive, and collaborative learning environments in particular gaming and virtual worlds. Specifically, she studies the effects of design choices on learning agency and outcomes, as well as learner experiences including engagement and motivation. Her research approach is a synthesis of mixed methods, qualitative to quantitative (focus groups, case studies, diary studies, content analysis, surveys, eye-tracking, true experiments).

Bruce Wexler graduated from Harvard College and the Albert Einstein College of Medicine. He studied psychiatry at Anna Freud's clinic and neurology at Queen's Square, London. He received his training in psychiatry at Yale University where he has been on the faculty since 1978. He has authored over 100 peer-reviewed scientific papers. His book "Brain and Culture" was published by MIT Press.

Elizabeth Zelinski studies mechanisms of longitudinal changes in memory, intelligence, and language in healthy adults aged 30 – 97. She believes that some of the negative change associated with aging can be reduced by engagement in challenging activities such as games. She served as a principal investigator of the IMPACT study, a large clinical trial of a program developed by Posit Science Corporation, that uses principles of brain plasticity. She recently found that modest improvements to healthy older adults' cognition with direct training were equivalent to the improvements seen with aerobic exercise interventions. Zelinski has been president of the American Psychological Association Division of Adult Development and Aging, is the Rita and Edward Polusky Chair in Education and Aging and professor of gerontology and psychology in the Davis School of Gerontology at the University of Southern California and is the inaugural Director of its Digital Aging Center.

Index

A

academic performance 210
Active Video Games 243
ADHD 207, 210, 218, 222-223
aging 192-194, 196, 200
AMSTAR 225, 229-231, 237, 243
anonymity 49, 80, 83-86, 88-90
artificial intelligence 155, 171, 246-247
athlete 184
attention 8, 36, 39, 50, 90, 131, 171, 183, 194-195, 198-199, 206-207, 210-215, 217, 219, 221-223, 236, 249, 254
attitude 57, 82, 94, 97-98, 100, 131, 137, 146, 219
avatars 50-53, 55, 57, 63-64, 66-67, 69-71, 80-81, 86, 89, 106

B

baseball 183-188
behavior 38-39, 45-46, 51, 53, 70, 90, 95, 103, 105, 107-108, 198, 207, 252
Big Data in healthcare 247
biological fidelity 103, 105, 109-110, 117-118

C

central line 122
Central Venous Catheter 120
characters 1, 12, 48-51, 53-57, 59-61, 63-71, 100, 105
chat room 81-83, 85-86, 88, 90
childbirth 154-164, 166, 169-176, 178-179
childbirth support 154-155, 171, 173-174, 179
cognition 62, 95, 100, 192, 195-198, 200, 206, 209-210, 215, 217-219, 222-223
cognitive decline 193, 199
cognitive development 222
cognitive interventions 198, 200
cognitive processes 94, 192-193

customer experience 18-19
customization 48-49, 51-54, 56-60, 62-71, 80-81, 86, 89

D

digital game 94-95, 98, 100, 132
digital health 246, 251-252
Dynamic Consent 246, 248

E

electronic medical records 249
emotion 2, 17, 19, 26, 35-36, 39, 41, 53, 136
exercise 26, 69, 86, 115, 134, 192, 195, 197, 210, 212, 214, 219, 223, 226, 231, 234-235, 243
exergames 225-226, 231, 236, 243
exergaming 225-226, 229, 231, 234-237, 243
experiment 50, 56, 80, 86, 146

F

flow 19, 26-28, 30, 34, 36-41, 52, 199, 227
Freemium 17, 20, 22, 26-28, 30, 32, 35, 40-41
functional outcomes 192, 200

G

game design 9, 32, 40-41, 65, 95, 122, 133, 188, 191
game user research 45
Games for Health 200
gamification 17-19, 41, 45-46, 131, 133, 136
gesture 2, 4-8, 11-13, 117
grinding 23-27, 29, 32, 38

H

health scores 103, 111-113, 115-116

I

identification 48-71, 83
identity 8, 50-51, 53, 64, 67, 69-71, 80, 82, 89-90, 248
Immersion 17, 20, 22, 28, 32, 35-36, 38-41, 51, 82, 85, 116, 131, 199
independence 192, 198, 200
interventions 104-106, 109-110, 192-200, 231, 234-235, 247, 251-252

K

Kinect 1-13, 28, 117

L

learning 3, 5, 13, 30, 33, 36, 39, 41, 47, 52, 68-70, 80-86, 88-91, 94-95, 98, 100, 107, 109, 112, 115, 117-118, 121-122, 128, 130-134, 136-137, 141-142, 144, 146-149, 154-155, 162, 193-194, 206-207, 210, 217, 222-223, 229, 249
ludic simulation 130, 132-134, 137-138, 144, 146, 148-149

M

magnocellular 184
marketing 200
math achievement 220
medical education 103
medical simulation 113, 115-116, 118
Microsoft 1, 3, 14, 117, 188
mixed method 48
MMOs 49-54, 64, 66-68, 70
motion gaming 1-3
motivation 20-21, 36-37, 46, 48-52, 54, 56, 62-64, 67-71, 90, 130, 137, 146, 199, 228, 235, 246, 252
MUVE 80-86, 88-91

N

neuroplasticity 194, 196, 199, 207, 209-210, 221, 223
non-digital game 98

P

parvocellular 183-186, 188
patient engagement 248-249, 251-252
perceptions 83, 95, 98-100, 173, 231, 235
physical activity 196, 210, 225-226, 231, 235, 237, 243
physical fitness 195, 199, 225-226, 231, 243
physiology 103-112, 115, 117-118, 184

physiology engine 104-106, 110, 115
play 3, 7, 12, 17, 19, 22-30, 34-40, 45-47, 49-50, 52, 54-56, 63-65, 67, 94-100, 107, 122, 125, 127-128, 130-132, 144, 146, 148, 172, 178, 183-186, 188, 194, 198-199, 212, 221, 226, 234-236, 247
psychology 4, 84, 99

R

reading achievement 219-220, 223
response inhibition 211-212, 215, 219, 222-223
retinal ganglion cells 183, 186

S

Second Life 70, 80, 89, 91, 174
serious games 69, 121, 251
serious gaming 120-121, 128
simulation 1, 81, 90-91, 103, 105-110, 113, 115-118, 121-122, 130-134, 136-139, 144, 146-149, 174, 176, 185
systematic review 225-228, 230-231, 237, 243
systems thinking 94-97

U

user experience research 17, 19, 39

V

value 17-20, 34-35, 38, 40-41, 59, 80-81, 90, 97, 130-132, 144, 148, 170, 222, 246-247, 249-251, 254-255
video games 1-2, 4, 19, 26, 28, 50, 53-54, 68-69, 112, 131, 154-155, 173-174, 176, 183-184, 188, 195, 226, 243
virtual world 50, 69, 90
vision training 183, 191
visual processing 183-185, 188, 191

W

working memory 192, 194-197, 199, 209-212, 214-215, 219, 221-222

X

Xbox 1, 3, 5, 12-13, 26-27

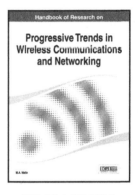

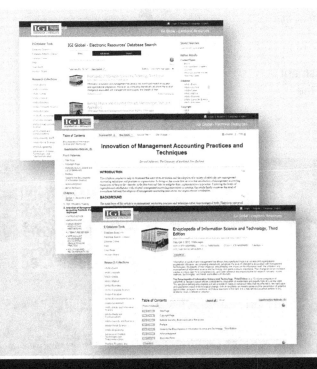

Become an IRMA Member

Members of the **Information Resources Management Association (IRMA)** understand the importance of community within their field of study. The Information Resources Management Association is an ideal venue through which professionals, students, and academicians can convene and share the latest industry innovations and scholarly research that is changing the field of information science and technology. Become a member today and enjoy the benefits of membership as well as the opportunity to collaborate and network with fellow experts in the field.

IRMA Membership Benefits:

- **One FREE Journal Subscription**

- **30% Off Additional Journal Subscriptions**

- **20% Off Book Purchases**

- Updates on the latest events and research on Information Resources Management through the IRMA-L listserv.

- Updates on new open access and downloadable content added to Research IRM.

- A copy of the Information Technology Management Newsletter twice a year.

- A certificate of membership.

IRMA Membership $195

Scan code or visit **irma-international.org** and begin by selecting your free journal subscription.

Membership is good for one full year.

Printed in the United States
By Bookmasters